KILLING FOR COAL

Killing for Coal

AMERICA'S DEADLIEST LABOR WAR

Thomas G. Andrews

HARVARD UNIVERSITY PRESS

Cambridge, Massachusetts

London, England

2008

Library of Congress Cataloging-in-Publication Data

Andrews, Thomas G., 1972–
Killing for coal : America's deadliest labor war / Thomas G. Andrews.
Includes bibliographical references and index.
ISBN 978-0-674-03101-2 (alk. paper)
1. Coal Strike, Colo., 1913–1914.   2. Strike and lockouts—Coal mining—Colorado—History.
I. Title.
HD5325.M631913 C736 2008
331.892′82233409788—dc22   2008020757

To my parents,

for loving me through thick and thin

Contents

Illustrations

Maps

KILLING FOR COAL

Introduction

Civil War, Red and Bloody

The shooting started around nine o'clock on a bright, breezy morning in a broad valley where the broken foothills of the southern Rockies tumble down onto the high plains. No one has ever determined who shot first, but participants and witnesses all agreed that within seconds of the initial gun blast, bullets began to fly thick and fast. Occupying the high ground was a small detachment of Colorado National Guardsmen. Thirty-four strong, this force and the dozen other militiamen encamped in the flats below consisted mostly of men formerly employed as guards by the largest coal mine operator in the West, the Rockefeller-owned Colorado Fuel and Iron Company.[1]

Seven months of shootouts and assassinations, executions and ambushes, had already earned the Colorado coalfield war the dubious distinction of being the deadliest strike in the history of the United States. On the morning of April 20, 1914, however, the conflict between Colorado state militia allied with the West's largest coal producers and mineworkers organized under the auspices of the nation's largest union erupted into open warfare, in what would become known as the Ludlow Massacre.[2]

Returning the guardsmen's fire were hundreds of striking coal miners of more than a dozen nationalities, all of whom resided in the Ludlow tent colony, "the largest of its kind in the history of this country," according to a

United Mine Workers (UMW) official, John Lawson. Union leaders had named the 1,200-person camp after the railroad depot about a mile away. The strikers, however, nicknamed it the White City, an apt description of the settlement's gleaming canvas facades, as well as an ironic reference to the dreamlike buildings that had housed the 1893 Chicago World's Fair.[3]

The sounds of exploding powder and shrieking bullets echoed between piñon-covered canyon walls, rousing the many strikers who had decided to sleep in, following Orthodox Easter festivities that had run late into the night. Women grabbed the children and hid with them in cellars dug into the hard adobe soil below the colony. The men of the camp, meanwhile, took their weapons, hurried to defensive positions via a nearby arroyo and returned fire in hopes of drawing the assault away from the colony.[4]

In the early afternoon a bullet hit Private Martin in the neck, inflicting a fatal wound that "smashed" his face "as if hit." Rifle fire also killed several strikers over the course of the day, including Frank Snyder. Just twelve years old, Frank had left the safe haven of his family's cellar either in search of food or to relieve his bladder—on this as on so many things eyewitness accounts differ—only to have a bullet tear off his head; "practically nothing above his eyes" remained. At some point in the late afternoon or early evening—here recollections again diverged—Ludlow's canvas dwellings caught fire under suspicious circumstances; soon the whole camp was ablaze. Two women and eleven children perished in their cellar hideout—asphyxiated when flames devoured the tents over their heads. Militiamen had also arrested and killed three men, including Louis Tikas, leader of the Greek strikers, who died of multiple gunshot wounds to the back.[5]

The family names of the eighteen strikers killed over the course of the day—Snyder and Tikas, Costa and Valdez and Pedregone—hinted at the diverse paths they had followed to the coalfields, as well as their unusual success at forging a common cause despite differences in race, ethnicity, and nationality. Back in September, the Denver journalist Don McGregor—a swashbuckling figure who would later join Pancho Villa's forces in the Mexican Revolution—had described the creation of Ludlow's sister tent colony at Walsenburg as "the outward sign of civil war, red and bloody, with its hates and its assassinations, its woes and its suffering." On April 21, 1914,

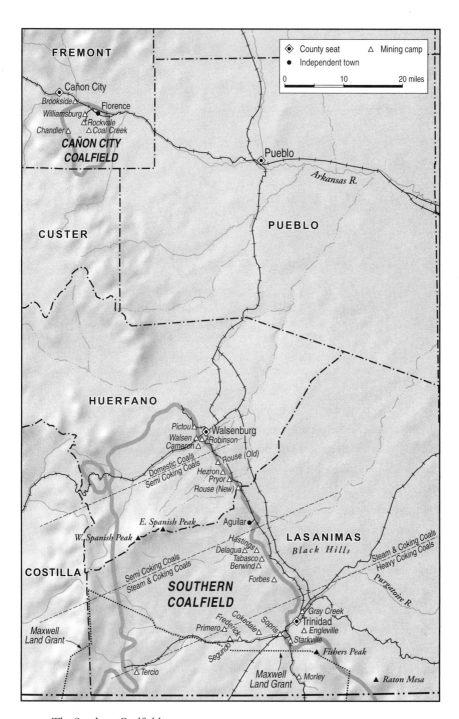

Map labels:

FREMONT

Cañon City
Brookside △
Florence
Williamsburg △
△ Rockvale
Chandler △ △ Coal Creek
CAÑON CITY COALFIELD

County seat ◈   △ Mining camp
● Independent town
0   10   20 miles

Pueblo
Arkansas R.

CUSTER

PUEBLO

HUERFANO

Pictou △
Walsen △ ◈ Walsenburg
Cameron △ △ Robinson
Domestic Coals
Semi Coking Coals
△ Rouse (Old)
Hezron △
Pryor △
Rouse (New) △

E. Spanish Peak   Aguilar ●
W. Spanish Peak ▲   ▲

Hastings
LASANIMAS
Delagua △ △   *Black Hills*
Tabasco △
Berwind △
Semi Coking Coals
Steam & Coking Coals
Steam & Coking Coals
Heavy Coking Coals
COSTILLA
Forbes △
Purgatoire R.

SOUTHERN COALFIELD

Gray Creek
Cokedale △   ◈ Trinidad
Frederick △   Sopris   △ Engleville
Primero △   ● Starkville
Maxwell
Land Grant
Segundo   ▲ *Fishers Peak*
Maxwell
Land Grant   △ Morley   ▲ *Raton Mesa*
△ Tercio

1.1. The Southern Coalfields

1.1. Militiamen in Action. Denver Public Library, Western History Collection, X-60548.

dawn's rays revealed the horrible fulfillment of McGregor's prophecy. Odd jumbles of metal furniture contorted by the heat, blackened coal stoves lined up like sentries on the plain, ethereal outlines seared into the ground where hundreds of tents had stood fast against rain and wind, snow, and gunshots for seven hard months—only vestiges remained of the hopeful strivings that had created and sustained the Ludlow colony.[6]

Journalists rushed to telegraph and telephone offices while the fighting still raged. The Colorado Coal strike had already attracted national press coverage, but a pitched battle between the United Mine Workers of America and the forces of the powerful Rockefeller family was headline news. "Little children roasted alive," as the irascible Mother Jones remarked, "make a front page story." The next morning, papers carried the shocking news of the strikers' deaths to millions of Americans, thus assuring Ludlow a place alongside Haymarket, Homestead, and Pullman in the annals of desperate struggle between Labor and Capital over who would bear the burdens and reap the rewards of American industrialization.[7]

4

1.2. The White City. Photograph by Bartosch. Denver Public Library, Western History Collection, X-60475.

How had all this come to pass—what forces had changed a former Rocky Mountain frontier into an epicenter of class war?[8]

Contemporary observers, unable or unwilling to rise above the chasm dividing working people and capitalists, generally made sense of Ludlow through two stories so different they sometimes seemed to describe altogether distinct events. Monty Bowers, a hard-driving executive dispatched by the Rockefellers seven years earlier to whip Colorado Fuel and Iron into shape, telegraphed the family's New York offices, "An unprovoked attack upon small forces of militia yesterday by two hundred strikers forced fight." At around the same time, Ed Doyle, the secretary of District 15 of the United Mine Workers, wired the union's international president with an entirely different interpretation. "For God's sake," Doyle implored, "urge the chief executive of this nation to protect the helpless men, women and children being slaughtered in southern Colorado."[9]

These two stories—of Ludlow-as-battle and Ludlow-as-massacre—proved remarkably enduring in the months and years ahead. The massacre story assumed a key place in the martyrology of the American labor movement and a striking centrality in the interpretation of the nation's history developed by several of the most important left-leaning thinkers of the twentieth century. Many union leaders and strikers held fast to memories of Ludlow as a cowardly act of slaughter perpetrated against defenseless women and children; Doyle's daughter later called it "an event that was to overshadow my father's entire life." The arch-muckraker Upton Sinclair wrote two novels about the coalfield wars. In 1946 the folksinger Woody Guthrie released his tragic lament "The Ludlow Massacre," which in turn inspired the people's historian Howard Zinn to write a master's thesis and several book chapters about the conflict. For his part, George McGovern wrote his Ph.D. dissertation at Northwestern on the subject and, as the Democratic presidential candidate, published a revised version of it as *The Great Coalfield War* during his unsuccessful 1972 election campaign. These works, together with union-sponsored publications such as Barron Beshoar's biography of the strike leader John Lawson, the public commemorations at the granite Ludlow monument dedicated in 1918, and oral tradition, solidified Ludlow's place as a signal event in the nation's history: a massacre of inno-

1.3. Ludlow in Ruins. Denver Public Library, Western History Collection, Z-199.

cents that exemplified the vulnerability of American workers to corporate rapacity, and the necessity of government safeguards to ensure working people's right to organize in defense of their lives and liberties.[10]

Adherents to the story of Ludlow-as-battle clung to their version almost as tenaciously. Coal executives, militia officers, and conservative apologists all sought to cast the killings as a regrettable consequence of a plan by strikers to drive the militia out of the coalfields, and hence to stop the companies from importing strikebreakers. The most famous and powerful exponent of this perspective was John D. Rockefeller, Jr. The pious, thin-lipped eldest son of America's richest man, John Junior oversaw the family's controlling stake in Colorado Fuel and Iron. The Rockefeller associate and Colorado Fuel and Iron director Jerome Greene nicely summarized the essence of the argument Rockefeller advocated in his public testimony before the U.S. Commission on Industrial Relations as well as in private correspondence. "The recent strike," Greene averred, "has been an attempt at forced unionization pure and simple, and not at all a rising of workers in protest against intolerable conditions."[11]

1.4. Guardsmen Firing from the Ruined Colony. Denver Public Library, Western History Collection, George Minot Collection, X-60558.

Rockefeller, unable to persuade most Americans to accept this version of events, took the advice of the author Charles Wayland Towne: "Get some vitality, pen-pictures and 'sobs' into your Casuistry, John, via the Press, and the tables will soon be turned in your favor." To spearhead this landmark public relations campaign, Rockefeller hired Ivy Lee. Widely hailed as an early pioneer in public relations for his work with the Pennsylvania Railroad and anthracite coal operators, Lee was reputed to be able to "open more office doors in New York than can any other person living." With Lee's help Rockefeller could bring to bear "methods of publicity" that he declared "new and in every instance most commendable," including a four-part series of "bulletins" and "an attractive, fully illustrated hand-book on the sociological and welfare work of the Colorado Fuel & Iron Company" to be distributed free of charge "to the President, to the members of the Cabinet, to all the members of Congress, to the editors of say the leading 5,000 newspapers in the country, possibly to the Mayors of the leading cities of the country, and to a further carefully selected list of people." In this manner, John D. Rockefeller, Jr., hoped to saturate the press and sway key opinion and policy makers with "facts" supporting the story of Ludlow-as-battle.[12]

Almost a century later, evocations of Ludlow still hew to the same story lines established as the fighting unfolded. The view of the Colorado coalfield war that has become the consensus is that workers were striking simply to achieve basic freedoms. Even though the miners suffered a crushing defeat, the blood sacrifices of Ludlow's martyrs prompted Rockefeller and his fellow capitalists to mend their ways and set American business on the path toward today's more enlightened labor relations. A Works Project Administration guidebook summarized this interpretation. Ludlow, New Deal authors argued, "aroused public opinion and brought about improvement of working conditions and civil liberties in the coal camps." Like most tales of the bad old days, such stories chart a narrative of progress. From this starting point, it becomes simply a matter of emphasis and tone to elicit either complacence or alarm lest we go back to the dark ages when big business reigned supreme and government forces served as the mailed fist of concentrated capital.[13]

Perhaps the biggest problem with the narrowly focused, polarizing memories of Ludlow inherited from the past is that they pluck a single day of killing from the stream of time, thus severing Ludlow from the vast and tangled web of events amid which it unfolded. In the process, they prevent us from understanding the larger contexts of imagination, power, and violence that caused the Colorado coalfield wars and molded their course.

The fighting that followed the destruction of the tent colony, a workers' uprising of such ferocity and effectiveness that contemporaries labeled it the Ten Days' War, is particularly difficult to square with what has become the consensus interpretation of Ludlow—and especially thick with implications for how we think about the endemic labor warfare that convulsed the United States throughout the Gilded Age and Progressive Era.[14]

Miners and their families assumed that the militia attack constituted the opening salvo in a long-feared offensive by mine operators and state troops to drive them out of the coalfields altogether. And so even as Ludlow smoldered, well over a thousand coal miners took up the arms they had cached, marched into the rugged foothills, and began to wage war against militiamen, mine guards, and strikebreakers. By the time the sun rose over the charred remains of the Ludlow colony two days after the fateful dawn of April 20, battalions of workingmen had "plunged" a massive territory "into a state of terror."[15]

Colorado's most powerful labor organizations—the Colorado State Federation of Labor, the Western Federation of Miners, and the United Mine Workers—endeavored to expand the scope and clarify the intent of these military actions in their "Call to Arms." Printed on broadsides and widely published on April 22 in newspapers throughout the region, this remarkable document solicited donations of arms and ammunition and asked volunteers to organize military companies "to protect the workers of Colorado against the murder and cremation of men, women and children by armed assassins in the employ of coal corporations." Money and materiel soon poured into strike headquarters. Cigar makers, colliers, and other workingmen and -women drilled in the streets of Denver and other towns. Union miners from around the country sent telegrams expressing outrage and vowing solidarity; workers from Wyoming, New Mexico, and Oklahoma notified their Colorado brethren that they were armed and ready to enter the fray.[16]

For some Colorado union leaders—the radicals of the Western Federation and the handful of Socialists within the United Mine Workers leadership—the moment seemed ripe for revolution. When else might the public look so approvingly on an armed union takeover of the mines and mining camps? Moderates retorted that upping the ante on the miners' rebellion would cause unconscionable loss of life, expose strike leaders to arrest and prosecution for treason, and erode newly awakened public sympathy for Colorado's coal-mining families. After fierce debate, union leaders decided not to unleash the dogs of war, but rather to sign a truce agreement with state officials.[17]

Just because labor leaders agreed to a cease-fire, though, did not mean that they were able to exercise authority over the brigades of strikers who had already scored several victories over guardsmen and company forces. The nature of the miners' struggles, as the ongoing fighting showed, transcended the union cause. For this was an uprising from below, an exorcism of frustration and pain that had accumulated over many decades, a conflagration that once ignited could not be quenched until it had consumed, at least for the time being, the unrest and deep-seated resentments that fueled it. Having already gained the upper hand, the striker-soldiers, distinguished by no other uniform than the crimson kerchiefs that earned union miners the derogatory nickname of "rednecks," had little interest in relenting simply because labor aristocrats in Colorado's distant capital had signed a separate peace.[18]

Though the militia boasted officers who had cut their teeth at Wounded Knee or at Cripple Creek, in the Philippines or during the Boxer Rebellion, state troops generally lacked combat experience. One of the National Guardsmen who fought the miners called them "ten times better soldiers than we were." And indeed among the strikers' ranks were veterans of broader conflicts: the Spanish-American War, Italy's North African campaigns, the Balkan Wars, and many others. "They was trained, them guys," recalled miner Bill Lloyd. Others had taken up arms not for God and Country but for Class and Craft. Organized under "General" John W. Brown, a "professional strike promoter," and "officers" such as Bernardo Bilitari, and using what one account described as "Greek war tactics," the strikers exploited their superior knowledge of the local terrain to ghost through the landscape.[19]

Materializing, then vanishing, then reappearing, these workers' armies executed a series of devastating attacks. By April 22, Las Animas County Sheriff J. S. Grisham reported that the "strike situation [was] absolutely beyond control," while the lieutenant governor and adjutant general of Colorado proclaimed the entire "coal camp country . . . helpless." Two days later, the strikers had taken "possession of all the country between Ludlow . . . and the coal camp at Rouse." Colorado's southern coalfields were an irregular, discontinuous set of rich coal deposits that stretched for a few dozen miles from the edge of the Great Plains into the foothills of the Rocky Mountains, and from the New Mexico border to Cañon City a hundred miles north. Once those coalfields were firmly in the strikers' control, the miners appeared to be "carried away by a sudden sense of their power," according to one observer. A week after Ludlow, the strikers had already taken an eye for an eye, a tooth for a tooth, and a life for each of the lives lost in the course of the tent colony's destruction. The deadliest day of the uprising, however, also proved to be the last.[20]

Trouble descended on the small company town of Forbes early on the morning of April 29 in the form of more than three hundred strikers. Greeks, Italians, Slavs, and "Mexicans" all figured prominently in the force that set out in the early morning cold from Camp San Rafael, a union tent colony that refugees from Ludlow had recently established. Rumors that an attack was imminent had reached Forbes the day before. Those who could fled the camp for Trinidad; those who remained, uncertain whether the state militia would answer their pleas for reinforcements, faced a sleepless night. The mine superintendent, notified around 4:00 A.M. of the strikers' approach, led the women and children of the town to the relative safety of an abandoned tunnel. At 5:30, two shots signaled to the strikers that they should sally forth against six state militiamen and more than two dozen mine officials and strikebreakers. In two skirmish lines of equal strength, the union men in parties of "ten or twelve" scurried "from post to post working their way down."[21]

At seven hundred yards, strikers opened fire with steel-jacketed bullets. The outgunned militiamen were unable to shoot back until they could "see rifles, and belts, and even mustaches" of the miners.

As the fighting raged, strikers marched many prisoners up to the surrounding foothills. Berating their captives—"'What you doing Scab work for . . . Son-of-a-Bitch [?]'"—the strikers robbed them and then set them free.[22] Though militiaman W. E. Lane, a machine gunner and Spanish-American War veteran, claimed to have shot two strikers, Forbes's defenders proved no match for the miners. The camp fell in less than an hour.

Down in Forbes, meanwhile, the rest of the strikers were showing less moderation. In the "lower part" of town they shot up the school, the saloon, and the superintendent's house. In the "upper part" the attackers "completely destroyed" the mine fan. Next, they set fires that destroyed a dozen buildings, including the stables and all thirty mules inside. The miners, as survivors later told a coroner's jury, "even shot the dogs." An hour after the strikers started their attack, they left the camp riddled with bullets, dancing with flames, and bloodied by corpses. Most of the ten dead were mine guards and strikebreakers. Edward Kessler, however, a sixty-five-year-old union carpenter from Denver whose wife claimed to have had a premonition of his death, was killed by gunshot wounds to the head, then "badly burned."[23]

Far from sating the union miners, the destruction of Forbes made them

1.5. Strikers in the San Rafael Camp following the Attack on Forbes. Denver Public Library, Western History Collection, X-60418.

hunger for more. Puffed up with victory, the worker-combatants marched on to each new target with their trigger fingers itching just a little more every time the battle cry of "Remember Ludlow" echoed off the canyon walls. "They was going to go the next place," miner Dan DeSantis recalled six decades later. Only the elements, it seemed, could stop them. "It started to hail, and rain and everything. They couldn't go no more," explained DeSantis. "Like the Indians who once owned these hills," a Denver journalist explained in an analogy meant to highlight the strikers' savagery and abandon. "The men [had] sallied forth, struck deep and hard and then returned to camp" by noon, caked with mud, "parad[ing] the streets of Trinidad with the guns upon their shoulders."[24]

Shortly thereafter, federal troops dispatched by Woodrow Wilson arrived from Fort Leavenworth bearing orders to reestablish peace in Colorado. At last the striking coal miners, entrusting the fate of the strike to Woodrow Wilson and a Democratic administration that seemed sympathetic to their plight, stood down. Major W. A. Holbrook of the U.S. Cavalry telegraphed the adjutant general, "Prominent citizens picture state complete terrorism existing in Trinidad"; during the previous week "armed strikers were openly drilling in streets, civil authorities powerless to execute laws." Though Holbrook and his men brought lasting peace to the coalfields, six mines, Forbes camp, and another company town lay in ruins. Upwards of thirty people had lost their lives in the Ten Days' War, the deadliest, most destructive uprising by American workers since Southern slaves had fought for their emancipation during the Civil War. Together with Ludlow's dead and the dozens killed in scattered assassinations, ambushes, and gun battles that had begun the previous August, the victims of the Ten Days' War pushed the total death toll for the Colorado coalfield war of 1913–1914 to at least seventy-five and perhaps as many as a hundred.[25]

Most participants and contemporary observers interpreted the attack on Forbes as they had made sense of the fighting at Ludlow, through stories that justified their actions and advanced their interests. The state of Colorado, reeling from the triple embarrassment of the Ludlow killings, widespread desertions by guardsmen sympathetic to the strikers or fearful of their might, and the rout of state troops at Forbes and elsewhere, treated the Ten Days' War as an insurrection. By 1915, United Mine Workers attorneys would face the impossible task of preparing defenses for a grand total of 369 murder indictments, 191 charges of arson, and 100 charges of assault with intent to kill. Most of the charges concerned the Ten Days' War. John Lawson, the international organizer in the southern Rockies for the United Mine Workers and perhaps the most influential strike leader, was convicted in April 1915 of murder and sentenced to life imprisonment at hard labor.[26]

Once Lawson and most of his fellow strikers were retried and released after years of legal wrangling, however, Forbes dropped out of the public eye, never to reappear. The exigencies of wartime production, the Bolshevik Revolution, the brutal suppression of strikes in southern Colorado and across the nation in 1919, the ascension of "100 percent Americanism" and Klan rule in Colorado—these and other developments gave coal miners plenty of reason to keep quiet about the uprising of 1914. Mine operators and the state were equally intent on downplaying the depth and extent of the miners' rebellion. The deadly force Colorado's mineworkers used to fight back against their oppressors and, for a few days at least, overwhelm them fitted poorly with the stories that capitalists, workers, and the state have chosen to tell about their shared past. Not surprisingly, not a single monument has ever materialized at Forbes or any other battlefield of the Ten Days' War, nor have any of these events ever been publicly commemorated.[27]

To fully understand the Great Coalfield War and its significance, we need to move beyond partial memories and polarizing stories. The perpetuation of the Ludlow-as-massacre story distorts our ability to understand the tumultuous relationship between mineworkers, mine operators, and the state. By making victimization the main story line of a struggle in which strikers actually inflicted more deaths than they suffered, historians have treated men, women, and children who demonstrated tremendous capacity for action as having been almost entirely acted upon. Such interpretations seem to underscore a key premise of twentieth-century politics: that working people can best achieve equality, fairness, and justice not through collective uprisings from below, but rather through the intervention of national unions, the Democratic Party, and the federal government.[28]

The key to moving beyond the standard history of the Colorado coalfield wars is to place the events within a broader context. Pushing our analysis backward in time recasts the story of Ludlow by transforming it from an aberrant outbreak of violence into the culmination of more than half a century of bitter struggle between capitalists and mineworkers. Extending our scope beyond the merely human, meanwhile, enables us to see the long history of struggle that gave rise to these events in ecological terms. The result is a more holistic interpretation, a new story of the coalfield wars in which these events figure not simply as a landmark moment in labor-management relations, but also as a window onto the still richer and more intriguing set of relationships that connected different groups of people—particularly capitalists, consumers, and coal-mining families—with the natural world.

Coal stands at the heart of the intertwined social, industrial, and environmental histories that were responsible for the Colorado coalfield wars. Fossil fuels simultaneously liberated Westerners from the previously insuperable constraints of aridity and geographic isolation and rendered them utterly dependent on coal supplies over which they had little control. Burgeoning Western metropolises, gold and silver mines in the Rockies, steel mills and smelters in Denver and Pueblo, farmsteads on the high plains, and the railroad networks that bound them all together—none of these could have adopted the forms they did in this dry, biologically unproductive land without the vast quantities of coal unearthed by southern Colorado's miners.

Recent scholarship and the emerging coalitions formed by red and green activists have begun to erode the boundaries between environmental history and labor history. Yet until we can tell stories about labor that tell stories about nature, too, we are destined to perpetuate a long Euro-American tradition of segmenting work and nature into discrete aesthetic, analytical, and geographical domains. By focusing on migration, mine work, and labor struggle, I attempt to move beyond this intellectual isolation and to advance our understanding of how working people have experienced and transformed the natural world, as well as how they have been transformed by it.[29]

Venturing back to the subject of work—and hence back to the earth in which colliers labored—we will explore how underground interactions between men and nature fomented decades of militancy in the southern Colorado coalfields. What was the nature of coal mines in this place and time? What physical, chemical, biological, and cultural processes made these spaces so dangerous and dynamic? How did mineworkers and mining companies seek to harness those underground dynamics which suited their purposes, while trying to avoid or contain those which threatened their lives and livelihoods? How did the various groups and individuals who depended on coal for wages, profits, or energy contest or reconcile their divergent understandings of and interests in what happened underground?

To answer these questions requires taking a journey through southern Colorado's coal mines and coal-mining cultures. But it also carries us back to the migrations that brought men, women, and children to the southern Colorado coalfields from all over North America and Europe, as well as parts of Asia. Since coal mining remained perhaps the least mechanized of any major American industry through the 1920s, companies needed to hire more workers if they wanted to meet the mushrooming energy demands of the Rocky Mountain West. Operators initially preferred to hire experienced craft colliers from Britain and the eastern United States. From the 1880s onward, though, mineowners increasingly turned to less experienced workers from labor hinterlands that stretched from the Hispanic plazas of southern Colorado to the distant countryside of southern and eastern Europe, as well as northeast Asia. Pushed from their homelands by a confluence of demographic, environmental, economic, and political currents, drawn by the promise of high wages in Colorado, and often whisked along on their journey by coal-powered railroads and steamships, mineworkers of many races and more than thirty nationalities eventually migrated to the Rockies to help satisfy the region's appetite for energy.[30]

Companies assumed that the differences in race, nationality, ethnicity, creed, and skill that separated these migrants would make it impossible for them to get along. And though the mining families of southern Colorado often found themselves divided—and hence conquered—they periodically managed to make common cause, most dramatically in the coalfield-wide strikes of 1884–1885, 1894, 1903–1904, and, of course, 1913–1914. These seasons of resistance always built on the tenets of craft pride, independence, solidarity, and pugnacious masculinity that British American miners brought to Colorado.[31]

The culture of opposition, born in the danger and dynamism of the mines and shared with newer migrants through an occupational ladder whose openness to migrants of almost every race had few counterparts in the industrializing West, fueled the miners' persistent discontent. When that discontent erupted above the surface in 1894, upwards of two thousand miners—joined by a few score women—marched dozens of miles through the rugged coalfields, tramping behind American flags and brass bands from mine to mine in hopes of persuading, or if necessary threatening, other miners to join their struggle. Mine operators, frightened but ultimately victorious against the mass mobilization, responded by building a new company town system, expressly designed to contain the opposition that underground work tended to generate. Yet far from pacifying the miners, the paternalistic campaign of landscape reform and social control spearheaded by Colorado Fuel and Iron would blow up in the operators' faces two decades later. When strikers again took up their march, they would carry not flags and musical instruments, but high-powered rifles and burning memories of Ludlow.

In these and other ways, the Great Colorado Coalfield War offers new perspectives on the interconnected social, political, economic, and environmental changes that we too casually subsume under the catchall phrase "industrialization." Colorado may seem an odd microcosm through which to approach a phenomenon more commonly associated with Manchester, Pittsburgh, or Calcutta. Popular myths and scholarly interpretations of the past of the American West have left little place for coal, coal miners, and coal-powered industrialization. Yet there are unexpected benefits to considering the history of a phenomenon as it manifests itself not at its unadulterated core, but on its messy periphery. And so even as this book claims a more central place in the history of the American West for the Colorado coalfield wars and the larger revolutions of industry that gave rise to the miners' struggles, it also illuminates how the close study of one small area of the world can improve our understanding of processes that now pose grave threats to the well-being of our nation and our planet.[32]

What begins as a study of Colorado's coal wars leads necessarily to an exploration of the interconnection of physical energy and social power in the industrial world. In the Rocky Mountain West, as in every other part of the world, fossil fuels and the energy they contained transformed environments, refashioned everyday life, and deepened divisions of wealth and status. Though power has always been a fundamental theme in historical analysis, energy has received little attention until recent decades. And if energy in general remains a marginal topic in U.S. history, it is even truer in the case of coal. Despite dozens of fine works on the subject, nowhere can we find a full analysis of coal's essential role in American expansion and industrialization. Taking another look at the part that coal played in U.S. history not only illuminates the gritty sources of the nation's prosperity and strength. It also helps us understand the roots of the nation's addiction to fossil fuels, as well as the origins of many of the other problems that industrialization continues to pose for our "postindustrial" society.[33]

Killing for Coal charts a course from the Cretaceous epoch seventy million years ago to the automobile age and ranges from the rural countryside of Japan, the Tirol, and southern Colorado to the smoking mills of Dickensian Britain to the booming gold camps and swelling metropolises of the American West. Great industrialists like the Rockefellers, soldiers like W. E. Lane, and strikers like Louis Tikas are not the only characters in this story. Mules and molten steel, arid climates and Irish potato plots, explosive gases and, most of all, a humble rock that burns all have roles to play. Together they tell the story of how half a century of contentious interactions between workers, capitalists, and nature set the stage for ten days of class warfare that brought southern Colorado to the brink of revolution.[34]

1

A Dream of Coal-Fired Benevolence

William Jackson Palmer, a wiry man five feet ten inches tall with wavy, reddish brown hair, a neatly trimmed moustache, and an aristocratic bearing that seemed at odds with his twin creeds of Quakerism and republicanism, had honed a daunting array of talents during his thirty years of life. Engineer, executive, soldier, romantic—each role played a part in leading him to traverse southern Colorado and northern New Mexico in the summer of 1867. Yet what mattered most during these weeks of intensive exploration was Palmer's oracular way of finding meaning in coal outcrops.[1]

To most people, rocks were just rocks: solid, unyielding *facts* that sat unnoticed and insignificant. To Palmer, the study of rocks opened windows onto an ever-changing past. A self-taught geologist who supplemented gleanings from the most current scientific treatises and lectures with practical knowledge gained on journeys through Britain, France, and the eastern states, Palmer saw rocks as repositories of history that not only recorded the past, but held clues to the future. He prided himself on his ability to discern these clues from outcrops of sandstone and shale, basalt and limestone and coal. And on this rugged southern Colorado frontier in the tumultuous wake of the Civil War, the prospects Palmer read seemed to tell of boundless power that could overcome the limitations of a stubborn land and create an industrial utopia.

William Palmer had been born in the Delaware countryside and had come of age in midcentury Philadelphia. An exemplary student, he nonetheless left Central High School before graduating, swooped up like many of his classmates at the elite public institution by an appeal to his ambition from one of the city's counting houses. Clerking failed to excite young Palmer, though, so he left the city. It was most likely while he was working as a surveyor for the Hempfield Railroad in the Alleghenies that the three guiding passions of his life—railroads, coal, and wilderness—first coalesced. More than any other career, engineering promised to unite these obsessions.[2]

A common thread ran through the biographies of many of America's small but growing pantheon of great engineers. Like many of the nation's painters and patricians, they had embarked on the pilgrimage to Europe. Inspired by their example, William Palmer set sail in 1855 for a grand tour of the engineering marvels of Britain and France.[3]

The eighteen-year-old tottered down the gangway of the *Tuscarora* and onto a Merseyside quay on a summer's day. In the nine months that followed, Palmer traced a snaking path through Britain's main industrial districts, as well as Paris and its hinterlands. Occasionally he rode the train; more often he walked, carrying only what he could fit into a knapsack and bearing letters of introduction from such distinguished figures as Lucretia Mott, who described Palmer's family as "warmly interested in our anti-slavery movement."[4]

Palmer's favorite uncle had loaned him money to pay for his passage. He met most of his other expenses by writing twenty-one long travel letters for the Pottsville *Miner's Journal,* the most influential newspaper in Pennsylvania's anthracite region. Published a decade after Friedrich Engels's *Condition of the Working Class of England* and a year after Charles Dickens's *Hard Times* first appeared in serialized form, each letter printed above the initials W. J. P. or the pseudonym Carbon earned the traveler four dollars. More valuable by far, however, were the contributions each made to Palmer's burgeoning reputation as a keen observer of British industrialism. J. Edgar Thomson, the head of the Pennsylvania Railroad and the preeminent entrepreneur of the day, found them so impressive that he arranged to meet their author on his next business trip to Britain.[5]

After disembarking in the "double-distilled Pittsburgh" that was Liver-

1.1. William Jackson Palmer, ca. 1870. Denver Public Library, Western History Collection, F-20207.

pool, the eager young Palmer rode a packet ship to Manchester, griping along the way that "the pretty Irwell which had flowed through green fields and scented meadows grew black and thick with the refuse from factory gutters until" the once pastoral river "resembled more a sewer than the winding watercourse" of its upper stretches. After this introduction to the environmental damage inflicted by Britain's industrial revolutions, Palmer approached one of the factories responsible for polluting northern England's air and water.[6]

The Wigan cotton mills filled Palmer with awe. In a lengthy letter to his uncle, Palmer wrote that the gargantuan factory had given him "a more exalted opinion of the power of machinery and of the genius of the great inventors . . . than all the panegyrics I could have read." Inside Palmer found "1,100 men, women and children" busily "guiding the almost automatic machines that perform with so much ease the manual labour. A thousand horsepower endlessly at work at as many different trades, varying in importance from the carrying of men and cotton up and down stairs to the setting in motion 800 looms, weaving the fabric so fast that you can hardly follow it with your eye." Wherever Palmer looked, he saw machines "conducting with perfect system the entire duties of the manufacture with slight superintendence from the pigmy race who brought them into life." The self-acting mule that spun cotton into thread struck the young American as "the most astonishing machine I ever saw," while the sight of the weaving room "looms doing their master's work with a regularity and speed that nothing but steam power could produce," he said, would "remain in my memory as one of the few things worthy of being remembered though everything else fail." As for the engines driving these machines, Palmer proclaimed them "undoubtedly the finest pieces of mechanism I have yet seen. Feeding their own coals[,] turning their own valves, pumping their own water into the boilers, registering their own force by guages [*sic*] . . . , providing themselves for the safety of their attendants in case of accidents, and giving motion besides to all the innumerable machinery and contrivances within the rooms of the factories, one could get a better idea of omnipotence . . . than the strongest imagination could otherwise furnish him with."[7]

Palmer found the scale, scope, and "perfect system" of the mills nothing short of sublime. Nowhere in the United States could he have witnessed anything like it. Yet even as the romantic in Palmer trembled in the presence of this modern wonder, the realist in him resolved to trace back to its earthly source the seemingly supernatural power that vitalized the mills' "inert matter." The next day, Palmer "occupied the hours of daylight in descending and ascending deep coal mine shafts in the neighborhood of Wigan and in crawling about with back and legs at an angle quite as acute as the pain thereby caused through underground passages that were apparently constructed for some lilliputian race yet to be discovered." Though he derided "colliers and collieries" as "decidedly the most unpleasing things," the traveler nonetheless focused most of his subsequent tour on the frequently unpleasant subject of coal. Palmer even published most of his letters under the wry title of "Underground Walks in England."[8]

The dawning realization that the sublime and the infernal aspects of British industrialism were intimately interrelated troubled the young American's Quaker morals, romantic love of nature, and republican distaste for fixed class distinctions. Tramping south from Lancashire to the Midlands, Palmer found farming and grazing "entirely sacrificed, for the fields beneath are more valuable than those at the surface." The sky in what Britons called the Black Country—"no name," sniffed Palmer, "could be more appropriate"— remained "always obscure and dusty" no matter how "bright the sky or sunny the day a few miles remote." Beneath the smoke and haze stretched a buckling, heaving landscape scarred by "abundant records of the work that has been going on below." Here in the Black Country, it seemed to Palmer, "no other business [was] thought of . . . than that of mining the Coal and Iron ore which underlie it and converting them to purposes of utility."[9]

The young American noted how coal and the industries it powered put not only the land, but also workers' lives and health in jeopardy. The sickly appearance of Sheffield's coke handlers appalled him; they looked "as though their lungs had become too familiar with sulphuretted hydrogen and . . . too ignorant of the pure, fresh air from which they are daily excluded." Worse still were conditions in the collieries which powered the British economy. Palmer expressed amazement at the policies and technologies that operators used to guard their employees against the hazards of mining; at the "fiery" Incehall colliery, for instance, he marveled at "the strict surveillance" carried out by mine officials called "firemen, who sit as if in judgment on benches near the foot of the pits" and at the steam engines responsible for "draining a mass of water which is never exhausted, in order that men may work and live in what would otherwise be only a vast pond." Yet despite such measures, acute and chronic dangers nonetheless lurked wherever Palmer ventured on his "underground walks." He decried such "fearful sources of danger and disease to the workman" as the explosive methane emitted from the coal seams into a Sheffield colliery with a "loud singing sound very much like that of a tea-kettle, close to the boiling point." He also recoiled at the complaints of colliers secreted away from "wholesome sunshine and the light of Heaven," who spoke to him "of the crouching, confined position which their labor necessitated."[10]

Most shocking of all to the young American, however, was the use of female and child labor in and around the mines. Depicting mining women as "a stout, muscular race, equipped with heavy boots," Palmer huffed that he had to take "a second look to assure" himself "that they [were] not in reality what they seem[ed] to be, men." Palmer was more sympathetic to the trapper boys who had to remain "sitting the whole livelong day without any light but such as would flash by them in the hands of the passing colliers," by no means "a pleasant substitute for the race over the green fields, the playground sports and attendant sunlight, in the midst of which an English lad is usually inducted into his teens." Mine work seemed to turn boys into drones, women into men, and manly laborers into "an inferior class of beings."[11]

Appalling as Palmer found the travails of British laborers, though, he was equally concerned about the tactics workers were using to improve their lot. After attending the meeting of a colliers' pit committee, Palmer grumbled that "these 'Unions' never stop with the redress of those wrongs which first caused them to be established." Palmer ardently believed that colliers deserved relief from poor ventilation and other occupational hazards. And yet his sympathies extended only so far. "The question of wages," he ominously warned, "will surely be entertained by those who have found that in 'Union is strength.'" Once miners began to feel their oats, strikes "with all their attendant evils" would inevitably "come to afflict" the industry, an eventuality that would deny workmen their wages, capitalists their profits, and consumers their fuel.[12]

Together, Palmer's dispatches reflected the future business giant's dawning recognition of coal's centrality to the industrial revolution. Palmer knew that the "omnipotence" so evident at the Wigan mills was possible only because of the "unpleasing" collieries below, just as he called coal "the real creator of all the wealth and prosperity we now witness" at Birmingham, the driving force that had turned this small town into "the iron depot of Europe and lined her streets with the shops and dwellings of princely manufacturers." Palmer had embarked on his tour of subterranean Britain largely because he needed material to fill his *Miner's Journal* letters. The more he saw of the leading industrial economy in the world, however, the more he became convinced that the real story of Britain's success was rooted as much in the collieries as in the engineering marvels they fueled. [13]

Thus William Palmer began to teach himself the art and science of reading coal strata. Palmer returned to Pennsylvania in the spring of 1856 intent on leveraging the knowledge he had amassed on his tireless wanderings through British collieries and coal-consuming industries into a career at the frontlines of America's nascent fossil-fuel-driven economy. He had already begun to court J. Edgar Thomson, the president of the Pennsylvania Railroad and one of the first American railroad executives to embrace the coal age. Thomson, described by one historian as having done "more than any one man who ever lived to establish, create, and perfect the railway system of the American continent," had taken note of Palmer's dispatches to the *Miner's Journal* and had even found time on a busy trip to London to squeeze the young American into his schedule. For the remainder of his trip, Palmer had provided Thomson with detailed reports on how British railroads used coal and coke. Once back in the states, Palmer began conducting extensive surveys of American coal properties for Thomson. Two years later, he performed a series of experiments that helped convert Pennsylvania's locomotives to coal from wood, which was fast becoming scarce and expensive in the Northeast. Even as these accomplishments earned Palmer membership in Philadelphia's prestigious Franklin Institute, he was supplementing his geological skills with business acumen. In 1857 he became secretary of the Westmoreland Coal Company at the early age of nineteen. Shortly thereafter, Palmer began a job that would change the course of his life, a four-year tenure as Thomson's private secretary, during which time Palmer worked closely with Thomas Scott and Andrew Carnegie.[14]

Lincoln's election in 1860 and the South's secession brought Palmer, raised like many of his fellow Quakers as an ardent opponent of slavery, to take up arms. He organized a "picked body of light cavalry" in the fall of 1861 and served as its commander for the duration of the war. Named the Anderson Troop, after Fort Sumter's defender, and later mustered into service as the Fifteenth Pennsylvania Cavalry, Palmer's special forces regiment swept down the Mississippi in 1862, then back to Pennsylvania for drilling and re-organization. As Robert E. Lee's army withdrew following the Battle of Antietam in September 1862, Palmer volunteered to spy behind enemy lines. Though captured in civilian clothes, Palmer managed to avoid summary ex-ecution by playing the role of W. J. Peters, a Baltimore-based mining engi-neer of Palmer's invention. After several months in the Confederate prison in Richmond known as Castle Thunder, as he related after the war in a *Harper's* article entitled "The General's Story," Palmer was freed in an exchange of prisoners. He went on to lead his men through two more years of fierce fighting in eastern Tennessee, Alabama, and Georgia. The soldier who "never expected to come back" from the fighting finished the war holding a brevet commission as brigadier general, making him the highest-ranking Quaker in either army.[15]

And though he laid down his arms at war's end "without a scratch" on his body, Palmer would always be marked by the war. Soon after returning to his regiment from prison, Palmer detailed to his father the new philosophy of life he had adopted at Castle Thunder. "If we do what seems for the best at the time, I think nothing further is required of us. Let Providence attend to the rest." This cast of mind, as Palmer would later admit, rendered him "too reckless to care for consequences, or the opinions of people." Foremost among the people whose "opinions" he dismissed were his troops, many of whom grumbled at their commander's merciless drilling and haughty de-meanor. His republican and Quaker tenets now hardened by militarism, Palmer set out to make his mark in the world with the self-assurance of a man who had served his country and cheated death while many of his friends were serving themselves.[16]

Even before the war ended, J. Edgar Thomson had offered Palmer a posi-tion of considerable authority and responsibility, as secretary-treasurer for the Union Pacific Railway, Eastern Division, renamed the Kansas Pacific (K.P.) in 1868. Thomson and his associates at the Pennsylvania Railroad had invested both their hopes and their money in this now forgotten transconti-nental pathway, destined to become one of history's great losers when the Union Pacific and the Central Pacific linked up in May 1869. Soon after ac-cepting the St. Louis–based position, Palmer boasted "of being instrumental in carrying the 'star of empire' westward across this Great Continent"—into the heart of a region he would transform into the most heavily exploited coalfield between Illinois and New South Wales.[17]

Traveling as hastily as possible during a summer marred by constant warfare between Plains Indians and U.S. troops, Palmer crossed the Kansas-Colorado border in late July 1867. Accompanied by his personal secretary William Colton, an African American servant nicknamed Tecumseh, Alexander Gardner, the famed Civil War photographer who had taken the last photograph of Abraham Lincoln before his assassination, and ten cavalrymen, Palmer hurried to intercept the Kansas Pacific railway survey. One of the largest, most ambitious, and least-heralded expeditions ever to explore the American West, the survey had set out from central Kansas in June under the command of General W. W. Wright. Complaints about Wright's poor leadership and fondness for drink led Palmer to assume personal command of the survey. Over the next seven months, Palmer would shepherd the two-hundred-man party as it charted thousands of miles of potential routes on the all-important leg from New Mexico to the Pacific. En route to Santa Fe, however, Palmer planned to spend some time looking into what he called "the paramount consideration," coal. On the road to Colorado Palmer had received a dispatch containing a chemical analysis of a coal sample from Raton Mountain, southwest of Trinidad. "If the veins in the Raton Mtns. are anything like the size reported," wrote one of Palmer's subordinates at the Kansas Pacific, "I should judge the Deposit more valuable that [sic] most of the Colorado Gold Mines."[18]

The news was encouraging, but the Kansas Pacific could not base its plans on a single sample. Palmer thus led a party consisting of geologist John J. LeConte, engineer L. H. Eicholtz, and others to reconnoiter the foothills between Trinidad and northern New Mexico in search of coal outcrops. Though American explorers had reported finding "stone coal" in the area in the early 1840s, the region's fossil fuel reserves remained relatively unknown to the wider world until Palmer's 1867 explorations. Eicholtz "brought in" a piece so fine that the general claimed it "might have been taken for Pittsburgh coal." LeConte found a twenty-five-foot-thick vein near Raton Pass that he compared to another well-known Pennsylvania coal. "An active week in hunting up and examining the coal beds" between Trinidad and the Maxwell Grant of northern New Mexico, Palmer reported to K.P.

president John Perry, "had revealed a greater number of coal veins . . . in crossing the Raton Mtn. than I have seen or heard of either in England or elsewhere in the United States." In the heart of an arid land where traveling by boat was impossible, fuel wood was scarce and expensive, and the soil could sustain only a portion of the population's needs, Palmer's party found immense reservoirs of power containing the accumulated chemical energy synthesized by untold trillions of ancient plants over the course of billions of days. One ten-foot-thick bed alone, the general estimated, held "enough coal in it, within an area of 10 square miles" to fuel two thousand locomotives for a hundred years.[19]

Coalification

Though Palmer's coal discoveries depended on his party's persistence in tracking down outcrops and their expertise in reading them, the general and his men could hardly conjure coal out of the thin Colorado air. Their findings were possible only because of events that had taken place at the time the Rocky Mountains were first formed, long before human life evolved.[20]

Most of the coal seams Palmer had investigated in Europe and the eastern United States and Europe dated from the Carboniferous period, between 360 and 300 million years ago. Colorado's coal deposits, by contrast, started forming during the Late Cretaceous, roughly 70 million years ago. At that time, a warm, shallow body of water that geologists inelegantly call the Western Interior Cretaceous Seaway extended deep into what is now Colorado. Sharks, marine predators such as the fifty-five-foot-long mosasaur, and a fifteen-foot-long razor-toothed bonefish swam through the seaway's tropical waters; *Tyrannosaurus rex* and other dinosaurs thundered along its shores; and above them pterosaurs with twenty-five-foot wingspans spiraled upward on the balmy air currents.[21]

On some long-distant day an unfathomably slow revolution began that would shape nearly every aspect of the region's natural and human history. The Rockies began to push up out of the water like a creature rising from the deep. Long-submerged seafloors in eastern and central Colorado gradually shook off the sea. Almost all of Colorado stood high and dry by sixty-nine million years before the present. As the shoreline slid eastward, a new coastal

environment of bays and deltas, of lazy rivers and sluggish swamps, materialized.[22]

Though Palmer and his fellow surveyors gloried in the dry, clear air and
snow-covered heights of the southern Rockies, Colorado's mountains had
begun their ascent in hot, sticky conditions, more like present-day Borneo or
the Everglades—a low-lying landscape of floodplains and swamplands. With
no frost, little seasonal variation in temperature, and prodigious annual rains
of 120 inches or more, the climate was ideal for plants. For millions of years,
ferns, mosses, cycads, figs, palms, and cypresses thrived in locales where
Palmer found only sparse grasses, shrubs, and scrubby evergreens in the
1860s.[23]

Plants, nature's fuel cells, grow by turning solar energy into chemical energy. Then as now, the most important inputs in the intricate series of reactions that drive this process are light, water, and carbon dioxide. The major
outputs include oxygen and carbohydrates, energy-rich organic compounds
that sustain a vast array of other organisms, including human beings.

The prodigious vegetation that grew year-round along the Cretaceous
seaway could synthesize and store vastly more energy in a single year than
could the stark ecosystems that Palmer traversed in Colorado tens of millions of years later. And since the swamplands flourished for thousands of
millennia, these ancient environments turned truly staggering quantities of
solar energy into forms that other species could exploit. Through death, decomposition, concentration, and compression, some of the carbohydrates
that sustained the ancient ecosystems of southern Colorado became trapped
in the lifeless black strata that would so interest William Palmer.

The first step in the formation of coal began when scavenging bacte-
ria feasted on leaves, branches, trunks, and other plant matter that fell into
waterlogged swamps. An initial stage of aerobic decomposition consumed
roughly half the plant matter. The remainder sank into the oxygen-poor
waters below, forming a dark muck rich in organic by-products of photosyn-
thesis.[24]

As subsequent generations of plants died, their weight pushed down on
their predecessors, compressing partially decayed remains into tangled
masses of peat. It took thirty to fifty years for a single inch of peat to form.
Shifting shorelines, fluctuating climates, and other paleoenvironmental

changes all affected the thickness and extent of peat beds. In places where peat deposition continued with little or no interruption for eons, however, beds of partially decomposed organic matter eventually measured dozens, even hundreds of feet from top to bottom.[25]

By the early Tertiary period (around fifty million years ago) the swamp-lands of southern Colorado had ceased to exist. Other sediments buried the thick beds of peat laid down over the preceding millions of years. Cut off from the life-giving rays of the sun, biological processes ground to a halt in these deposits. Physical forces then became the main engines of coalification. Though there is more than a measure of truth in the characterization of coal as "buried sunshine," the earth's own energies also helped transform porous, tangled peat, a substance so soft you can pick it apart with your fingers, into coal, a denser, more concentrated material that can be worked only with spe-cial tools and explosives. Once a peat bed had been buried beneath about a hundred meters of material, pressure from overlying sediments and geother-mal energy conducted outward from the earth's core resulted in rising sub-terranean temperatures with every additional meter of depth. Deposits that had formed in swampy conditions began to dry out. Injections of thermal energy drove chemical reactions, some of which sheared molecules of oxy-gen and hydrogen off the carbohydrates catalyzed by ancient plants. By and by, the remaining material grew more compact and rich in carbon.[26]

The Coal Age

While Palmer the geologist pieced together the explanation of how these coal strata formed, Palmer the entrepreneur was beginning to look beyond what *was* to what *could be*—the work these stores of solar energy could perform. Amid the detritus of the Rockies' distant past, Palmer discerned clues to Britain's recent history.

Palmer's expedition for the railroad was representative of the vanguard of industrial America, which was turning its energies westward after the Civil War. The survey's mission was to determine how to bring the coal age to a frontier world of foot trails and wagon roads, Indian pueblos, Anglo home-steads, and Hispano plazas in which the muscles of humans and domestic animals afforded the main type of motive power. In this world, wood, animal droppings, and other organic fuels kept the home fires burning, and everything made out of iron or steel required expensive, time-consuming transport from furnaces and manufactories hundreds or thousands of miles away. The leaders of the Kansas Pacific wanted to change all that by supplanting muscle power, wood, and dependence on imports with a coal-fired industrial economy based on Great Britain's pioneering example. Palmer's grand tour of Britain and France in the mid-1850s had inspired his efforts to realize a reformed industrial order in the Mountain West.

As a young engineer, Palmer had grasped that industrial expansion would rely on fossil fuels. It was an obvious connection to make, yet one entirely ignored by Britain's great classical economists, Adam Smith, Thomas Malthus, and David Ricardo. Though the world these thinkers inhabited was in the throes of a process that one present-day scholar calls mineral-intensive industrialization, the economic orthodoxies they established failed to account for the essential role of fossil fuels as a catalyst of rapid economic and demographic growth. Such eminent Continental political economists as Johann von Thünen and even Karl Marx overlooked coal just as completely. Palmer, by contrast, looked at southern Colorado's rich coal prospects in 1867 and asked a question that would change the course of Western history: If coal could revolutionize the British economy, why couldn't it transform the sleepy Colorado frontier?[27]

Though he did not put it in so many words, Palmer realized that the rapid growth of British industry depended on the momentous transition from an economy in which most energy and materials derived from organic sources to a mineral-intensive economy in which fossil fuels and metals (particularly iron) played a much more important role. This transition, which actually unfolded in two overlapping stages, had begun at least a century before Palmer's tour: first, the island nation had shifted from an agrarian economy capable of only very gradual growth to a more intensive organic economy in which agricultural improvement and the greater exploitation of windpower and waterpower facilitated somewhat more rapid growth; next, Britain led the world headlong into a coal-powered age of iron, steel, and unprecedented expansion.[28]

Palmer's encounter with the Wigan mills had revealed the new potential that coal could unleash. Whereas organic energy sources fluctuated from season to season and year to year, fossil fuels provided a more or less constant supply of energy. Plants grew only seasonally. Animals wore out; winds died down; streams abated. And yet the Wigan mills continued to churn out fabric with uninterrupted "regularity and speed." Remaining "endlessly at work," they provided steadier returns than any investment that was subject to nature's fluctuations. Vastly more productive than older technologies, the mills' steam-powered machinery greatly increased the amount of thread or fabric a single worker could produce. Coal power made it easier to concentrate workers and machines at a single site, thereby generating considerable economies of scale. All this productivity remained possible only so long as colliers continued to toil in the strata below.[29]

Palmer concerned himself with the realities of 1850s Britain, whereas Smith, Malthus, and Ricardo had sought to understand an idealized world in which all the necessities of life came from the land itself. Food, shelter, clothing, heat, mechanical energy, raw materials—all derived from the bounty of the soil. Virtually all economic goods—cloth and firewood, wheat and meat, motive power and the very roofs over people's heads—required the diversion of energy produced by plants, animals, water, or wind. Because only a finite amount of solar energy reaches the earth's surface each year, the productivity of organic economies remained strictly delimited, as historian E. A. Wrigley explains, by "the annual inflow of energy from the sun."[30]

Economies based on organic energy sources could and did expand, of course. The expansion of cultivation onto previously marginal lands, the introduction of New World crops such as potatoes and maize, improvements in means of transport, colonial conquests, the development of chattel slavery, breakthroughs in harnessing the energy of the wind and rivers, and other factors could all facilitate growth as measured in output per capita. In *The Wealth of Nations* (1776) Adam Smith used the example of the division of labor in pin production to elucidate still another way to increase productivity: by increasing, in Wrigley's words, "the efficiency with which an energy *flow* can be utilized." Yet "as long as the main sources of power and heat were organic," and hence limited by the fixed land surface of the earth, growth through improved efficiency was destined to remain "necessarily quite modest."[31]

Smith acknowledged "that there would be an upper limit to the productivity per man attainable," but Malthus's forecast proved gloomier still. He predicted that economic upswings would inevitably sow the seeds of their own destruction. Demographic expansion would multiply the quantity of "necessaries" needed to maintain human life. Mounting demands would eventually overtax limited supplies of land. Pauperization and starvation would ensue, Malthus prophesied, until populations ebbed to their former levels.[32]

Ricardo best expressed the ironclad limits to growth in organic economies through the principle of diminishing marginal returns. Farmers could increase agricultural yields, for example, by introducing such "improved" methods as new crop rotations or application of manure. Yet every technique they could devise for eking out an additional unit of output required "an increasing proportional input of labour, or capital, or both." Farmer Jones might spend one extra day plowing, and hence harvest enough wheat to feed his family for two days. But the second additional day of plowing might yield just enough wheat to eat for a day and a half, and the third would produce still less. In such a scenario, it was only a matter of time before the work Jones expended in growing an additional day's worth of wheat required more energy than it produced. Expanding output beyond that point, Ricardo claimed, was impossible. Thus an economy composed almost entirely of farmers had no way of achieving the rapid, more or less sustained growth that citizens of mineral-intensive economies now take for granted. The essential dilemma of diminishing marginal returns, Ricardo declared resignedly, was the absolute dependence of organic economies on "the laws of nature, which have limited the productive powers of the land."[33]

As long as people relied on current flows of solar energy to meet virtually all their needs and wants, the mechanisms detailed by Malthus and Ricardo continued to constrain human societies. By delving below the earth's surface, though, producers could set changes in motion that made ongoing expansion possible across "a large and growing sector of economic activity. Each step taken made the next easier to take." While organic economies remained subject to the limited flow of solar energy, mineral-intensive economies could draw on the accumulated capital of eons past—the fossilized plant matter that had piled up over many millions of years in Britain and Colorado alike.[34]

A Stagnant Frontier

The Colorado frontier through which Palmer traveled in 1867 could not have seemed more different from industrializing Britain. A land of rugged topography and startling splendor, it had a dry climate and a sparse population. The economy of this territorial outpost was stagnant, and the inhabitants were so isolated that they were driven to the point of distraction. Native populations had plummeted because of disease, warfare, and environmental change. Even non-native populations had ebbed since the Pike's Peak Gold Rush crested in 1859. The region's fabled gold mines had consumed more wealth than they produced. Unscrupulous hucksters were destroying the territory's reputation in financial markets. Locusts were devouring the crops.[35]

All was not well, in short, with Colorado, for behind these afflictions loomed problems that seemed intractable. Despite the blood spilled during the conquest of the territory, the toil expended in its transformation, and the capital invested in its prospects, growth had stalled. The geologist William H. Brewer summed up the dire straits in which Coloradans found themselves by the late 1860s when he observed that a "premature decriptude [*sic*]" was descending on the territory.[36]

Colorado's stagnation flew in the face of one of the most pervasive myths of national life. Americans liked to believe that a higher power had charged them with a sacred duty to subdue the continent and dispossess its native peoples. A strain of thinking that led back to the Puritan idea of the "city on a hill" promised that those who carried out this divine mission of conquest would profit morally and financially. The ideology of manifest destiny denied the possibility that the frontier might fail to reward the extravagant hopes Americans had invested in it. And yet as many emigrants to Colorado were discovering, neither westward expansion nor the economic advancement it promised was inevitable.

The troubles that beset the Colorado frontier at the time of General Palmer's 1867 visit originated in the fundamental challenges the region's climate and geography posed to human economies. As Palmer and other members of the Kansas Pacific survey discovered, the interrelated problems of isolation and aridity lay at the heart of Colorado's woes. The core of western North

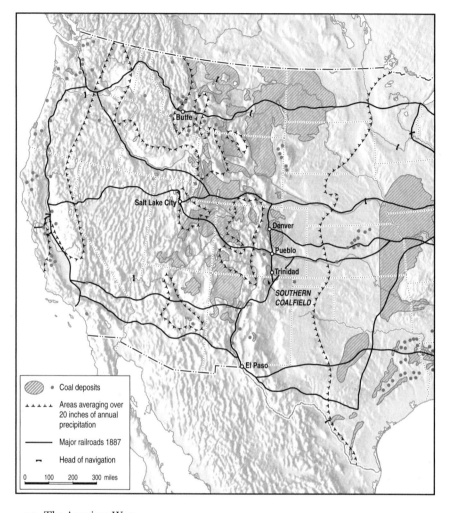

1.1. The American West.

America lay too high and dry for water travel. From southern Canada to
northern Mexico and from the hundredth meridian to the Pacific crest lay a
vast, virtually unnavigable expanse. By the 1860s, commercial steamships
were plying the Missouri River as far as Fort Benton, Montana; the Colorado
to Callville, Arizona; and the Sacramento–San Joaquin and Columbia-
Willamette systems into the interior valleys of California, Oregon, and Washington. Small craft could travel still farther up some of these waterways. Even
so, boats of all descriptions inevitably scraped up against the edge of a new

country, the first American frontier of any extent to be explored, settled, and developed without the benefit of transportation by waterway. Only lunatics, daredevils, and John Wesley Powell believed that the shallow, sluggish streams of the plains or the raging, boulder-strewn rapids of the mountains could take them anywhere they wanted to go.[37]

The only reliable way to move people and things was to travel over the rugged land itself—hardly an ideal solution. Boats glided over flat, slick surfaces. Humans and animals on foot and the conveyances they hauled, by contrast, had to negotiate rough terrain that ranged from gentle slopes to some of the steepest grades on the continent. Gravity challenged travelers at every turn. Even relatively easy journeys such as Palmer's gallop along the Santa Fe Trail entailed gaining and losing many hundreds of feet of elevation; travel became exponentially more difficult as a person headed from the Rocky Mountain foothills westward. Overcoming friction and gravity took time, skill, patience, and considerable expenditure of energy. Slow and expensive travel imposed the equivalent of a heavy surcharge on every transaction that required traversing Colorado's rugged land.

Capturing the energy flowing through Colorado waterways proved only slightly easier than traveling on them. On the plains, most rivers and creeks lazed along, too shallow and broad to drive millwheels. Mountain watercourses, meanwhile, hurtled down with awesome and often unpredictable force. Hemmed in by canyon walls, they funneled melting snow and summer rains into torrents capable of wrecking any timber structure. Though Palmer and his K.P. surveyors found gristmills, sawmills, and stamp mills in operation in different parts of the territory in 1867, use of waterpower was nonetheless proving less practicable in Colorado than almost anywhere else in the United States save the Western deserts. Moving water had driven the first generation of British and American factories, but Coloradans faced grave difficulties in channeling sufficient energy from the region's rivers and streams to duplicate the earlier successes.[38]

Low biological productivity, another consequence of aridity, placed a third check on organic energy economies in Colorado. Only in parts of the high country—a land whose poor, rocky soil clung tenaciously to steep slopes that experienced some of the shortest growing seasons in the continental United States—did the annual average precipitation exceed twenty-four inches per year; the most heavily settled portions of the territory generally struggled by on ten to twenty inches of moisture annually. The region's plants had evolved plunging taproots, waxen leaves, and other remarkable strategies to cope with scant, uneven precipitation. Even so, plants grew more slowly and sparsely in Colorado than in more temperate climes. Woodlands covered less than a fifth of Colorado in the mid-nineteenth century, and none of the region's forests could compare in heft or bulk to those in the Northeast, in the upper Midwest, or on the Pacific Coast. "The mountains are generally clothed with a growth of pines," Cyrus Thomas of the Hayden Survey wrote in 1869, "but these are often of a very inferior character, especially along the eastern slope nearest the arable lands." From eastern Kansas to the base of the Rockies, Kansas Pacific surveyors found "all rolling Prairie—no timber excepting a little along the streams." No wonder that Palmer proclaimed the high plains "the least valuable country on the whole route to the Pacific."[39]

The soil's limited capacity to provide the necessities of life mothered no end of human inventions. Over many millennia, Colorado's indigenous peoples had developed ingenious lifeways that enabled them to survive on the plains and in the mountains by acquiring and sharing vast stores of knowledge about the organisms and landscapes from which they obtained food, fuel, shelter, trade goods, and spiritual sustenance. Agriculture, a far more intensive strategy for channeling solar energy toward human purposes, had taken hold of parts of southwestern and eastern Colorado in the first millennium A.D. Within just a few centuries, however, catastrophic drought and other factors led virtually all Indian peoples in the territory to either abandon farming or retreat to more favorable climes. Thus Colorado supported perhaps the least dense Indian population on the eve of European contact of any part of North America east of the Western deserts and south of the boreal forest.[40]

In the 330 years between the first Spanish incursions into what would later become Colorado and the K.P. survey, two primary sets of biotechnologies had revolutionized how people in the region interacted with one another and the natural world. Since time immemorial, hundreds of generations of Coloradans had taken life one step at a time, as they transported all their belongings either on their persons or atop dog-drawn travois. Horses, initially obtained from the Spanish or seized during the Pueblo Revolt of

1680, enabled Indians to let someone else do the walking. With every stride, horses extended Indian horizons, by making much more of the energy trapped by plains grasslands accessible to native peoples than ever before. A new era of mobility began for Indians once they learned to care for, breed, and ride these strong and noble creatures. Horses, writes Elliott West, represented nothing less than a "liberation."[41]

The Kiowa Nobel laureate N. Scott Momaday likened the resulting amalgam of people and equines to the centaurs of Greek myth. It would probably be still more apt, though, to imagine an even more complex and powerful metamorphosis, a symbiosis among humans, horses, and buffalo. With the decline of the bison, the native peoples of the mountains and plains faced a crisis. From bison the Indians had obtained virtually everything they needed to survive and even thrive on the same lands that seemed so "impoverished" to K.P. surveyors. Already by 1850, bison were becoming scarce along the Colorado piedmont and extinct in the mountain valleys. Once-plentiful herds thinned in part because of increased hunting by native peoples who had grown dependent on the trade goods that bison products could purchase, in part because Indian horse herds crowded bison out of the wooded valleys on which buffalo relied for pasture and shelter. Bison were also killed off by drought, exotic bovine diseases (acquired from the oxen and cattle brought west by overland emigrants), and other factors. After the discovery of gold in 1858 lured upwards of a hundred thousand fortune seekers into the region, bison populations began to fall even more precipitately. By the time of Palmer's visit in 1867, the "black forms of buffaloes" which had "dott[ed] the rolling prairie" and stood "out against the horizon miles away" had disappeared to such a degree that no bison, "no Indians, nothing but level plains covered with short tufts of grass" populated the expanses that stretched out before the general and his men.[42]

A second energy revolution, the reintroduction of agriculture following a centuries-long hiatus, played a part in both the destruction of the buffalo and the native peoples' dispossession of most of eastern and central Colorado by 1867. Farming and ranching enabled Anglo and Hispano settlers to harness the sun's energy for their own ends with greater efficiency than could the horse-mounted buffalo hunters. In a migration that the geographer Donald W. Meinig has astutely declared "a little-known event of major importance," northern New Mexicans began around 1850 to settle long-coveted lands in the San Luis Valley; a decade later, a second stream of *pobladores* settled irrigable valleys in Huerfano and Las Animas counties, the future heart of the southern Colorado coalfields. Beginning around 1859, Anglo farmers had also begun to cultivate the fertile floodplains along the streams fanning out from the base of the Rockies, from the St. Vrain Valley north of Boulder to the Purgatoire Valley west of Trinidad.[43]

Wherever these farmers and their ranching counterparts settled, they replaced wild grasslands and riparian woodlands with farms and ranches. Charles Green, a lanky Ohio farm boy who had been wounded in both arms at Chickamauga, expressed relief and delight when the K.P. survey encountered the first farms since it had left central Kansas a month earlier. After hacking through a "great Wilderness" of sagebrush and greasewood along the Arkansas, Green gloried in the sight of "the picturesque, cultivated and fertile valley of the Huerfano." At last the surveyors "could realize that [they] were in a civilized country."[44]

More than nostalgia, of course, led Green to find a simple visit to a Colorado farm so transporting. Successful transplantation of advanced organic energy economies to the base of the Rockies depended on the construction of irrigation works and the concomitant exploitation of peons and other laborers. "Every Farm has its ditches for irrigating," Green noted from the Huerfano. "Rain is very uncertain," declared A. R. Calhoun, a *Philadelphia Press* reporter who accompanied the survey. Irrigation was "the first thing necessary" for settling the country, but "farming by this means is difficult and requires hard labor." Comparing the oppressive system of debt-peonage employed by many large Anglo and Hispano landowners on the St. Vrain Grant to bondage in the antebellum South, Calhoun found "very little difference between slave labor and the system whereby they get work from the Mexicans."[45]

The advanced organic economy that newcomers to Colorado had constructed gave them decisive advantages over indigenous peoples. By focusing the "productive powers of the soil" on a small number of plant and animal species selected and bred over many millennia to maximize the quantity, quality, and security of nutrition humans could coax from the land, farming and ranching helped the intruders overwhelm native peoples militarily and demographically. Only in remote mountain fastnesses and in bison refugia such as the Smoky Hill country did Indian peoples retain their former autonomy by the time of Palmer's 1867 journey.[46]

Advanced organic energy economies, for all the benefits they provided, failed to liberate Euroamerican newcomers from the limitations imposed by climate and geography. The majority of Colorado's population consisted of townspeople and miners, all of whom were dependent on foodstuffs imported from distant markets over the few roads that stretched east across the dry plains to the river towns of Kansas and Nebraska. Native peoples recognized these narrow arteries as the interlopers' greatest vulnerability. Anglos in Colorado, isolated and hard-pressed to sustain even their own metabolism without supplementing their diet through trade with the plains, understood just how tenuous their existence was, and how dependent they were on the outside world for food supplies. The merest rumor of Indian attacks along the trade lifelines thus gave rise to a siege mentality. If confirmation of supposed "outrages" reached the settlements, the mood spiraled from anxiety to paranoia and finally to rage. "None but the men who passed through the dark and despairing days when everything appeared to work disaster and to threaten annihilation can realize the state of public feeling," claimed Frank Hall, an early settler and Colorado historian. "Colorado seemed to be cut off and set aside as a barren region not worth saving."[47]

Forest depletion and freight rates offer some measure of the difficulties under which the economy labored. Settlers had stripped the river corridors of the plains and piedmont of much of their timber; meanwhile what Palmer's associate A. C. Hunt decried as "wickedly wasteful" lumbering and the sharp increase in forest fires attendant on Anglo settlement cleared growing swaths of timber around Central City and other mining camps. By the late 1860s, many of the Front Range foothills lay "denuded." The dwindling of the forests drove wood prices skyward: $14 per cord in Central City in 1864, $75 in Denver in 1867, and $100 to $150 on the northeastern plains in the same year. Such high prices made heating with wood expensive, and fueling factories with it impossible.[48]

Given that water transport was infeasible, overland travel laborious and expensive, waterpower largely impracticable, fuelwood scant, and agriculture limited by the availability of irrigable land and the vicissitudes of some of the most erratic weather in the United States, the Colorado frontier was suffering through nothing short of an energy crisis at the time of Palmer's coal discoveries.

A Vision of Industry

Having studied the coal outcrops of southern Colorado and northern New Mexico thoroughly enough to "dismiss the fuel difficulty" that arid Western lands posed to energy-hungry railroads, William Palmer rendezvoused with Kansas Pacific survey crews in Santa Fe. While his new men gorged themselves on peaches sold by Pueblo Indian women, Palmer lobbied New Mexico's power brokers to support his railroad.[49]

The general revealed the import of his recent coal discoveries in an address before an assembly of Anglo and Hispano men and women who intended to petition Congress for the construction loans and land grants needed to subsidize the Kansas Pacific. Palmer began by evoking several commonplace themes in transcontinental railroad promotion. The K.P., he claimed, would help the nation rebound from the internecine conflict and financial strain of the Civil War. By subsidizing the railroad, the government could also solve the so-called Indian question by stimulating rapid population growth that would make Western settlements "strong enough to protect themselves and the surrounding country; and the Navajos, Apaches and Comanches will either squat down peacably [sic] on their farms as the Delawares and Wyandottes have done—or else betake themselves, as I hope and believe, to regular employment on the Railroad itself." The Kansas Pacific would facilitate American expansion not only into the Indian Country of the Great Plains and Southwest, but also into Mexico, "bring[ing] about peacefully those relations with Old Mexico which the people of the United States have so much at heart." Last, the Kansas Pacific would reroute "the course of trade throughout the world." In the process, the railroad would secure for the United States "that wonderful commerce of the eastern seas, which from time immemorial has built up populous cities along its channels, and enriched every nation through whose hands it has passed," while ensuring that "the old dream of Columbus" would finally be "realized, and the East . . . found at last by sailing to the West."[50]

Such grand promises—that federal railroad financing would effect the re-construction of the war-torn republic, the conclusive conquest of native peoples, the economic incorporation of northern Mexico, and the fulfillment of the grand mercantilist project that had inspired Columbus to seek Asia across the uncharted Atlantic—might have been uttered by any Western railroad promoter. But toward the end of his speech, Palmer departed from conventional themes in transcontinental railroad advocacy to sound a more novel note. "It requires no prophetic power," he declared, "to foresee the future of the regions [the railroad] will develop." It seemed to him but a matter of time before the Mountain West would duplicate the industrial revolution that had transformed Britain and the American Northeast. The coal outcrops the general and his men had located ensured that "where only the miner's ranche [*sic*] is now visible, furnaces and factories will be built, and cities will spring from the earth at the call of intelligent labor." By exploiting the region's thick coal seams, Palmer believed, Colorado and New Mexico could escape the limitations of isolation and aridity under which they were laboring. He foretold a utopian future for the Rocky Mountain landscape, one powered by the same forces responsible for revolutionizing the British economy.[51]

A Grander and Happier Columbia

More than two years later, in late January 1870, William Palmer, staying in the stately American House Hotel in Denver, described to his young fiancée how "a sight burst upon me which was worthy of God's own day." While the general had spent his weeks supervising the construction of the Kansas Pacific from western Kansas to Denver, by letter he had courted Mary Lincoln "Queen" Mellen, the doe-eyed eighteen-year-old daughter of a prominent Long Island attorney, whom he had met in the spring of 1869. During their separation Palmer beguiled Queen with fantasies of the better world they would create together in Colorado.[52]

His vision that January morning contrasted sublimely with the torpid settlement's dirt streets and false-fronted buildings: "The 'Range' all covered with snow arose, pure and grand, from the brown plains." The beauty of the scene made him wonder, "Could one live in constant view of these grand mountains without being elevated by them into a lofty plane of thought and purpose?" He thought not, for the majestic Rockies glistened "like the shore of a glorious New Land, a newer and grander and happier Columbia than that which greeted the great sailor on the beach of Santa Domingo."[53]

Twenty-eight months earlier in Santa Fe, Palmer had invoked Columbus to symbolize the old American dream of commercial expansion. As he looked westward from the American House in 1870, by contrast, he enlisted the worthy mariner for another purpose altogether: to frame a grand historical drama with himself in the starring role. For decades, cartographers had depicted the plains as "the Great American Desert." To Palmer, however, these vast, desolate expanses seemed more an Atlantic than a Sahara, and the settlements lining their western edge more beachheads than oases.

The moment seemed as auspicious as the setting. America was not only reconstructing itself after the Civil War, but reinventing itself, too. The meaning of freedom, the rights and responsibilities of labor, the relationship between state and nation, the place of women, African Americans, native peoples, and immigrants—all were in flux. A time of great optimism, it was also an era of trouble and terror. Amid such civil strife, many of the displaced and the optimistic looked westward for refuge or redemption.[54]

Palmer was no exception. After returning to St. Louis following the successful completion of the Kansas Pacific survey in early 1868, he had grown disillusioned with business as usual. He confessed to Queen that his conduct following the war had been decidedly "chequered"; he even claimed to have behaved more reprehensibly than "the wickedest man in New York," damning self-reproach indeed for a Philadelphian. More troubling to Palmer than the self-indulgence of his private life—his un-Quakerly taste for expensive wine, fine cigars, and cashmere suits—was the immorality of his dealings for the K.P. "Men in active life," he explained to Queen, "must have a thousand relations with people that they cannot anticipate or control. They are subjected to a great variety of temptations in consequence." Immersed in what he called "the hot competition of this American business life," Palmer confessed, he found it "a great temptation to be a little unscrupulous." Disillusioned with transcontinental railroading, Palmer waited for the opportunity he needed to make a break with the Kansas Pacific and set out on his own.[55]

That opportunity finally presented itself in all its splendor as Palmer beheld the view from American House during a business trip in January 1870.

The Front Range in all its winter glory can take anyone's breath away, but what made this scene such a revelation to Palmer was the blessing it seemed to bestow on the plans he had been hatching for building a better society in the shadow of the Rockies. Two visions lay at the heart of the bright future the general had described to his intended over the previous months: first, an "ideal railroad" that would eliminate competition, end labor disputes, and "solv[e] . . . a good many vexed social problems"; second, a home in nature that would combine the best features of Western wilderness and European refinement.[56]

Palmer began to envision his home in nature on a lovely day in August 1869. He wrote Queen a breathless letter describing Monument Park, at the foot of Pikes Peak about seventy miles south of Denver. He lovingly detailed the "almost perfect" ponderosa-cloaked valley: the "green slopes" rising above, the "wealth of coloring" of its wildflower meadows, and "the softened outline of earth blending with the sky" that "reminds you constantly of the ocean, on whose shore you seem to be standing." Palmer envisaged how he and his bride could transform this "wild Government land now waiting for some-one to take hold of it" into a place where life "would be poetry" it-self. They would begin by securing "several thousand acres" of land at the "Government price," $1.25 an acre. Next, he would rename the place Bijou (French for "jewel"), to signify the transformation of an open and public landscape into an intimate possession "containing likewise the most pre-cious stones of all kinds together with everything that is and ever will be of any real value to me on this earth." The home he designed to make with Queen promised "more leisure, more books, more quiet opportunity to think and plan"—more time, in short, to "bring [himself] back constantly from all this artificial and headlong struggle to Nature, with its toning influ-ences."[57]

Palmer equated struggle with artifice, yet he had no qualms about refash-ioning this landscape. In dreamy prose, he waxed eloquent about how Queen would select a site anywhere "on one of the bold pine-topped hills near the mountain foot" for the couple's "Castle." Their family and friends could build estates nearby, so that the Palmers would never "be without society when we wished it, for sharing in the grand estate should be the houses of our friends—those really our friends." Between these country seats would wind "fountains & lakes and lovely drives and horse back trails through groves," while the valley below would hold "the farms of industrious rancheros that will supply this Eden with what is required for the material wants of its occupants."[58]

When the Palmers and their friends tired of "society," they could retreat to a rugged, primitive "deer park" stocked "with antelope and black-tailed deer and the range for our buffalo—& all other animals native to the Plain, not forgetting even the little Prairie-dog with its 'twinkle of a tail.'" Palmer's time in the West had convinced him that these creatures were "soon to disappear before the advancing tread of emigration," so he took it upon himself to ensure that these creatures "should here all be preserved," together with "a few Indians." Palmer's misgivings about the Indian Wars and the decline in game populations that each extension of the K.P. precipitated probably inspired this scheme to protect vanishing plains natives. But a form of imperialist nostalgia also led the general to conceive of the deer park as a living time machine that would "recall more vividly the wild prairie life—which the Americans of a few years hence will know only from the pages of story books."[59]

By building a home in the midst of nature, Palmer and Queen would blend the primitive virtues of "wild prairie life" with the comforts of domesticity. He predicted that their future in this fantasyland of country castles and pleasure drives, thrifty farms and wildlife reserves, would be a veritable "idyll . . . of the kind that gives wing to the imagination, and allows no foothold for it to halt upon, short of infinity." A beautiful dream, this vision wooed Queen westward (though health problems eventually led her to abandon Colorado for a succession of rented English estates) and inspired Palmer to establish a town colony near Monument Park, on a dry tract that one of Palmer's enterprises disingenuously named Colorado Springs. Before Palmer's lavish vision of a home in nature would be realized, though, the people working in the coalfields would pay a tremendous price.[60]

Palmer's New West

Palmer's daydream of a better model for railroad organization complemented the plan for Bijou. Traveling by train furnished the general with his "favorite time for thinking, not perhaps good hard square business thinking—or formation for plans of life—but that delicious dreaming which does one more good than either, and leaves an aroma of the spirit land for some time." Five months after singing Monument Park's praises to Queen, and a few weeks before his stay at the American House, Palmer indulged in a particularly fruitful spell of daydreaming, envisioning a "model way of" doing business that seemed sure to forestall competition, eliminate labor conflict, and assuage a conscience troubled by eight years of military and commercial combat.[61]

Palmer believed that the best way to create a more benign industrial order was to operate monopolistically. He blamed capitalism's woes on competition, which induced firms to despoil the landscape and operate against the interests of their employees and customers. He thus saw Colorado's isolation as an asset instead of a liability, for the oceanlike expanses of the plains would protect Palmer's railroad from rivalry and give the general the free hand he needed to exercise benevolence while pursuing profit.[62]

Palmer recognized that although geography could facilitate monopoly, it could not prevent internal discord. Like most military men, he favored autocracy and hierarchy. When he dreamed of an "ideal railroad," he dreamed of quasi-military chains of command that would carry out his will unimpeded by the "jealousies and contests and differing policies" that had handicapped the K.P. His favorite officers from the Anderson Troop would occupy the various managerial positions, "the most fitting man" assigned to each. To "occupy the various positions of inspectors, agents, clerks, conductors, brakemen, engineers, mechanics etc.," Palmer planned on recruiting a "host of good fellows" from the regiment. In this manner, he hoped to secure a workforce that would "carry out unimpeded and harmoniously" all his "views in regard to what ought and ought not to be done."[63]

A series of benevolent policies would keep everyone working "heartily and unitedly towards the common end." Palmer would pay his workers "wages enough," he explained to Queen, to "save something and these savings they should be furnished with opportunities of investing in and along the Road." Stock options and profit sharing, two precocious practices that became commonplace only in the twentieth century, would further encourage its employees to become "capitalists themselves in a small way." Soon, workers would come "to feel as though it were their own Road and not some stranger soulless corporation." Once they recognized the company as "their own business and that they were adding to their store and growing more prosperous along with the Road," the laborers of Palmer's imagination would realize that "all their interests would be the same as their employers'": all "waste" and "careless mismanagement" would evaporate and the railroad would become "quite a little family."[64]

Paternal concern for employee welfare would produce happiness, efficiency, and loyalty. "Everybody should be looked after," he fantasized, "to see that there was no distress among the workmen and their families." In *Palmer's* New West, "there never would be any strikes or hard feelings among the labourers towards the capitalists." By forestalling competition, eliminating conflict, and fostering harmony of interests between capital and labor, Palmer felt he had devised "a model way of conjoining . . . usefulness on a large scale" with "a new model of making money."[65]

Even as the would-be railroad entrepreneur was regaling Queen Mellen with these and similar portraits of a utopian future, he was assembling the component parts of an integrated industrial network at the foot of the Rockies. Palmer started acquiring lands throughout Colorado using capital from J. Edgar Thomson and a small clique of other investors from Philadelphia and England. On these tracts he projected the building of lumber operations, irrigated farms, cattle ranches, tourist resorts, townsite developments, and other enterprises.[66]

Once connected by the tracks of his "ideal railroad," these seemingly disparate initiatives would energize the stagnant Western economy and restore virtue to an American nation sullied by political corruption, capitalist excess, and immigration. "We shall have a new and better civilization in the far West," Palmer bragged in a letter suffused by the mid-nineteenth-century reformers' characteristic blend of republicanism, white supremacy, and Protestant perfectionism. In the "newer and grander and happier Columbia" conceived by Palmer, "the people [would] never get to be as thick as on the Eastern seaboard. We will surrender that briny border as a sort of extensive Castle Garden [precursor to Ellis Island as New York's immigration station] to receive and filter the foreign swarms and prepare them by a gradual process for coming to the inner temple of Americanism out in Colorado, where Republican institutions will be maintained in pristine purity."[67]

All Palmer's imaginings rested upon the coal outcrops of southern Colorado. And so he set about surveying and purchasing coal lands, assembling a veritable empire that would eventually encompass thousands of acres of ancient swamplands in southern and western Colorado. The fuel these tracts contained drove the locomotives of Palmer's Denver & Rio Grande Railway, paid for the Palmers' lavish estate at Glen Eyrie, just outside the Garden of the Gods, and made the general's Colorado Coal and Iron Company the largest coal mine operator in the Mountain West.

To Palmer, his interlocking visions held the promise of a better society, where business would be more profitable, human interactions with the natural world more harmonious, and relationships between capitalists and workers more amicable than in the eastern states and Europe. But even as fossil fuels initiated a mineral-intensive industrial revolution that would fundamentally transform the region, they also replicated the environmental devastation, human disfigurement, and class conflict that Palmer was endeavoring to avoid. Balancing the interests of humankind and nature, capitalists and workers, would prove much more difficult than the general dreamed.

2

The Reek of the New Industrialism

The odors of the Rocky Mountain Empire tickled the nose with their contradictions. If we could have followed William Jackson Palmer around Colorado in the late 1860s, we might have breathed in smells of dust and dung, blasting powder and sawdust, pine needles and wood smoke and rotting flesh. On the eve of the great coalfield wars, we would have found many of those odors overwhelmed by the acrid aroma of burning coal and such accompaniments as sulfurous smelter smoke and ozone, newly milled steel and stewing sugar beets.

Indeed, the smell of coal became so pervasive between the 1860s and the 1910s that Coloradans and visitors alike came to take it for granted. The reek of the industrializing West is lost to us, but ample evidence attests to the speed and pervasiveness with which fossil fuels penetrated the very foundations of economy and society, the physical structure of the region, and even its culture. Photographs, drawings, buildings, and ruins provide eloquent testimony to the central role of coal in Western history. Though today we see these images through a different lens than did Coloradans of the late nineteenth and early twentieth centuries, their past and our present nonetheless converge around a shared dependence on fossil fuels and a troubling propensity to overlook the human suffering and environmental destruction that our appetite for energy inflicts on distant hinterlands. But before we can see these connections, we must first abandon American frontier mythologies that make the notion of an industrial West seem like a contradiction in terms.

Surprisingly few photographs of Colorado during this era betray direct evidence of coal. Instead, they attest to the protean nature of energy and its incredible capacity for disguise. The impact of fossil fuels runs as a hidden theme through many of the stock images of the era, whether of the monstrous mechanical drills used by silver miners, the combines that harvested the fields beyond which barbed-wire fences fell away to the horizon, the generating stations dispatching electricity to brighten city streets and department store windows, or the great hard-rock miners' strikes pitting members of the Western Federation of Miners against state militiamen and mine operators. Indeed, by the early twentieth century, even pictures of Main Street facades signaling triumph and permanence, or domestic scenes depicting respectable middle-class families gathered around the hearths of their suburban residences, demonstrated the centrality of coal to Western life. To understand the place of the Colorado coal miners' struggles in the history of the West, we must learn to discern the many ways in which this fossil fuel shaped Colorado's landscape, social character, and political economy.

Railroad Smoke, Coal Fire

Paragons of progress, harbingers of modernity, trains seemed to nineteenth-century Coloradans the restless, relentless symbol of American conquest. "The pioneer locomotive has flashed the keen brilliancy of its headlight against the window panes in the Capital of Colorado," declared the Georgetown newspaper *Colorado Miner* in 1870, signaling a watershed development:

> Those notable journeys "across the continent," behind horses of special speed, bottom and beauty, are experiences of the past. The days . . . when some of us went sailing across an ocean of land instead of an ocean of water, have been met and passed and nearly forgotten. And now we are to be provided with "silver-palace sleeping cars," "restaurant cars," and all the exquisitely luxurious rolling salons that have come into vogue within the last few days. Farewell to the rocking Concords of

the olden time! Farewell to the accomplished and picturesque whips! Denver has conquered her isolation.[1]

The trains that effected this conquest marked their passage with inky plumes. For there to be smoke, of course, there had to be fire; and coal fired the engines of the Western railroads. Railroads and coal mines, which had sprung from common British origins, advanced westward in tandem, together transforming landscape and labor alike.

Two lines of descent linked the railroad to the coal mine. The first led back to the early modern era, when European miners and quarrymen devised wooden rails to speed the transport of stone, ore, and coal in human- or horse-powered cars to the outside world. The second common point of origin lay in the steam engines invented by James Watt, Thomas Newcomen, and other eighteenth-century inventors to pump water from British coal mines. Profligate consumers of fuel, these engines remained tethered to the collieries for more than a century. By the early 1800s, however, improvements in design and machining finally made it possible to free the steam engine from its fuel supply. George Stephenson, a mineworker's son who labored outside the pits of northeastern Britain for more than a decade, united these two lineages by taking the prime mover first devised to drain mines and resituating it atop the parallel rails miners had used for centuries to carry coal and rock from pit to market. Stephenson's first locomotive consummated the railroad-colliery relationship by towing an inaugural cargo of thirty tons of coal. His first railways of any length sealed the union by connecting the coal pits with ports and industrial centers, first in County Durham, then in Lancashire and Merseyside.[2]

Both rails and steam engines appeared on the American scene by the early 1800s. And though in the summer of 1830 anthracite fueled the locomotive Tom Thumb in its maiden voyage along the Baltimore & Ohio, the nation's first recognizably modern railroad, the vast flows of organic energy contained in American forests and the embryonic state of the U.S. coal industry quickly impelled most early railroads in the United States to substitute wood for coal. By the time of the Civil War, however, the depletion of America's eastern woodlands reunited trains and coal. When J. Edgar Thomson and other transportation magnates turned their energies westward following the Union victory, they well understood that their plans to incorporate the isolated, sparsely timbered expanses of the plains and mountains into the nation's rail networks would hinge on fossil fuel.[3]

William Palmer, that reader of coal seams, exclaimed that he "would not give a fig for any railroad that had no promise of a coal traffic." Like any successful railroad executive, he recognized that companies depended on coal not simply for fuel but also for freight. So Rocky Mountain railroads—Palmer's Denver & Rio Grande (D&RG) and its competitors—took care to locate their lines to take advantage of the Cretaceous and Tertiary legacy. The general's engineers tucked the Kansas Pacific tracks along lignite outcrops on the northern edge of the Monument Divide; by the early 1870s, the K.P. and several other companies had also laid tracks connecting the northern coalfields with Denver, the Clear Creek mining districts, and agricultural communities along the base of the mountains. Palmer's D&RG was simultaneously building out to the Fremont County coalfields, where Palmer opened his first collieries in 1872; then it extended south to Huerfano County in 1876, Las Animas County in 1878, Crested Butte in 1880, and other western Colorado coalfields thereafter. The Atchison, Topeka, & Santa Fe (AT&SF) and the Denver, Gulf, & Fort Worth (later renamed the Colorado & Southern) soon built competing lines to the southern fields, and several railroads vied with the D&RG in the Western fields throughout the 1880s. Though the Santa Fe and some other railways withdrew from the coal business—the managers reasoned, "There is coal enough on the line and enterprise enough in the public to develop these mines to our advantage, without our material assistance"—the pattern of coal-driven railroad development nonetheless continued into the twentieth century. The D&RG's North Fork Extension reached coalfields northeast of Delta, the so-called Moffat Road penetrated the rich seams of northwest Colorado, and Colorado Fuel and Iron subsidiaries extended tracks into the coal-rich Purgatoire and Crystal valleys.[4]

These railroads tapped into several distinct deposits, suited by their varying chemical and physical properties for different applications. The northern fields of Boulder, Weld, and Jefferson counties contained lignite, ideal for heating homes and generating electricity. The more dispersed fields of western Colorado held a full spectrum of coal types, including anthracite, the cleanest- and hottest-burning of all. In the southern fields, meanwhile, coal deposits ranged from sub-bituminous to bituminous. Long episodes of volcanic mountain building along the New Mexico border had subjected Las Animas County's seams to considerable heat and pressure. These forces, though they destroyed some of the county's coal deposits, elsewhere left behind rich beds of coking coal, a peerless industrial fuel. Just to the north, Huerfano County straddled a transition zone; its coal displayed what one commentator termed "a noticeable variance of composition," some varieties being "highly adapted for domestic purposes" and others used mostly "for steaming." Finally, the Fremont County seams lay distant from the ancient forces of volcanism; though lower in carbon content than its southern counterparts, coal from the Cañon City area nonetheless surpassed Huerfano and Las Animas County varieties in its suitability for household and smithy use.[5]

Railroad corporations set up most large-scale coal mines in Colorado through wholly owned subsidiaries; locomotives consumed much of the fuel unearthed during mining's formative stages; and railways continued to connect the fossil-fuel-producing hinterlands with markets throughout the state and region even after railroad managers divested themselves of their coal industry holdings in the 1890s and 1900s. Without railroads, coal mining would have remained a marginal industry. But what of the converse: How would the railroads of the Mountain West have fared in the absence of such rich and varied coal deposits? There is no way to know for sure, but certainly Colorado's rail networks would ultimately have looked much different. Railroad companies would have built many fewer miles of track; not only would they have had no need to bend and extend routes to trace the contours of coal deposits, but higher fuel costs might have rendered some routes unprofitable. As for Palmer, he surely would have set his sights on landscapes more capable of satisfying his dream of coal-fired benevolence.[6]

The combined might of railroads and coal mines first eroded, and then destroyed, the isolation that had so vexed inhabitants of frontier Colorado. Incorporating the Mountain West into the nation, trains reoriented the way in which the region's inhabitants experienced time, space, and mass.

Step by step, rail networks crisscrossed and tamed some of the most recalcitrant topography on earth. As they compressed the distance between points, they rendered Colorado a smaller, less isolated place. Even in the late 1860s it took several weeks to reach the Rockies from the Missouri River. By the early 1880s, steam trains had reduced the journey to one long day. And by century's end the Atlantic seaboard lay just two nights' travel from the Rockies. Places that had felt impossibly far away now seemed startlingly close. Coal-powered rail travel expedited the transport of people and cargo, thus integrating the Mountain West more fully into national and international markets for labor, capital, and leisure. As immigration to Colorado increased, the "briny border" of the eastern seaboard, which William Palmer had envisioned as an "extensive Castle Garden" to be entrusted with preserving "Republican institutions . . . in pristine purity," lost whatever power it had formerly exerted to "receive and filter the foreign swarms and prepare them by a gradual process for coming to the inner temple of Americanism out in Colorado."[7]

Coal-powered railroads changed the way people experienced their world, as the hands of virtually every clock and watch in Colorado were shortly to demonstrate. In February 1871, just eight months after work crews completed Denver's first rail connection to the East, a newspaper reported that the city's jewelers had "decided to adopt a system of time that will approach uniformity. They will get Chicago time each day by telegraph and regulate their timepieces accordingly." Many Coloradans welcomed the eclipse of frontier chaos and the advent of modern standardization. "As it is now," the paper explained, "every man has his own time and will swear by it." If the new "Chicago time" seemed "a little fast," the paper announced, "we will get used to it."[8]

Railroads tended to make time more homogeneous in other ways, too. In the early 1880s, before railroads reached the San Juan silver mines, M. K. Ihlseng explained, "The outdoor working season extends from June to January, the softening of the snows render[s] the roads difficultly passable until July, then the regular rains for a fortnight impede freighting—the implacable elements thus discourage, if not entirely suspend, active operations until late in July." Harsh mountain weather made mining impossible for half the year; worse, seasonal shifts in weather, in road conditions, and in the availability of feed shortened the work year still further by hampering the progress of wagons, sledges, and mule trains. Unlike these older transportation technologies, railroads relied on fuel derived from the fossilized energy that colliers steadily extracted from distant subterranean chambers. Avalanches and floods would continue to pose "a serious expense" to railroad companies, yet wherever locomotives marked the sky, once-seasonal work such as mining and logging became practicable for more of the year. In the process, coal-powered railroads helped reset the rhythms of labor to industrial time. The availability of jobs and the pace of work now depended more on business cycles and capitalist caprice than on nature's fluctuations.[9]

The immense motive power of the railroad may have proved even more significant than its superhuman speed or its ability to defy the seasons. Since time immemorial, the lack of navigable water in the West had forced people to move from place to place overland. The region's rough land surfaces and often convoluted topography forced people, draft animals, and conveyances to overcome a great deal of friction and gravity in the course of any journey. Freight costs in the regional organic-energy economies consequently assumed astronomical proportions. Trains, by contrast, ran on hard, smooth wheels of iron or steel that glided on sleek metal rails laid atop roadbeds carefully engineered to level out the land's natural irregularities. Locomotive boilers rounded out the advantages of the railroad by bringing to bear the power of hundreds of horses. Freight rates fell correspondingly. In mountain regions without rail connections, the historian LeRoy Hafen found, "the average charge was about $2.50 per hundredweight for ten miles"—roughly $5 per ton per mile. The first through freight train from Denver to the East Coast, by contrast, left the Colorado capital in 1870 carrying ten tons of Central City silver ore to the docks of New York City, and from there on to English smelters, at a *total* charge of $38 a ton. In the two decades that followed, railroad freight rates fell still further. The average tariff of .6 cents per ton per mile in 1889 made it possible to transport a thousand tons of goods on the railroad for the same amount it cost to move just one ton of goods by wagon. Freight rates fell still further in the years ahead, as locomotives grew faster and larger; the engines used on mountain portions of the D&RG in 1913 outweighed that company's first locomotives by more than 1,800 percent and traveled 233 percent faster. In the heyday of the organic economy, commodities and finished products had trickled into and out of Colorado; businessmen purportedly griped that they could "get no goods, no machinery out from the States under a year from the time of ordering." In the mineral-intensive economy of rails and coal, however, unprecedented quantities of goods flowed into the Rockies. During the first full year of railroad service, 234 million pounds of freight in all reached Denver, a steep increase from 17 million pounds four years earlier.[10]

This figure reflected not simply an acceleration in exchange, but also a shift in its composition. Before 1870, most goods hauled across the plains were either valuable (gold), essential (wheat), or capable of making up for high transportation charges (mining machinery). With coal-powered trains, though, traffic in bulky, low-value commodities skyrocketed. Colorado railroads quickly grew to depend on mineral products. In an annual report for 1912, one railroad claimed that coal, coke, ore, rock, and bullion accounted for 85.5 percent of its freight and perhaps 50 percent of its earnings.[11]

By making Colorado's wide range of coal and coke varieties available and affordable, railroads redirected the region's development along new channels. Locomotive smoke in the sky symbolized the arrival of a mineral-based energy economy powered by stores of energy excavated from the earth, rather than flows of energy derived from rivers and winds, plants and animals. As enormous quantities of power began to course through a world long restricted by low precipitation and limited biological productivity, a spiral of radical but uneven transformations ensued. Among the most dramatic was population growth, the most rapid the territory had ever experienced, from 39,864 non-Indians in Colorado in 1870 to a total population of 412,198 in 1890 and 799,024 in 1910. Even as the combination of railroads and coal mines was freeing people from age-old limitations, however, it was fast binding Coloradans into new and troubling dependencies.[12]

A Vast Industrial Ecosystem

The habit of seeing railroads as essential to the development of the West while overlooking coal is just one aspect of a larger gap in understanding. To bring coal, coal miners, and coalfield struggles back from the margins of the Western past, it is necessary to follow the trail of coal as it moved along what environmental historian William Cronon calls the "paths out of town."[13]

Initially, the Colorado railroads consumed almost every ton of coal their subsidiaries mined. Within just a few years, however, trains were hauling much more coal than they burned; just three years after the general's crews

2.1. William Henry Jackson's Denver, early 1890s. Copyright Colorado Historical Society, WHJ PANO.

broke ground, for instance, Palmer's D&RG was already hauling two and a half times as much fuel as its engines consumed. Most of the coal freighted by rail ended up in towns and cities in the region. There coal shaped the character of urban growth by fueling rapid industrial expansion, deepening divisions between rich and poor, and sowing the seeds of conflict.[14]

William Henry Jackson, a photographer who first made his name in the 1860s and 1870s by capturing striking Western landscapes on film for the Union Pacific Railroad and the U.S. Geological Survey, captured one of the fullest visual representations of the remarkable growth that fossil fuels had made possible in the Front Range cities. On a clear summer day in the 1890s on the eastern edge of downtown Denver, Jackson climbed to the top of Colorado's new capitol building, set up his tripod, and exposed five glass plates, each overlapping with the next, to create a stunning panorama of Denver with the snowcapped Rockies in the background.

Nary a chunk or pile of coal can be seen in Jackson's iconic, widely reproduced vista. Yet Jackson's scene nonetheless rested on long-buried sunshine. The treeless plains and sparsely wooded foothills in the background of the

© Colorado Historical Society

panorama testified both to the harsh constraints imposed by aridity and topography and to the strain that decades of Anglo settlement had placed on local forests. The city dominating the image materializes as if from nowhere. A crown of smoke hovers above rows of brick homes, stores, and factories. Between these buildings forged thanks to the alchemy of coal and clay run rows of utility poles and streetlights, streetcar lines and railroad tracks, tangles of electrical wire and powerhouse smokestacks. Coal-generated power courses through all these conduits, the quickening current of the region's dominant urban center. Jackson captured the image of a fossil-fuel-powered metropolis, a city as dependent on the yield of the earth's depths as on water and the bounty of the soil.[15]

Historians have long treated the cities of the Front Range as Gold Rush and railroad boomtowns. Denver leveraged its location along what William Palmer called the "shore of a glorious new land" to become, in effect, a great port city "uniting mountain and plain." Multiple transcontinental lines eventually connected the city to points east, and a web of mountain railways radiated westward into the Rockies. Pueblo, a hundred miles to the south, became the second most important transportation hub in the region and the self-proclaimed "Pittsburgh of the West." As rail junctions, these cities enjoyed many advantages over less fortunate rivals. Perhaps the greatest was the presence of competitive energy markets that arose because multiple railroads were transporting many grades of coal and coke to the Front Range from mines throughout Colorado and Wyoming. Though coal companies and urban dealers periodically colluded to maintain artificially high fuel prices, in these cities consumers could nonetheless buy coal more cheaply than could those in the outlying regions who were dependent on the railroad monopolies for fuel supplies. No less important was the measure of protection that competitive energy markets offered to city dwellers against coal miners' strikes and other disruptions. When cut off from one source of supply, Denverites and Puebloans could substitute coal from elsewhere with relative ease. This boon to businessmen and householders seeking stability in an uncertain world meant greater insecurity for coal miners, who periodically sought to improve or maintain their situation by cutting off the flow of energy from mine to market.[16]

Together, the railroads and coal mines stimulated rapid economic growth and demographic expansion in both Denver and Pueblo. Once track gangs linked the capital with American rail networks, a prodigious boom lifted Denver from its post–Gold Rush lethargy. The city's 1870 population of 4,759 doubled in 1871. As coal began to flow into the metropolis the following year, another 5,000 people became Denverites. By 1880, the capital's population had swelled to over 35,000, and by 1914 it exceeded 200,000, making the Western upstart larger than the Philadelphia of Palmer's boyhood. Pueblo also flourished after coal and the railroad arrived; by the time of the Ludlow Massacre more than 50,000 people called the town home. Thus did another of Palmer's dreams—that "the people never get to be as thick as on the Eastern seaboard"—dissipate like a high plains mirage.[17]

As Jackson's panorama suggested, coal fueled industrial development and commerce in both these Front Range cities. By 1900, Denver boasted 1,474 manufacturing establishments with a total of 10,926 workers on their payrolls and annual revenues of $41.4 million, and Pueblo's 241 manufacturers employed nearly 5,000 people and produced $30.8 million in goods. Some of these establishments used organic energy sources—particularly wood and water—to process animal, plant, and other organic inputs. Denver and Pueblo, like Chicago before them, were growing into Nature's metropolises.

But they also stood at the epicenter of a mineral-intensive industrial revolution. Grain elevators, flour and paper mills, breweries, stockyards, lumberyards, packinghouses: all harnessed fossil energy. The sooty industrial districts of Denver and Pueblo, however, also boasted hundreds of factories—brickyards and ironworks, railroad shops and mining-machine factories whose ingenious inventions "predominated in all the mines of the west" and were even exported to Canada, Mexico, and parts of South America and Asia "in large quantities." All these facilities employed the power of coal to transform minerals into forms of greater value and utility. Far and away the largest and most important consumers of coal in these cities, however, were blast furnaces, mills, and smelters. Without high-quality coke, energy-hungry metallurgical establishments could never have done business in Colorado. With coke, these smoke-belching plants spurred economic growth along the Front Range, solidified urban dominance over the mining hinterlands, and replicated many of the ills Palmer had consciously tried to avoid in composing his vision of a New West.[18]

In 1881 Palmer's Colorado Coal and Iron Company (CC&I), precursor to Colorado Fuel and Iron, completed the first and only integrated steel mill to be erected west of the Missouri before World War II. A correspondent from the *New York Daily Graphic* predicted a bright future for this plant, which turned iron ore, coke, and limestone first into iron, then into raw steel, and finally into rails and other finished steel products: "The starting of this furnace at South Pueblo marks the commencement of a great iron industry at the foot of the Rocky Mountains." Hopeful prognostications aside, however, the operation would struggle for its first two decades. Discriminatory rates set by transcontinental railroads at the behest of eastern steelmakers such as Palmer's old friend Andrew Carnegie made it impossible for Pueblo steel to compete in many Western markets, and episodic busts in the regional economy periodically destroyed demand for rails and other products. By the early 1900s, though, the newly consolidated Colorado Fuel and Iron resolved many of its most pressing problems to become "the most self-sufficient and elaborate of all steel-making companies. It is more than a business," journalist Herbert Casson declared: "it is a civilisation." The Pueblo mills stood at the core of a vast industrial ecosystem encompassing iron and manganese mines, limestone quarries, retail and wholesale stores, immense hydraulic systems, two subsidiary railroads, a telephone company, a cooperage for making nail kegs, sales offices stretching from Los Angeles to Kansas City and from Spokane to Fort Worth, and, of course, more than a dozen collieries and several coking plants.[19]

Every ton of iron and steel turned out by the Pueblo works owed its origins to fossil fuel. More coke than any other ingredient was loaded into the plant's blast furnaces. Other parts of this "busy city in itself" also burned coal and coal gases to heat ingots, pump sixty million gallons of water through the works each day, and drive a veritable stable of engines collectively rated at 60,000 horsepower. By 1907, the Pueblo works was consuming well over half a million tons of coal and coke annually—roughly 5 percent of Colorado's total output. Ancient energy helped forge all the metal goods and tools Westerners produced to tame a recalcitrant land. "Embedded" fossil fuel thus underlay the rails facilitating the passage of people and goods; barbed wire fencing in the open range; pipes transporting water, sewage, and petroleum to their destinations; and the plates and bars fashioned by other manufactories into such products as carriages, agricultural implements, and mining machines. Rails made at Colorado Fuel and Iron even made the passage on Pacific steamships to Hawaii, Japan, Siberia, Manchuria, and Australia.[20]

Devil's Workshops

The price of the iron and steel products churned out at the Pueblo mills rarely reflected the heavy toll that industrial labor levied on the five thousand to seven thousand men who labored at Colorado Fuel and Iron's Minnequa Works during the early twentieth century. Most worked six or seven ten- to twelve-hour shifts each week. Shop employees sometimes stayed on the job for thirty-six or even sixty hours straight when machinery broke down. Heat and hazards only aggravated the physical and mental strain of long shifts. Death on the job was common and often grotesque. "The steam, the fire, the fluid metal, the slag and the whir of machinery," declared one manager, "all ma[d]e it look like it was the Devil's Workshop."[21]

Conditions proved just as diabolical in the smelters of Denver and Pueblo. Colorado's first gold- and silver-refining establishments were clustered near the precious-metal mines in the mountains. Once railroads reached the high country, however, canny industrialists, led by Nathaniel B. Hill, began to relocate their smelters along the Front Range. "The sagacious superintendent," one admirer explained of Hill's decision to move his Boston and Colorado Smelter out of Black Hawk in the late 1870s, realized "that, to keep in the lead, he must be at the place where the railroads of the State concentrate, and where fuel and general expenses of living are cheapest." As Hill grasped, Front Range smelters possessed a comparative advantage over their mountain counterparts. Significantly more coal than ore was consumed by metallurgical works, so it paid to locate them nearer to collieries than to gold and silver mines. Moreover, because smelters functioned most profitably by mixing different types of ore, Denver and Pueblo producers benefited from their ability to combine ores hauled downhill to the Front Range from mining districts spread across Colorado and other parts of the North American West. In conjunction with lower labor costs, these factors led Hill's competitors to establish three large smelters in Denver within a decade, and three more in Pueblo. Soon the Front Range smelters had lowered the charges that ore producers paid to refine precious metals by 80 to 90 percent by comparison with the sums charged by Colorado's older metallurgical works. Savings on that scale enabled silver- and gold-mining companies to exploit ever lower-grade ores at a profit. By the early 1900s, however, almost all the mountain smelters had been decommissioned. These closures and the Guggenheims' acquisition of the so-called smelter trust (formally known as the American Smelting and Refining Company, or ASARCO), placed Colorado's lucrative ore markets under the control of just a few firms, a move that had both the labor leaders and the mining barons of the West crying foul. In this as in so many other instances, mineral-intensive industrialization helped accelerate the concentration of wealth and power in the hands of trusts that brooked no challenges from workers or would-be competitors.[22]

Smelters and steel mills influenced not only the economies of Denver and Pueblo, but also their demographic composition and physical form. Metallurgical plants initially relied on the practical knowledge of skilled workers imported from established ore-processing centers like Wales, Saxony, and Pennsylvania. During the late nineteenth century, though, managers successfully replaced many high-wage craft workers with machines and unskilled operatives drawn from other, supposedly more tractable populations. The Sicilian Fasula family, who came in the 1890s via Louisiana—"too many mosquitos there," the Ukrainian Jewish Edelstein family—"junk people" who bought scrap metal from throughout the West and sold it to Colorado Fuel and Iron, the Slovak Hrusovsky and Baltazar clans—drawn to Pueblo "because of the steel mill and the smelter": all crowded together with other southern and eastern Europeans, Hispanos, Mexicans, and African Americans into the working-class enclaves sprouting up around smoky mills and smelters. Capitalists located most of Denver's metal refineries beyond the city limits, in such company-owned towns as Argo, Globeville, and Swansea, where land was more affordable, workers easier to control, and municipal taxes and nuisance regulations easier to evade. As for the polyglot inhabitants of Pueblo's Bessemer, Goat Hill, Grove, and Peppersauce Bottom neighborhoods, civic leaders complained that they "liv[ed] like live stock in large numbers in small houses and single rooms."[23]

Surely the most startling of the state's "foreign quarters," though, was Pueblo's "Mexico." A three-acre Hispano barrio built in the 1870s, this adobe "remnant of the days when Pueblo was a frontier village and trading post" housed just 4 Hispano families by 1903. The rest had been displaced by 150 Italian families, 3 blacks, 2 Frenchmen, and 1 Arab, who "built in between, above and below the adobes of the Mexicans, and burrowed dugouts and caves," so that "the flat, dirt-covered roof of one dwelling—they could scarcely be called houses—formed the dooryard of the one immediately above." This "Mexico" evoked other places and times. It probably reminded its inhabitants of Palermo or Naples. Eastern visitors, by contrast, made more fanciful associations as they struggled to square their expectations of Western primitiveness with the realities of modern industrialism. Asked to describe Pueblo, one tourist purportedly remarked: "'That's the place with the smelters, the big steel plant and the settlement of Pueblo Indians.'"[24]

As smelting and steelmaking were spawning industrial enclaves and new centers of migrant life, these industries were also damaging the air, water, soil, and living beings. A small anecdote hints at the larger dimensions of industrial toxicity. In 1902, Mr. Milleson, a beekeeper who lived near Denver, reported that he had "lost eight or nine colonies within a month last spring." Milleson had "invested in bees twenty-five years ago, when there was no

2.2. City of Coal: Denver from the North Side. Photograph by L. C. McClure. Denver Public Library, Western History Collection, MCC-1409.

smoke in the neighborhood, but now he is surrounded by the smelters, and all the garden flowers and fruit-bloom, and the grass, are continually coated with a deposit from the smoke, and not one of his colonies is in first-class condition." The harm done to human health, of course, prompted even greater concern. Remarkably few contemporary accounts attest to the medical problems that pollution from smelter and steel works caused; better documented is the toxic legacy passed on by the Colorado industrial revolution to the poor, mostly minority residents who today live on or near the sites of old smelters.[25]

City dwellers a century ago tended to look on pollution differently than we do. One Pueblo booster claimed that though "unsightly perhaps in themselves," the city's smoke-spewing factories "nevertheless contribute their quota to the general fund of beauty. If we follow the injunction contained in the motto of the Business Men's Association, and 'Watch Pueblo's Smoke,' we shall see many impressive pictures in black and white, and even in colors running from slate and deep blue, on through opalescent gray to chrome yellow and rich red." Economics offered still greater cause than aesthetics to celebrate smoke. Following the settlement of a hard-fought strike in 1899 in which smelter employees organized by the Western Federation of Miners sought to limit the workday in these hazardous workplaces to eight hours, a *Denver Times* cartoonist depicted the welcome return of inky black billows to the urban skyline above a caption that said it all: "Prosperity."[26]

Urbanites of all classes may well have equated smoke with economic vitality, yet neither prosperity nor pollution was evenly distributed. In Denver and Pueblo alike, urban dwellers of means fled the smoking metallurgical plants and the migrant "others" who crowded around them. Denver's wealthy had once shared downtown neighborhoods with poorer folk, but increasingly the rich and the middle classes that emulated them left the center city for new suburban neighborhoods located upwind or uphill from emerging industrial districts. Desirable residential neighborhoods, like Capitol Hill, University Park, Berkeley, and Montclair, all lay comfortably removed from the increasingly polluted Platte Valley. Promoters of Highland, on the bluffs west of the river, bragged, "True to her name and nature, she stands high and sightly," with "no smelters, factories, or emitters of smoke within her borders." A few miles to the northeast, meanwhile, the overwhelmingly Slavic workforce of the Globe smelter choked on a thick miasma of airborne pollutants. Even as the wealth produced by the smelters flowed to the suburbs and to Eastern financial centers such as New York, the toxic by-products of refining silver, gold, lead, and other metals remained in the laborers' backyard.[27]

The environmental inequalities that continue to characterize mineral-intensive economies rendered certain parts of Front Range cities healthy and pleasant, others sickly and squalid. But coal-burning technologies not only pushed well-heeled Coloradans away from congested, polluted manufacturing districts; they also pulled them out toward the healthier, more spacious suburbs. Commuter railroads, electric tramways, and cable cars—generally powered either directly or indirectly by coal—"enabled men of moderate means," Denver historian Jerome Smiley explained, "to acquire homes for

2.3. Chinese Denverites at Home, November 1914. Copyright Colorado Historical Society, William W. Cecil Collection, 20003534.

themselves in pleasant places away from the business center." In Denver and Pueblo as in other American cities, streetcar promoters who doubled as real estate developers, expanding their efforts farther and farther outward, built ring upon ring of suburbs promising refuge from smelter smoke and urban squalor. By the early twentieth century, Denver's streetcar lines covered more than two hundred miles. Pueblo, Colorado Springs, Boulder, Cripple Creek, Trinidad, and other cities also constructed extensive transit networks. Tourist Richard Harding Davis described Denverites' love affair with cable cars, "beautiful white and gold affairs" that "move with the delightfully terrifying speed of a toboggan. Riding on these cable-cars is one of the institutions of the city," Davis declared in 1892. "Every one in Denver patronizes this means of locomotion whether on business or on pleasure bent, and whether he has carriages of his own or not." Well into the 1920s, hundreds of thousands of Coloradans used coal-powered mass transit every day, most of them to journey between center city and suburb, others to reach industrial enclaves and parks such as Lake Minnequa, the steelworks reservoir that offered "the only place of amusement" for operatives and their families. As these fossil-fuel-dependent systems bound ever larger stretches of land together into coherent metropolises, they simultaneously deepened the environmental and social rifts along the Front Range. However far streetcar cables and wires reached, after all, these sprawling webs all led back to the downtown generating stations and powerhouses responsible for at least some of the smoke and soot so many wealthy and middle-class folks were moving to the suburbs to avoid.[28]

Coal shaped *how* city dwellers of different classes lived as well as *where* they lived. Depending whether they were rich or poor, people burned varying kinds and amounts of coal in their homes, obtained their fuel by different means, and used it for distinct purposes. Imagine three hypothetical Denver consumers of the late 1880s and early 1890s: a mining mogul holding court from a mansion perched atop exclusive Capitol Hill, a young clerk and his wife inhabiting a modest Highland bungalow, and a widow sheltering with her offspring in a makeshift hovel in the Platte River Bottoms.

The mogul would have purchased clean-burning Crested Butte anthracite in lots of a ton or more, paying eight or nine dollars per ton. He—for virtually all moguls were men—would enjoy many benefits from this fuel, but he and his family would touch it with neither hands nor tools. It was servants' work, after all, to feed furnaces, stoves, and boilers—and female servants' work to clean up the comparatively small quantities of dirt and soot that the most efficient household devices of the day emitted into the mansion. The Highland bungalow dwellers, meanwhile, would have bought a ton or half-ton of low-smoke domestic coal from the northern or Cañon City fields at four or five dollars per ton. The clerk might have rolled up his sleeves to stoke boiler and furnace, his wife spending some of her long workdays kindling stove and hearth and still more time tidying up the mess made by the house's various coal-burning devices. As for the widow mired in the Bottoms, she would have had little choice but to spend part of every day walking alongside the railroad tracks with children in tow, scrutinizing them for bits of coal dropped by passing trains. Returning home, they would have fed these leavings into a leaky old stove, whose heat took the edge off the chill and cooked their meager meal, while smoke and soot filled their shack. Coal offered all three of

2.4. "Gas Is Nice": Middle-Class City Dwellers at Home. Copyright Colorado Historical Society, Harry H. Buckwalter Collection, 20030792.

these households some measure of liberation. Yet in the new industrial order, some Coloradans could procure more of such freedom from the elements than others.[29]

When urban dwellers gathered around the proverbial hearth, bathed the city grime off their limbs, gazed out on winter scenes from toasty parlors, or labored over the stove, which one domestic engineering manual called "the pivot around which a people revolve and live," they could not ignore the centrality of coal in their lives. Easier to overlook were the large quantities of coal that urbanites consumed indirectly in the form of gas and electricity. These energy sources tended to make the homes of wealthier Coloradans brighter, cleaner, and healthier than those of humbler folk, while further insulating the rich from the negative consequences of their profligate energy use.[30]

Not long after Colorado's first gashouse started transforming coal into illuminating fuel, Denver's streetlights burned so bright that miners could sometimes see them from Ward, a mile higher and fifty miles to the northwest. Two years later, in 1873, ten thousand lamps were lighting Denver's nights. By the 1880s, Leadville, Pueblo, Colorado Springs, Gunnison, and other cities had mimicked the example of the capital.[31]

After electricity began to supplant gas, Denver started calling itself the City of Light. Parisians would have scoffed at such presumptuousness, but the commercial elite of this Western upstart took the claim seriously enough. A light-studded arch welcomed train travelers as they crossed the street from Union Station; a few blocks away, more than thirteen thousand lightbulbs decorated the new Denver Gas & Electric Company headquarters, completed in 1910. "There is no city in the country that can boast better street lighting and private lighting than Denver," one souvenir volume declared. Another celebrated the city's "wonderful night illumination" for accentuating Denver's "artistic appearance" and "contributing to the public safety."[32]

Gas and electricity did make public space more attractive and secure; the municipal franchises under which these utilities operated also made a small cadre of capitalists incredibly rich. Junius Brown, a cofounder of Denver Gas & Electric, built a special gallery in his gray stone mansion on Capitol Hill, then filled it with one of the most impressive collections of paintings and sculptures in the West; Charles Boettcher, a leading force in the Colorado electricity, cement, and sugar beet industries, furnished various rooms of his mansion with Colonial American antiques, Japanese handicrafts, and Delft tiles and Oriental rugs purchased on family holidays to the Netherlands and the Middle East. Many Coloradans perceived conspicuous consumption by such grandees as resting on ill-gotten gains, for the region's gas and electric companies priced their services so high that most city dwellers could not afford to bring those superior sources of energy into their homes. Until an innovative early twentieth-century executive, Henry Doherty, "fashioned a strategy for boosting consumption of gas and electricity," the historian Mark Rose contends, consumption of those two forms of energy in Denver was restricted to a "small group who occupied prestigious office buildings and whose lovely homes and apartments were located in neighborhoods established for the well-to-do." In contrast with people of humbler means who had difficulty forgetting where their energy came from, elite Coloradans were experiencing what David Nye, a historian of technology, calls "an unintended collective effect" of fossil-fuel-driven technologies: "enmeshed in systems, families consumed energy—often without thinking about it—whenever they turned a tap, threw a switch, twisted a valve, or lifted a telephone receiver."[33]

Evidence of the existence of the systems behind such household apparatuses permeates William Henry Jackson's panoramic photo of Denver, and the impact of mineral-dependent industrialism becomes more visible still when we turn from infrastructure to superstructure. Consider first the mass and height of the downtown district that dominates the center of the shot. Denver, as Richard Harding Davis declared, was fast becoming "a thoroughly Eastern city—a smaller New York in an encircling range of white-capped mountains." Denver's "towering office buildings" shared with the skyscrapers of Manhattan or Chicago a reliance on fossil fuels. The Denver Gas & Electric Building, celebrated on one tourist postcard as "the best-lighted building in the World," its thousands of bulbs shining "like a flashing diamond" below an illuminated sign that urged urbanites to "USE A GAS WATER HEATER" and "USE G&E COKE," declared this dependence with unusual frankness. The deep-lying foundations that rooted these structures in the earth were excavated by coal-burning steam shovels; the steel that braced their soaring walls had been forged in Pittsburgh; and an array of energy-hungry technologies, including elevators, central heating, and electric lights, made their inner spaces habitable.[34]

"Brick," proclaims a recent architectural guide to Denver, "made this city." And more often than not, coal made brick. Fossil-fuel-run kilns started operating in 1871; within a year a writer claimed, "The business part of the city is built almost exclusively of brick, and very many of the private dwellings as well." Other towns and cities throughout the region were also constructed

2.5. "The Best-Lighted Building in the World," 1910s. Photograph by Charles
M. Smyth. Denver Public Library, Western History Collection, X-24889.

largely of brick, sometimes locally produced, sometimes shipped by rail from
Denver, Golden, or Pueblo. By the early 1880s, Denver firms were turning
out hundreds of millions of bricks a year; so brisk had the demand become
by the end of that decade that brickmakers turned to steam-powered machines to increase production. Without a device nicknamed "the Chief," one
journalist wrote during a construction boom, "a brick famine would have
surely resulted, and the inevitable necessity for importation of brick [would

have] forced their price up so high, that many of our building improvements would have been greatly delayed, if not abandoned altogether." Constructing with brick, a sensible adjustment to building where suitable clay was abundant and lumber dear, received an added boost from building codes; Denver, to give just one example, banned wooden structures after an 1863 fire razed much of the city. Brick was eventually used for all sizes and shapes of buildings, from tiny outbuildings to huge factories; it also lined sewers, blast furnaces, and streets. Coal even helped transform lime, silica, and gypsum into Portland cement—both a key ingredient in the mortar that held together those billions of bricks and the main constituent of foundations, bridges, sidewalks, dams, canals, and other structures.[35]

The hard angles and burnt orange and red hues of the Front Range cities fittingly evoked the elements of fire and earth that lent their industrial economy its strength and power. The smoke-belching smelters, mills, and factories of the urban West, the extensive technological systems providing transportation, heat, and light, not to mention the glaringly unequal ways in which the costs and benefits of all these technologies mapped onto urban space, together helped account for the radical transformation separating the "newer and grander and happier Columbia" that William Jackson Palmer had glimpsed in 1870 from the burgeoning cityscape that William Henry Jackson depicted two decades later. In a single generation, Colorado's capital and its smaller urban counterparts had grown outward and upward with astonishing speed. The architectural artifacts of a coal-powered "age of steam, electricity, and the various inventions for annihilating time and distance" bore little resemblance to the timber-framed houses of the American frontier or the adobe dwellings of the Southwestern borderland. Instead, the urban landscape had become recognizable to Richard Harding Davis and many others as a Western variant of Eastern industrial centers. Colorado cities might be more scenic and less fetid, but they hardly embodied the new utopia Palmer had endeavored to build.[36]

Industrializing the Hinterland

From the gold- and silver-mining districts to the farms of the plains and mountain valleys, other Westerners were also turning to fossil fuels to escape the limitations of climate and ecology. Yet like their urban counterparts, those who lived in the vast hinterlands of Denver and Pueblo would find that their desire for power in a place where energy had always been scarce caused almost as many problems as it resolved.

That coal had no visible presence in stereotypical portrayals of gold and silver mining reveals the wide abyss that separated the gilded myth from industrial realities. Scholars have rightly assailed the popular image of the prospector, a grizzled loner with pick in hand and burro in tow, for fostering misconceptions: the stereotype, it is claimed, gives the false impression that the racially diverse mine workforce was predominantly white, writes women out of mining history altogether, obscures the collective character of underground labor, and trivializes the alienation that often accompanied it. Our stock prospector fails to convey the complexity of the past in at least one other crucial respect: we are given to believe that he was a rugged individualist whose success or failure hinged on his brains and brawn, along with the pluck of his surefooted burro, in a frontier world where men were men and coal was just another rock in the ground.

In fact, mining camps placed heavy burdens on fuel resources. Along with forest fires, the demand for cordwood, building materials, and mine timbers denuded ever-widening circles of forest around the gold and silver camps. Railroad construction crews aggravated wood shortages by clear-cutting right of ways and harvesting lumber for ties and bridge timbers. Once coal-powered trains began to run on wood-lined rails, though, the possibility of a serious "timber famine" in the mining camps evaporated. One of Leadville's largest wood dealers reported only "150,000 feet of native lumber on hand at present" at the end of 1881, yet "a large supply of Chicago pine and California redwood" stood ready to compensate for the "thinning out" of regional forests caused by "the rapid extension of our mining industries." In addition to transporting billions of board feet of lumber into Rocky Mountain mining camps from distant woodlands, railroads also hauled tens of millions of tons of fossil fuel into the gold and silver districts. "'The necessities of the people following the exhaustion of timber on the mountain sides,'" as state geologist J. Alden Smith explained, "'were met by cheaper and better fuel brought up from the coal beds of the plains.'"[37]

We may nostalgically associate mountain living with a crackling wood fire, but denizens of the mining camps often fed their fireplaces and stoves with coal. "Don[']t growl anymore about cold weather," one Gunnison hardware store advised. "Go to Schluter & Spengels and buy a coal stove." Per pound, coal provided more heat than wood and made it possible to dispense with the bother of felling, hauling, drying, and splitting timber. Breweries, laundries, gasworks, and generating stations supplying electricity to transit networks and homes—all consumed still more coal, which was freighted in to the gold and silver districts from the collieries below.[38]

The biggest consumers of fossil fuels in the mountains, though, were always the mines themselves. Indeed, fossil fuels played an unacknowledged but essential role in the success of gold and silver mining. Colorado's rich mineral belts posed two formidable problems. First, the vast wealth of the mountains lay not in the easily worked surface deposits known as placers, but rather in lodes and veins that plunged deep into the earth. Second, most of the gold and silver in Colorado consisted not of pure flakes or nuggets, but rather of so-called refractory ores, stubborn compounds whose molecular bonds held precious minerals fast.

Fossil fuels proved essential for solving both these problems. The most widely practiced technique for unearthing ore from buried lodes and veins involved blasting shafts and tunnels through solid rock using so-called hardrock or quartz mining practices developed in Saxony and Cornwall and later improved on Nevada's Comstock Lode. Colorado's early mining history showed that synthetic explosives, muscle power, and wood-burning steam engines generally sufficed for starting a mine. But as shafts and tunnels followed veins and lodes farther underground, an array of complex technological systems were required to sustain life and labor. Pumps, fans, hoists, haulage mechanisms, and so forth, all consumed prodigious quantities of energy. Though organic energy sources remained important, coal nonetheless powered most of the state's largest mines from the late 1870s onward.[39]

Fossilized energy made deep mining possible, yet it also changed the nature of underground labor. During the industry's early days, craft miners directed tools, explosives, and sheer bodily force against solid rock. In 1870 all this began to change. In that year the steam-powered mining drill made its successful Western debut at Georgetown, Colorado. Such fossil-fuel-driven machines placed vast quantities of power at the disposal of miners and the capitalists who employed them. Power drills advanced through solid earth at "more than five times the speed of hand-drillers." The tourist John Codman noted the impact of these technologies along Clear Creek in 1879: "The great crowd have left the exhausted placers for the mountains, where, under the organized system of capitalists or corporations, there is either great wealth to be gained or disastrous failure to be experienced. The poor man, instead of working for himself is a day-laborer for hire, and the rich man becomes either a millionaire or a bankrupt." Three decades later, a travel guide explained that Cripple Creek's fabled riches lay "hidden deep in the granite's close embrace . . . Far beyond the simple appliances of the old-time miner, and as impossible to reach with unaided human hands as if it were in the very center of the earth, these treasures of the mountains yield themselves only to the impact of drills driven by electricity."[40]

Mechanization increased labor productivity and decreased mining costs. In the process, it degraded the miners' craft and eroded their autonomy. Labor-saving mine machines cost many men their jobs. Those who remained employed, meanwhile, found that their labor increasingly resembled that of factory workers: it was closely supervised, performed for a wage, and oriented around such tasks as operating machines, maintaining technological systems, and performing whatever menial labor still needed doing. To make matters worse, devices that ran on fossil fuel often introduced new dangers to already hazardous mines. As a Montana mining inspector lamented, "it seems that death lurks even in the things which are designed as benefits." Electrification brought exposed wires underground; the cages that workers rode down deep shafts had a propensity for dashing miners into rock walls or smashing them against the shaft bottom; and power drills thrust thick clouds of rock dust into miners' lungs, where it eventually caused silicosis, a painful terminal condition that shortened the lives of thousands of Colorado mineworkers. Little wonder that gold and silver miners organized to fight the new work world that coal-powered industrialism introduced. And so the Colorado mountains became fertile ground for a succession of unions, culminating in the Western Federation of Miners. An anarchosyndicalist union devoted to overthrowing the capitalist system, the federation's members squared off repeatedly against mineowners and their state allies during the same years that southern Colorado colliers were waging industrial struggles of their own.[41]

Even as some coal-powered technologies amplified underground hazards in metal mines, others were helping to overcome the second great challenge of Colorado geology: almost all of the state's gold, silver, and other precious metals were not only buried deep underground, but also entrained within refractory ores. Refining and smelting techniques imported from California, Nevada, Mexico, and Europe could unlock only a fraction of the silver and gold from these ores. "The tailings and refuse of the mills," one early historian noted, "were more valuable than what was saved from them."[42]

After years of experimentation, metallurgists and skilled smelter workers learned to overcome these problems, usually with the aid of prodigious quantities of mineral energy. The process of freeing precious metals from the complex compounds in which they were trapped often began in stamp mills that used waterwheels or wood- or coal-burning steam engines to pound rock into smaller particles. Many Colorado ores next required "roasting," a process in which coal or charcoal helped burn off sulfur and other impurities. The final and most energy-intensive stage of refining ores was smelting. None of Colorado's tree species in their native form contained enough thermal energy to liquefy solid rock. Braziers established a niche in the mining economy by stripping the foothills and mountains of trees large and small, then piling the timber up in pits or kilns. When burned in low-oxygen conditions for a day or more, this wood turned into charcoal, a purer, more concentrated fuel capable of raising rock to temperatures of 800 degrees or higher. Given the limited supplies of wood in Colorado and their rapid destruction, however, charcoal could not sustain the smelters' voracious energy requirements. "The fuel around the mills & mines must rapidly disappear," one commentator rightly predicted in the 1870s, "and its place must be supplied with coal, or coke." And indeed, the 2,500 braziers supplying charcoal to the Leadville smelters subsequently worked themselves out of business by deforesting large stretches of the upper Arkansas River in the 1870s and 1880s, while their counterparts in the Platte watershed west of Denver were fast "cut[ting] everything down to four inch diameter over all the country."[43]

Given the escalating cost of charcoal, the capitalists who operated mountain smelters eagerly welcomed the railroads that would ultimately destroy their business. Ore processors in southern and western Colorado had been importing coal and coke at prices as high as $160 a ton, but fuel prices fell precipitately after the advent of rail transport to the larger gold and silver camps. Ore processors quickly switched from organic to fossil fuel (though they still mixed in roughly one part charcoal to every nine parts coke). An "over-hanging cloud of smoke" was now draped over Leadville and other large mining camps, shrouding them with a "blanket of noxious black and yellow" pollution. As the railroad undercut the competitive advantages that mountain smelter owners had initially enjoyed, though, the skies above many mining camps cleared. Fuel and labor, as we have seen, were cheaper in Denver and Pueblo; meanwhile, downhill hauls from the mountains and the convergence in these cities of rail lines from multiple mining districts made it easier and more affordable for metallurgists along the Front Range to maximize profits by mixing complementary ores. As early as 1888 one authority proclaimed, "Smelting in Leadville has never been a success." In Cloud City and throughout the mountains, ore processors joined the swelling ranks of losers in the West's new industrial economy.[44]

In the final reckoning, coal and coke made daily life more comfortable in mining communities and spared the mountain forests from complete devastation. The combination of coal and railroads also considerably reduced the cost of extracting and refining ore, thereby making it possible for many otherwise marginal mines and mining districts to produce at a profit. "Metallurgical science," one railroad booster declared, "has revolutionized the primitive methods formerly employed in the extraction of precious metals." Gold and silver ores could now be "mined at an expense of cents where it formerly cost dollars, and are transported for a song." But that was only part of the story. Polluted skies and streams, pockmarked landscapes littered with tailings, a political economy dominated by financiers and industrialists based in the Front Range cities and in more distant metropolises—these and other features of the Rocky Mountain mining districts all served notice that beneath the glitter of gold and silver lay the grime of coal.[45]

Fossil Fuels and Farming

The silver crash of 1893 and the ensuing collapse of mineral production hit fuel markets hard. Gold booms in Creede, Telluride, and most of all, Cripple Creek, the last of which had yielded more than $300 million by 1911, stanched the hemorrhage of Colorado's economic lifeblood, but the twentieth century failed to yield even a single bonanza. Unstable metal prices, labor-management strife, and escalating production costs together plunged the industry into a downturn from which it has never recovered. In 1910 a state official complained that fewer "men [had] been employed in the mines and smelters than at any time within the last twenty years." The population of Hinsdale County, in the San Juans, shrank by 60 percent in the first decade of the twentieth century, while counties surrounding Cripple Creek, Leadville, and Central City lost 50 percent, 41 percent, and 38 percent of their populations, respectively.[46]

As settlers abandoned the mining regions nearly as fast as they had reinhabited them, demand for coal in silver and gold camps collapsed. Several western Colorado collieries closed as a consequence. Mines in the southern fields suffered, too, yet operators there were in a better position to tap into other markets. At the height of the silver panic, Colorado Fuel and Iron executives reassured investors, "While the production of silver adds materially to the success and earnings of our properties and is the largest single industry we depend on aside from railroads, the greater portion of our most *profitable* business is in supplying domestic coals to the agricultural sections of Kansas, Nebraska and Texas."[47]

Much as CF&I promised, booming agricultural districts on the high plains and in the mountain valleys combined with swelling urban markets to consume much of the excess supply freed up by the mining crisis. Irrigation transformed tens of thousands of acres of arid land on Colorado's Western Slope into flourishing farms and orchards; as a result, the populations of Delta, Mesa, and Montrose counties all doubled between 1900 and 1910. Demographic expansion proceeded even more rapidly in eastern Colorado, where reclamation, dry farming, high crop prices, and relentless boosterism combined to triple the populations of some eastern Colorado counties over the same period. Growth was equally brisk in many counties of western Kansas, Nebraska, and Oklahoma, and a St. Louis journalist found the Texas Panhandle in the throes of "an agricultural revolution."[48]

The success or failure of harvests and herds continued to depend on the interplay of sun, soil, and water with plants, people, and other animals. And yet coal provided newcomers to the region with much more power than their Indian, Hispano, and Anglo predecessors could eke out of the Western soil.

"Many an emigrant from the woods of the Middle States," agricultural historian Alvin Steinel claimed, "was appalled to find here a country without fuel." When the straggling woodlands that bordered the streams and rivers soon gave out, farmers, ranchers, and orchardists confronted unpleasant choices. Wood was expensive to import, sod difficult to cut and dry, animal droppings unpleasant to collect and smelly to burn. The memoirist Hal Borland recalled his father complaining, "'The only thing about this country I don't like is there's nothing to do with. No timber, not even any rocks. . . . There's sod. And cow chips. Why, there's not even any old boards.'" First considering, then dismissing, the notion of burning sheep dung on his hearth, Mr. Borland concluded, in a way that was fast becoming second nature throughout the plains and valleys, "'We'd better get some coal.'"[49]

Agricultural settlers, like the city dwellers and miners they fed, stoked fires in their hearths, stoves, and boilers with coal; farmers, like their counterparts, also relied on fossil fuels to help them produce, transport, and process goods. Even the cultivation of peach orchards along the Colorado River, where coal oil smudge pots bade "a final 'good-bye' to spring orchard frosts," benefited from mineral-intensive industrialization, but the example of wheat offers the best illustration of coal's impact on Western agriculture. Bituminous coal powered Colorado's first deep irrigation well in 1885; in 1908 a newly built "steam-powered electric station" near Garden City, Kansas, began to pump water from the ancient Ogallala aquifer to the thirsty wheat fields of western Kansas by way of more than two hundred wells. Farmers invested not only in steam-powered irrigation, but also in coal-burning machinery such as the Reeves tractor, described by historian Donald Worster as "a miniature locomotive weighing several tons." Oxen, horses, and mules continued to provide the power for planting and sowing many fields, but come harvest time, most wheat farms on the plains relied by the early twentieth century on enormous combines "fired," as one CF&I attorney dramatically phrased it, "on indignation and Colorado coal." The slow but inexorable substitution of mineral energy for organic sources helped farmers wrest more from the soil with less labor. In 1830 the average American farm exerted 61 man-hours of labor to produce twenty bushels of wheat, but by 1896 the figure had dropped to 3.19 man-hours. With coal meeting an ever-larger percentage of their energy needs, farmers could also increase the amount of land devoted to wheat. Farmers typically fed draught animals by consigning some of their land to pasture and feed; by replacing animals with machines, farmers freed up these lands to grow more wheat.[50]

The impact mineral-intensive industrialization had on agricultural hinterlands only intensified after the crops were harvested. Had people in the Front Range cities and mountain mining camps traced the bread they ate backward from bakery to farm, they would have found that coal was used to bake their loaves, coal to mill the flour, coke to refine the sugar beets that sweetened the bread, coal to power the elevators that sorted and stored wheat kernels before milling, and coal to power the locomotives that hauled golden streams of grain and piles of beets from countryside to metropolis. By the 1910s, calories extracted from coal seams helped produce a considerable percentage of the food calories Westerners ingested. In the increasingly industrial food system on which everyone from silver kings to ranch hands, store clerks to coal miners was growing to depend, did anything remain truly organic?[51]

City dwellers generally welcomed the bounty that fossil fuels made possible, but the farm population wrestled with its implications. Steam-powered tools and other factory-made goods enticed farmers into debt, empowered them to destroy the soil on which their livelihood depended, and encouraged them to abandon time-worn practices to restore the nutrients that crops drew from the soil. Draught animals, for instance, helped replenish depleted soil with manure, but steam-powered implements left only ash and smoke in their wake. More immediately, growing reliance on coal increased farmers' dependence on the railroads, whose subsidiaries monopolized the coal trade in many agricultural regions. Farmers consequently paid some of the highest fuel costs in the region; hence the confidence CF&I executives expressed when they reassured investors rattled by the collapse of silver by explaining, "The greater portion of our most *profitable* business is in supplying domestic coals to the agricultural sections of Kansas, Nebraska and Texas."[52]

The coal companies' gain, of course, was the farmers' loss, as Hal Borland learned. Having resolved to "get some coal," Borland's father hitched up his team and drove his wagon to town. Pulling up to one of two lumber and coal dealers in Brush, he walked inside and inquired about the price of coal. The dealer "mentioned a figure." Hal Borland recalled that "Father shook his

2.6. Boiler Room, Sugar Beet Factory, Fort Collins, Colorado, ca. 1900. Denver Public Library, Western History Collection, X-10891.

head. 'It seems pretty high,' he said." Father and son proceeded to the second coalyard, only to find the same price prevailing. Both retailers, it seems, bought their fuel from the same source, and neither could deviate from the price mandated in a Denver or Chicago office. Borland bristled at his dilemma, yet he knew that his family could not survive winter on the treeless plains without fuel. And so father and son left town with a ton of coal in their wagon and the bitter burden of powerlessness weighing on their shoulders.[53]

Like the Borlands, most people who lived in the farming and mining hinterlands of Colorado had grown to depend on coal by the time of the Ludlow Massacre. Coal not only heated their homes and cooked their meals. It also greatly increased their ability to plow, drill, dig, drain, and harness recalcitrant Western lands, waters, and organisms into more productive and profitable configurations. Each of the millions of tons of coal they burned freed them a little more from the constraints of isolation and aridity. Yet in the process, farmers all too often compromised their autonomy. In the New West that the labor of southern Colorado mineworkers was making possible, liberation and dependence stood in close, often paradoxical relation.

Crossing an Industrial Rubicon

In both the city and the countryside, then, Coloradans burned coal to break the bounds that had long constrained natural ecologies and human economies in the region. Fossil fuels gave people newfound power—to transcend bodily limitations, transform matter, and haul unprecedented quantities of goods, information, and people farther, faster, and more cheaply than ever before. With every passing year, Westerners demanded more heat, light, and motive power, more food, gold, steel, and electricity—and hence more coal. By the time of the coalfield wars, fossil fuel was in enormous demand for industry and homes alike. Less conspicuously, coal was the crucial component that produced and delivered the foods Westerners ate, the goods they bought, and the tools they used. It helped determine the work they performed and the places they called home; it was present in the very air they breathed and even in the cells that made up their bodies.[54]

Every ton of coal provided clear economic gain; every ton provided a store of additional power that people could use to change their world. Rough figures on per capita coal consumption offer one index of the boost that fossil fuels offered. In 1870 the average Coloradan consumed perhaps .3 tons of coal; in 1880 at least 2 tons; in 1890 6 tons; by 1900 almost 8 tons; and in 1910 over 12 tons. A few comparisons illustrate the magnitude of the fossil-fuel dependency these figures reflect. At the time of William Palmer's tour in the 1850s, Britons consumed fewer than 4 tons of coal per capita; current coal consumption in the U.S. averages 3.5 tons per capita; and Australia, the most voracious consumer of coal today, burns about 7.2 tons for each resident. By 1914, Colorado's collieries had yielded nearly 185 million tons of coal. Obtaining an equivalent amount of energy from wood would have necessitated the destruction of at least 8 million acres of forest. By the 1910s, 600,000 acres—around 1,000 square miles' worth of timber—would have needed to find its way from Colorado's wooded hinterlands every year in a state that possessed fewer than 18,000 square miles of woodland, much of it sparsely forested and slow to regenerate.[55]

Economic growth under Colorado's organic-energy regimes had generally been slow, hard-won, and ephemeral. The mineral-intensive industrial economy that took root after 1870, by contrast, grew in a manner E. A. Wrigley likens to "mutation, in its suddenness, its unpredictability, and its scale." And a defining characteristic of mutation is its irrevocability. By the early twentieth century, life without coal was unimaginable.[56]

Had coal suddenly vanished on a winter's day around 1900, a long-forgotten silence would have replaced the clanking, whistling, screeching world of steam. Virtually all train traffic in the West would have stopped, halting the flow of people and goods between hinterland and metropolis, Western cities and outside markets. Mines excavated by men and machines would have filled with water and poisonous gases. Most construction would have ceased. Smelters and mills, tractors and combines would have run out of steam. Country folk, cut off from so many necessities of life, would have scurried to pantries and cellars to see how long their stores of food and fuel could last. City dwellers, meanwhile, would have maneuvered around streetcars stopped dead on their tracks. For a time, horse-drawn wagons and buggies cobwebby with disuse might have been drawn into service. But before long, horses, livestock, and poultry would have devoured every last vestige of browse, grass, and refuse—if the hungry human population had not eaten the animals first, that is. Only those trees guarded by force would have remained standing, for people would have needed wood not simply to stave off the cold, but also to cook their diminishing food supplies. The energy crisis would quickly have moved from the public to the personal sphere, from the social organism to the individuals that composed it.

No such doomsday scenario was ever likely, of course. The revolutions initiated by Palmer and his competitors ensured that coal had become too thoroughly imbricated in the very structure of the region's political economy and society, its ecology and built environment, for such a nightmare to have become reality. If the worst had come to pass and not a single ton of Colorado coal had made its way from mine to market, the railroads would have hauled it in from other states—at a premium. Hooked on fossil fuel, Western industries and consumers alike encountered the same dilemma Mr. Borland had confronted when he sought to purchase a winter's supply of fuel on the high plains. The Denver Chamber of Commerce ominously summed up the situation in a 1907 report on coal: "'We cannot exist without it.'"[57]

The region's dependency on fossil fuels generated considerable fear and foreboding. As early as 1872, editor John J. Lambert of Pueblo's *Colorado Chieftain* lashed out at the unexpected consequences of crossing the industrial Rubicon. "Heretofore we have been entirely dependent upon wagons for our coal supply, which has been laid at our doors at prices ranging from ten dollars to fourteen dollars per ton. With the completion of the branch road to the coal fields"—the D&RG extension linking Pueblo with Fremont County—"this system has been revolutionized." Palmer's trains made the transport of coal cheaper and faster. Yet so long as the general retained his "exclusive monopoly of the carrying business," the editor warned, "it [did] not look as though we were destined to reap any great advantage from the change." For Palmer's enterprises charged prices so high that they could be "viewed in no other light than that of an extortion . . . which the railroad company will find out sooner or later, our citizens will not submit to."

Land fraud perpetrated by coal companies, alleged price-gouging by the region's "coal trust," the polluted skies, the heavily publicized mine disasters that offered periodic reminders of the heavy price colliers paid to keep everyone else's home fires burning—all these generated no shortage of criticism. If denizens of the coal-powered economy often acknowledged the deleterious consequences of their dependency, though, they nonetheless lacked both the will to change the way they lived their own lives and the power to alter how others conducted their affairs.[58]

As for the coal miners, they knew full well that their labor made this world go round. And though it was a radical collier indeed who fantasized about an absolute fuel blockade, mineworkers understood that if they could shut down the flow of energy, they might be able to use the region's fossil-fuel dependency to secure concessions from Palmer, his competitors, and their successors. United and coordinated action, in short, could win mineworkers formidable power. The difficulty lay in unifying men, women, and children drawn to the southern coalfields from the four corners of the globe. "The earth has been transformed," a Greek immigrant to the West wrote, in one of the forlorn poems he jotted down in his journal between stints of work. "And I ride the wave to survive."[59]

3

Riding the Wave to Survive
an Earth Transformed

When a group of British colliers arrived in Dawson, New Mexico, each carried a flat trunk bearing the most precious tool of the colliers' trade: a safety lamp, its glass globe enshrouded in clothing to guard against the perils of their journey from the eastern shore of the Atlantic to the Rocky Mountain West.[1]

Twenty tramps jumped off a freight train in 1893 in southern Colorado with gunnysacks slung over their shoulders and issued a prediction: if the impending session of Congress could grant "no relief to the people, they expect[ed] the laboring people out of employment to rise up in arms." The tramps told a newspaper reporter they anticipated "a war and [were] ready to fight."[2]

Few could have brought along with them more than Mary Thomas did. The young Welsh bride came with 156 wedding presents, including "a beautiful Bible" she had received from her church, a gold bracelet, and $1,500 cash—perhaps two years' wages for the average coal miner in Colorado.[3]

Mrs. Micek, who had always kept geese outside her cottage in the Moravian coalfields, "had to bring her featherbeds with her, and her pillows, and her kids," her daughter later remembered. "She said she didn't care if she left anything else back there." After a twenty-two-day crossing from Hamburg to Galveston, she bundled her children and her bedding onto a train and set out to rejoin her husband. The train crashed, leaving Mrs. Micek "sitting on the prairie at midnight in a strange country, thousands of miles from home, not knowing where [she was] going to, three little kids, and [her] feather-beds."[4]

The people who came brought shotguns for hunting, revolvers for protection, rifles as soldierly mementos. They bore battle wounds from wars— waged to gain national liberation, satisfy imperial ambition, or pacify civil discord in the Balkans and Africa, the Philippines and Cuba, the Mississippi Valley and Mexico.[5]

Their pockets bulged with paper: tickets from the Santa Fe Railroad and the North German Lloyd line, passports issued at ports of embarkation from Trieste to Bremen to Hiroshima, medical certificates and landing papers dispensed in ports of entry from Halifax to Boston to New Orleans, names and addresses of relatives and fellow villagers and labor contractors, photographs of family members, cheat sheets for eluding the immigration restrictions, which one ill-fated Chinese sojourner incarcerated on San Francisco's Angel Island declared "harsh as tigers." Among all these sheets of varying size and shape, thickness and value, the most important to retain were the instructions telling migrants how to get from where they were to where they wanted to go.[6]

The newcomers had skin of many colors: pinks that usually counted as "white," a spectrum of browns generally collapsed into "black," or some curiously classified as "yellow." But many skin colors seemed harder to describe. "Mexicans" (mostly Americans of *nuevomexicano* descent), Italians, Greeks, and some others were neither "white" nor "yellow," neither "black" nor "red." They did not fit anywhere, it seemed—at least not yet.[7]

Their bodies were often marked in other ways, too. Pocks betrayed where smallpox and other diseases had ravaged their flesh. Deep tans distinguished the men who worked outside from the sallow-faced mining men among them. Calloused hands, missing fingers, and prosthetic limbs testified to lives of toil, and there were other manifestations: glass eyes and bluish black "coal tattoos" left when blasting powder and falling rock drove carbon particles under the skin. The newcomers displayed less-accidental evidence of their occupations, too. The Scotsman Alexander McBride rolled up his right sleeve in front of a county clerk to reveal an "Anchor Cross and Haert [*sic*]," and his left sleeve to expose a star and the letters "N. A. M.," in all likelihood a reference to a British union, the National Association of Miners.[8]

They brought along ideas that drew them together and ideas that set them apart, prejudices of race and nationality, ethnicity and region, trade and party and union. The Welsh and Scots despised the Irish, the French bore a grudge against the Germans, and the Germans claimed superiority over the Poles, who could not forgive the Austrians, who despised African Americans, who distrusted Yankees, who saw Hispanos as dirty, lazy, and primitive. The divisions shifted, sometimes deep as the mines in which the laborers had come to work, sometimes ephemeral as the wind rippling the wheat on the prairies outside their train windows.

The migrants hefted the pain of dispossession in their hearts, but the dreams in their heads led them onward. Many of the farmers and peasants among them pined to return to the soil, to climb back out of the mines with enough cash in hand to purchase land back home. Those who had grown up underground, meanwhile, transported with them dreams of "beautiful mines," colliers' nirvanas where the coal lay in thick veins, clean and solid. Still others, a restless multitude with uncertain aspirations, simply wished for enough work to get by until better prospects materialized.[9]

Those who came brought traditions of conflict, a volatile mix of trade unionism and rural resistance, radicalism and conservatism—and held fast to memories of ancient struggles against oppressive landlords and of recent strikes. The tattooed McBride made no effort to hide his politics, but the organizer Mike Livoda could not afford the risk of showing his United Mine Workers of America card when he left the unionized mines of Montana to organize in Colorado. Southern Italian villagers did not need membership cards to identify which of them had supported the popular Fasci movement as agrarian protest spread from Sicily to the Abruzzi and Molise in 1892.[10]

They brought "history of things carried inside them," Zeese Papanikolas writes in his peerless saga of the Ludlow martyr Louis Tikas and the Greeks he led—a sense of the past that

> informed every gesture, every inflection of their voices and summed up their whole notion of what it was to be a man in the world. They brought it with them in the packets of Greek earth they had sewn to their cloth-

ing like amulets, in the Old Country costumes they would bring from their trunks on feast days, and in the songs of the *Turkomachia*—the Turk wars—carried down from generation to generation, which they would sing in America not with some vague nostalgia, but with the sense of an epic and living presence more real, even, than the machines and pits they worked among and the men who drove them.[11]

The others with whom these Greeks worked and lived bore within them histories of their own.

They abandoned some of these things even as they clung to others. And whether they looked back with yearning, bitterness, or resignation, they harbored the dawning resolution that these histories pointed forward as well as backward. For through the act of migration—of picking up and setting out or, more commonly, of returning to the strategies of mobility they and their people had long practiced—they had begun to sense a power, perhaps even a destiny, to wage battles of their own, win victories of their own—make histo-

3.1. Italian Family, Las Animas County. Trinidad Collection. Copyright Colorado Historical Society, 20004874.

ries of their own that many tongues would relate, new-world epics that would resound from the Colorado coalfields back to the homelands from which the migrants had come.[12]

Who were these coalfield migrants, and what do their origins, journeys, and experiences reveal about work and struggle in the Colorado collieries? Whence did they come, and why? By explaining the peopling—or, more appropriately, the repeopling—of the southern coalfields, we can move past timeworn understandings of industrial struggle in the region and begin to answer two important riddles: If the way in which such migrants habitually responded to trouble was simply to move on, why did they repeatedly decide to take a stand and, in the face of formidable odds, fight powerful corporations? And why did these struggles continue to erupt, even as the mine workforce and coalfield population became increasingly diverse?

Migrant Tracings

Labor was relatively scarce in Colorado through the 1870s, particularly during upswings in the West's boom-and-bust economy. Few people possessed the skills needed to develop and operate coal mines; those who did usually pursued brighter prospects in silver and gold. And so Palmer and the other capitalists who launched collieries began to look not only to the Hispano settlements of Colorado and New Mexico, but also to the Eastern states, Europe, and Asia. The result was a series of migrations, some of them direct, others involving numerous stops and starts, whose scale, pace, and complexity had no precedent in Colorado's long history of human habitation.

These migrants—distinguishing between the immigrants and so-called natives among them obscures more than it reveals—usually left little trace in the historical record. Few could write in any language, and almost no writings by them survive. Government and company officials proved anxious to control, categorize, and tally the migrations. Yet the records and statistics that officials produced offer only snapshots of much larger and ever-changing tableaux—snapshots compromised by their limited temporal and geographic scope. But if we can know much less than we would like to about the people who sought work in the coal mines, we can still shed some light on their lives.[13]

They inhabited a shifting world, neither the world apart that William Palmer hoped Colorado might become nor the bordered, static domain that cartographers and governments were seeking to impose on the earth and its peoples, but rather a transnational space in which states and corporations often lacked the will or the power to contain fluid ideas and institutions, energies and populations. Migrants, though they inhabited a world structured by all sorts of inscrutable forces beyond their control, nonetheless retained some power to choose, shape, or at least influence the course of their own lives. In addition to the journeys the migrants made, there were paths not taken, abandoned before the goal was reached, or retraced. For the vast majority of migrants, after all, the Colorado coalfields represented a place that they were much more likely to travel *through* than *to*. [14]

The travelers came for many reasons. For some, Colorado lay at a safe distance from things they wanted to leave behind. Others came because journeying to Colorado to work underground now took no longer than it once had to walk to a neighboring prefecture to plant rice or to move herds of sheep from the Sangre de Cristos to the San Luis Valley or to leave the Croatian countryside for the Ruhr coalfields.

They came because the land no longer needed them, no longer even had room for them; because steam power was making the world a smaller place; because William Jackson Palmer had dreamed of a new Columbia and because the general and men like him had come to Colorado to build railroads and steel mills and colonies and tourist resorts; because the bonanza mines of Leadville, the smelters of Pueblo, the streetcars of Denver, and the combines of the Great Plains were all developing an insatiable appetite for a rock that burned.

The migrants came because they wanted to reassemble families separated by the wedge of industrial change. Or a steamship agent had visited their village, beating a drum and promising that fortune lay across the ocean; or a silver-tongued recruiter had deceived them into signing up as scabs; or their husbands or uncles or fathers or rivals, their cousins and friends and fellow villagers, had sent letters extolling this far-off country.

They came because some of the envelopes arrived containing tickets and money along with letters. Besides, the migrants knew they could retrace their steps if they wished. And so they imagined heroic homecomings, in which the travelers' pockets would be stuffed as full of dollars as Mrs. Micek's featherbeds were with down.

The Irony of Coal

Capitalists all over the world encountered tremendous obstacles when they sought to replace coal miners with coal-mining machines. Indeed, the coal industry paradoxically remained one of the last sectors to experience the full impact of mineral-intensive industrialization. Even as the adoption of fossil fuels in other sectors of the economy was liberating city and country, agriculture and industry from the constraints of organic energy regimes, coal mining itself continued to rely overwhelmingly on human muscle power and skill. Given that labor productivity in the collieries increased incrementally, while regional demand increased exponentially, coal companies in the southern Colorado coalfields could never have satisfied the West's growing appetite for fuel without the migrants who flocked in from many American states, as well as three dozen countries on four continents.[15]

The first documented effort to mechanize a Colorado coal mine, the 1881 experiments of Palmer's Colorado Coal and Iron Company at the Engle mine opened a few years earlier southeast of Trinidad, illustrates both the motivations that led companies to experiment with mechanizing collieries and the combination of natural, social, and technological obstacles that hampered these efforts. Hoping to erode the control that skilled colliers exerted underground, Colorado Coal and Iron officials contracted with the South Pueblo Machine Company (SPMC). The cutting machines, air compressors, and skilled operators freighted together by the machine company to Engle seemed to promise the mining company "a valuable adjunct," as a later report phrased it, "especially in the matter of controlling labor and wages."[16]

A four-man team led by the machine foreman David Jones set up its equipment in the spring of 1881 and went to work. After these "machine men" had loosened the coal from its bed, laborers hired from nearby Hispano plazas would load it into cars. The coal company directors imagined that the combination of machine technology and unskilled labor would break the control colliers had exerted over production in the coal industry's first decade. Soon after the deafening screech of the machines first echoed off the mine walls, a combination of forces began to undercut the undercutters.

Local mine officials posed one problem. Drawn from the colliers' ranks, they had little respect for machine operators who were untutored in the miners' craft. Skilled workers had still more reason to oppose the machines. Some colliers intentionally held up the contraptions by leaving debris in their path. Others expressed their misgivings by forsaking the collieries for the San Juans. "Men are leaving us daily for the silver mines," the harried superintendent George Engle lamented, "& as a rule, these are our best men." Mine blacksmiths dragged their feet on making simple repairs, then charged astronomical prices, while miners pleaded with or perhaps threatened machine operators. "Two good men I first brought out here from Ohio at considerable expense," machine company executive E. S. McKinlay complained, "were in some way persuaded that this was not a good country." At wit's end, McKinlay surveyed the accumulated obstacles and saw evidence of a "concerted plan" whose object was "getting rid of us & our machines."[17]

The CC&I and the SPMC anticipated opposition from skilled workers and managers. They did not expect trouble from Hispanos. Long portrayed by Anglos as tractable manual laborers, the local residents of the southern coalfields proved as irascible as the colliers the companies wanted them to replace. For the many *nuevomexicanos* who belonged to Penitente groups, the public rituals during Holy Week defined their obligations to God, community, and self. Work counted for little by comparison—particularly the labor of loading up rubble dislodged by deafening machines in a dark, dusty mine. When Holy Week began in April 1881, so many Penitentes refused to work that the coal company had to shut the Engle mine down. Still more surprising, the Penitentes refused to work the next week, too. Operators quickly ran out of room to work without loaders to clean up the coal they had cut, and further cutting became impossible. Most disconcerting of all, though, was a "Strike of Mexicans" that began on April 29. Hispano laborers "came out" of the mine en masse to protest low wages, and they stayed out well into the following week.[18]

Environmental factors exacerbated the mechanizers' woes. Cutting machines were powered by compressed air that was generated by coal-burning boilers, but Engle occupied dry strata underlying arid lands. Even after

CC&I built an underground cistern and filled it with Purgatoire River water freighted in at great expense in tank cars, supplies sometimes ran too low to generate steam, and Jones and his men were forced to shut down their machines. Even when the operators had plenty of water and sufficient laborers to load the coal that was cut, the machines still let them down. One breakdown after another maddened machine operators and infuriated the company officials that had hired them. Only after these glitches were worked out did it become clear that even under the best of circumstances the cutting machines were inadequate for the job. After an operator worked one machine for ten straight hours, he reported that it "could do no more." Less than a week later, Superintendent Engle informed his superiors with secret satisfaction that the machines could not keep pace with the market. "At present," he reported, "the machines with full work & more men than they need, cannot cut the coal we require—and we will therefore have to put on regular miners."[19]

In the three decades that followed, mining machinery improved immensely. Mechanization did eventually succeed in places where "the nature of the coal" favored it, particularly in the thin seams of Fremont and Huerfano counties. And even in thick or gassy seams less suitable for machine mining, the devices exerted what one executive pronounced "an important influence in controlling the miners," not only "reduceing [sic] the cost of mining" but also "lessen[ing] the liability of strikes and labor troubles." Partial mechanization of cutting combined with the use of steam and electricity for haulage and an intensification in traditional hand mining to double the productivity of Colorado's mineworkers between 1885 and 1910. In the end, though, the most significant feature of the incremental increases in productivity was their inadequacy. The 293 cutting machines working Colorado collieries in 1913 accounted for 24 percent of the annual coal output for the state—a good deal more than the 8 percent of coal cut by machine in Britain that year, but well below the U.S. national average of 40 percent.[20]

To satisfy an eightfold increase in coal consumption between 1885 and 1910, Colorado coal operators followed George Engle's advice by employing more men instead of more machines. Employment in and around Colorado's coal mines mushroomed. From just a few colliers in 1870, the figure rose to around 1,500 in 1880 and approximately 6,000 in 1890. The depression of the mid-1890s left thousands of mineworkers jobless, but recovery brought the workforce to 7,000 by 1900; agricultural booms, urban expansion, and industrial recovery drove the total number of employees up to 15,000 by 1907 and to a peak of 15,864 in 1910, before it fell to around 14,000 in 1913. Though a far cry from the 1.2 million mineworkers laboring in Britain or the 800,000 working in Pennsylvania at the time, Colorado's mine workforce nonetheless accounted for fully 10 percent of those employed in the state—enough to sustain a large population of 60,000–75,000 dependents in the Rockies and well beyond, while competing in energy markets that served upwards of 1 million people.[21]

The paradox of coal, then, was this: even as the introduction of fossilized energy into transportation, gold and silver mining, metallurgy, manufacturing, domestic technologies, and urban infrastructure was "reduc[ing] human muscles to" what geographer Vaclav Smil regards as "a marginal source of energy," the provision of the new energy forms remained utterly dependent on human brawn and organic energy supplies. This seeming contradiction served as the impetus for migrations every bit as compelling and significant as the gold rushes and overland sagas that have long dominated Western myth and memory.[22]

Journeys

They had left because people like them were being dragged out of their homes and killed simply for being brown or black or "Dago." Few suspected that the same thing could happen in Colorado, too, but Stanislao Vittone, Lorenzo Andinino, and Francesco Ronchietto learned this deadly lesson during the so-called Italian massacre of 1895, in which a posse attacked several Italians accused of murdering the Rouse saloonkeeper A. J. Hixon.[23]

Or they left because they had exhausted the coalfields in which they had labored. Or they were younger brothers who stood to inherit little, or no one required their strength or skill. Or they wanted their sisters to find good husbands. They left because no company would hire them after they had risen up only to fall back down in defeat.[24]

They wanted more security against the vicissitudes of environmental changes, the cruelty of landlords, the parsimony of corporations, more money and what it could buy: food and possessions, status, and especially land. But most of all, they left because they dreamed that their journey might lead to a better life, whether in the new country or the old.[25]

Henry Johns, like many other men who made their way into Colorado's coal camps, was born into a coal-mining family in the colliery town of Stepaside, in southwestern Wales. And though he managed to postpone his entry into the mine labor force longer than most—he stayed in school until the age of ten, long enough to master the written English and basic math that would later give him an advantage over later migrants to Colorado's coalfields—he would nonetheless recall with pride and perhaps a tinge of regret that his "boyhood days were spent in coal mining."[26]

Once Johns started working underground, a second and, in many ways, more significant phase of his education began. Working his way up a well-defined occupational ladder, Johns was eventually apprenticed to a master collier. By the time the twenty-seven-year-old boarded a steam-powered ocean liner to cross the Atlantic, he had become a skilled miner with a deep respect for the dangerous, dynamic underground environments in which he labored. Leaving behind his fiancée, Margaret Thomas, who worked as a domestic servant, Johns set out to make a better life for himself and his family in Fremont County, Colorado. When Johns arrived in November 1886 (direct from Wales, it seems), the county's domestic fuel mines employed upwards of five hundred Welshmen—enough to support Methodist churches, singing societies, Welsh literary clubs, and the *Eistedfod,* a "blessed old institution" through which Cambrians celebrated their distinctive cultural and national heritage.[27]

Mining companies tolerated and even encouraged the Welsh commitment to education, devotion, and cultural pride. They looked much less kindly, however, on one of the migrants' cherished traditions: trade unionism. Johns arrived to find his countrymen still reeling from a disastrous strike of 1884, in which colliers organized by the Knights of Labor had been crushed by the operators, and then blacklisted; according to the community's chronicler, William Jones, the unsuccessful campaign organized by the Knights of Labor to protest wage cuts and other affronts had caused "our nation . . . much trouble," leading "many of them to leave."[28]

Johns, who was intent on being reunited with his fiancée, earned a reputation as a company loyalist who preferred the Methodist Church, the Cambrian Singers, and fraternal orders to labor unions. Within three years, his savings had enabled him to send for Margaret. They married in 1890, had their first child later that year, and three years after that another. Refusing to join his fellow miners in the marching strike of 1894, Johns made the most of his basic schooling, his mining expertise, and his successful completion of correspondence courses at the International School of Mines in Scranton, Pennsylvania, to win an unusually rapid series of promotions: to fire boss in 1897, mine boss in 1898, and superintendent in 1902. He remained at the Rockvale mine for the duration of his career, after which he retired in 1920 with thirty-three years of service to Colorado Fuel and Iron or its predecessors and more than half a century in the mines.[29]

Let us consider next the path that brought Sam Vigil's father from southern New Mexico to the Huerfano County mines. As a youth, Vigil had set out from the farms around Las Cruces, north toward the railroad town of Chama. Unschooled and presumably unable to speak much English, Vigil probably found work as a common laborer for the railroad, lumber, or livestock industries. But after three years, rumors of higher wages to be had at the coke ovens near Trinidad prompted Vigil to move again. Perhaps hitching rides on passing trains or simply traveling on foot, he ventured across Chama Pass and into Colorado, then across the San Luis Valley and La Veta Pass to Cucharas. In this predominantly Hispano community outside Walsenburg, Vigil met "people that came from Taos," his son later related. They "said that there was chokecherries, apples, grapes, and cherries abundantly here and many of them stayed here in Cucharas because of that." Whether it was the people or the fruitfulness of the place that appealed to Vigil, he cut his journey short. Instead of continuing south to Trinidad, he found work in the coal mines that Palmer and his rivals were developing in Huerfano County. Although Vigil eventually became nearly as skilled at the collier's trade as men such as Henry Johns who had grown up in the mines, the *nuevomexicano* remained "a farmer too, you know. In the winter he worked in the mines and then in the summer he worked in the farm," a small patch in North Veta on which the family kept milk cows, horses, pigs, and chickens.[30]

In contrast to Vigil, Emilio Ferraro arrived in Trinidad precisely as planned. Three of Ferraro's uncles had already followed a much-traveled path of migration from the southern Italian village of Grimaldi to Colorado. With funds and instructions provided either by his relatives or by John Aiello, a Grimaldi-born saloonkeeper, merchant, and banker who served as a broker between Colorado Fuel and Iron and people from his native village who were seeking work, Ferraro ventured first to the provincial capital of Cosinza—whose prefect reported to the Italian government in 1894, "'Going to America has become so popular recently that young men feel ashamed if they have not been at least once.'" From there he went on to Naples, the busy port from which several million Italians would emigrate in the late nineteenth and early twentieth centuries. A few weeks later, he passed through Ellis Island and then caught a westbound train. Ferraro's uncles met him at the Trinidad depot some three days later, allowed him to rest, and then took the green Italian to "this shoe shop." Ferraro recalled that "the shoemaker he was an Italian fellow from Sicily. I say, you give me work? Oh sure, I'll give you work, I got lots of work." "How much you pay me?" Ferraro asked. "One dollar a day," the shoemaker responded. "How can I make a living?" the young Italian cried. "My uncle tell me, no, no, no. Shoot, you cannot stop here. You come with me." The pair headed to Starkville, a camp whose mines and coke ovens fueled steel mills and smelters throughout the Rocky Mountain West. After a quick streetcar ride south from Trinidad, Ferraro arrived in Starkville, where, his uncle promised, "I get you a job making two dollars a day . . . And then if you learn how to pull ovens, you get 98¢ more." Ferraro "started at Starkville working. But when I find out that [Cokedale] was a new camp coming up . . . , my uncle tell me, he says, there is lots of work. If you want to go on up there, why not, there's lots of work." In the years that followed, the villager from Grimaldi combined stints of shoemaking and bartending with longer-term positions as a skilled coke worker, car maker, and brick mason.[31]

The far more circuitous route that George Pezell's father followed to Colorado was probably more characteristic of coalfield migrations. Though a citizen of the Austro-Hungarian Empire, Pezell was an ethnic Croatian from Smiljan, a tiny hamlet best known as the birthplace of the famous inventor Nikola Tesla. Most likely a younger son who stood to inherit nothing, Pezell decided to leave the countryside to work for wages, first as a cabin boy on an Italian ocean liner, then in the collieries that fueled the rise of Germany, and finally in the copper mines of Bingham Canyon, Utah. After seven years there, Pezell returned to his home village in 1907 and married a local girl. The following year, he made his third and final journey across the Atlantic. An experienced collier who now spoke Italian, German, English, and Serbo-Croatian, he easily found work as an interpreter in West Virginia's mines. Acting as a mediator between inexperienced immigrant mineworkers and British American foremen, Pezell soon saved enough money to send his bride passage to West Virginia. Not long after his wife's arrival in 1909, the couple moved to an iron-mining town in northern Minnesota, where George was born in 1910, before they moved again, first to Ruby, a coal camp west of Walsenburg, and eventually to a Utah coal camp.[32]

The journeys of coalfield women are often more difficult to reconstruct, but a story Louis Guigli told about his mother's path to Colorado hints at some possible aspects. Mrs. Guigli (her son did not mention her maiden name) had left her parents' home in the Italian province of Modena at the age of fourteen "to go to work for the rich." After five years of domestic service, she returned to Modena and married a man named Guigli, then emigrated with him to Chicago. After a stay of unknown length, the Guiglis moved to Kansas, where Mr. Guigli started mining coal in Cherokee County. Frustrated with the difficulties of laboring in seams scarcely more than a foot thick, Mr. Guigli "said this coal is too low for me I believe I'm goin to Colorado." Guigli left his wife behind in Kansas and set out with a cousin "to work in the high coals around Walsenburg Colorado." Eventually, he sent for his wife and children. After an operation by an inept camp doctor killed her husband on the family's kitchen table, Mrs. Guigli, like many coalfield women, supported her family by taking in boarders.[33]

Compatriots and relatives welcomed Johns, Vigil, and Ferraro to Colorado, and no one seemed to oppose the arrival of Pezell or Guigli. A group of Japanese workmen, by contrast, received a much less friendly reception in 1902. After word spread that Delos Chappell, head of Victor Fuel, had imported "a non-union labor delegation of Japs" from Fresno, California, a mob of "white" union miners composed of Britons, Americans, Italians, Austrians, Hungarians, and others gathered at Chandler in Fremont

County.[34] Chappell addressed the assembled miners, explaining, "'The company does not want to employ Japanese and Chinese and [*sic*] more than the men want them'"; but recent efforts to secure more miners through labor agencies in the East had failed. "It is just a question of getting any labor at all,'" Chappell concluded. A skeptical unionist retorted:

> It is the known intention of the Colorado Fuel and Iron company to cut down the wages of white miners when they have got enough foreign labor to weather them through the strike that would be sure to follow. They are, in a sly, underhand way, gradually putting Chinese and Japs in the mines everywhere and excluding in preference to them experienced American miners of which there are hundreds unemployed in this very state and the neighboring states. The Chandler miners have spunk, and they have had an inkling of what the company is up to. They have a strong union and are able to make a stand that will eventually, if the men hang to it, bring about the exclusion of Asiatic labor in all the districts of the great trust.

The union miners' opposition forced Chappell to announce that his company would "abandon the attempt to introduce any sort of 'yellow' labor in the Canon district hereafter." But the United Mine Workers could not prevent the capitalist from exacting his revenge. Chappell spitefully closed the Chandler mine at the height of the late-winter peak in domestic fuel demand, when colliers expected to work the longest hours and bring home the thickest pay envelopes of the year; then he shipped the Japanese workmen to Huerfano County, where the men "were put to work" despite protests from local union miners and "threats of violence against the Japs." Chappell's maneuvers led a seasoned coalfield editor to conclude that "one thing is certain—Japanese miners and laborers will stay here just as long as the Company or companies want them here. Those who refuse to work with them can go elsewhere. These newcomers will be protected by the authorities and all other well behaved people."[35]

Within a few years, more than a hundred Japanese had migrated to the southern coalfields. Like Pezell, Ferraro, Guigli, Vigil, and Johns, these Japanese men and their families participated in one of the most influential processes in human history: the mass migration from the countryside and older industrial regions of North America, Europe, and Asia to the busy centers of the mineral-intensive economy.

Composing the Mine Workforce

The maturation of the Rocky Mountain West's fossil-fuel-based economy coincided with population movements of unprecedented scale and scope. As exponential growth in coal consumption necessitated a massive influx of workers to underground workplaces, many parts of the globe were suffering from overpopulation, unemployment, political instability, racial tension, national rivalries, and a surfeit of ostensibly "natural" calamities. The coincidence in time of energy revolutions and mass migrations was less accidental than it might have seemed. Indeed, those processes have generally proved to be so closely connected that a stretch of the imagination is required to conceive of one without the other.

The labor force in the Colorado mines can be classified loosely into three groups. The first consisted of artisan-colliers, most of whom were skilled white miners, like Henry Johns, with origins in Britain, Ireland, and coal-mining states, such as Pennsylvania and Illinois. Manuscript census rolls from 1880, for instance, record the small force developing Palmer's new coal banks in Walsenburg as consisting of five Irishmen, three Pennsylvanians, two Welshmen, two Scots, two New Mexicans, a German, a Canadian, and one migrant each from Wisconsin, West Virginia, Illinois, and Iowa. Though their short-lived monopoly on work underground ended by the late 1870s, British Americans, such as the colliers who arrived at Dawson in 1913 with their lamps carefully wrapped, continued to migrate to the Western American coalfields well into the twentieth century, their arrival replenishing the skilled miners' ranks and belying outdated distinctions between "old" and "new" migrations. Usually reaching the Rockies after one or more intermediate stops in the northeastern, Appalachian, or Midwestern collieries, these craftsmen pioneered the work at new pits and founded many of the state's early coal camps. Such men not only introduced the skills, methods, and ideologies that shaped mine workscapes and work cultures, but continued to predominate in supervisory positions and union hierarchies well into the twentieth century. Beginning in the 1880s, smaller numbers of artisan-colliers of more varied heritage—African Americans, Belgians, French, Germans, Polish, Mexicans, and others, such as George Pezell's Croatian father—began to make their way to Colorado.[36]

Supplementing, then overwhelming this movement of skilled miners was a second and larger stream of unskilled, inexperienced laborers, including Sam Vigil's father, Emilio Ferraro, and the unnamed Japanese miners who met with such an unpleasant welcome at Chandler. The historian John Laslett has termed similarly recent arrivals to the Lanarkshire and Illinois mines newcomer-rebels, and for good reason. These laborers, no matter how far-flung their native lands, generally had common origins as agricultural or rough laborers, though tradesmen, like the coke-working cobbler Ferraro, along with former factory workers and men who had experience mining precious and base metals, were also represented. Hispanos began to seek mining work in Huerfano and Las Animas counties in the late 1870s and quickly became numerous enough to organize actions such as the Engleville Penitente strike of 1881. By the early 1880s, Northern Italians, Tyroleans, and a few Scandinavians had followed, often entering the mines after stints building railroads and hewing ties. The Union Pacific employed Chinese at a subsidiary mine in South Park, until a horrific explosion in 1890 ended the only concerted effort to employ that nationality in Colorado's collieries. The first African Americans, meanwhile, arrived in the southern fields aboard shuttered trains during the strike of 1884. Enticed on false premises by labor recruiters, the new arrivals refused to work as scabs, but other blacks took up mining after the strike ended. They were joined in the 1890s by southern Italians, Hungarians, Serbs, Russians, Moravians, Croats, Bohemians, Ruthenians, Poles, and others. Many of these migrants came directly to Colorado, but others had worked stints in the collieries of Germany, Silesia, Appalachia, and the Midwest. After 1900 or so, Greeks, Bulgarians, Koreans, Mexican nationals, Japanese, and other inexperienced mineworkers diversified the workforce still further. An unknown number of tramps, both native- and foreign-born, rounded out Colorado's underground workforce.[37]

Already by 1890, the confluence of these movements in southern Colorado was producing a mine workforce of remarkable diversity. By the 1910s, it brought together as mixed a group of workmen as had yet labored together on American soil. Federal census takers polled coalfield residents only once a decade. Because the categories employed often obscured more than they revealed—"Austrian," to cite just the most notable example, masked such disparate ethnicities as Tyrolean, Croatian, Slovenian, Polish, Ruthenian, and German—and because mining families were so mobile, robust statistics on coalfield demography are lacking. Colorado Fuel and Iron employment figures from the eve of the 1903 strike reveal a composite of coalfield migrations, albeit one distorted somewhat by the inclusion of steelworkers, iron miners, and other non-coal-mining personnel: 3,700 "Americans," 3,500 Italians, 2,000 "Austrians," 1,000 "Mexicans" (including both local Hispanos and recently arrived Mexican nationals), 900 Irish, 800 English, 600 Slavs, 600 "Colored," 400 Hungarians, 400 Welsh, 300 Scots, 300 Germans, 250 Swedes, 200 Poles, 200 Greeks, 150 French, 100 Swiss, 50 Belgians, 50 Finns, 25 Bohemians, and 25 Dutch. A census of 3,500 Huerfano County colliers on April 1, 1915, offers another snapshot of coalfield demography, tallying 896 Italians, 602 "Mexicans," 506 "white" Americans, 429 Austrians, 270 Greeks, 248 "colored" Americans, and 101 Hungarians leading the twenty-nine "nationalities."[38]

A final and equally important group of migrants remains utterly invisible in mine employment statistics. Men and adolescent boys typically embarked in search of work alone, with male relatives, or with male compatriots, so most colliery camps were populated overwhelmingly by men, particularly in the industry's early decades. Even so, growing numbers of women and children also ventured to the southern fields, some directly from the old country, others by more roundabout routes. Emotional, sexual, and social pressures motivated some reunions and family migrations. But opportunities for male children to enter the mines and for women such as Margaret Thomas and Mrs. Guigli to reestablish a viable household economy also figured into the calculations families made. Women might supplement the family income by taking in boarders, doing laundry, or selling milk, eggs, vegetables, and other foods they raised themselves. They also contributed by discharging the seemingly endless array of unremunerated duties that census takers lumped under the catchall term "housekeeping." By the early twentieth century, family migrations brought ratios in the coal camp population closer to parity between the sexes. A Colorado-born group of artisan-colliers had emerged to work below their native ground.[39]

How much, too, the miners left behind. Home. At the center of the seven-acre Adamic freehold in Slovenia stood a two-story house. During the long winter, the family's livestock occupied the ground floor, while a dozen family members crowded into the rooms above each night to sleep.[40]

Emigrants left behind spring moons that told them when to plant; soils they had tilled, animals they had birthed and named and nursed; railroads they had built, tunnels they had hacked out of the earth. They left wives and children, parents and grandparents; the bones of their ancestors; friends and enemies; kings and emperors and landlords. They left poverty and repression; work that was too hard and pay that was too low; promises and dowries, mortgages and debts, strikes and wars and blood feuds.

They left behind many things they would miss—things they knew as well as the back of their own hands. As they abandoned the comfort of known worlds—the burn of grappa, the swish of scythes cutting through barley, Dolomite mountain crags glowing rosy yellow in the sunset, the melody of familiar place-names rolling off the tongues of family and friends—the absence of such things wore a hole in their sense of themselves.[41]

Bursting at the Seams

Far and away the most important pull the southern Colorado coalfields exerted was the relatively high-paying work in jobs that were essentially open to anyone willing to take them. Companies often hired men with little or no experience underground. And unlike the copper mines of the Southwest, the sugar plantations of Hawaii, and many other Western enterprises, American coal corporations paid "Mexicans," Asians, and other nonwhites the same rates and wages as were paid to British Americans, an average of around $10 a week in the nineteenth century and up to $15 a week by the 1910s. Colorado coal companies boasted that they offered the highest tonnage rates in the United States. Though seasonal fluctuations in demand, cyclical downturns in the regional economy, mining disasters, and other factors all limited the number of days colliers could work, an unskilled migrant still had good reason to anticipate annual earnings of at least $375, and quite possibly $500–800—attractive figures indeed at a time when the typical unskilled Italian sojourner in the United States could expect to make $300, "prosperous peasant famil[ies] in Italy" earned the equivalent of from $50 in the Marches to just over $100 in the Piedmont, and Hungarian field hands averaged just $22 per year. Kinship networks and the formation of ethnic enclaves in the coalfields exerted another strong pull. Many migrants left their old countries or earlier migration destinations for Colorado to rejoin husbands, brothers, mothers, comrades, and countrymen. Finally, less tangible factors—the worldwide appeal of America's mythic frontier, Colorado's reputation for healthfulness, perhaps even the similarity of the Rocky Mountain landscape to homelands in the Tirol, Slovenia, and New Mexico—may have heightened the allure of Colorado.[42]

The factors stimulating people to leave their old countries during the late nineteenth and early twentieth centuries were even more complex than those pulling them to the coalfields. We can nonetheless draw useful distinctions between idiosyncratic, sociopolitical, and economic-environmental pushes. Some people left their homelands because of private circumstances; a Greek named Condas sought to escape an arranged marriage, for example, while Ed Tomsic fled to thwart his parents' plans for him to join the priesthood. Less random forces motivated most others. Young men facing conscription often reasoned that it was better to venture out into the wide world than risk death fighting in foreign wars or domestic insurrections. Others were fleeing revolution or racial or ethnic violence. A surprising number of coalfield migrants sought refuge in the American Southwest from conflict-ridden borderlands in the Tirol, northern Mexico, Crete, and elsewhere. Also seeking refuge were African Americans terrorized by the violence and repression of the Jim Crow South, Christian Slavs seeking to evade partitions and Ottoman oppression, radicals exiled from many homelands, and blacklisted unionists.[43]

In most instances, though, economic factors seem to have provided the greatest motivation for emigrating. Nick Halamandaris's father, for instance, left Greece to work as a stonemason in Asia Minor. Years of back-breaking work enabled him to amass no more than twenty-five dollars. Coming to the

United States made sense to Halamandaris and others "because their country that they come from couldn't support them." The Colorado collier Dan DeSantis used similar language to explain why he left Italy at the age of fifteen: "There was nothing to make a living over there; there was no money. So we came over here to make a better living." Mickey Judiscak remembered the stories his Czech parents told: "They were very poor and from what they told me things were tough. They didn't talk too much about it—they were glad to be away from there. I don't think they had too many pleasant memories of the old country. My mother did say that wealthy people owned all the land. She said her people were sort of like tenant farmers; making only enough to live. Except for food and shelter they had very little."[44]

As the recollections of Halamandaris, DeSantis, and Judiscak all attest, many parts of the world could provide their inhabitants with only the paltriest of livings. Why? Government policies deserve some of the blame. In parts of Slovenia, Italy, and Japan, for instance, exorbitant taxes left smallholders little more than a pittance. Feudal holdovers also helped mire some rural areas of Europe and Asia in poverty. "The land is held almost exclusively by the aristocracy and the church," a U.S. immigration inspector reported from southern Italy, "and the peasantry are afforded practically no opportunity to acquire possession of even small tracts."[45]

These long-standing problems, however, only partially explain the mass migrations of the late nineteenth and early twentieth centuries. Larger forces were clearly at work. Problems that might be described in purely economic terms—rock-bottom incomes, high food prices, narrowing access to agricultural land, falling wages, the abandonment of handicraft industries, and so forth—almost always resulted, at least in part, from some underlying ecological factor.[46]

Let us start by looking at the most powerful force driving migration, the global population boom that produced labor surpluses in rural regions and industrial centers in many parts of the world. The population of Europe, which was 140 million in 1750, swelled to 250 million by 1845 and 468 million by 1913. Japan's boom began later but quickly assumed analogous proportions. Hovering between 25 and 27 million from 1721 to 1846, the number of inhabitants in the island nation grew to perhaps 33 million in 1868 and 56 million by 1920. Mexican demographic expansion remained more gradual but was substantial nonetheless; from 6 million people after independence, it had grown to 15.1 million by 1910. North of the Rio Grande, immigration and the decimation of indigenous populations facilitated the most prodigious increases of all, from perhaps 6 million inhabitants in 1800 to well over 100 million a century later. All told, the world's population increased from around 900 million in 1800 to around 1.6 billion in 1900.[47]

Fundamental changes in the way people related to one another and their environment constituted both a cause and an effect of population growth in all these places. One particularly influential set of dynamics involved humans, microbes, and their habitats. Advances in medicine and public health served to moderate the impact of infectious disease, the single greatest cause of death in most human populations before the twentieth century. Changes in the external environment reinforced the transformation of the body's internal environment. Improved disposal of sewage and garbage; campaigns against such vectors of disease as rats and mosquitoes; and the development of technologies and regulatory structures that ensured a growing minority of the world's citizens access to clean water, pasteurized milk, and uncontaminated food all helped inaugurate a new era of human population dynamics. This new regime of relationships between and among people, germs, vectors, and landscapes marked a turning point in the history of the planet. From this fork in the road, some societies would travel toward famine and starvation, others toward seemingly boundless plenty.[48]

Whatever factors helped determine which path a society would take, however, the calculus of energy proved inescapable. To put it in stark terms, declining death rates led to population growth only if the people spared by disease could obtain the food they needed to survive. In all the migrant source regions that supplied laborers to the Colorado collieries—Johns's Wales, Vigil's New Mexico, Halamandaris's Greece, DeSantis's Italy, Judiscak's Bohemia, and so forth—the sanitary revolution of the late nineteenth and the twentieth centuries would surely have fizzled out if it had not been for agricultural revolutions that multiplied the consumable energy available to fuel human metabolisms.

The age of European discovery, as Alfred Crosby has emphasized, initiated a series of uneven biological exchanges. The Old World offered its smallpox and rats and weeds, its wheat and its livestock, in return for seeds and cuttings in whose genes were encoded millennia of patient, skillful, and serendipitous collaboration between New World peoples and the plants they used to turn the sun's energy into food. American plants circulated along global trade corridors first as novelties, then as necessities.[49]

Consider the humble potato, a prolific plant that yielded more calories per acre than almost any other crop. This once-despised tuber—sixteenth-century Europeans blamed it for causing leprosy—eventually facilitated tremendous increases in population. In Ireland, just an acre and a half of potatoes—about a football field's worth—could "keep a family hearty for a year," according to Crosby. The extension of hundreds of thousands of such plots enabled an island whose soil provided 3.2 million inhabitants with the barest of livings in 1754 to support perhaps 10 million by the 1840s. Thanks to the potato, Britain, Scandinavia, Germany, Poland, Russia, and other parts of northern Europe also experienced rapid demographic growth, if less dramatic than Ireland's. When an American pathogen known as the potato blight first crossed the Atlantic in the early 1840s (surviving, it seems likely, in the hold of a fast clipper ship), many of the people who had come to depend on the tuber for food had either to emigrate or to starve.[50]

If we trace the genealogy of any Colorado coalfield family back far enough, we are quite likely to find the family tree spreading its branches during the period when these epidemiological and agricultural revolutions began: the 1600s in parts of Britain, the early nineteenth century in much of the United States, Germany, and other parts of Northern and Western Europe, and the late nineteenth and early twentieth centuries in southern and eastern Europe, Japan, Korea, and Mexico. As a result of fundamental transformations in how humans related to their environments, some combination of unemployment, underemployment, and low wages almost invariably ensued. Some of the peasants who suffered these woes rebelled; the eras of agricultural change were consequently times of tumult—of peasant revolt, social banditry, and everyday forms of resistance that loomed large in the collective memory. Many more, however, sought to free themselves from the land. Writing of southern Italy in the early twentieth century, the traveler Robert Foerster argued that leaving the known patterns of agricultural life through migration was "simpler and ... surer than revolution."[51]

The distance laborers put between themselves and the farms they left offers one measure of the shift in relationships between working people and the natural world. Moving to find work was hardly a novel practice. Instead, demographic transitions intensified and amplified older patterns of migration. First in Britain and then elsewhere, too, growing numbers of tenant farmers and farm laborers began to embark on seasonal migrations. Between 1660 and 1730, during the height of England's agricultural revolution, for instance, 76 percent of rural women and 68 percent of rural men moved away from their native villages at some point in their lives. A century later, many *nuevomexicano* men were leaving their lowland farms for months at a time, to herd sheep in the foothills and mountains. Across the globe in Japan, men known as *dekasegi* had long left home to work as harvest hands. In the Tirol too, many men "spent the major part of their lives as nomads," according to the anthropologists John Cole and Eric Wolf. In the early 1700s, such men moved for part of the year to Italy, Austria, and southern Germany to work as migrant agricultural laborers or itinerant peddlers selling handicrafts produced in home workshops; a century later, some of their descendants began to range even farther afield during the building season, to work in the construction trade. Colorado's coalfield migrations grew out of these earlier movements in which Tyrolean wanderers, Japanese *dekasegi*, Hispano *pastores*, and others left home for several months of the year to find work.[52]

The forebears of mineworkers' families generally came not from the stationary class of peasants with deep roots to a single locale, but rather from the wayfaring folk who survived their rapidly changing world by moving from place to place.

They came however they could—by wagon and oxcart and on foot; by boarding newly finished railway cars, cramming into third-class coaches, piling out of cramped holds in smelly deepwater ports. From Kobe and Le Havre, Liverpool and Fiume, they traveled in steerage on ships so large they bore the names of monarchs, nations, and myths—*Kaiser Wilhelm, Mauretania,* and the *Titanic*'s older and more fortunate sister ship, the *Olympic.*

From American ports, Mexican mining towns, eastern coalfields, Canadian construction camps, and Western cities, they made their way, sitting or standing aboard trains stenciled with every sort of acronym: NYCRR and GTRR, PRR and UPRR and CPRR, C&S and AT&SF and D&RG. They came in passenger coaches and special cars whose blacked-out windows concealed their human cargo from the view, reach, and insults of the strikers who called them scabs.

Industrializing Migration

Mineral-intensive industrialization—the substitution of mineral for organic energy stocks and the corollary substitution of mineral inputs for organic raw materials—was not only the single most important factor in defining the challenges and opportunities migrants faced in Colorado and their old countries. It also blazed the paths these migrants took to the coalfields. Some coalfield migrants had spent their lives in coal mines; others had never ventured underground. Yet all inhabited places were being reshaped in one way or another by fossil fuels and steam-powered technologies.

Human migrations formed the nexus for economic, ecological, and social transformations in three primary respects. First, the transition to fossil fuels and mineral inputs pushed many people from their native lands by accelerating population growth, ecological degradation, and social dislocation. The expansion of mining and manufacturing and the accompanying industrial pollution that so troubled young William Palmer on his Black Country tour of the 1850s made it impossible for some people to remain on their land. Far more significant was the application of mineral fertilizers and fossil fuels to agriculture, first in Britain and then in much of Europe, northeast Asia, and North America. By the early twentieth century, farmers in many parts of the world had chosen, like their counterparts on the eastern plains and in the western valleys in Colorado, to embrace so-called modern methods. The bonds of organic energy systems loosened as agriculturists began to replace draft animals with coal- and gasoline-powered tractors and implements, work nitrates and other minerals into the soil, and process their harvests in steam-powered mills, canneries, and factories. Yet even as mineral-intensive industrialization helped sustain booming populations, it inexorably depressed demand for agricultural labor throughout migrant source regions.[53]

Coal pushed people out of some places, but it also pulled them to others. The reconfiguration of existing patterns of migration and the charting of new paths from country to colliery and factory thus began to connect the southern coalfields of Colorado with many migrant source regions in a second way. Itinerant agricultural laborers or peddlers increasingly gravitated toward rapidly growing industries with acute labor demands, such as mining, manufacturing, and railroad construction. Sometimes gradually, sometimes decisively, seasonal itinerancy metamorphosed into full-time wage work. Tyroleans increasingly extended older patterns of migration that had taken them to Swabia to tend fields, Innsbruck to sell handiwork, or Vienna to build houses: they now built railroads through the Alps. Entrepreneurial Hispanos left their flocks to haul railroad ties and drive bull teams ferrying freight between plains railheads, Front Range cities, and mountain mining camps. Peasants, tenants, sharecroppers, and *dekasegi* abandoned large estates and small plots in Japan, the Mezzogiorno, the Scottish Highlands, Serbia, the U.S. South, and many other places for the promise of high wages in burgeoning coal mines. Wherever men mined coal, it was possible to find migrants who had crossed racial, regional, and national borders to labor alongside artisan colliers and locals who had been displaced from farms and cottage industries. In Westphalia, Poles and Croats accompanied Germans underground; Irishmen ventured into Lanarkshire's pits alongside Scots; Italians labored in West Virginia with African American freedmen and Scotch-Irish mountaineers; and so on. Though adult and adolescent males predominated in the initial stages of this shift from agricultural labor and seasonal itinerancy to coal mining, women and children accompanied or followed their menfolk in sufficient numbers to transform the energy boomtowns of the world into new centers of family life and community formation.[54]

The use of fossil energy in transportation innovations forged a third and still stronger link between the Rockies and migrant source regions. Railroads and steamships lowered both the cost and the risk of travel, thus accelerating movement of people from places where labor was plentiful and poorly compensated to places where workers were scarce and wages high. By the late nineteenth century, Colorado collieries lay within one month's journey of the most densely populated regions of the world. The railroads built by William Palmer, his predecessors, and his rivals reduced the journey to the Front Range from almost anywhere in the United States and much of Canada and Mexico to under five days. The extension of rail networks throughout Europe and parts of Asia brought long isolated backwaters within a few days' travel of deepwater ports. The advent of large, fast ocean liners powered by steam meanwhile slashed the duration and expense of ocean crossings; by the 1890s, New York lay just six days away from Le Havre and Southampton, while even the longer journeys from Bremen to Galveston or from Tokyo to San Francisco rarely consumed more than three weeks. Heavy competition drove ticket prices sharply downward to an average transatlantic fare of thirty dollars, leading one historian to declare that "it was the steamship . . . that caused the America fever to grow from isolated outbreaks into an epidemic."[55]

By making travel faster and cheaper, railroads and steamships reduced the stakes and risks involved in long-distance migration. Now that America seemed "'so near,'" one Irishman declared in expressing a common sentiment, "'that it was just round the corner,'" those already laboring in the established collieries of Europe and the United States found it easier than ever before to seek out higher pay, surer work, and better conditions in the industrializing Rockies. Seasonal itinerants also extended their journeys. Some became self-styled "birds of passage" crossing the seas for part of the year, whereas others embarked on longer journeys from which they nevertheless hoped to return home. Jim Dimante explained that Greek miners in Utah, to cite just one example, liked to drink to shouts of "Kalipa threva," a toast that celebrated their common goal: "They were all planning on going back to their good *katathreva*," the Greek motherland. Ten Italians fulfilled similar ambitions when they left a Colorado coal camp "for their native land, with a goodly supply of Uncle Sam's gold."[56]

Trains and steamships, in short, formed a "bridge linking the two worlds" of Eurasia and North America. Obscured behind the metaphor of a static structure lay the power of coal and the cumulative human labor required to extract coal and burn it. "The fastest steamships" of the 1890s, one Colorado-based German entrepreneur noted in an account of transatlantic travel, burned three thousand to four thousand tons of coal per crossing—roughly two hundred railcars' worth, enough to keep fully a third of the *Kaiser Wilhelm der Grosse*'s crew of 480 "tend[ing] the fires" in the ship's bowels. After descending the steel stairs leading to a ship's power plant, the businessman described the "horror resulting from our comfort" as "truly terrible, if one has once been in such a boiler room and has observed the naked figures, dripping sweat from the strenuous work in a ship sometimes tossed by rough seas; one learns how these people have to be carried out unconscious after a few hours of work—very often during a crossing deaths occur as a result of the heat," an unfortunate side effect of the increasingly dense network of fast, affordable, secure transportation that workers used to travel to the Colorado coalfields from all over the world.[57]

The Migration Business

In truth, that network of steamships and railroads was formed of many strands. Capitalists hoped to profit from the transport of passengers across continents and oceans and, in concert with labor agents and other entrepreneurs, made migration their business.[58]

One sector of this business specialized in providing credit to the many prospective migrants who, despite a decline in transportation costs, lacked sufficient money to purchase train and steamship tickets. The American immigration commissioner John Gruenberg reported in 1908 that "the number of peasants who could and would migrate was comparatively small as long as it was confined and limited to those only, who could raise enough cash money to pay for their railroad and steamship transportation, and it was therefore the 'credit system' which stimulated the emigration as much as any other factor." Gruenberg and other U.S. agents found that "money lenders or village bankers" constituted one source of credit, and steamship agents "located in the great emigration centers" another. The transatlantic lines disavowed any connection with these agents, but American officials maintained: "It is obvious that there is a community of interest between these parties and the transportation lines, namely, the procurement of as large a number of passengers as possible."[59]

Loans attracted some, but steamship agents also employed other techniques. In southern Italy, for instance, they kept a lookout at the post office for incoming letters from American emigrants, then "avail[ed] themselves to the utmost of this means of advertising; calling the attention of prospective customers to the fact that some one of their neighbors [had] received such a letter and inducing them to read it." In eastern Europe, agents dispatched "a vast army of agitators or runners" to journey "from one village to another," seeking "to form groups of peasants to induce them to emigrate to America and to coach and instruct them how to evade the Contract Labor Laws by false answers." In Japan, emigration companies "bound together" with steamship lines "by a very close tie of mutual interest in money making" also marketed migration. An English businessman described how "some half-a-dozen Japanese with drums, banners &c." marched noisily into a remote district and attempted to entice young men into contract labor on Hawaiian plantations. The impact of such spectacles is unclear, but the success of the immigration companies was undeniable; between 1899 and 1903, they accounted for 63 percent of Japanese who left for the United States. A few years later, the most notorious of steamship labor agents in Europe, Frank Missler, used the same strategy, filling steerage on the North German Lloyd line by sending percussionist-recruiters to almost "every village and hamlet" in Austria-Hungary, Bulgaria, Serbia, and Macedonia. After drumming up attention, Missler's agents announced to "all those, who now want to go to America" that they could "get their tickets passports, information, etc. from" a government-appointed agent, usually an "influential citizen" of the locality. Undoubtedly the most important "information" Missler and other old-country labor agents provided involved wages. One broadside issued by Missler's Belgrade office, and preserved by a U.S. immigration investigator, explained in Serbian that "in the states of Texas, Colorado and California labor is paid highest; because, in these states, workmen are scarce." Similar claims brought thirty-five Bulgarian "work-seekers" in 1907 to Trinidad, where they started in the collieries at $1.95 a day, a hefty sum in the old country but slim pickings in the land of dollars.[60]

Western American railroads, generally more concerned with boosting settlement and tourism along their routes, played a less intentional role in inducing migration to the southern Colorado coalfields. Each surge in construction sent railroads and the firms that built them scurrying to secure the most tractable and inexpensive workforce possible. When the track-laying booms inevitably crested, then crashed, "large numbers of men" found themselves thrown "out of employment." After one such crash in the late 1880s left hundreds of Italians and Tyroleans stranded in the Rockies without work or passage home, the Colorado coal mine inspector explained: "As there has been a marked degree of development going on in our coal fields and new mines being opened, the [collieries have] offered an opportunity for employment, with fairly good wages, . . . tempt[ing] many inexperienced men to take to coal mining."[61]

Many Mexicans, Japanese, Greeks, and others would find their careers taking a similar turn in the decades ahead. And though most of those who ended up in the mines found their own way to southern Colorado, many other coalfield migrants moved from old country to new—and often from track labor to underground work—thanks to the shady dealings of labor agents. Coal companies secured mineworkers from agencies in American cities as far-flung as Pittsburgh, Chicago, and Joplin, Missouri. Recruitment via such channels increased markedly during labor disputes, when picket lines and threats by unionized colliers reduced walk-up employment in the pits, and when the agents who plied Denver's Larimer Street tenderloin struggled to round up men who would be willing to break strikes. Padrones, Missler's new-world counterparts, also sought to profit by brokering deals between workmen and employers. Leonidas Skliris, the Salt Lake City–based "King of the Greeks," played a major role in initiating the movement of Greeks into Colorado's collieries following 1900, while a "couple of well dressed, bright looking Japs in American attire" that a pro-union newspaper reported as having met with Colorado Fuel and Iron officials in 1901 played a similarly significant role in the arrival of Japanese miners, such as the party from Fresno that so enraged colliers at Chandler the following year. Even after the Colorado Bureau of Labor began to crack down on padrones through licensing requirements and the creation of Free Employment offices, immigrant entrepreneurs based in the southern coalfields continued to procure workers for the region's coal companies. Italian union miners, for instance, claimed that mine officials relayed hiring requests to a "large body of businessmen who have become rich by our labour." The Tarabino brothers, who were merchants and saloon owners, and John Aiello, whose diversified enterprises included a bank, a saloon, and a general store, played pivotal roles in bridging the distance between a handful of southern Italian villages and Las Animas County, and an Austrian Slav named Corich served much the same function by helping bring men from his homeland to the coalfields. The active correspondence these entrepreneurs maintained with relatives and associates in their home villages often specified the "numbers of fellow country-men whom the person addressed is instructed to bring with him for the ac-ceptance of the promised employment." Letters sometimes enclosed fare for passage and instructions for evading interrogation at the gateways to the "great Eldorado" of America.[62]

Through the Grapevine

Naturalization records and oral histories document the presence in the coal-fields of numerous migrants from Aiello's native village of Grimaldi, demon-strating the importance of ethnic entrepreneurs as mediators between the demand of Colorado coal-mining companies for labor and the supply of work seekers in the labor hinterlands. Many migration chains, though, seem to have developed without inducement. The gambits of railroad and steam-ship companies as well as the machinations of padrones and coalfield king-pins propelled many toward Colorado, but these factors probably exerted less influence on migrants than many critics supposed. "What may be de-scribed as the personal element," an immigration report stated in 1908, "has now become almost, if not quite, the most important feature of the emigra-tion question." President John Osgood of Colorado Fuel and Iron put it still more succinctly when he claimed, "The best employment agency we have is the men working in our mines."[63]

Improvements in communications abetted this "personal element," for they greatly increased the quantity and quality of information available to po-tential migrants. Telegraphs, steam-printed newspapers, and national labor unions brought word of high-paying jobs in Colorado's coal mines to the at-tention of potential workers throughout the United States. Transportation improvements and modern mail service made even more of a difference. "So many foreigners have become domiciled in the United States," American in-vestigators claimed, "and so extensive a correspondence is carried on be-tween those located in the United States and their friends and relatives still in the European countries, that it is impossible to overestimate the effect pro-duced by this personal influence." The letters that migrants sent home from the industrializing West helped people back home assess the dangers and benefits of emigration. Mail from Colorado and other states "to country villages in Italy and Hungary, and other such countries," the Dillingham Commission found, had "become practically public property and pass[ed] from hand to hand, and even from village to village." In Calvi, Italy, a former leader of the Knights of Labor, Terence Powderly, discovered that "when a letter is received from anyone located in the United States it is read and reread by others, so that it is soon memorized by hundreds of people." In the Habsburg Empire, "Every mail delivered, even in the remotest villages . . . brings glad tidings from friends and relatives located in America to the effect that work is abundant and wages princely, by comparison with those paid in their native land." Such letters, as in Italy, were "read and reread until their contents [could] be repeated word by word." The money orders and bank transfers that often accompanied outbound letters from the Colorado coalfields sometimes helped transform villages in the old country. By 1906, 846 million lire were flowing each year from the Americas to Italy. In the southern part of that country, "where for centuries, the farmers have been unable to do more than pay the interest on their mortgages," the labor statistician Ethelbert Stewart explained, "hundreds and thousands of farms have been cleared of debt; new, bright homes have been built, better farming implements have been purchased and land has been improved by fertilizers; all with money sent by the father or son who 'went to America.'" Here was concrete confirmation that the potential rewards of leaving home justified the attendant risks. Indeed, glowing letters and gleaming farmsteads cumulatively prompted so close an association between America and prosperity that in Europe, as in Asia and Mexico, "the words 'United States' were greeted with smiles and manifestations of pleasure."[64]

Perhaps more important, though far harder to reconstruct, were the informal networks through which news about wages, working conditions, prices, and the availability of work circulated between North American collieries, Western industrial outposts, and migrant source regions. Thousands of men first heard of Colorado through the grapevine. Return migrants, for their part, represented a particularly compelling source of information. The disillusioned among them tended to agonize in silence and shame. The fortunate, the prideful, and the mendacious, by contrast, portrayed America as a land of milk and honey. The residents of Japan's prosperous Aichi Prefecture, for instance, so eagerly absorbed the "tempting stories" related by a man named Ito "to advertise his own achievements" that less than a year after Ito's return, "more than one hundred persons [were] said to have emigrated to the United States." A few anecdotes from oral histories suggest the importance stories like this played in luring laborers to Colorado and Utah. A German collier "heard that America was the finest place in the world to live"; in Italy, August Andreatta's grandfather, a man who had journeyed back and forth from his homeland to America four separate times, told anyone who would listen, "Boy, the United States is a beautiful Country." And in Greece, Anast "Ernest" Chipian recalled, "everybody that [had] been to America and come back to the home town were bragging so much about America being the richest country and a golden opportunity for everybody." The wealth some return migrants displayed confirmed such stories of opportunity. "The prosperity of the United States is so thoroughly advertised by . . . the personal appearance, manner of dress, and prosperous look" of returned migrants, a U.S. immigration inspector wrote, "that, when one observes the effect produced in his native village by the return thereto of a former emigrant, the only wonder is that America does not receive a larger influx of these foreign people than it does."[65]

They found all manner of things: wide open spaces and deep snows and parched air that sucked the moisture from their lips; clanking, rumbling machines standing outside man-swallowing tunnels; bustling, fuming cities built on coal. Migrants to the West found sprawling, sparsely peopled farms as different from the little plots onto which some of the newcomers had formerly crowded as they were from the plantations, haciendas, and estates where others had toiled. They had clothes to wash, husbands and children to bury, wounds to heal.

They found people to trust and people to fear; unfamiliar writing and even more unfamiliar faces. The immigrants often took new names, sometimes of their own choice, more often an invention of officials who had no expertise in transliterating Magyar, Greek, or Japanese. And whether the new arrivals saw these monikers as an insult or a liberation, some found their world shaken loose from its moorings, until everything seemed alien, themselves most of all.

They found people they knew, people with whom they had risen in the world. They found codes of race, deep hatreds packed into words uttered in a hiss: *Nigger, Dago, Jap, Hunky.* They encountered privilege, indignity, and different ways of thinking about what it meant to be a man, along with color and class and gender, creed and country, region and village.

They found pay envelopes filled with dollars.

Looking at the adobe huts and low-eaved log cabins of the coal camps where they earned those dollars, some migrants occasionally found themselves transported back in memory to Taos or the Tirol. Closing their eyes in front of the stores run by Aiello or the Tarabinos, they breathed in the aromas of salami, olives, and sharp cheese and felt the planet shrinking. That sense of the closeness of home comforted but also tormented them, for when the illusion of proximity vanished, many found that they had washed up on the shore of a land so different, so distant from the one they had known, that they cried or raged at the dislocation.

Many found the foul taste of blood and coal and last night's drink in their mouths in these unfamiliar places, where the coal barons and their henchmen ruled just the way other overseers had governed the lands left behind: *signori* in business suits, *hacendados* in bowlers, *massas* piously extolling the virtues of free labor. When Joe Strampa met death waiting in the mines, his wife took their three children back to Austria. In the face of such everyday tragedies, others felt reassured that their lives were not so bad, that there were worse places, that they were never going to find nobler or more highly paid work than coal mining.[66]

They found work inside the earth, deep grumblings of discontent, men who held out the promise that the people of the coalfields, newcomers and old-timers alike, could throw off their chains—if only they joined together to fight.

They tripped over questions. If they did not join the battle here, then where? Did they still have anything left to lose after they had given up so much, hoped for so much, and sometimes gotten so little in return? And so from time to time they found in their hearts a great resolve: they would take this new home and shake it until it fulfilled their extravagant hopes.

Mobility and Militancy

Some migrants made a beeline to meet family members, honor labor contracts, or join fellow villagers who had pioneered in forming migration chains.

For most who came to the Colorado coalfields before and during the big strike of 1913–1914, though, Colorado was neither their initial nor their final destination. They were people who realized full well that their ability to move from place to place was one of the few strategies at their disposal. In negotiating the pitfalls and possibilities that industrial capitalism presented, they knew that all too often, the best they could do when times got tough was to set out once again in search of brighter horizons.

Migrants had embarked, after all, in search of opportunity, money, and freedom. At least some who viewed mine work as a means to some other end found what they sought and returned home from their quest, like the Italians who left the Rockies with heaps of "Uncle Sam's gold." Mobility enabled the less fortunate migrants to continue their striving. "Miners of those days," as John Brophy recalled, "had to lead a gypsy life," and many left to find work mining coal in northern Colorado, Utah, Montana, New Mexico, or elsewhere. Others joined family and countrymen to work as loggers in the Chama Valley, unearth precious metals in the Rockies, harvest wheat and sugar beets on the plains, labor in the steel mills or smelters of the Front Range cities, raise sheep on the Western range, or build railroads. Still others bought land or homesteaded around the coal camps. No small number, in defeat rather than triumph, retraced the path that had led them from the old country to the new.[67]

The mobility of coalfield migrants raises crucial questions about the militancy that erupted from the southern mines in major strikes during 1884, 1894, 1903, and 1913, as well as in dozens of local disputes. How did the men, women, and children who had come to Colorado from so many different places—artisan colliers and "green men," old-timers and newcomers—begin to make common cause and organize themselves? How did a migrant population accustomed to mobility manage to band together in order to take on some of the most powerful corporations in the United States, not just once but repeatedly? The answers lay underground, in the mine environments where boys and men from around the globe labored in some of the most perilous conditions imaginable.

4

Dying with Their Boots On

In January 1884, after "kissing loved ones and bidding them good-bye," ninety men and boys stumbled from their boardinghouses and homes out into the darkness of a bone-chilling dawn. In their heavy boots, some walked alone, others alongside friends and family in little clusters, but all trudged toward the same destination, a spot perhaps five hundred paces west of the town center that cast an infernal glow on the mountainside above.[1]

The men swung lunch pails and traded stories as they walked. Their accents and their names—Anderson, Laux, Williams, O'Neil, Lodenwald, Hughes, Creelman, Hular, McGregor, Probst, Donegan—hearkened back to two continents and many nations. Brogues and burrs, singsongy Welsh and guttural Pennsylvania Dutch echoed off the false facades of this archetypal Old West mining town: isolated, makeshift, fraught with the possibility of violence.

A few were just boys. Morgan Neath and little Tommy Lyle were only twelve years old, and Morgan's big brother William was seventeen. Of the rest, most were in the prime of life; a few had passed it. Perhaps half the men were married. Six lived with their families in Crested Butte, but the others had left behind wives and often children in the old country.[2]

The destinies of these marked men would soon diverge still more sharply than their origins. Fifty-nine of them were walking to their death, victims of

Colorado's first major colliery disaster. Like the gunslingers of Western lore, most would die with their boots on. Some of those boots were hardly charred, others were left with jagged bone and ragged muscle protruding, and twenty-three pairs in all lay twisted and torn amid "a mass of raw and bleeding flesh . . . distorted all out of human shape." A reporter for the *Denver Tribune* portrayed the carnage with breathless ghoulishness:

> The clothing was burned and blackened, the faces in many cases were bruised out of all semblance to humanity. Hands were raised as if to protect the face, the skin and flesh hanging in burned and blackened shreds, arms broken, legs broken, and in some cases boots torn off by the force of the blast. Skulls crushed in. One man had both arms blown off, another was found on his back, his head in a pool of water, and when they lifted him up the back of the skull and brains fell with a sickening splash into the blood puddle. Another man has a hand raised, the fingers bent like talons, the skin and flesh gone to the wrist, leaving only a horrible claw.[3]

The fate of these men—the day shift at the Colorado Coal and Iron Company's Jokerville mine—and the thousands of other Western coal mine workers who perished on the job in the following decades make the association between violence and the Wild West appear curious, even negligent. After all, on-the-job accidents and workplace disasters claimed many more lives than range wars and gunfights ever would. The gruesome industrial violence that resulted when colliers unintentionally detonated the immense energies latent in the ancient coal seams where they labored has been almost entirely overlooked by novelists, filmmakers, and historians alike. The mining families of the Colorado coalfields, by contrast, could afford no such luxury.[4]

The Ludlow Massacre and the miners' rebellion of 1914 emerged from hidden histories made deep underground. Dozens or hundreds of feet below the surface of the Colorado coalfields, the interactions of living beings with earth, air, water, and fire helped create, sustain, and sometimes destroy what I call mine workscapes. In one way or another, these workscapes constituted both the source of the southern colliers' persistent discontent and a unifying

4.1. Charles Graham, *The Disaster at Crested Butte, Colorado, Harper's Weekly*, February 16, 1884. Denver Public Library, Western History Collection, Z-4004.

factor that drew coalfield migrants from remarkably diverse backgrounds to make common cause.

What is a workscape? On the most basic level, it is a place shaped by the interplay of human labor and natural processes. Whereas "landscape" refers to a particular stretch of ground, a scene that can be taken in at a glance and represented on a single canvas or within a photo frame, "workscape" implies something more complex: not just an essentially static scene or setting neatly contained within borders, but a constellation of unruly and ever-unfolding relationships—not simply land, but also air and water, bodies and organisms, as well as the language people use to understand the world, and the lens of culture through which they make sense of and act on their surroundings. Impossible to bound, own, or represent in two-dimensional space, workscapes straddle material realities, the ways in which people have tried to perceive and direct the course of shifting realities, and the identities people have created out of these material and perceptual building blocks. Going beyond the hoary dualisms that separate "man" and "nature" in much of Western thought, the workscape concept treats people as laboring beings who have changed and been changed in turn by a natural world that remains always under construction. Ultimately, exploring the mine workscape reveals much about how nature shaped the lived experience, identity, and politics of Colorado mineworkers.[5] Wherever people work, in short, the boundaries between nature and culture melt away.

Subterranean Crucibles

"Watching coal-miners at work," as George Orwell once wrote, "you realise momentarily what different universes different people inhabit." Like scuba divers or astronauts, colliers ventured into an environment fundamentally different from those in which our species evolved. Conditions underground, like those in space or beneath the sea, threaten the human organism with expiration at any moment. To make sense of the labor-management conflicts that frequently erupted at collieries like the Jokerville mine, we must take a closer look at these subterranean crucibles of industrial struggle.[6]

The Jokerville day shift had started innocuously enough. Carpenters, tracklayers, blacksmiths, and engineers reported for work at the mine offices

4.2. Entering the Mine Workscape, 1910. Denver Public Library, Western History Collection, Z-6303.

and workshops; some then headed underground to perform maintenance on the mine's transportation and ventilation systems. The drivers, mostly young or inexperienced, turned off toward the stables to feed and harness the mules responsible for carrying coal on the first leg of its journey out of the earth and on to the market. For their part, face workers, the majority of the mine work-force responsible for the actual work of mining, would have filed toward the shed covering the mine entry, past Luke Richardson, the mine's fire boss, and into the tunnels beyond. Investigators would later blame the ensuing explosion on Peterson, a Swedish miner who allegedly ignored Richardson's warning about the dangerous levels of methane that had built up in his work-room.[7]

That outcome lay in the future, though, as sixty-seven of the men walked through a portal of stout timbers and into a familiar world. Those of us unaccustomed to underground mine labor might have felt out of place. Unmoored from our everyday realities and thrust into a dark, claustrophobic, utterly alien environment, we would soon have confronted the limitations of sensory organs designed to decode radically different surroundings.

Railroad and coal company executives used information obtained through their own explorations as well as from geological consultants to determine where to invest the hundreds of thousands of dollars of capital generally required to launch an industrial coal mine. Crews of expert colliers and other skilled workers then began to build the infrastructure of the mine workscape. The techniques and tools used to extract coal were of little use for penetrating the comparatively harder rock that separated fossil fuel deposits from the surface, so development workers had to master not only the craft of coal mining, but also skills more commonly associated with hard-rock mining or railroad building. Driving their picks into the earth and blasting their way through impediments, miners drove main tunnels through dozens, even hundreds, of feet of rock. If the tunnel they excavated to reach a coal seam plunged vertically, colliers called it a shaft, if it dipped at an angle, it was a "slope," and if it was aligned horizontally, they referred to it as a drift.[8]

Having driven at least one passageway between the coal seam and the surface, development workers next proceeded to lay out the rest of the mine. Old colliery maps reveal an underground arrangement of space not altogether different from the grid commonly used for Western towns and cities. Though geological irregularities, surveying errors, and diffuse authority over these underground environments led practical miners and coal company engineers to depart freely from right angles, it is nonetheless helpful to imagine a coal mine as a gridded space or underground town. Haulageways known as entries functioned as main avenues; "side entries" worked like side streets; and "rooms" and "pillars," the former destined for removal, the latter intended to stay in place and support the roof until all the coal in that district of the mine had been removed, comprised the city blocks. The support systems threaded through this grid—car tracks, compressed-air pipes and hoses, electrical wires, air courses, pumps, fans, and so forth—facilitated the movement of energy, materials, and creatures such as mules, mice, and men between the mine workscape and the outside world.[9]

Once this infrastructure was in place, the work of extracting coal could begin. Soon colliers began to labor in dozens or even hundreds of active rooms, each bordered by an entry to the rear, the blocks of standing coal known as pillars on either side, and a working face at the front. Salaried employees known as mine bosses had the authority to assign miners to rooms, but once a miner reached his room, he entered a space where companies exerted little supervision and exercised only rudimentary authority. In the small earthen workrooms distributed around the mine grid, miners—generally working in pairs—employed techniques and tools that traced their origins to Europe and the northeastern United States. The precise methods used varied, depending on the thickness of the seam, the concentration of methane, the expertise of the colliers, the weight of the overburden, and several other factors. The basic process usually began when a miner swung his pick against the lower portion of the coal face. He next picked up an augur and drilled several holes in the shelf of coal he had just undermined. After filling some of these holes with cartridges—hand-rolled and filled with either black powder or giant powder taken from kegs placed in the crosscuts or side entries where miners from adjacent rooms congregated for meals and breaks—a collier proceeded to light the wicks or "squibs" that hung out from the cartridges, then hurried to a relatively safe spot to wait for the powder to explode (by the early twentieth century some collieries used electric shot-firing systems operated by specialists). Preindustrial rhythms and craft skills persisted in the collieries well into the twentieth century. In contrast with hard-rock miners and the many others whose crafts were destroyed or compromised by coal-burning machines, colliers owned their own tools, started and stopped work at will, toiled at their own pace, and worked not for wages but for tonnage rates.[10]

Colliers, once they could see through the smoke and dust the charge had thrown into the air, returned to the room to load the coal and rock broken off the face by the blast. If necessary, miners split large chunks into more manageable pieces, then used crowbars, shovels, and even bare hands to pack their cars tightly with several tons of coal, then pushed the cars along iron or steel tracks to the side entry. Next, the young men or recent immigrants who performed the comparatively unskilled work of driving mules or locomotives collected these cars and took them either to a shaft, where they were lifted up to the surface, or directly out the mine tunnel to a scale outside; in either case, a car's journey might cover hundreds of yards in a new or small mine, but upwards of five miles in the larger collieries. Company officials weighed the cars and recorded each collier's tonnage on a ledger. From the scale, the mine cars proceeded either to the coke plant or to a large wooden-framed structure outside the mine mouth known as the tipple, where mechanical devices dumped the coal out of the mine cars and into railroad cars. Thus did generations of Colorado coal miners earn their living—and thus did the fossil fuel unearthed by the miners' toil begin to make its way out of the ground and toward the market.

Of Mice and Mules and Men

Prodigiously lethal places, the Colorado coal seams had once ticked and hissed, hooted and howled and roared with exuberant life. In a very real way, colliers devoted themselves to opening a channel thanks to which the buried life force of the distant past could invigorate the Rocky Mountain economy. When mining began, Colorado's coal seams were almost as lifeless as the surface of the moon. Mine development work began to breathe vitality back into these long-dead places. People and animal interlopers from the surface world sojourned underground; meanwhile, rodents, microorganisms, and mules started to make a permanent home in the collieries.

Canaries and coal mines seem to go together like swallows and San Juan Capistrano. In Colorado, though, the miners' canary was usually a mouse. Quite a variety of rodents, including native pack rats and exotic house mice— all referred to simply as mice—unintentionally hitched a ride into the mines in the loads of oats and hay that would fortify the mules for their day's work. Creatures that survived the passage and found a mate began to reproduce prolifically; one female mouse could bear as many as 150 young in a single year.[11]

Apart from mule feed, the most reliable source of organic energy underground was to be found in colliers' dinner pails. Hungry or resourceful mice often begged miners for food; at least some men obliged by throwing scraps to the rodents or even feeding them by hand. As men and mice shared food, a strange symbiosis began to develop. At first, one miner recalled, rodents would "go about their business." Mice let down their guard, as Dan DeSantis told an interviewer, only when a miner "le[ft] them a piece of bread." Over time, mice grew to trust colliers. Workmen even began to anticipate the rodents' appearance at their daily meal: as one group of mineworkers ate their dinners, for instance, "four or five beady-eyed little scroungers" would venture out of their holes and commence "waiting," as another miner remembered, "for bits of food to be thrown to them."[12]

Miners learned to differentiate between their lunch companions on the basis of their markings and behavior; some even began to name mice, a practice that signaled the miners' growing sense of familiarity with the rodents that inhabited their rooms. "Oh yeah," Dan DeSantis recalled with a smile, "the little buggers they knew their name, yeah, Pete this and that, boy they come out of the crack and they get that close with you. Little by little you could just about feed them by hand." In the camps above, the act of breaking bread together often cemented communal bonds across deep cultural divides; in the mines below, sharing food across the boundary between species helped colliers turn rodent fellow travelers into friends.[13]

"We take care of them," DeSantis explained; "we like them." Such colliers as DeSantis appreciated mice for both emotional and practical reasons. Making pets of playful, friendly, harmless creatures took men's minds off work, while dispelling the boredom and tension that often developed as pairs of men labored side by side for long hours in dark, isolated, and dangerous workscapes. Moreover, most miners had migrated from agricultural or protoindustrial regions; for some of these men, befriending mice may have reminded them of rural life back home.

Making mice into pets brightened workers' days, but coal-mining folklore also taught miners to value the rodents' presence for another reason: the animals were preternaturally sensitive to danger. Mice, like canaries, would lose consciousness or die when exposed to even small concentrations of carbon monoxide; their delicate hearing and sensitivity to vibration also alerted them to a cracking roof overhead. Canny miners kept an eye on their rodent friends. If a mouse started to scurry away at top speed, if it grew lethargic, or if it simply keeled over, then miners knew to "watch it. You better be careful," as DeSantis put it, "because something's wrong, either gas or cave-in." Building bonds with mice thus helped men forestall danger, even as it alleviated the monotony and alienation they sometimes experienced in the course of a day's work.[14]

Mules, of course, were altogether different animals. Hybrids whose existence and propagation depended on human intervention, mules are among the newest of the world's mammals. The veterinary historian Juliet Clutton-

Brock explains, "Different species of Equidae will not normally interbreed in nature and it requires the guile and expertise of man to bring it about." Clutton-Brock surmises that Sumerian herders assisted the conception of the first mule by tricking a male ass into mating with a female horse. This mule, like almost all mules, was sterile. Indeed, the animals would quickly have vanished if humans had stopped finagling horses and asses into mating. The immense utility of these hybrids, though, prevented that outcome and soon made them a mainstay of labor in the Old World; possessed of "more stamina and endurance" than either the ass or the horse, "more sure-footed," and capable of hauling "heavier loads," the mule constitutes, in Clutton-Brock's words, "a perfect example of hybrid vigour."[15]

The first mules to arrive in Colorado accompanied Spanish conquistadores in the sixteenth century. Many more followed, as Hispanos, and later Anglos, dispossessed native peoples and initiated an agricultural revolution. The industrialization of the Mountain West set in motion by William Palmer's dream of coal-fired benevolence only intensified reliance on the energy and instincts of these beasts of burden. Singly, in pairs, or in teams, mules helped haul practically every ton of coal extracted in Colorado up through the 1920s. Haulage took place in two stages: first, the movement of loaded mine cars from the colliers' rooms to sidings along entryways; and second, the trip from these sidings to shaft or tipple. Machines began to displace mules from the second of these tasks in the late nineteenth century. Whether driven by steam, by compressed air, or by electricity, technologies reliant on fossil fuels required no food or veterinary care, and little rest. Properly serviced, they could "stand up to the work all day and all night" for many years, thus offering companies an estimated cost savings of 50 percent over animal power on main haulageways. Between 1902 and 1916 CF&I proceeded to retire half its mules. Even so, mules continued to work in Colorado mines well into the twentieth century because they posed less risk of igniting methane and were capable of maneuvering in tight spaces much more effectively than machines. As late as 1937 more than three thousand mules were still at work underground in Colorado, one for every two coal mine workers. Most worked only on the first stage of haulage, though some continued to work the main entries of gassy mines through the 1950s.[16]

The need to feed so large an equine workforce provided a stimulus to lo-

4.3. Mine Mules, Rouse. Copyright Colorado Historical Society, Trinidad Collection, 20004922.

cal economies and transformed local ecosystems in many parts of the coal-fields. Mine operators initially bought hay and alfalfa for their mules from ranchers along the Cuchara River and other local growers. But just as coal companies integrated backward by building railroads and starting stores, so did at least one company seek to control its own supply of animal feed. Colorado Fuel and Iron purchased the Maxwell Land Grant west of Trinidad, kicked settlers off their lands, and then started a company farm on which some of the very families they had dispossessed were hired to tend feed crops on shares or for wages.[17]

Several factors made mules the draft animals of choice in the Colorado collieries. First, the creatures varied greatly in height. Mate a burro with a pony and the progeny will be short; cross a Clydesdale with an ass and you get a much bigger beast. These variations enabled companies to fit mules to particular mines. Colorado Fuel and Iron, for example, bought short mules from Texas to ply Fremont County's thin seams, and taller mules from Missouri and Nebraska to work the thicker seams of Huerfano and Las Animas counties. Horses and donkeys varied in size, too, but hybrids possessed several advantages over their parent stock. A Welsh miner remarked of mules that it was "truly wonderful the hard work they stand," adding that "no horse can stand the same amount of work." Coal companies employed mine mules for their brains as well as their brawn. Drivers could readily train the animals to respond to four universal voice commands—"giddap" for "go," "whoa" for "stop," "gee" for "right," and "haw" for "left." "All you had to do was just tell them what you want to do," driver Dan DeSantis recalled, and "they'll do for you." In fairly short order, mules learned their "run," a relatively fixed route connecting a set of rooms and entries.[18]

It was the job of drivers to coax or compel these creatures to apply their formidable energy and intelligence to the hard work of moving coal. Colliers and rodents developed symbiotic relationships that revolved around mealtimes and moments of danger; drivers and mules, however, engaged in battles of will day after day for nine hours or more. Though drivers and mules sometimes collaborated harmoniously, mulish desires tended to diverge from driverly duties. Horses, donkeys, and people made mules, but mules made their own decisions. Stubborn and powerful, the animals offer a whinnying, kicking metaphor for the central problem mine workscapes posed for workers and managers alike: these hybrids created and maintained by a combination of human artifice and natural processes proved all too capable of eluding human control.

Partnerships between drivers and mules ranged from respectful to dysfunctional. Alex Bisulco fondly recalled a "gentle" mule named Jack. Like the mice that skittered below him, Jack became particularly friendly during lunch breaks. Approaching Bisulco and his co-workers, "He'd eat all the sandwiches . . . bananas everything we'd give him all the peelings and all that kind of stuff." Mules such as Jack "were just beautiful," Bisulco wistfully recalled. But then he qualified his praise: "There was some mean ones. Very mean ones."[19]

Mules, as Bisulco knew all too well, could be ill-tempered and extremely stubborn. The organization of production underground made mules' willfulness all the more infuriating. Under the tonnage system, colliers' earnings depended to no small extent on the efficient flow and equitable distribution of cars between their rooms and the surface above. A driver who failed to curb his mules' recalcitrance thus constituted a liability to the miners he served.[20]

Drivers sometimes enticed balky mules with food, but most masters used the stick rather than the carrot. The resulting abuse contributed further danger and violence to workscapes already beset by falling rock and exploding gas. Interviewed in the late 1970s, Bisulco reminisced while holding his old braided-wire "popper" behind his neck. This whip, he recalled, would "cut the mules every time. . . . Sometime it'd draw blood on them poor mules." The old driver quickly reined in his sympathy, though: "If the mule needed whipping," he claimed, "well, they sure got it." Poppers cut into mule flesh, but sprags—thick wooden sticks used to brake descending mine cars—could inflict blunt-force trauma. By beating mules with little restraint or regret, drivers sometimes blinded or even killed their equine assistants.[21]

Intriguingly, a few former drivers likened their animal co-workers to people. Mules, claimed retired driver Victor Bazanele, "had sense like a human." On a couple of occasions, drivers extended their anthropomorphic analogies. Bisulco, for instance, remembered a female mule named Nelly that always made him "fall behind" in his work. When Nelly "run true" to her womanly "breed" and revolted, the driver explained, "by jingle, I'd just lose my patience" and "really beat [her] up. . . . Those balky mules was awful," Bisulco concluded, "worse than any balky woman you ever saw."[22]

Drivers even likened the mules' resistance to their own struggles. Victor Bazanele joked that mules "knew when starting time was and quitting time was." When "quitting time came around," he declared, "you couldn't make those mules do nothing." Bisulco concurred; the animal workforce, he claimed, "was unionized before some of us."[23]

Even though Bisulco and Bazanele were jesting, the humor conveys a serious message about the contradictory nature of power in coalfield society. By telling stories that cast mules in the role of women and unionists, drivers hinted at the manifold connections that knit together mine workscapes, domestic spaces, and industrial struggle. Such comparisons captured the ambiguous social position that drivers occupied: just as surely as they were dominated by the companies, they in turn dominated mules and women.

Likening obstreperous animals to strikers or women marked mules as subordinates. At the same time, it portrayed the animals as actors fully capable of resisting their subjugation. With their sharp hooves and sturdy legs, strengthened by pulling many tons of coal a dozen miles or more a day, the animals sometimes maimed or even killed drivers. After a "vicious and ill-tempered" animal scraped its back against the roof of the Brookside mine, for instance, it erupted into a rage, knocked down a young Italian driver, and dragged a string of cars over both his legs. Mules, in short, were rebels with a kick; heaping abuse on them was just as likely to provoke them as it was to break their will.[24]

Mules, along with mice and other creatures, enlivened mine workscapes. The close, often violent relationships drivers forged with mules shaped the nature of labor for thousands of underground workers. Mules gave way to machines on main haulageways, yet continued to play a role in the mine work of rooms and side entries, thus demonstrating both the limitations and the surprising persistence of old-fashioned horsepower. Crossbreeds in more ways than one, these sturdy creatures embodied the close relation between labor and natural processes that made colliery workscapes so violent and contradictory.

When the Earth Grows Restless

Every mine tunnel driven into the side of a hogback opened a portal into another world, another nature. For those who labored under the earth, there was no getting away from it. Earth surrounded mineworkers: it formed the floors beneath their feet, the roof over their heads, the walls on all sides. Most other Coloradans stood on solid ground, but colliers paced the mine workscape with anxious strides. Geological irregularities threatened to block their progress and hamper their work. Worse, the unpredictable coal and unstable rock that encased them was liable to fall down at any moment. To toil in such conditions was to embark on a close, complex, and sometimes fatal relationship with a capricious environment.

Miners knew that ancient geological processes had formed the coal seams in which they labored. In the course of their daily work, colliers encountered impressions of seaweed and clam shells, not to mention recognizable remains of figs, palms, redwoods, breadfruit, and other tree species altogether different from the scrubby junipers and piñons that grew outside the mines. The miners' craft thus bound its practitioners to a past when the dark seams in which they toiled had been teeming swamplands dappled by the sun's rays.[25]

Variations in these ancient ecosystems determined the thickness of coal seams and their character. Peat accumulated faster in some places than others; conditions fostering its deposition also prevailed longer in some parts of Colorado than others. Coal deposits consequently varied in thickness from around three feet in Fremont County to between five and eight feet in the rest of the southern field to forty-five feet in a thick bed near New Castle aptly known as the Mammoth seam. The geography of prehistoric peat swamps shaped not just the thickness of deposits, but also their extent and composition. Most coal seams were shaped like an elongated lens; near their edges, where roof and floor converged, miners knew the deposit to be "pinching out." Other geological irregularities occurred less predictably. Ancient streams and rivers had sometimes carved channels through peat swamps, leaving behind troublesome features that miners called washouts or rolls. More uniform but equally problematic were layers of shale or other rock; these "bands" or "partings" of "bone" or "boney" had formed when volcanic eruptions, catastrophic floods, droughts, or other cataclysms deposited ash, silt, or sand on top of Cretaceous and Tertiary swamps. Thicker layers of valueless rock between bands of coal, so-called split seams, had resulted from more drastic and enduring shifts in depositional environments.[26]

By molding the physical environment of the mine workscape, geology structured colliery labor. The thin seams of Fremont County, for instance, made it impossible for miners to work standing up and ensured that they would remove less coal in a day's work than their counterparts in other parts of the state. Companies consequently had to pay colliers a higher tonnage rate to attract and retain miners to work these cramped mines.[27]

The character of mine earth varied not simply from field to field, but from entry to entry and room to room. Coal seams were thicker here, thinner there, split and parted from place to place, pinched out on the edges. This uneven underground topography fomented tension between mineworkers and their employers. Room assignments proved particularly contentious. Since miners were paid only for the coal they extracted, subterranean geological variations translated into large disparities in the wages colliers could potentially earn in different rooms with the same expenditure of time and effort. Mine bosses assigned miners to the various rooms of a colliery. Invariably drawn from the ranks of British American craft colliers, mine bosses parlayed their intimate knowledge of the contours of risk and reward in the mine workscape into power and sometimes even profit. Suspected union organizers, colliers of some other race or nationality, malcontents, and men who simply got on a mine boss's nerves customarily received the worst assignments; friends, relatives, countrymen, and colliers loyal to the company were given the best rooms to work. Some bosses, however, learned that a little flexibility could go a long way. A miner who wanted to keep a good place knew to treat the mine boss to drinks at the saloon; a few colliers were allegedly so desperate for good places that they pimped their wives and daughters to mine bosses—or so went one rumor that made the rounds of the strikers' camps in 1913–1914.[28]

Even more problematic than the geography of reward, however, was the workscape's cartography of risk. As men excavated tunnels and rooms far below the surface, they created perilous spaces in which the immense potential energy of the earth above their heads threatened to become kinetic energy at any moment. Miners would have faced great danger even if they had merely removed coal from the ground; but they ran a heightened risk because they also brought in air. The moment mineworkers exposed a coal face to oxygen, it began to weather rapidly, for all coal seams formed in oxygen-poor environments, then lay sealed off from the atmosphere for eons. Pyrites entrained in coal could ignite spontaneously, though this was a rare occurrence in Colorado, given the low sulfur content of Western coals. Far more troublesome was the rapidity with which microscopic fissures and cracks could widen. Wherever miners labored, they weakened the earth around them, as the flaking shale roofs and sloughing coal faces of the mine workscape attested.[29]

Such problems were nothing new in the coal industry. Colliers had long mitigated the danger of falling rock and coal by employing two types of roof support. First, miners periodically left solid coal intact, in "pillars," the generous proportions of which served to prevent overlying strata from crashing down all at once. Second, miners wedged rough-cut timbers of pine or spruce between floor and ceiling, to support the expanses of roof that spanned the space from pillar to pillar. Operators procured mine timbers in two ways: through multiyear contracts with logging companies and through short-term contracts with Hispano *properos* (prop cutters), Italian migrants, and local Anglos. The amount of lumber in the subterranean workscape increased in direct proportion to the rising demand by regional consumers for fossil fuels, stimulating companies and contractors to enlist muscle and steam power to fell and haul in an ever-growing number of trees from the forests of southern and central Colorado.[30]

The boundaries between organic and mineral-intensive economies blurred in the mines—and all too frequently collapsed altogether. Falling roof and walls struck workers down in ones and twos, inflicted head wounds, pinned men down, and even squashed colliers flat, "like a newspaper." Though such accidents attracted less notice than dramatic mine explosions such as the Jokerville blast, they nonetheless accounted for the greater part (814) of the 1,708 on-the-job deaths in the Colorado collieries between 1884 and 1912.[31]

Props, if structurally sound and properly placed, protected workers from most of the rocks and coal detached by undercutting and oxidation. There was a knack to setting props that some miners never acquired, however. Worse, dry rot, corrosion inflicted by chemicals in mine air, and inherent irregularities in the wood could all bend or break even expertly positioned timbers. Even when timbers were sound and well placed, gaps remained. Geological features known as potholes and water slips had a bad habit of loosening large chunks of rock between props. Miner Sam Goffatt received a fatal knock on the head in 1898 when a "small rock" fell through the props of his "exceptionally well timbered" place. On a few rare occasions, massive stretches of mine roof could even break free. Paul Pulto probably never knew what hit him when an "enormous" block of sandstone measuring perhaps eighty feet in length crashed onto his head.[32]

Though pillars and timbers made mining possible, they could not make it safe. Simple bad luck could fell the most careful collier. Read through enough accident reports, though, and you will quickly see that happenstance alone is not sufficient to explain most deaths caused by falling earth.

The tonnage system of payment left miners little choice but to gamble with their lives. By compensating miners solely on the basis of the amount of coal they extracted, companies rendered timbering a form of "dead work," the colliers' grim name for tasks that were necessary but uncompensated. This system forced mineworkers into constant and complex calculations. To cast these life-and-death decisions in cold economic terms, miners had simultaneously to assess their exposure to risk and to estimate the comparative costs and benefits of devoting time to setting timbers instead of extracting coal. Or to put it more unequivocally, men had to decide whether to safeguard their lives or to tempt fate. Miners who pushed their luck in hopes of earning a little more money sometimes paid with their lives; more cautious comrades sacrificed wages for safety. This devil's bargain seems more infernal still given the insecure, often seasonal nature of work in the mines, the widespread indebtedness of colliers, and the dream of economic advancement that had drawn so many migrants to the coalfields in the first place.[33]

A different but related calculus explains some of the other choices workers made in the face of underground risk. Just as the drive for extra tonnage could motivate a mineworker to court danger, so too could a man's need to demonstrate his masculinity lead him to ignore his better instincts. John Bonomo, for instance, was working with five other men to remove coal at Crested Butte in 1897. The "coal was free on one side," Bonomo later related, "and unsupported" by timbers. The six men "all knew that the coal was about ready to fall of its own accord." Bonomo "remonstrated with them that it should be taken down rather than taking any more chances." Frank Norden and John Pilone replied to Bonomo's entreaties by "ridiculing his cowardice." Stung by his comrades' derision, Bonomo shut his mouth and labored on. As he shoveled coal and kept "out of danger" as best he could, "suddenly the whole mass fell" on Norden and Pilone. "A few minutes after the coal fell the overlying slate fell," further crushing Norden and Pilone and "caus[ing] great delay in extricating their bodies." Bonomo survived, but his comrades, like many other mineworkers, suffered fatal injuries when they allowed masculine insecurity to outweigh self-preservation.[34]

Miners butted up against earth at every turn. It butted right back, with less intention but much greater might. Try as miners would to control the powerful physical and chemical forces that their work unleashed, they could not turn back the clock. The collier-bard John W. Brown cut to the heart of the matter in verse: "Pick! Pick! Pick! / In the tunnel's endless gloom / And every blow of our strong right arm / But helps to carve our tomb." Only by learning the colliers' craft and absorbing the knowledge of mine workscapes so integral to their trade could mineworkers begin to balance the need to earn wages with the will to stay alive and save face.[35]

If colliers made trouble for themselves, however, they were not the sole authors of their predicament. When the earth grew restless and miners died, the working people of the coalfields blamed their suffering on their employers—and for good reason. Dependence on fossil fuels had hidden costs, which miners and their families often paid with their lives. Instability and violence underground invariably engendered more of the same on the surface.[36]

Deadly Currents

Before examining either type of violence more closely, let us first reconsider our assumptions about terra firma. The ground beneath our feet, after all, is porous and permeable, as well as solid and seemingly dependable. As rocks go, coal is unusually riddled with cavities. Overlying strata tend to fill pores and larger fissures in coal in two ways: by pressing water into them, and by blocking the escape of volatile gases released from ancient swamp deposits. Mine workings intruding into preexisting hydrologic systems released methane into the mine workscape and introduced dangerous gases underground. Through their labor, miners helped turn mines into toxic, volatile environments incapable of sustaining human life without the aid of vulnerable technological systems.

Groundwater reflected the qualities of scarcity and abundance that had long characterized human economies on the surface. Mines in Las Animas County tended to be the driest. The lack of water at the Engle mine contributed to the failure of Colorado Coal and Iron's 1881 mechanization drive. On balance, however, underground aridity hurt miners more than it helped them. Picking and blasting in dry mines sent clouds of dust into the mine atmosphere, where they aggravated acute and chronic hazards to human health. Sprinkling, the most common dust mitigation technique, also became more difficult in the absence of a steady water supply. Companies could escape this vicious circle only by hauling water to the mines by rail, but this solution was costly. One mine inspector admitted, "There are several mines in this State situated so far away from the source of water supplies that sprinkling as profusely and thoroughly as is suggested would incur an expense so nearly equalling the margin of profit that they would be forced to cease operating." Parsimonious executives primed mine environments for disaster when they balked at the expense. Inadequate sprinkling contributed to a spate of mine disasters that claimed hundreds of lives in the early twentieth century.[37]

A little water could make labor safer, but there can always be too much of a good thing. Most collieries in Huerfano County lay just beneath sand and gravel deposits. These alluvial sediments could conduct large flows of water from streams and arroyos into the mines below. The wet conditions that resulted sometimes forced workers in the mines around Walsenburg to labor in water up to their waists, thereby causing much discomfort and disease. Southern Colorado mines suffered no tragedies such as the White Ash disaster near Golden, in which water from a neighboring mine, inundating a colliery, killed ten. Flooding posed problems nonetheless. Geologist James Gardiner had warned William Palmer that mining the Walsen tract would "always" involve the risk of large influxes of water. After the general ignored Gardiner's advice, miners and managers suffered the consequences. When in 1889 "a large water pocket was struck," the mine flooded completely; fifteen years later, storm waters, pouring through the intervening alluvium, again filled the mine.[38]

Other Huerfano County collieries flooded, too, but a more common problem throughout the coalfields resulted from less-spectacular dripping and seepage. In Colorado, as on most other terrestrial expanses, the ground holds much more water than the surface—over sixty times as much. Since time immemorial, falling rain and melting snow had percolated down into bedrock through pores and fissures. Impermeable strata eventually slowed the downward course of the water and forced it to collect in more porous strata known as aquifers. Southern Colorado's richest coal horizons occupied the Raton and Vermejo formations, two of the most important aquifers in the region. Together with their neighbors, the coal-bearing strata of these formations form a basin, a bowl-like geological structure that dips down in the middle and curves upward at its edges. The western lip of this basin outcrops in the mountains on the Upper Purgatoire, where rain and melting snow soak into the earth and charge the aquifers with water, which then creeps down the sloping contours of the basin's western rim. Though these bodies of groundwater move downward and eastward at a rate of just thirty-two feet or so a year, the high elevations at which they start their downward journey give them considerable hydraulic head—enough in some instances to push water back up the basin's eastern slope.[39]

The flow of water into mine workings accelerated as entries and rooms penetrated ever deeper into subterranean aquifers. Surprisingly enough, some operators made the most of an otherwise trying situation by piping the water pumped out of mines into coal camps, where it sustained mining families and draft animals. *Camp and Plant* described the water thus obtained as "pure and wholesome, with just enough sulfur in it to make it healthful"—a dubious description at best, considering that the water passed through a workplace where hundreds of mules and men labored for long days without privies.[40]

Wherever groundwater flowed, it seemed, easy distinctions between nature and artifice dissolved. Invariably, the flow of water into the workscape accelerated over the life cycle of a mine. In fact, rising waters and the mounting costs they imposed were an important factor in the closure of some of CF&I's most productive Huerfano County collieries. Even in the comparatively arid mines of Las Animas County, the growing influx of groundwater made mine workscapes more expensive for companies to operate, more challenging for workers to labor in, and more difficult for either to control.[41]

Problematic though the intersection of mine workings and groundwater hydrology proved, the air in mines presented still greater risks and dilemmas. The peril that mine air posed was a direct consequence of the first fact to confront almost anyone who set foot in a coal mine: darkness. Boys and men frequently suffered disorientation, even terror, the first time they ventured underground. "'Mother I don't want to go into that dark hole,'" one fifteen-year-old cried after his first day on the job. "'I'm afraid to go in there,'" the boy begged. "'I'll do anything if I didn't have to work there.'"[42]

The absence of natural light meant that humans could survive in mine workscapes only through artificial means. Mines lacked the living plants and algae whose photosynthetic capabilities had created and maintained the surface atmosphere in which human beings had evolved. Coal mines, like space-craft or submarines, intruded into alien environments incapable of supporting higher life forms. That collieries were exponentially larger than such craft and possessed neither a firm outer shell nor advanced technologies to monitor and ventilate the air within gives some notion of the immense dangers miners faced once they passed through the mine portal.

Miners obtained a measure of protection against airborne dangers by observing the fine-tuned reactions of mice, cultivating their own senses of smell and sight, and learning to identify hazardous gases by the way the flames of their lamps burned. These techniques enabled colliers to distinguish between two broad categories of mine air. The first, "good" air, resembled the surface atmosphere: relatively unpolluted, replete with oxygen, and neither too hot nor too cold. "Bad" air, by contrast, contributed to the dangers of the mine environment in several ways.

First of all, heat was a common characteristic of bad air. The oxidation of mine earth, the respiration of human and animal workers, geothermal energy, the weight of the atmosphere above, and other factors all warmed the mine atmosphere. Underground temperatures in Colorado's collieries never approached the searing heat of Nevada's Comstock Lode or Bolivia's Potosí, though the heat made workers "not as lively" and less able "to get out of the way when [danger] approache[d]."[43]

A second characteristic of bad air was its impurity. Merely by breathing, animals and colliers depleted the mine atmosphere of oxygen. As a consequence, workers sometimes became so "depressed, fatigued and indifferent" that they lacked "the desire and ambition to accomplish a good day's work, or of earning a full day's pay." Accidents also became more frequent in "a misty mine atmosphere." Colliers laboring in rooms filled with dust and smoke, a state mine inspector explained, "cannot see or hear warnings of danger as quickly"; moreover, "disintegration of the roof and sides and the decomposing of timber and ties," the same inspector argued, "are noticeably hastened in the presence of highly contaminated air. . . . The falls of roof and sides occur oftener and the decaying of timber is quicker."[44]

Bad air thus revealed the interconnectedness of mine earth, mine air, and the organisms that labored underground. Miners drew still more precise distinctions about workspace atmosphere, which offer further insights into the dynamism and danger of the Colorado collieries. Stinkdamp, blackdamp, afterdamp, firedamp, and so forth—their names all build on an old Teutonic term meaning "an exhalation, a vapour or gas, of a noxious kind." As this etymology might suggest, these appellations referred not to elements isolated in a chemist's laboratory, but rather to real-world compounds formed during the interaction of human labor and natural processes.[45]

Stinkdamp, to begin with the most innocuous of these mixtures, owed its name to the rotten-egg stench of hydrogen sulfide. A by-product of blasting, spontaneous combustion, or the decomposition of sulfates and submerged timbers due to the action of microorganisms, stinkdamp was comparatively rare in Colorado, though it did occasionally sicken miners.[46]

Slightly more dangerous was blackdamp. Formed by the combination of carbon dioxide (exhaled by mammals and given off by burning lamps, exploding powder, oxidizing coal, decaying timbers, and smoldering mine fires) and nitrogen, this heavy, potentially fatal mixture "invariably" accumulated in the "worked out and abandoned portions of mines." From there it occasionally surged into active workings. Between July and August 1891, for example, the Robinson mine suffered a spate of blackdamp incidents. The gas raised the respiration rates of seven workers until they lost consciousness; one reportedly "knew Nothing" for two days.[47]

These men eventually recovered, but miners who breathed in afterdamp were rarely so fortunate. A compound produced by the explosive combustion of gas and dust, afterdamp contained heavy concentrations of carbon monoxide. The majority of casualties in Colorado's mine explosions probably resulted not from the force of the blasts, but rather from carbon monoxide poisoning as afterdamp seeped through the workings. Perhaps the most dramatic case unfolded at Starkville in 1910. Rescuers there found a cluster of dead bodies surrounded by empty dinner pails. Since the explosion had occurred not long after dawn, investigators deduced that the group had survived the explosion, then banded together to look for an escape. Finding that they were trapped, the men sat down and waited for help. Lunchtime arrived with no sign of rescue, so the men sat down to share a meal they must have known would be their last. Carbon monoxide claimed one, then another, until all lost consciousness and died.[48]

Stinkdamp, blackdamp, and afterdamp poisoned miners who breathed these mixtures into their lungs. In a letter to the *Denver Post,* three experienced colliers described firedamp as "the monster most dreaded by the practical coal miner," and for good reason. Its main ingredient was methane; the most dangerous forms of firedamp also contained carbon monoxide. Methane, commonly called "swamp gas," was produced by the decomposition of ancient vegetal matter. Like groundwater, the gas occupied pores and fissures within coal seams. As miners excavated tunnels and rooms in these gas-filled strata, methane began to flow—silently and slowly under ordinary conditions in most noncoking mines, much more rapidly in many collieries in Las Animas County and the western fields. In "gassy" properties such as the Jokerville mine, methane hissed out of the earth and into the mine atmosphere through so-called blowers. On very rare occasions, it even burst forth from the mine face, heaping rock and coal on unlucky miners. Mineworkers always dreaded firedamp's "dangerous nature" and horrifying potential, but those in coking-coal mines had particular reason to fear, for methane concentrations in such mines were much likelier to reach 5 percent to 15 percent, the range of greatest volatility for the gas.[49]

Damps and the explosions they caused poisoned miners, and tore their bodies to pieces, but another component of mine air proved just as inimical to human life. Dust—produced by picking and blasting and often jostled back into the air by miners and mules—presented both chronic and acute risks. Colliers inhaled large quantities of airborne coal as they labored; the resulting buildup of coal dust in their lungs eventually caused a debilitating, painful, and often fatal disease. Ink-black sputum first announced its presence; over months or years, the malady developed into pulmonary fibrosis. Progressively blocking oxygen from reaching the bloodstream, the condition asphyxiated its victims with agonizing slowness. Known in the Colorado coalfields as miners' consumption, asthma of the mines, or miners' asthma, the disease is now called pneumoconiosis or black lung disease. The presence of coal particles in the mine atmosphere not only eroded the pulmonary health of Colorado's mineworkers but could also ravage their bodies with sudden, irresistible force. Suspended dust could catch fire indirectly—as it did when firedamp exploded or a miner's shot "blew out" to detonate methane and other mine gases—or directly, as it did when a spark from an electric wire ignited coal particles in the mine atmosphere. In either case, a chain reaction of devastating proportions quickly ensued.[50]

Colliers contributed in manifold ways to the airborne hazards that plagued mine workscapes; they also stood to lose the most when disaster struck. Mineworkers developed various techniques to "read" mine air, but the construction and maintenance of the increasingly elaborate technological systems required to ventilate the mines were largely entrusted to supervisors, engineers, and so-called company men. In the 1880s the ace coal company geologist R. C. Hills had observed, "The matter of ventilation will, more than anything else, determine the limit of profitable working" in the Colorado coalfields. Three types of ventilation helped extend these limits in the decades ahead.[51]

The first and simplest of the systems, "natural ventilation," employed two mine openings constructed at different elevations; pressure differentials caused air to flow into one tunnel and out the other. Unfortunately, the method proved "uncertain and unreliable," for natural ventilation stopped altogether when surface temperatures equaled those underground. A second and more complicated form of ventilation, furnaces, relied not on organic energy flows, but rather on the combustion of fossil fuel at the bottom of a shaft to draw a current of air through the mine from an intake shaft. Furnaces were more reliable and provided a stronger flow of air than natural ventilation did, but they suffered from two serious drawbacks: most Colorado mines were too shallow for the optimal operation of furnaces, and they introduced open flames into highly explosive environments. The third ventilation technology, fans, avoided both these problems. Powered by coal via steam, compressed air, or electricity, mine fans employed giant rotating blades or cylinders. Operated in one direction, they propelled spent air out of the mine atmosphere; when reversed, they sucked fresh air in underground.[52]

The superiority of fans led companies to invest large sums in them by the late nineteenth century. Nevertheless, ventilation in collieries remained poor. "The difficulty in the provision of air in many mines," as an 1893 mining guide asserted, "is not so much because sufficient air does not enter the intake, but on account of the inefficient distribution throughout the workings." Bringing good air into all the entries and rooms of sprawling mines and expelling bad air from every point on the underground grid was no simple task.

Most mineworkers not employed at the coal face spent some or all of their workdays building and maintaining trapdoors, cloth brattices, concrete stoppings, air tunnels, and other structures that collectively directed air along a zigzagging path that sometimes extended half a dozen miles. Trapper boys opened and closed haulageway doors, timbermen erected props and set timbers to keep entryway roofs and walls from collapsing, fire bosses inspected mines for gas, engineers and mechanics serviced and operated fans, and labor gangs erected diversions and removed obstacles from air courses.[53]

Together, human labor and technology helped sustain an underground atmosphere capable of supporting mammalian life. Yet mine workscapes nonetheless remained disaster-prone places; in fact, they grew deadlier as time wore on. Between 1884 and 1912, Colorado coal mines averaged 6.81 fatalities per year per thousand workers employed—more than twice the national average of 3.12 deaths during the same period. By the early 1910s, though, a rash of explosions pushed Colorado's annual average mine fatality rate above 10 deaths per thousand. Mineworkers, as they toiled away in workscapes linked only by a precarious circuit of tunnels and rooms to the surface atmosphere hundreds of feet above, must have shivered in their boots. Every breath they took, after all, depended on the competence of other workmen, the capricious forces that their work underground unleashed, and the good faith of employers who passed up few chances to exploit them. The persistent solidarity and militancy of Colorado mineworkers makes more sense when we realize their vulnerability to airborne hazards capable of inflicting incredible devastation on every boy and man underground. When the industrial struggles rooted in the pits surfaced from the mines and spread throughout the southern coalfields, it is small wonder that battalions of striking colliers exacted revenge in the wake of the Ludlow Massacre by dynamiting any mine they could.[54]

Disaster

If mineworkers breathed easier at the end of a shift, it was both a reaction to inhaling the comparatively clean air outside and an expression of relief at having eluded harm for yet another day. Danger, they knew, stalked miners in many guises. Obstinate animals could kick with deadly force, the earth was unstable, groundwater might flood mine workings at any time, and toxic substances filled the air. Yet mining companies and mineworkers feared fire more than any other danger. Falls of rock and coal actually killed and injured more men, but these accidents struck miners down one or two at a time. Fires and mine explosions, by contrast, killed mineworkers by the dozens.

Fires take place when three elements come together: oxygen, fuel, and an ignition source. Mine workscapes possessed all three in abundance. Ventilation and circulation systems brought oxygen underground. Fuel was everywhere—coal's ability to burn, after all, was what impelled men to burrow deep into those ancient deposits. Mine work, meanwhile, filled the air with dust and explosive gases, while introducing powder, timber, hay, and other flammable materials into the collieries. Only slightly less ubiquitous were ignition sources: miners' lamps, powder squibs, electric sparks, matches, pyrites capable of bursting spontaneously into flames on exposure to oxygen, and so forth. Encased by a rock that burned; filled with flammable implements and by-products of mine labor; well-supplied with oxygen; and rife with more triggers than a Wild West Show, the Colorado coal mines were better primed than most places to catch fire. When the latent possibility of disaster became a reality, mine explosions revealed both the sinews of bravery and solidarity that braced mining communities, and the grievances that fueled mineworkers' discontent.

Common fires occurred when solid substances, such as coal or hay, smoldered or flamed. In November 1910, for instance, a fire broke out in the underground stables of the Bear Gulch Mine. One man succumbed to the "dense smoke," but a heroic rescue effort spared 173 others "by the narrowest of margins." As this case shows, underground blazes posed a real danger, yet a second kind of fire could prove far deadlier.[55]

Explosions resulted when fire, oxygen, and an ignition source combined in a confined space. Contained between earthen walls, roof, and floor, explosions roared through mine workscapes much the way gunpowder blasts through the barrel of a gun. Firedamp and coal dust thrown into the mine air caught fire, then burst outward with incredible force, initiating chain reactions that released extraordinary amounts of energy into the mine. An 1888 explosion at Starkville, for example, "dislodg[ing] the massive entry timbering in both directions like saplings before a tornado," catapulted logs so large a grown man could hardly wrap his arms around them the distance of more than three football fields. Only two unfortunate men were working underground at the time. "Had there been five hundred," state mine inspector McNeil believed, "not one could have possibly lived after such a blast."[56]

Each colliery explosion was distinct; each had its own saga of death, hope, heroism, and malfeasance. Most disasters began when a miner's lamp or a misfired blast of powder (known as a blown-out shot in colliers' parlance) ignited firedamp or coal dust. The resulting explosions behaved chaotically. Some simply knocked men down; others ripped their bodies apart. Some drove particles of coal dust deep into mine timbers and human flesh; others inflicted no visible ravages on the men they killed. Some wrecked timbers and dislodged rock; others left little trace. Extending their "deathly influence," as one state mine inspector described the 1904 Tercio disaster, to "every point in the workings," explosions exhausted the available supply of oxygen and fuel within seconds.[57]

Once a blast had run its course, survivors began to struggle with its aftermath. Usually some number among the mine workforce evaded instant death, but their troubles were hardly over. As deadly afterdamp seeped through the workings, blast survivors faced wrenching decisions: Should they stay in their place to await rescuers or retreat to a safer place to erect a barricade against afterdamp? Should they abandon injured comrades and workmen who succumbed to afterdamp, or jeopardize their own safety by staying with their fellows? And which of the many routes from their room to the mine portal was the most promising way to safety?

Panic reigned outside as well as in. Explosions could often be heard for miles around. The miner Harry Bailey claimed of the booming Sunshine blast that he and his friends had "never heard anything of that kind before." Off-shift miners and colliers from neighboring properties, wives and children of the men underground, townspeople, and sometimes tourists hastened to the mine workings. The "wildest confusion" prevailed. The hopes of this anxious, wailing crowd were lifted and dashed with every piece of news, every rumor.[58]

The rescue effort began immediately, for there was no time to lose. Local colliers and mine managers arrived first, soon joined by men who had come on foot or had boarded special trains from neighboring mines. After forming

parties led by mine bosses, mine superintendents, and sometimes state officials, rescuers began to penetrate the choked depths of the mine. Fallen earth
and shattered timbers usually blocked their way. Crumbling roofs and caving
walls threatened to fall at any time, while invisible, generally odorless afterdamp crept through the tunnels and rooms. In the 1900s crews of colliers
trained in mine rescue techniques joined these parties; arriving in dedicated
mine cars owned by Colorado Fuel and Iron or, after 1910, by the U.S. Bureau of Mines, they donned special breathing apparatus that enabled them to
reach areas where unaided rescuers would have died.[59]

Rescue work was hard, heroic, and dangerous. Afterdamp posed the greatest threat, sneaking up on crews with little warning. Those who regained
their senses after succumbing to carbon monoxide almost invariably rejoined
the rescue effort. An unfortunate few never recovered, having sacrificed their
lives in trying to fulfill perhaps the most sacred obligation of their craft: to aid
a fellow miner in need. Moreover, colliers knew many stories about men surviving for a week or more after explosions. Imagining themselves in their
comrades' boots, rescuers worked around the clock. Picking their way
through smoky air, fallen rock, splintered timbers, and other debris, they
searched for their comrades, improvising air courses as they worked, while
vigilantly watching for signs of afterdamp. Crew after crew took its turn. Each
pushed forward systematically but with great urgency, relenting only when it
could do no more; then another plunged into the darkness, the mood of the
crowd outside changing with every advance and retreat.[60]

Rescue shaded into recovery. The grim work of finding and extricating
the dead—often dismembered or badly decomposed because of corrosive
mine gases and water—could continue for weeks; in at least one instance
some bodies were never recovered at all. Crews gathered up the remains of
their comrades with stoic resolve. As one old miner put it, "Well, it makes
you feel bad but what you going to do, that's one of those things that we got
to put up with it." Men who worked underground knew that death came with
the territory.[61]

Rescuers carried injured miners to the camp doctor's office or, more rarely,
to the depot for transportation to such facilities as Colorado Fuel and Iron's
state-of-the-art Minnequa Hospital in Pueblo. The dead, meanwhile, were
usually placed in improvised morgues. From there, some corpses traveled by

rail or sometimes steamship back to the places from which they had come. Family members carried most others to the front parlors of their homes, where undertakers worked their strange magic, endowing blasted, decomposed corpses with the illusive appearance of peaceful slumber. The Trinidad photographer Fred Aultman even recalled two separate occasions when women called him to take a family portrait with their dead husbands propped up and all visible signs of their expiration disguised. A few days later, survivors and the families of the victims joined with churches, fraternal lodges, mutual-benefit societies, miners' unions, and townspeople to bury the dead. Only then could the survivors begin to put their lives back together again.[62]

The reckoning, meanwhile, had begun along with the rescue. Blame flew fast and furious. Company officials pointed the finger at reckless workmen or union agitators. Mineworkers, labor unions, and muckrakers blamed the tragedy on corporate carelessness. Most newspapers and public officials pursued a more moderate course. Coroners' juries impaneled to determine the cause of death also reserved judgment on occasion, though more commonly they attributed mine disasters either to company negligence or to the actions of an individual employee.[63]

In the legal, moral, and rhetorical blame game that followed almost every blast, professional mining men, particularly the state coal mine inspector, played a prominent role. Rushing to the disaster site on the next available train, the inspector—invariably a British American craft collier of long experience—assisted in the rescue while simultaneously launching an investigation. Inspecting the underground workings in meticulous detail and taking testimony from blast survivors, supervisors, and experienced miners familiar with the stricken mine, he tried to reconstruct the cause and course of the disaster. On many occasions, these investigations conclusively identified the reason for the blast. Sometimes, though, inspectors admitted that despite their best efforts, the source of an explosion nonetheless eluded their comprehension.

After the 1896 Vulcan explosion, for instance, Inspector David Griffiths claimed that although he had carried out his duties "conscientiously," all his "endeavors were fruitless, and . . . no definite cause could be found." According to Griffiths, even "if the most competent fire boss had examined the mine a minute previous to the explosion," the official "would have proclaimed the mine to be perfectly safe," for "our present mode of detection of danger is too crude and the danger line is much too high." The mine foreman B. L. Davis sounded a similar note in testimony before a coroner's jury impaneled to investigate the Sunshine mine disaster:

> Q. You believe from your experience as a miner that there is an element causing these explosions that we know nothing about?
> A. *Yes, several of them.*
> Q. Why do you believe that?
> A. *Because when you can't discover what has caused the thing, there must be something mysterious about it.*

The 1907 Primero disaster was just as much of a mystery to State Mine Inspector Jones. "In all other explosions," he asserted, "I have been able to come to a definite conclusion as to inception and point of origin." At Primero, by contrast, Jones claimed that multiple "evidences of conflicting forces make it a most difficult task to come to any absolute conclusion as to the origin of this explosion."[64]

Mine officials and mine inspectors often asserted that the elemental force of fire defied not only human control, but human understanding. Predictably, mineworkers saw things differently. Even though they knew better than anyone else the complexity and capriciousness of underground environments, they tended to attribute mine disasters not to the mysteries of nature but to the misdeeds of corporate overlords. The companies' successful suppression of the inconvenient truth concerning coal dust suggests that workers had good reason to attribute "mysterious" explosions to employer negligence.

As far back as the late 1880s, State Coal Mine Inspector McNeil blamed coal dust for a deadly blast that sent three miners hurtling fifty feet out the New Castle mine entrance. This case and many others in collieries worldwide notwithstanding, Colorado Fuel and Iron and its competitors insisted that it was impossible for coal dust to explode without the prior ignition of methane or another accelerant. State mine inspection reports, citing ongoing debates in the international mining literature about the volatility of coal dust, lent some legitimacy to the companies' assertion. The veil of denial parted only when a series of three dust explosions killed more than two hundred men in 1910. Before a coroner's jury impaneled to investigate one of these tragedies, the CF&I attorney Fred Herrington proclaimed that the recent explosions had "'established a hitherto unrecorded fact in mining science, that under certain conditions dust may explode without the contributing agencies of gas or fire.'"[65]

The volatility of coal dust was, however, not an "unrecorded fact"—John McNeil had noted it more than a quarter century before—but an officially suppressed fact. The consequences of denial became all too clear when coal companies, having skimped on sprinkling and other dust abatement methods, set the stage for disaster in the volatile atmosphere of the coking collieries in Las Animas County. Though mineworkers recognized the mysteries of mine workscapes, they had ample reason to attribute mine explosions to employers' perfidy.

Mollyfication

Mine disasters such as the Jokerville blast were significant events in their own right. Yet they also hinted at the abiding connections linking the violence of the Colorado mine workscape to the struggles mineworkers waged on the surface above. Colliery development in southern and western Colorado fostered the florescence of a regional economy based on fossil fuel and drew wage-seeking migrants from adjacent valleys, neighboring states, and nearly every corner of the globe. Following these men and boys underground to the workscapes formed by their toil teaches us much about how elemental dynamics shaped life, labor, and death in the coalfields. It also demonstrates why contemporaries associated explosions in the mines with eruptions of labor violence.

Not long after the Jokerville mine blew up, stories began to circulate. "The air," a *Denver Tribune* correspondent reported from Crested Butte, "is full of rumors," and "the wildest excitement prevailed." Another journalist noted that "grave fears were entertained that at any moment an outbreak of some nature would take place." Colorado colliers, many people worried, were bent on avenging their dead.[66]

Anxieties about an imminent "outbreak" fastened on two particular groups. Suspicion fell first on the colliers of Baldwin, a Union Pacific mine tucked below Ohio Pass, about a dozen miles southwest of Crested Butte. One day after the explosion, sixty of the sixty-five men on the Baldwin day shift joined the foreman, Joe Cumiskey, at the railroad tracks just beyond the tipple to catch the next train to Gunnison. From there they planned to transfer to a Crested Butte–bound Denver & Rio Grande train. Many Baldwin miners "had friends working" at Jokerville, so Colorado Coal and Iron officials assumed, as one reporter phrased it, "that the miners did not wish to go to Crested Butte for the purpose of aiding in the recovery of the bodies, but to create a disturbance and perhaps resort to bloodshed." The D&RG, still conjoined with the CC&I under William Palmer's control, therefore ordered its crew to steam out of Gunnison "as the train from Baldwin approached," that is to say, just "in time to avoid them."[67]

If the railroads controlled steam transportation in the Rockies, however, they had yet to monopolize workers' ability to move across the land. After the D&RG refused to take them to Crested Butte, about thirty colliers returned to Baldwin, lashed snowshoes to their boots, and trekked to Crested Butte through avalanche country. "Straggling parties" began to arrive in Crested Butte on the afternoon of the twenty-fifth, some aboard a horse-drawn sleigh, but "most of them coming on snow-shoes across the mountains." Trailing down the valley, they marched straight to the Jokerville mine. Without stopping to rest, they made sally after sally—not against coal company officials, but rather against the mine workscape. Several succumbed to afterdamp, but their fellows dragged them out before it was too late. Not until the final pair of badly decomposed bodies had been recovered, six days after their daring mountain crossing, would the Baldwin miners return home.[68]

The second focus of suspicion proved equally misguided but far more surprising. "A new danger was discovered last night," alleged a widely circulated report published two days after the disaster. "It seems that there is here an organization of Mollie Maguires." The Mollies, a secret society formed by Irish mineworkers in Pennsylvania's anthracite region, had supposedly been crushed by the combined force of the mineowners' association, Pinkerton detectives, and the state. Two days after Jokerville exploded, however, a mine boss named Gibson was underground aiding in the rescue when "a miner rushed into the tunnel, handed [him] a gun and told him to protect himself as a gang of Molly Maguires were coming to lynch him." Five years after the last Mollies convicted of capital crimes swung on a Pennsylvania gallows, the organization had supposedly resurfaced half a continent away.[69]

As it turned out, the working people of Crested Butte seem to have agreed with the *Denver Tribune*'s editor that "there [were] enough dead people around . . . now to meet all immediate necessities." One outpouring of violence did not merit another—at least not yet. The rumored revival of terrorism among Colorado mineworkers failed to materialize—perhaps it was the specter of the Mollies and not the organization itself, after all, that had journeyed westward. Whatever the case, guards protected Gibson the mine boss, while "the streets [were] patrolled by men on the watch for any appearance of an outbreak from the Mollies." Meanwhile, the weight of testimony given before a hastily assembled coroner's jury fixed blame for the disaster not on Colorado Coal and Iron, but on Peterson, the "green" or inexperienced Swedish miner who had ignored the "positive orders" the fire boss Richardson had given him at the mine mouth, by entering his own underground work room with an open flame. In this case as in so many others, death underground set off not an immediate eruption of violence, but instead a simmering discontent.[70]

Five days after the fateful morning on which the Jokerville day shift had proceeded to its doom through the icy dawn, around two thousand men, women, and children assembled in a "large frame building" thrown up by the coal company as a temporary morgue. Before forty-six coffins, a Protestant minister recited a "prayer and a short selection from the scriptures"; then the congregants sang a few hymns. After a "very touching and beautiful sermon," twenty-eight of the coffins were loaded onto sleighs. A long cortege of miners—led, oddly enough, by Gibson the mine boss, the Mollies' purported enemy, and followed by sheriff's officers, the priest and altar boys, and "friends and citizens"—strode silently through "streets draped in mourning and flags at half-mast." A raging storm had turned the perfect little valley in which Crested Butte sits into a "wilderness of snow," forcing the procession to struggle for perhaps a mile through snow "three feet deep on the level." Despite the "great difficulties" that these conditions presented for the grave diggers, the bodies of twenty-eight Jokerville colliers were nonetheless lowered slowly back into the ground on a little rise above the Slate River, not far from the bodies of their comrades buried by fraternal orders in separate ceremonies, and almost within sight of the Jokerville mine in which they had perished. The earthly remains of at least sixteen others had already been taken to the little frame depot on Elk Avenue. From there, they retraced the star-crossed paths that had brought the miners to Crested Butte from other parts of Colorado, as well as Illinois, Ohio, and Pennsylvania.[71]

5

Out of the Depths and on to the March

Even in an era marked by populist insurgency, convulsed by economic crisis, racked by strikes, and patrolled by so-called industrial armies led by Jacob Coxey and other self-styled generals of the unemployed, the march was an unexpected sight. In late May 1894 some two thousand striking colliers and a few dozen coal camp women descended on Rouse, a mining town tucked into the Rocky Mountain foothills south of Walsenburg. "The north and the south have met," one witness declared, "and their meeting was like the convergence of two murmuring streams." One stream of marching strikers had set out on foot from Fremont County, more than eighty miles away; the other had trekked from the coal camps of Las Animas County, thirty-five to fifty miles distant. As for Rouse, the miners had chosen it as their rendezvous because they had come to believe that their collective fate hinged on this particular piece of ground. The strikers' aim was first to advance into the streets of the town, then to persuade the men still working there to come out of the mine and join the march.[1]

Knowledgeable observers expected that the remarkable marching strike of 1894 was nearing a decisive moment. Much more hinged on Rouse, however, than the fate of the largest miners' strike yet organized in southern Colorado. The shift from migration to mass mobilization as a strategy for betterment, the translation of underground tensions into surface conflicts, the coalescence of local disputes into regional and national strikes, the union of fragmented identities and narrowly defined interests in collective movements championing the rights of coalfield migrants as workers, citizens, and human beings—these and other trends seemed at the tipping point.

This was, of course, neither the first nor the last time southern Colorado mineworkers would strike. The southern coalfields' catalogue of labor woes stretched back to 1873, when colliers at Coal Creek had walked out of the mines in an unsuccessful bid to reverse William Palmer's effort to cut their wages from $1.50 to $1.25 per ton. Organized miners had scored their inaugural victory in December 1879. Amid a "general advance in wages, and in cost of supplies," Colorado Coal and Iron miners in Fremont County and Walsenburg had secured wage increases, though at Engleville "the strike was successfully resisted by the prompt employment of Mexican labor." Two years later, as we have seen, Engleville's *nuevomexicanos* had silenced company machines by refusing to work during Holy Week, and in June 1882 miners struck again at the mine in a fruitless effort to resist the imposition of new work rules at the property.[2]

These early disputes tended to be highly localized affairs, sometimes spontaneous, sometimes initiated by committees drawn from the miners' ranks or from the camp lodges of a national union called the Miners' National Association. The strike of 1884–1885, which affected Colorado's southern and northern coalfields, as well as the Wyoming collieries, set a much clearer precedent for the marching strikes and coalfield wars to follow. The strike was organized by the Knights of Labor, the first national labor organization to recruit workers without regard to craft or ethnic group. When Colorado Coal and Iron followed a Santa Fe Railway subsidiary in slashing wages and rates in the Fremont County mines, "an immediate strike" erupted. Though colliers managed to cripple production of domestic fuel during the winter heating season, the companies nonetheless derived a "great benefit" from the strike, for it enabled them "to introduce in[to] the various channels of consumption, where Canon coal only was known," fuel from Huerfano County. This "benefit" evaporated in October, however, as miners from Huerfano and Las Animas counties joined the dispute and demanded "that the miners at Canon be reinstated at old prices." When the companies sought to arbitrate with their workmen, Colorado Coal and Iron explained in its annual report to shareholders, they discovered the miners to be "controlled by an association called the 'Knights of Labor,' who demanded that before work be resumed the Company should recognize their body." Believing that the Knights were "assuming unwarranted power" and preventing the company "from enjoying its natural advantages," CC&I allied with its competitors to crush the strike. The company imported strikebreakers (mostly Italians and African Americans), discharged alleged troublemakers, and imposed wage cuts on workmen, who found themselves pushed to "'the eve of starvation.'" With the Knights of Labor forced to retrench and the region entering a boom cycle, seven relatively quiet years ensued; labor-management relations in Colorado were aptly described in the *United Mine Workers' Journal* as "'not friendly, but peaceable.'" Beneath the surface, though, trouble was brewing— trouble that would lead hundreds and eventually thousands of men to walk off the job, join together, and embark with a few dozen women on one of the most remarkable mass mobilizations in the history of the American West. In ways these miners could not have predicted, what Jacob Coxey called "a petition in boots" would lead the southern coalfields away from the harmonious relations that both operators and miners desired, and toward the all-out labor wars of the twentieth century.[3]

The Madness of Markets

Markets and workscapes lay behind this long history of labor-management conflict in the southern coalfields. Mineral-intensive industrialization transformed the Western economy in ways that made it virtually impossible for colliers and coal companies to find common ground. Annihilating Western isolation, coal and railroads made it cheaper and easier for work-seeking migrants to reach Colorado. Labor, scarce and thus richly remunerated on the Rocky Mountain frontier, became plentiful by the 1880s. Prevailing wages throughout the region plunged accordingly.[4]

Railroads imported coal as well as people. Shipments of fuel into Colorado from Wyoming, Utah, and other states exacerbated the often cutthroat competition that pertained in Denver and other markets served by multiple rail lines. Imports also jeopardized the ability of Colorado coal miners to force concessions from operators through strikes, since the worst effects of even an all-out work stoppage could now be averted by supplies of fuel hauled in by railcar from coalfields beyond the state borders.[5]

The fossil-fuel-driven regional economy, like the organically fueled economy that had preceded and still sustained it, also ebbed and flowed from season to season and year to year. Complicated interactions of coalfield geology, Western ecology, and the international economy subjected industrializing Colorado to both regular rhythms and unpredictable crises; together, the variations had troubling consequences for mineworkers. The home heating market, for instance, picked up by late summer, as dealers stocked up on domestic coal, and then collapsed between January and April, depending on the severity of the winter. So even as men who worked the coking- and steam coal seams of Huerfano and Las Animas counties were enjoying regular employment, their comrades in the domestic coal mines of Fremont County were enduring months of slack work or layoffs. The high plains droughts of the early 1890s also caused a downturn in coal consumption in eastern Colorado, Nebraska, Kansas, and adjacent areas, as farmers undertook "forced economies" that "greatly curtailed their winter consumption of coal."[6]

Business cycles wrought still greater havoc than climatic cycles. Demand for coal increased exponentially between the 1870s and the 1910s, yet industry fortunes nonetheless declined whenever hard-rock mining, railroad construction, and urban expansion veered from boom to bust. Coal companies reduced output and cut prices during economic downturns such as the panic of 1883–1884. Strikes ensued as operators, pressed by financial challenges of their own and emboldened by the ready availability of workers discharged from other industries, tried to cut labor costs.[7]

The companies' efforts to reduce tonnage rates (for miners at the face) and wages (for the other underground and surface workers, collectively known as company men) owed as much to the structure of the coal industry as to the vicissitudes of the Western economy. William Jackson Palmer had assailed the "hot competition of American business life" for preventing employers from treating their workers properly; however valid this notion, the general's failure to secure a coal monopoly boded ill for Colorado colliers. Competition and increased production together pushed retail energy prices steadily downward from the 1870s on. Profit margins in the industry declined apace, from nearly three dollars per ton of coal in 1880 to perhaps ten to forty cents in the 1900s. Already in 1890 one large firm, the Colorado Fuel Company (which merged with CC&I two years later to form CF&I), was warning its stockholders: "Competition has reduced the profit on a ton of coal or coke to so low a figure that no considerable reduction [in prices] can be made in the future." Since rates and wages accounted for perhaps 60 to 80 percent of the cost of producing each ton of coal, and since mechanization and other strategies for rendering extraction more efficient made only halting headway, operators chose to accommodate consumers' cries for cheaper coal—not to mention their own desire for profit—by cutting mineworkers' pay. Strikes, though troublesome, provided operators with a golden opportunity to slash labor costs by replacing militant craft miners with inexperienced newcomers, as well as a fighting chance to impose a victor's peace on miners reduced to hunger and despair by weeks or months without pay.[8]

No wonder southern Colorado's coal companies earned a reputation as inveterate foes of the unions. And though executives often resorted to ideologies of free labor or social Darwinism to justify their opposition to labor organization, their intransigence remained at heart a practical strategy for controlling mining costs. Elevating collective interest above selfish individualism, mineowners in the southern coalfields cooperated during strikes with even more gusto than they competed during peacetime. Unionization in the collieries also presaged higher fuel costs for other industries, while offering a precedent that might inspire other workers to organize. And so during colliers' strikes the small clique of men who controlled the railroads, streetcars, smelters, hard-rock mines, factories, and banks of the Rocky Mountain West hastened to lend moral, financial, and strategic support to the coal barons. Supremely conscious of the stake their own class had in the outcome of the coalfield struggles, the overlords of the fossil-fuel-driven economy closed ranks to present a united and formidable front.[9]

William Palmer's vision of Colorado as a "newer and grander and happier Columbia," a utopia of labor harmony and natural balance, vanished well before the marching strike of 1894 erupted. In place of his dream of coal-fired benevolence, the harsh reality confronting miners was one of a regional economy that was at once wildly erratic, brutally competitive, and closely controlled by the few dozen industrial oligarchs on whose actions the livelihoods of hundreds of thousands of women, men, and children turned.

From the Welshmen who represented the driving force behind the strike of 1884 to the Italians and Austrians who were so eager to march a decade later, mineworkers of every nationality, race, and ethnicity suffered from irregular employment, wage cutting, and union busting. But just as mine air exploded only when fuel, oxygen, and an ignition source combined within a confined space, so too did colliers' strikes erupt only when miners could come together in spite of the social divisions that tended to pit various migrants against one another.

Colliery work cultures characterized by craft pride, inclusiveness, autonomy, and solidarity exacerbated the madness of markets. Interactions between miners and mine workscapes—the uneven topographies of risk and reward underground, the devil's bargains posed by tonnage rates and dead work, the potential of mine disasters to kindle unrest in the camps above, and so forth—did much to generate and sustain militancy in the southern fields. Still, it would be foolish to explain industrial struggle in Colorado as a simple or direct consequence of shifting earth and explosive air. Nor should we underestimate the depth or force of the factors setting mineworkers against each other. Though some British commentators likened colliers to "Nature's noblemen," a diverse, far from angelic assortment of boys and men labored within the buried swamplands of the Mountain West. Distrust and dissension, fomented on many occasions by the companies, pervaded the mines. Discrimination and interethnic violence were rampant in the camps above. In the context of the economic segmentation, legal and extralegal discrimination, and racial violence that characterized the North American West during this era, however, the more interesting phenomenon is not that miners often had trouble banding together, but that they periodically managed to overcome their differences and to carry out mass mobilizations, such as the marching strike of 1894.[10]

Pride and Practice

Despite the widespread perception of coal mining as menial labor, most men who toiled underground took immense pride in their work. They knew what we tend to forget: that mine labor imparted a deep knowledge of underground nature. Since very few sources exist to document the contours of this knowledge in the years leading up to the marching strike of 1894, we have little choice but to extrapolate from later sources. Oral histories gathered in the 1970s offer particularly rich insights into how aging mineworkers remembered their careers during the 1900s to the 1930s. Since basic mining methods remained relatively unchanged through the late 1920s, the interviews offer evidence about the connections between underground work cultures and mineworker militancy in the late nineteenth century, while illuminating the deep roots of coalfield violence in the early twentieth century.[11]

It is useful to recall that even as coal liberated city and country from the Malthusian constraints of organic energy regimes, the extraction of fossil fuel continued to depend on the embodied knowledge of mineworkers and mules. The colliers' craft endured, even as most coal-powered industries replaced animals and skilled workers with machines and unskilled machine tenders. Miners honed, then passed on, their craft as they ascended an informal occupational ladder.

Though at least a few craft colliers first entered the mines as young boys or even as toddlers, most began to learn their trade well before puberty as "trappers." Former Colorado miner Bill Lloyd described trapping as "a job that kids always done. That was where they started in the mines, when their dinner bucket drug the ground." British American miners often started working underground at eight or ten; the deaths of two twelve-year-olds in the Jokerville explosion suggest that in this as in so many other respects, the Colorado mining industry replicated old-country practice. As they opened and closed underground doors so that mule trips could pass, trappers faced a lonely initiation into the hazardous and alien environment of the mines. In the process, boys learned from older males how to act like men. A miner related his father's experience as a boy of thirteen entering the mines; he was young enough that "if a piece of coal fell on his toe or he suffered some other minor injury . . . he would cry and my grandfather would tell him to pick up his bucket and go home and send one of his sisters in to help my grandfather work." Trappers' work, though mundane and poorly paid, brought grave responsibilities. In places where leaving a single door ajar for just a few minutes could short-circuit the flow of good air and enable firedamp to reach dangerous concentrations, one boy's negligence could cost dozens of lives.[12]

Boys who survived this introduction to mine workscapes were usually promoted to driving, the next rung on the ladder, by the time they reached their late teens. As they distributed empty mine cars and collected full ones, drivers embarked on fraught relationships with their animal co-workers. As they grappled with their mulish charges, the colliers whose rooms drivers served educated them in the culture of manly labor that prevailed underground. Miners depended on drivers to maintain the "turn," a custom through which colliers sought to control output and equalize earning opportunities by ensuring that each miner would receive the same number of cars during a workday. As drivers conversed with more experienced men and learned to read signs of danger underground, their knowledge of colliery workscapes and work cultures expanded.[13]

Although some men continued to drive for the rest of their lives, most eventually exchanged their reins for picks, augurs, shovels, and powder. The room-and-pillar system of mining was well suited to educating newcomers in the ways of the collieries. Pairs of miners generally worked together in each of the work rooms that made up the city blocks of the mine grid; often, one man (known variously as a helper, buddy, or partner) was serving an informal apprenticeship beneath a more experienced relative, countryman, or stranger. Helpers were primarily responsible for loading coal that the master collier loosed from the face. Loading was physically challenging, but men soon developed the calluses, muscles, and discernment needed to shovel many tons of coal a day. As they sweated through this grunt work, they were also learning the miners' trade through observation. "I see them working," Pete Aiello explained, "and I done the same." Craft miners taught "green" men how to "read" important workscape signs such as the visible pattern of cleavage on the mine face, which suggested where to place powder charges; the various sounds rock made when tapped with a pick, which provided clues about the soundness of the roof overhead; and the distinctive effects produced on the flames of a miner's lamp by various mine gases, which warned of the presence of poisonous or explosive "damps."[14]

The knowledge that craft colliers imparted to their apprentices was at once physical, mental, and cultural. During lunch breaks and other slow points in the day, "there was a good deal of visiting back and forth," the union leader John Brophy later recalled. Master miners sometimes took advantage of the opportunity to instruct less experienced men in the lore and customs of the pits. Mineworkers, like other people surrounded by capricious forces of tremendous power and mystery, had a healthy appetite for stories that seemed to explain the inexplicable. Collieries, saloons, and boardinghouses

5.1. Partners at the Face, Western Colorado, 1915. Photograph by L. C. McClure. Denver Public Library, Western History Collection, MCC-2228.

echoed with cautionary tales about how to avoid death underground. Interwoven with the humorous stories and fanciful lore—Don't set foot in any mine visited by women or white rabbits; lay off work for at least a day when a dream of muddy water wakes you—were deep and bitter memories of past injustices. "From earliest childhood," Utah collier Walter Morgan Donaldson recalled, "we were steeped in the lore" of the mines. "We learned at an early age," Donaldson recalled, about the "tragedy of the mine disasters" and "what the word scab meant."[15]

In the classic British American scenario, mineworkers had generally trapped, driven, and "helped" by their late teens or early twenties. Such men were said to have "grown up" in the collieries, a phrase that reflected how men and mine workscapes shaped each other's development. Bodies and minds, personalities and identities—all matured through a peculiar education carried out in constant contact with the underground environment.[16]

Miners schooled not only sons and younger relatives in the craft and customs of mining, but also older countrymen and complete strangers. "You took your son in," recalled Henry "Welchie" Mathias, "or you took your neighbor, or whatever, and they didn't work in the mine before, they'd put in with an experienced miner. I'd been in the mine 30, 40 years, well you'd get this new guy to come with you, see, to work. Show him many things—you got to detect gas, know the working conditions about the roof and that kind of stuff, you know, and a man wouldn't know it till he's worked." Adults who arrived in the coalfields lacking underground experience sometimes started as trappers. Victor Bazanele, born in Italy but raised in Germany, recalled the scorn that miners heaped on the immigrant men who performed this boys' job; the treatment was "terrible. We were called dago, mackerel snapper, all kinds of words." Many newcomers began with driving to avoid such epithets and insults, others jumped straight into helping, but in either case such "green men" eventually served apprenticeships that lasted for months or even years. Working day after day with the same master collier, they learned the skills, traditions, and even the politics first carried to the southern fields by British American miners. A single workman's inexperience could kill off an entire shift, but self-interest alone could not fully account for the unusually inclusive attitudes skilled miners expressed. "I had to work a lot of overtime, you know," Laurence Amicarella recalled. "Green men, huh. I stayed with them, worked with them. I didn't want to. I stayed with them to show them how to, you know, not to get hurt. Cause at the Columbine, I'd seen 17 or 18 of them get killed while I was in the mine." At least some colliers, Amicarella's comments suggest, felt a moral duty to instruct incoming migrants about the perils of the mine workscape.[17]

In time, both green men and migrants who had grown up in the pits became "full miners," men competent to work alone. Most had to hone their skills for at least another decade or two before earning the esteem of their fellow workmen as "practical miners," an honorific reserved for expert colliers of broad experience who often played an important role in developing new collieries and spearheading mine rescue work. Oral histories and accident reports filed by the state mine inspector—an office invariably filled by a British American practical miner—offer ample evidence that some Hispanos, Austrians, African Americans, Japanese, Italians such as Amicarella, and other migrant newcomers eventually won the regard of their fellows as "practical" or "experienced" miners.[18]

Local supervisory positions, by contrast, remained the preserve of British American men well into the 1920s. Several factors combined to bar other migrants from the positions of fire boss, mine boss, and superintendent: simple discrimination, the superior craft knowledge of men raised in the mines, and the English-language and arithmetical skills needed to pass the required correspondence school courses and state certifying exams. Decades after college-educated engineers and managers had taken the helm of most gold and silver mines in Colorado, coal companies continued to draw virtually every local mine official in the southern fields from the ranks of practical miners. At a 1916 convention, former state mine inspector John McNeil—lauded by the *Denver Times* as "perhaps the best posted man in the West on coal"— explained the advantages men such as himself enjoyed over parvenus. Let those "who entered the mines in their early boyhood days remember," McNeil declared, "that they have already graduated in an important branch of coal mining that cannot be acquired in colleges, and in this you excel over college-bred engineers who enter the coal mines later in life. It is difficult for me to define what this is; that something which enters in by the tips of the fingers, as it were; something that is mirrored on the retina of the eye; an innate consciousness to feel the throbbing, practical pulsations of a coal mine."[19]

Such embodied knowledge—a "consciousness" that seemed innate but was actually acquired through years of on-the-job education—could not be learned from books or theoreticians. "Lots of people tell you that you never get warned in these accidents," former collier Tony Hungaro explained, "but you always get warned, but the only thing is you got to be awake and listening." The practical experience that trained "the tips of the fingers" and "the retina of the eye" vastly improved an expert miner's chances of being "awake and listening" when danger threatened.[20]

Colliery work cultures resided more in the body than in the mind, more in practice than in symbolic systems of language. Those who have earned their bread in other ways have consequently tended to look down on mineworkers in Colorado and elsewhere with what E. P. Thompson once denounced as "the enormous condescension of posterity." Colliers, however, saw their work as a "challenging and . . . an honorable occupation." The collier Joe Crump declared, "Once anybody start working at the mine, they won't do anything else. They just fall in love with it somehow, they just like to work there." Welchie Mathias phrased the same sentiment somewhat differently. "Boy, I'm telling ya, that goddam mine, it put something in you, see, that's what it does." Other colliers joined Mathias in characterizing their craft as the outcome of a process that seemed almost biological. "I don't know how to put it," said Amicarella, "just that it grows on you, just grows on you, being a coal miner."[21]

Miners' Freedoms

Together, craft pride and the inclusive occupational ladder through which it was transmitted inspired a third core characteristic of colliery work cultures: a fierce sense of independence that stimulated and sustained decades of conflict in the southern fields. What Carter Goodrich called the miners' freedom, in his 1925 study by that name of the American coal industry, took root in Western soil because coal companies and British American colliers largely re-created the physical, economic, and moral structures that had long underlain craft miners' independence. Other migrants to the coalfields subsequently joined their own traditions of autonomy to the independent traditions imparted by master colliers. Laurence Amicarella bluntly expressed the close connections between experience, craft knowledge, and industrial struggle. "I worked the mine 50 years," he told an interviewer. "Each day I worked I learned something. I learned to tell the boss to kiss it." For Amicarella and many other miners in the southern fields, occupational cultures easily metamorphosed into oppositional cultures.[22]

A collier's time, to begin with, was his and his alone. Operators tried to establish shifts of nine hours or longer. Yet although drivers, tracklayers, and other company men had to abide by company time, colliers usually set their own hours. "Everybody," Victor Bazanele recalled, "could go in every time he wanted to in the mine." Some arrived early, to get a jump on their work; others straggled in later. But most arrived more or less in around the same time, as the victims of the Jokerville explosion had on that fateful January morning in 1884. Colliers also decided for themselves when to knock off, take a break, or skip work altogether. Funerals, fishing trips, sickness, religious and national holidays, ill portents and rumors of portents, elevated workscape hazards, especially fierce hangovers—each offered the occasion to lay off work for a day or more.[23]

Operators, though they surely bristled at the control miners had over their own hours, possessed neither the will nor the means to reform such customs. The tonnage system placed the opportunity cost for slacking or skipping work squarely on colliers' shoulders, thus removing employers' main financial incentive for mandating rigid schedules. Moreover, since the vast majority of Colorado mineworkers used their own tools, not their employers', coal executives could not enlist machines in their attempt to control workers or the labor process.[24]

The freedom of the miner resided not simply in his command over time and tools, but also in the power he exerted over the room or "place" in which he worked. His place constituted both the object of his labor and the focus of his most thorough workscape knowledge. A collier generally labored in a single room until he and his partner had removed all the coal it contained. Miners asserted quasi-proprietary claims over the places they had hewn from the earth. Such claims lacked legal standing, but mine officials often honored them nonetheless. Ill and injured miners, as well as colliers who decided to lay off work, expected to return to the same room and to find it unmolested, no matter how long they had been absent. Strikes were even known to end with miners' resuming work in their old places.[25]

It is little wonder that workmen who labored according to their own schedule and with their own tools, in places they considered their own, bristled at authority. As the Jokerville disaster demonstrated, mineworkers sometimes defied fire bosses such as Luke Richardson, who warned Peterson the Swede not to start working in his room before clearing out the firedamp that had accumulated inside. Mine bosses and superintendents rarely visited a collier's place more than once a week. Even these occasional visits, though, were greeted with indifference or hostility; some colliers even laid down their tools and refused to work in the presence of their ostensible superiors. Mineworkers who flouted their bosses' orders probably had a greater chance of being crushed to death or blasted to bits than they did of being dismissed for insubordination.[26]

Two brief comparisons with other mining cultures of the American West illustrate the unexpected degree of independence colliers enjoyed. Gold and silver miners started and ended their workdays on fixed schedules determined by their employers and announced by steam whistle; worked for a daily wage unrelated to their output; performed most of their work using machines that ran on fossil fuel and constituted not their own property, but the owners'; and frequently toiled under direct supervision by engineers and managers. The hard-rock miners' craft, once the warp and woof of labor in the gold and silver districts, had unraveled. Only through drilling competitions and other nostalgic, largely symbolic demonstrations of obsolescent skills could gold and silver miners fleetingly reclaim their old manly independence.[27]

The longwall system of coal mining offered an even more direct contrast with the room-and-pillar system used in all but a few Colorado collieries. Although the basic tasks of picking, blasting, and loading remained identical in the two systems, longwall miners worked in groups of a dozen or more to advance in unison along the single face or "longwall" of a very large room. The aptly named mining expert Thomas Collier explained the interdependence that resulted: "A good Longwall miner," Collier claimed, "realizes more than any one else the importance of being regularly at his place every working day." For even a single "day lost causes his place to fall behind the others which makes his work harder and his daily output is further reduced by the amount of small [and hence unmarketable] coal that is liable to result from the excessive pressure where the face falls behind"; worse still, "the bad results are also felt by" his neighbors, who had to work harder in his absence because "the coal does not break as well as when the face is kept in a uniform line." So different were the demands of the two systems that Collier claimed that "a good room and pillar man may not be successful in Longwall work."[28]

Hard-rock mining transplanted many of the fundamental characteristics of industrial production to mineral extraction. Longwall mining depended on coordinated group effort, time discipline, and direct supervision. Room-and-pillar mining, by contrast, was a throwback to an earlier age. Coal mine workscapes remained a refuge of muscle power and craft autonomy, at the same time as they propelled a regional economy characterized by the dilution of skill, the triumph of machines, and the domination of production by capitalists instead of workers.

Mining and Militancy

Much as mineworkers prized their independence, colliery work cultures were hardly anarchical. Colliers acknowledged extensive obligations toward their fellows. The mutualism and solidarity that prevailed in mine work-scapes drew men together underground, even as the culture of camp life on the surface above pushed them apart.[29]

Consider the capacity of colliery labor to turn "white" skins black, and thus to undermine the distinctions of color on which American notions of race depended. "When you see me come out of the mine," Italian-born collier Dan DeSantis joked, "you see the nigger come out." An African American collier, Alfred Owens, made a similar point more delicately when he asserted, "Practically everybody's the same in the mines." Owens recalled how he and his white partner would josh each other at day's end. "When we'd come out I'd look at him and his face would be all dirty, we didn't see nothing but white, with his teeth, and I'd laugh at him. . . . He'd say, what are [you] laughing at? I'd say, you're so black. He'd say, well, what do you think about yourself?" In the collieries, Owens recalled, "We didn't have no Jim Crow stuff like that. Everybody was just what you are, that's what you was."[30]

The sense of common identity and of common cause that Owens expressed resulted from the conjunction of migrant traditions, subterranean conditions, and coalfield realities. British American colliers arrived in Colorado bearing strong traditions of mutualism. We have already encountered three key strands of this heritage: the duty to throw oneself into rescuing fellow mineworkers when disaster struck, the obligation to "educate" unskilled boys and inexperienced migrants, and "the turn" by which drivers equitably distributed mine cars to enforce a moral economy in which each collier "got to . . . make a living like the other guy."[31]

Other distributive practices shored up the underground commonwealth. When work became scarce because of warm weather or economic depression, colliers allocated shifts among themselves. And when a man missed work because of sickness or injury, his comrades helped him out. Tony Hungaro recalled that even during the machine-mining era, "Guys [would] donate their time and donate their money" when their buddies were injured, to "get the guys through. . . . If one guy don[']t feel too good everybody else picks up the slack. . . . You get him through so he could have some groceries for his family." Pete Gerglich recalled, "I see guys go down in the mine, he can't carry a pick. We had to help him. The guys help him take his tools down to the mine. . . . He had to go, he had to work if he want to eat."[32]

Such practices fostered intense feelings of camaraderie. "Once you were down in the pit," as one miner succinctly put it, "you worked together, you helped one another and that was it." Workscape hazards cemented such bonds. In the process, they helped transform mutualism—cooperation for the common good—into solidarity—what the nineteenth-century philologist Archbishop Richard Trench once called "a fellowship in gain and loss, in honor and dishonor, in victory and defeat, a being, so to speak, all in the same boat." Like the coal dust that blackened white and brown skins alike, workscape dangers held the power to overcome race, ethnicity, and other distinctions.[33]

Boys and men realized not long after they first set foot underground that their lives and livelihoods depended not only on their own skill and luck, but also upon their co-workers' actions and abilities. Every miner's room occupied just one part of a larger matrix. An accident anywhere in the pit could have sudden, often deadly, ramifications throughout the pit. Bonding across cultural divides offered some protection against such hazards. "It didn't make any difference whether you were a Mexican or—see, the Mexicans were the last ones to come in there. Italians and Bohunks [Slavs] and the Welsh and the English," Henry Mathias claimed. "They come in in swarms, in bunches at different times down thru the mining career. And he drinks outa your bucket, you drink outa his bucket. If your bucket is closer to him when he wants a drunk, why he goes and takes a drink out your bucket. . . . And that's the way you are, down below there. . . . When you get down there, you're a family."[34]

Kinship, of course, can adopt a number of forms and serve a variety of functions. Here Mathias seemed to use "family" to mean relationships formed between relatively equal, autonomous, yet interdependent men and cemented together in the face of great peril—a "band of brothers," similar to those often found among soldiers and sailors. John Tomsic seconded the contrast Mathias drew between "down there" and the surface. "The guys that you work with in the mine," Tomsic reflected, "they are so close together in the mine. . . . One was watching the other one, protecting the other guy all the time you know and any danger that would come up or anything else. It ain't like outside. But in there it just seemed like it just drawed the men right together. You just couldn't imagine how guys get in there."[35]

Laboring together in spaces where a danger to one could instantaneously erupt and become a danger to all, men began to lay a foundation for collective action. Entries, air courses, and other realms of company authority and responsibility stood between the miners' places. Explosions and other dangers that traveled through those channels and into the colliers' rooms revealed the limits of the miners' independence. If "continuing struggle," as a former collier, Bill Davis, put it, "created a common bond that lasted forever," no small part of that struggle consisted of pressing companies to ventilate mine air, mitigate coal dust, maintain haulageway roofs, and otherwise prevent disaster from spreading into the colliers' places via the areas where corporate control prevailed.[36]

Notions of manliness were interwoven with the miners' occupational culture of solidarity, independence, and craft pride: the rugged masculinity one collier celebrated when he called a miner "a goddamned good man," the respectable masculinity epitomized by "practical miners," the paranoid masculinity for which the mere presence of women underground tempted fate, even the stupid masculinity that led some mineworkers to risk their lives simply to silence their co-workers' taunts. The mineworkers' diffuse yet everpresent perception of themselves as men became more focused and pugnacious when threatened. Unions—first the Knights of Labor, then the Western Federation of Miners and the United Mine Workers—succeeded in organizing the southern colliers only insofar as they could build on the pride, independence, solidarity, and understanding of masculinity forged in the daily struggles between mineworkers and their workscapes.[37]

The World Above

The interrelationship among regional fuel markets, volatile mine workscapes, and colliery work cultures fostered chronic tension and instability in the Colorado collieries. Fortunately for employers, the mineworkers' capacity to build effective social movements on the promising foundations laid underground was often hampered by internal dissension, social dysfunction, the quest for upward mobility, and coalfield migrants' resumption of the wandering ways that had brought them to the southern fields in the first place.

Though Colorado never yielded a *Sons and Lovers* or a *Germinal,* the desperation and familial discord evoked by Lawrence and Zola permeated coal camp life in the Rockies. Mining fostered pride, but it also caused pain, frustration, and fear. When "everything go wrong in the mine," Josephine Bazanele told an interviewer, miners would "come out and they take it out on the woman you know, or the kids. My old man used to do [so]. . . . Something was wrong in the mine and [he] got to let the steam go someplace else."[38]

Anger sometimes resulted in deadly violence. Between 1880 and 1920, Las Animas County's homicide rate—thirty-four murders per year per hundred thousand people—exceeded that of Omaha, New York, and Boston by five, eight, and twelve times, respectively. Men perpetrated 99 percent of these murders, and though women and children numbered among the victims, most of those killed were other men. Quarrels, which frequently had an interethnic dimension, started most of these incidents; others were connected with strikes, domestic disputes, police violence, or vendettas.[39]

Alcohol did much to fuel the mayhem. Colorado's mineworkers, like their relatives in most migrant source regions, were a notoriously hard-drinking lot. Many colliers flouted company policies and state laws by drinking on the job. Some brought wine underground in their lunch pails; others slipped bottles of liquor into their pockets. After work, an estimated 90 to 95 percent of miners headed to saloons, most of which catered to a particular ethnic, national, or racial clientele. Any coal camp worth its salt provided miners with a remarkable range of drinking opportunities. Enterprising camp residents, most of whom seem to have been former colliers or women widowed by the mines, established seven watering holes to serve Rockvale's force of a few hundred, and Sopris, a somewhat larger town, once boasted nineteen saloons. Miners sidled up to the bars of these establishments thirsting not simply for refreshment, but also for release from the anxiety, loneliness, and anger that mine work tended to inflict on them. "They gather," a coke oven worker, Emilio Ferraro, later recalled, "lots of people down [at] the saloon.... That was their life of the miner, anyplace you go." Drinking often served to solidify bonds developed underground, yet it also bore at least some responsibility for the exceptional level of violence among colliers. The overwhelming majority of murders documented in Las Animas County occurred in or near saloons and bars; a still higher percentage involved victims or assailants who had been drinking.[40]

Like internal dissension, mobility was an obstacle for mineworkers who tried to organize collective movements. The quest for individual, family, or community betterment that had brought most migrants to the Rockies led some to pursue economic advancement for themselves at the expense of others. Practical miners who were promoted to boss or superintendent often turned their backs on the miners they ostensibly managed, their former fellows. In the camps above, meanwhile, company patronage elevated John Aiello, the Tarabinos, and other coalfield padrones to positions of power that reinforced preexisting divisions within migrant groups.[41]

The vast majority of people who came to the southern fields, however, were more likely to move out than to move up. Coal miners in Colorado probably moved as often as any workers in the industrializing world. Some found what they sought, then returned home flush with cash and brimming with stories. Most arrived in the Rockies after extensive migrations; few had any intention of staying a day longer than it suited them. If the work was too hard, the mine too gassy, the pay too low, the housing too squalid—"if you didn't want to stay with it" for any reason, as Laurence Amicarella put it—"you moved." The father of Bill Lloyd, to give a dramatic example, brought his family to the northern field camp of Lafayette from Monmouthshire, Wales, by way of Pennsylvania. "When the work slacked off up there," the Lloyds headed to Rouse, then to Rugby, where Mrs. Lloyd opened a boardinghouse. After the senior Lloyd was transferred from Hastings to Delagua "to open up them mines," Bill Junior began his mining career. Father and son soon quit and moved to Piedmont, then to Cokedale, to Bowen, and finally to Lester. In little more than a decade the Lloyds moved at least ten times.[42]

Such mobility was not uncommon. Of some 2,500 coal miners working in Las Animas County in 1900, only 750 remained anywhere in the county just three years later, and earlier generations of mineworkers may have been more transient still. Far more than upward mobility or collective mobilization, migration constituted mineworkers' default strategy for dealing with the many difficulties they faced. As a union miner lamented in March 1894, "'Tis bad to find a place where there are so many men going into and out of a camp, as those of Southern Colorado."[43]

The mineworkers' pragmatic assessment of their chances against the operators also helped ensure that what happened underground usually stayed underground. The solidarity and militancy engendered by mine workscapes tended to be highly localized. Any struggle waged by men from a single colliery was doomed to fail, but organizing several mines at once required more time and effort than hard-working miners could usually spare. Could the colliers at the next pit be trusted? Would the mine operators concede, or would they push back? If the companies did fight, how were miners to survive weeks or even months without pay, and what was to be done if employers punished strikers with layoffs, blacklists, or worse? Such dilemmas were liable to haunt any collier weighing the costs and benefits of united action.

What Triggered the Miners' March

Mass mobilizations such as the marching strike of 1894 resulted from a complex mixture of causes. The groundwork for decades of industrial struggle had been laid by an oppositional work culture and by fuel market conditions that constantly drove down mineworkers' wages. Among the factors keeping the volatility in check were internal divisions within the mining population, drinking, various forms of mobility, and the grim calculations men made as they contemplated what it might take to organize an effective challenge to the companies' power. By the spring of 1894, however, a deep depression and the expansion of the recently formed United Mine Workers of America into Colorado combined to ignite the powder keg of discontent.

In summer 1893 the revocation of the Sherman Silver Purchase Act devastated a Rocky Mountain economy already weakened by trouble in the crucial agricultural, railroad, and banking sectors. "Our people are in debt," William

5.2. Coxeyites in Camp, March 1894. Copyright Colorado Historical Society, Harry H. Buckwalter Collection, 20030902.

Palmer anxiously exclaimed. "Wages are being reduced, incomes stopped or diminished, men being discharged, while many of the 'well-to-do,' who formerly could have assisted their neighbors or the unemployed to tide over a season of disappointment or misfortune, are now uncertain whether they will themselves come out 'even with the world.'" Banks suspended business or failed outright, leaving depositors empty-handed. Real estate, vigorous since the mid-1880s, crashed down like a high-country avalanche to wipe out fortunes large and small. Silver mines throughout the mountains, Denver's smelters, Pueblo's steelworks, and other firms halted production. By winter more than 20 percent of the workers in the region had lost their jobs, including more than 90 percent of its hard-rock miners.[44]

Few coal miners numbered among the throngs of unemployed massing in the Front Range cities in search of relief. Though most collieries remained open, the broad crisis suffered by coal-consuming industries and households led to many canceled or scaled-back orders. Mine managers, needing to limit production, responded by imposing shortened work weeks. Colliers, as was consistent with their ethos of mutualism, distributed the shifts remaining, while complaining that the mines were "'overcrowded'" and the "'turn at times slow.'" Though wages and rates remained unchanged despite the crisis, pay envelopes grew thinner and children's cheeks hollower.[45]

Coal companies precipitated the marching strike by making those already-trying times worse for their employees. Bank panics in Denver and Pueblo had made cash so scarce that it became difficult to make payroll. Claiming financial necessity, Colorado Fuel and Iron, Victor Coal and Coke, and others started compensating workers with paper certificates known as scrip, redeemable only at company stores. By the spring of 1894, miners throughout the southern coalfields had endured several months without pay; those in Fremont County had particular cause for concern, as demand for the county's peerless domestic fuel melted away along with the winter snow. Investigations by State Coal Mine Inspector Reed "proved conclusively that the irregular payment of miners, and the scrip system of payment, were the mainsprings that precipitated the strike."[46]

Equally significant, however, was the expansion of the United Mine Workers of America onto Western soil. Founded in 1890 with the amalgamation of Knights of Labor Assembly 135 and the Ohio-based National Miners' Federation, the United Mine Workers quickly became the most important organization of American colliers. The preamble to the union's constitution asserted: "There is no fact more generally known, nor more widely believed, than that without coal there would not have been any such grand achievements, privileges and blessings as those which characterize the nineteenth century civilization. . . . Those whose lot it is to daily toil in the recesses of the earth, mining and putting out this coal which makes these blessings possible," the organization resolved, "are entitled to a fair and equitable share of the same." In battle the United Mine Workers evinced all the toughness of its rough-and-ready membership. During periods of peace the organization was businesslike and pragmatic. United Mine Workers leaders realized that the best way to ensure the survival of their union and the prosperity of its members was to incorporate every mineworker in the United States and Canada into the union fold. And though the organization retained many of the racial and ethnic prejudices of the British American colliers who represented its driving force, it probably made greater strides toward interethnic and interracial solidarity than any other major union prior to the New Deal. United Mine Workers leaders developed an organizational structure designed to channel the local grievances of mineworkers dispersed across the continent into one cohesive international movement. Organizers drawn from backgrounds almost as varied as the nation's coal-mining populations used their language skills and access to migrant networks, along with their knowledge of particular workscapes and familiarity with local conditions in the coal camps, to enlist miners of many races and nationalities.[47]

This peculiar combination of inclusiveness, militancy, and expansionism soon made the United Mine Workers one of the biggest and strongest labor organizations on the continent. It also set the organization on a collision course with southern Colorado's adamantly antiunion mine operators.

Taking on King Coal

When the union prepared to launch a massive strike in 1894 to push for new contracts in the core fuel-producing states from Pennsylvania to Iowa, it requested Colorado's colliers to stop work, too. If Western miners continued to labor, union leaders reasoned, the coal they dug could undercut the union's campaign in the East and Midwest. When 125,000 to 150,000 mineworkers from bituminous collieries around the country walked off the job on April 21, 1894, the *Denver Republican* confidently remarked, "There is little probability of the coal strike reaching Colorado." The United Mine Workers, however, had organized the Western colliers much more effectively than the *Republican* and most observers recognized.[48]

Not long after the union's creation in 1890, a group of British American miners from Erie, in the northern fields, had founded the first local of the union in Colorado. Two years later, the United Mine Workers dispatched its international vice president, P. H. Penna, to organize in the Rockies; within five months Penna reported that eight hundred Colorado miners had joined the union, including many Knights of Labor transferring from such colorfully named lodges as Anti-Monopoly in Walsen, Australian Ballot in Trinidad, and Star of Hope in Coal Creek.[49]

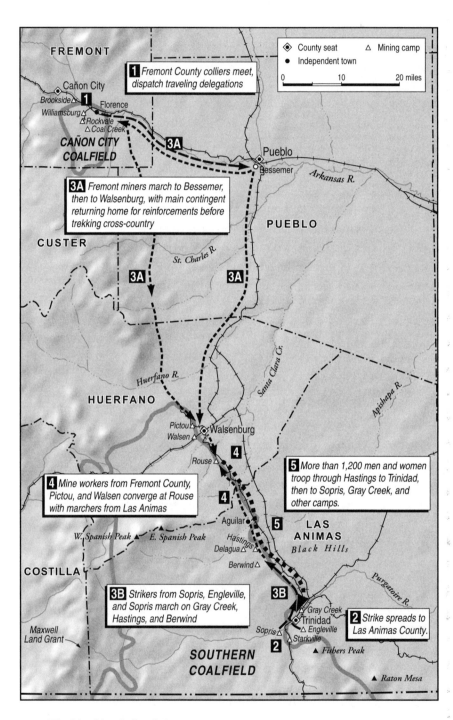

FREMONT

Cañon City

Brookside △
Williamsburg △
△ Rockvale
△ Coal Creek

Florence

CAÑON CITY COALFIELD

County seat ◈   Mining camp △
Independent town ●

0   10   20 miles

1 Fremont County colliers meet, dispatch traveling delegations

3A

Pueblo
Bessemer

Arkansas R.

3A Fremont miners march to Bessemer, then to Walsenburg, with main contingent returning home for reinforcements before trekking cross-country

PUEBLO

CUSTER

St. Charles R.

3A   **3A**

Huerfano R.

HUERFANO

Pictou △ ◈ Walsenburg
Walsen △

Rouse △

4

4 Mine workers from Fremont County, Pictou, and Walsen converge at Rouse with marchers from Las Animas

4

Santa Clara Cr.

Apishapa R.

5 More than 1,200 men and women troop through Hastings to Trinidad, then to Sopris, Gray Creek, and other camps.

Aguilar ●

5

LAS ANIMAS

Black Hills

W. Spanish Peak ▲   E. Spanish Peak ▲

Hastings △
Delagua △
Berwind △

COSTILLA

Purgatoire R.

3B Strikers from Sopris, Engleville, and Sopris march on Gray Creek, Hastings, and Berwind

3B

Gray Creek
◈ Trinidad
△ Engleville
Sopris △   △ Starkville

2 Strike spreads to Las Animas County.

Maxwell Land Grant

2

▲ Fishers Peak

SOUTHERN COALFIELD

▲ Raton Mesa

5.1. The Marching Strike of 1894.

Fremont County quickly became the center of United Mine Workers' organizing in the southern fields, and it was there that colliers shocked Colorado's coal-consuming public by joining the nationwide mineworkers' strike of 1894. Feelings of solidarity with the national cause combined with such local grievances as nonpayment of wages to ensure that "when the whistle sounded" on April 24 to call the men to work, "there were but few responded, and those who did respond were not allowed to go to work" by their peers.[50]

The next day, mineworkers from Coal Creek, Rockvale, Williamsburg, and other camps gathered at McDonald's Grove for the first of several mass meetings. After extensive deliberation, the assembled colliers voted "to follow their brothers in other districts and abandon the mines" and further resolved to "stay out for one week to ascertain the feeling of miners elsewhere in the state." Traveling delegations fanned out to Las Animas and Huerfano counties, Colorado's western and northern fields, and the coal camps of northern New Mexico. The marching strike had begun.[51]

A week later, six hundred Fremont miners learned in the course of a second "mass meeting" at McDonald's Grove that "they had not received any encouragement to strike from any source." Their brethren in New Castle, recently forced by Colorado Fuel and Iron to accept a humiliating 30 percent wage cut after a three-month strike, "advised the Fremont county miners not to strike. The same advice came from the northern camps." Worse, "nothing" had been "heard from the south," the all-important pits of Huerfano and Las Animas counties, "where the miners were all working."[52]

Nor did the operators seem concerned. When a reporter asked J. A. Kebler, head of Colorado Fuel and Iron's Fuel Department, to detail the miners' demands, he dismissively replied that "the strike is simply a sympathy one and intended to encourage their cause elsewhere. They say they have only gone out for a week, but it will prove to be an expensive week." Anxious to unburden his firm of obligations that a predecessor company had undertaken in a contract signed with colliers in the late 1880s, Kebler relished the opportunity to inflict the same punishment on the Fremont County miners as he had imposed on their New Castle counterparts: a 10 percent cut in wages and rates for every month they remained on strike.[53]

Kebler's stance drew on Colorado Fuel and Iron's established customs of wage cutting and union busting. One of the largest industrial corporations in the nation, CF&I had been created by the 1892 merger of John C. Osgood's Colorado Fuel Company with the Colorado Coal and Iron Company, established by William Palmer in 1881 to consolidate the various coal, town, and steel-making operations that the general had founded to realize his utopian visions. Osgood, who had been born in Brooklyn and orphaned at the age of twelve, was just the sort of leader Colorado Coal and Iron had so painfully lacked following Palmer's 1884 ouster by Wall Street investors.[54]

After quitting school at fourteen, Osgood worked briefly as an office boy at a Rhode Island cotton mill, then returned to New York. Supporting himself as an errand boy and clerk, he acquired "an excellent knowledge of bookkeeping and accounting," thanks to night classes at Cooper Institute. When a friend offered him a job in the offices of the Union Coal Company in Ottumwa, Iowa, the nineteen-year-old turned his sights westward. Osgood began working soon thereafter for the White Breast Mining Company, a close ally of the Chicago, Burlington & Quincy Railroad.[55]

The Burlington dispatched Osgood on his first visit to Colorado around 1882. The seemingly boundless potential of the state's coal seams evidently appealed to the young entrepreneur, for he moved to Denver and incorporated the Colorado Fuel Company in 1884. Colorado Fuel initially functioned as a broker, reselling northern Colorado coal to the Burlington at a healthy profit. By the late 1880s, though, Osgood and his inner circle had begun to buy up existing mines, as well as to launch collieries in Rouse and elsewhere.[56]

Soon after overtaking Colorado Coal and Iron as the state's largest coal producer, Colorado Fuel engulfed Palmer's old company to form one of the most powerful corporations in the nation. Numbers convey some sense of CF&I's size: over $13 million in authorized capital, 7,050 employees, in excess of 77,000 acres of farming, town-building, grazing, iron-mining, and oil-bearing land, 71,837 acres of coal land containing an estimated four hundred million tons of fuel, fourteen operating coal mines, and a share in fuel and steel markets that sprawled from Kansas to the Pacific and from Canada to Mexico.[57]

Osgood, Colorado's combative King Coal, shared Palmer's disdain for unions. The labor organizations of Osgood's mind—unwieldy, antiquated bureaucracies commanded by self-interested parasites and utopian radicals—obliterated the individual worker's drive for personal advancement, challenged the company's control over property and production, and jeopardized the operators' profitability. Worst of all from Osgood's perspective, these organizations threatened to unleash the savage propensities of the inferior races that manned the mines.[58]

Few miners among the crowd at the second meeting at McDonald's Grove would have taken lightly the threats Kebler made on behalf of Colorado Fuel and Iron. "The older miners and married men" reportedly "cautioned the meeting against hasty action in declaring a strike." To no one's surprise, "at one stage of the meeting" a journalist found "the sentiment was strongly against continuing the strike." Collective doubt neared its apogee. Then younger, more militant colliers astutely called a fifteen-minute recess. When the meeting resumed, "the feeling took another turn," for reasons that no paper bothered to specify. Before filing out into the crisp spring night, the men passed a resolution that "'the miners of Fremont county abstain from work until ordered in by the president of the United Mine Workers of America.'"[59]

The *Denver Republican* prophesied doom. "Before the miners of Fremont county resume there will be want and suffering, as this is the dull season for selling coal and, as all the other mines are working, there will not be much need of coal." But what if "all the other mines" stopped working? Then there would be "much need of coal," the colliers reasoned—enough to force even the mighty John Osgood to bend to the miners' collective will.[60]

Particularly encouraging was the favorable reception enjoyed by the traveling delegations dispatched after the first meeting at McDonald's Grove to Las Animas County. Colliers at Engleville, where workers had helped thwart CC&I's mechanization campaign thirteen years earlier, joined the strike on May 2. Their comrades from Sopris and Starkville took their tools out of the pits a few days later, then dispatched delegates of their own to New Mexico, who "waited on the miners . . . to induce them to lay down their picks." Soon, between three hundred and four hundred New Mexican miners had struck "in s[y]mpathy with their Eastern brethren and the grand effort which they are making to secure living wages and to free themselves from a condition which is little, if any, better than the condition of the black man previous to the 'late unpleasantness.'"[61]

The failure of the Fremont colliers to make headway in Huerfano County, though, augured ill for the strike. On May 7 "a large congregation of miners" meeting at Stanley's Hill, "midway between Walsenburg and Rouse," voted down three separate strike provisions. In a region laid low by hard times and haunted by hunger, it seemed the miners agreed with a local correspondent that during the throes of a regional depression "half a loaf is better than none." As they also recalled, "About ten years ago representatives from Coal Creek induced the miners here to go out on a strike and then deserted them in their hour of need. The result of that strike is felt to this day. The men who have been trying to get our miners to strike at this time are from Coal Creek, and remembering their former experience our miners are a little shy at listening to their advice." Nine days later, with many "Mexicans," Slavs, and others returning to work, the *Pueblo Daily Chieftain* claimed, "the backbone of the strike seems to be broken."[62]

Instead of giving up, however, the union miners made a momentous change in tactics, by abandoning traveling delegations for mass mobilizations. The marches that culminated in the great convergence of miners on Rouse began around midnight on Friday, May 18, as several hundred Las Animas County miners formed themselves "into armed companies." Parading behind American flags and brass bands, the miners stomped from Engleville, Starkville, and Sopris north "through Trinidad," past the future site of the Ludlow Massacre "to Berwind and Hastings to compel the miners there to cease work." In one of the injunction suits that CF&I filed against the marchers, company counsel singled out Italians and Tyroleans—Chris Passevento, John Brazio, Luca Previs, and Giacomo Toller—as the leaders of the six-hundred-man-strong "crowd." The company alleged that the strikers had "urged and endeavored to persuade the Coal miners" at Berwind "to quit work and strike," thus placing "the safety of the lives" of its miners "in imminent peril from the defendants and those whom they might induce to join with them, and participate in their unlawful and evil designs ... [of] riot and blood-shed." Meanwhile, coal company toughs were beating up and firing on strikers at Sopris. They crippled one, in addition to throwing "men, women and children out of their houses, on only five days' notice," though the families in question owned their homes and had occupied them for "months and years." They even blew up the Sopris home built and inhabited by a Swiss-German collier named Oberosler and his family; Emma Zanetell, Oberosler's daughter, later recalled that her family "lost everything" in the blast.[63]

As a U.S. marshal charged with enforcing the injunction against the Las Animas strikers rode the train back to Denver with a flag—"red and blue stripes and five stars painted on one side of a white banner while on the reverse side were printed in large letters 'HOBO'"—"taken from the miners ... as a trophy," the coordinated mobilization of the Fremont County colliers set the stage for the dramatic descent of around two thousand strikers on Rouse. On May 19, over six hundred miners, most from Coal Creek, gathered in the railroad town of Florence. "Having no money," one report alleged, they planned to commandeer a train. The Denver & Rio Grande tried to sabotage this plan by ordering its trainmen to bypass the town. Yet just as Baldwin's colliers had subverted a similar move by the railroad by snowshoeing through the high mountains in the wake of the Jokerville tragedy, several hundred Fremont County colliers began "footing it" to Bessemer, a steelworks suburb just south of Pueblo. Twelve hours and thirty miles later, the miners reached their destination, having kept up a remarkable pace that illustrated both their resolve and the stamina they had developed mining coal. "Under the favoring shade of a few cottonwood trees they sat down to rest," while George Edwards, one of the strike leaders, explained their goal to a reporter: "to get to Walsenburg to confer with the working miners, whom they believed they could get to strike simply through the persuasive power of argument."[64]

It took just one night waiting for a train to no avail, then lying "down on the bare ground to sleep," to convince the Fremont miners that if they wanted to get to Huerfano, they would have to do so under their own steam. One contingent started walking directly. The remainder caught a train back to Florence and melted into the group of "seven hundred miners with flags and preceded by the Coal Creek brass band" that had commenced marching "overland to Rouse" by way of Walsenburg. A Pueblo paper remarked, "Some of the best citizens in the camps are going with the army," before noting that "the majority seem to be Italians and Austrians." The group decided that "owing to the extreme old age of some of their number," they would break their journey into four day-long marches of fifteen miles each. A Pueblo paper soon reported that the marchers had been seen "striking across the country at a lively rate [and] apparently in the best of spirits."[65]

While these columns of Las Animas and Fremont County miners were "tramping along over the hills," the colliers from two large Huerfano County properties, Pictou and Walsen, were anxiously looking toward the nearby camp of Rouse. The men there, they believed, "hold the key to the coal strike situation. . . . Toward the miners [t]here all strikers have been bending their efforts . . . , for they feel, it is said, that if Rouse strikes they gain a big point; if not, the movement lacks much of unanimity."[66]

Paternalism, Place, and Power

As we have seen, outdoor meeting places such as McDonald's Grove had played a vital role in the strike's inception, as had the marchers' strategy of rallying by the hundreds in the camps outside the mines to plead with—and probably threaten—the men still at work. Colliers' amorphous local griev-ances, once coordinated with the United Mine Workers' national strategy, had developed into a coherent coalfield-wide movement that had spread throughout several thousand square miles of territory. Now the fate of a strike that had germinated in mine workscapes and sprouted quickly in outdoor meeting places and workers' communities turned on the miners' ability to take Rouse—not only the most productive colliery still in operation, but also the prototype for a new kind of company town, expressly designed to con-tain militancy and exclude unionism.[67]

Over the preceding four weeks, the strike had gained ground wherever miners had successfully built communities of their own during the preceding years. Yet marchers made little progress in places where operators owned most of the housing and land. This messy geography of power was a legacy of the half-hearted paternalism that had characterized coal company policy during the industry's first two decades in the southern fields. During the strikes of the twentieth century, coal company officials would claim that "nat-ural" conditions of geographic isolation and social hierarchy gave them no choice but to build and operate their own camps. The first two decades of company policy in southern Colorado coal camps, however, paint a more complex and contradictory picture of the coalfield landscape, revealing the arrangements of place and power that gave rise to the marching strike of 1894 and helped shape its course.

Colorado Coal and Iron's hospital plan represented the only vestige of William Palmer's utopian vision that ever extended to coal-mining employees. There is little evidence that southern Colorado's coal companies spent money during the 1870s and '80s on schools, churches, workmen's clubs, or other focal points of corporate paternalism common in other coal-mining regions of the world. Nor had company stores taken hold as forcefully as they later would. Colorado Coal and Iron ran stores in a few camps, as did Osgood's Colorado Supply Company, but mining companies generally preferred to contract with independent merchants to provide store services.[68]

Particularly ambivalent were the companies' housing policies. Operators usually viewed the construction of houses and boardinghouses as a necessary adjunct to mine development. Once built, though, worker dwellings presented managers with a choice: rent or sell?

Leasing promised two principal advantages. First, it helped companies recoup some of the wages they disbursed. "At Rouse," the Colorado Fuel Company's 1892 annual report explained, "it was thought advisable to erect additional miners' houses," because such accommodations would "return a good revenue in rentals as well as facilitate the securing of additional miners." Second, leasing provided a measure of control over the cost of living—a particularly important concern, given the companies' need to drive wages downward. From Crested Butte, for example, where "the Company have . . . no accomodations [*sic*] whatsoever," consultant Joseph Simons proclaimed the excessively high rates colliers charged to be "the best evidence what bad influences missing facilities upon the scale of wages exert."[69]

Renting afforded the companies revenue and a mechanism for controlling labor costs, yet coal company officials revealed themselves to be reluctant paternalists. Simons, for instance, noted approvingly that wages remained low at Coal Creek, "owing mainly to the fact that most of the laborers live in their own houses, and through irrigation near Canon City living there has become cheap and pleasant." Even at Engleville, a camp that anticipated some elements of the later company town system, manager George Ramsay, who argued "that it would be better for us to let the miners build their own houses," explained "that miners who own their own homes will always be on hand when the busy season opens up, while the miners who have no particular place to call home will go wherever they can get the best work for the time being." Executives sometimes found such arguments for worker-owned housing persuasive. In 1888, for instance, Colorado Coal and Iron's real estate committee authorized the sale of lots in its two primary company towns, Engleville and Walsen; the next year, the Colorado Fuel Company board of directors passed a similar measure regarding company-owned houses at Rouse and Sopris.[70]

Whatever the impact of these policies—Rouse, at the very least, remained largely company-owned—they paled in significance to the widespread practice on the part of local mine officials of tolerating and perhaps even encouraging employees to build their own homes on company land. Photographs capture the fascinating architectural heterogeneity that developed as colliers constructed hundreds of dwellings according to their own notions: log cabins resembling those built by miners in gold and silver camps; shacks and boxcar dwellings similar to those erected by industrial workers in the Front Range cities, and even architecture in vernacular styles, such as Hispano adobes or Tyrolean chalets, that evoked migrant homelands.[71]

The companies' reluctance to assume paternalistic obligations combined with mineworker initiatives and the pragmatism of local mining officials to map a spectrum of power relations onto the coalfields. A few camps, such as Walsen, constituted little more than extensions of preexisting Hispano and Anglo settlements. Free-standing open camps such as Coal Creek consisted, in turn, mostly or entirely of houses that miners built or owned themselves. Such places met the great landscape scholar J. B. Jackson's definition of a "vernacular landscape" because they were "identified with local custom, pragmatic adaptation to circumstances, and unpredictable mobility." So-called closed camps, such as Rouse and Berwind, by contrast, matched Jackson's description of "political landscapes." Built by companies in response to strikes and other labor woes, these company-owned, company-controlled towns consisted of "spaces and structures designed to impose or preserve a unity and order on the land."[72]

In the towns and camps, as in the workscape below, the boundaries between zones of corporate control and labor autonomy were unstable and

5.3. Little Italy, Sopris: A Vernacular Landscape. Copyright Colorado Historical Society, Jesse F. Welborn Collection, 20004991.

hotly contested, as the first month of the marching strike had demonstrated. The conflict, born of workscape militancy and the United Mine Workers' expansion, flourished in vernacular landscapes but foundered in political landscapes. Strike leaders recognized this pattern. Fearing that their efforts were doomed to fail unless they could open up the closed camps, they marched en masse, with the intention of encircling and neutralizing Rouse, which was at the same time a symbol of the coal companies' desire to "impose . . . unity and order" on the land and a material threat to the colliers' campaign to halt the flow of fuel into Western markets.

Making Their Move

With the miners of Fremont and Las Animas counties heading their way, colliers from the Huerfano County pits at Walsen and Pictou decided to lay off work. After another meeting, hundreds of colliers signed a public statement. "We feel that we would do anything for the benefit of our Eastern brethren, for we know they are trying to better their conditions." Careful to portray the strike as more than a matter of sympathy, the miners assured the public that they also had "many grievances of their own, and God knows we need to have our condition bettered in this place. The citizens all know that we have worked half time for the last twelve months and have endured much hardship, and the time has arrived when we must and will make an able stand to demand our rights."[73]

The following day, May 25, a vanguard of seventy-five colliers arrived from Fremont County and made "their headquarters at Tony Bartolero's saloon." No institution posed a greater threat to the companies' power than places like Bartolero's. For despite the dissension that alcohol fueled, saloons served to galvanize the culture of opposition fostered underground. Bars gave mineworkers room to socialize, obtain news from back home, celebrate their national and racial identities, borrow money, eat free food, bond with other men, and cultivate their reputation for generosity, toughness, humor, and other valued traits. Because alcohol loosened men's tongues, watering holes were also important places for mineworkers to share complaints about bosses, wages, and conditions. Saloons, as one historian puts it, provided "the gateway to comradeship." Tony Bartolero and other saloonkeepers even allowed unions to meet in their rooms, a practice that in the wake of the strike did much to generate unprecedented concern about temperance in the minds of John C. Osgood and other hard-drinking coal barons.[74]

The main contingent of the Fremont marchers arrived in Walsenburg a few hours after the vanguard had filed into Bartolero's. Some had turned back, but more than four hundred men had stuck it out, "some . . . armed with shot guns, which they had taken, they said, merely to hunt with." Accompanying them were sixteen women and "several well loaded commissary wagons" stocked with a ton of flour and "a large quantity of salt meats, potatoes, and other provisions," as well as "numerous four-wheeled and two-wheeled vehicles." Once this procession reached Walsenburg, it turned the corner onto Main Street, where the marchers "gave a cheer. Two horsemen led, followed by 115 Walsen miners who had gone out to meet" their Fremont brethren. A band played "a lively air" as strikers walked four abreast, "without regard to step or time," carrying blankets and "little grub bag[s]" on short sticks. After passing down streets "lined with people eager to see the strange procession about which so much has been said and which they have looked for with some misgivings," the Fremont miners made camp in "a beautiful little grove."[75]

The next day, a group of fifty "prominent Pueblo business men" called on the strikers. Sharing the marchers' belief that if Rouse joined the strike, the miners still working elsewhere in southern Colorado would swiftly cast their lot with the union, the businessmen planned "to encourage the Rouse men in their determination to continue at work and . . . if possible dissuade the Coal Creekers from trying to get the Rouse men out." But the miners stood resolute. When one of the visitors beseeched the miners to consider the impact of an all-out colliers' strike on the people who labored in Pueblo's smelters, steel mills, and other coal-burning factories, the union organizer Sam Chambers replied that the strikers "could not help the crippling of other industries." Rebuffed, the "Pueblo gentlemen boarded their train and watched the miners headed by their band march and countermarch for the amusement of the visitors."[76]

Hundreds of miners from all over Las Animas County were even then nearing Walsenburg, buoyed up on their march by the rallying cry "Rouse miners must come out." As word of the southern strikers' approach reached Walsenburg on May 28, the Fremont miners mustered together with the colliers of Pictou and Walsen. "The whole army was formed into line and, 900 strong, started for Rouse." Flanked by horsemen and accompanied by "wagons and buggies," the miners made brisk time. Two and a half hours and seven miles later, they mounted a hill and "looked across the valley to the south and beheld a long column coming down the hill in the direction of Rouse. They were their friends from Las Animas county, who had camped near that place during the night, and who had been watching for their arrival."[77]

Half an hour later, "the two columns met near the station and only a short distance from the offices of the company." A great roar filled the air, for the joining together of between 1,700 and 2,200 colliers constituted "a great occasion for the miner, and he gave his lung free action." Parading "amidst continuous cheering and waving of flags," the allied forces "marched back through Rouse to a place adjoining the lands of the coal company where they struck camp." An already diverse mixture of migrants from throughout Europe and North America had joined together not simply to show their allegiance to a vision of American promise, but also to defy Colorado Fuel and Iron to displace them. Meanwhile, back in Las Animas County, women of Tyrolean, Italian, and Swiss-German descent "all got out of their homes while their husbands was all away on this march up there." With few miners left to defend them against company guards and sheriffs' deputies, Emma Zanetell recalled eight decades later, they "felt braver all together."[78]

Endgames

Newspaper reports are oddly mute on what happened next. All we know is that two hundred Rouse miners "quit work" the next day "and joined the body of strikers." Perhaps two hundred others, however, remained on the job. The "pivot" of the struggle had refused to tip in the colliers' favor.[79]

So southward to the closed camps of Las Animas County the strikers headed, once again on foot. Delaying their departure by a day was "one of Colorado's celebrated out-pourings that reaches the roots of all vegetation." Miners bivouacked in their fellow workers' houses in Walsenburg and the surrounding camps. While miner-built, worker-owned dwellings sheltered them from the storm, their longtime connections with small businessmen and agriculturists throughout southern Colorado kept them "well fed. Trinidad sent up 1100 loaves of bread and other edibles," while the small towns of La Veta and Cuchara had "donated largely" and "given liberally." Seven cattlemen had "each offered a fat steer and Leonidas Valdez [had] given them forty sheep and a ton of flour." Last but hardly least, the colliers "sent out committees to forage and the Mexican people, though poor, done well by us." All told, Anglos, Hispanos, and other folks had "shown their liberality and large-heartedness." A week after having "marched up there," as Emma Zanetell recalled, the strikers "all come back" to Las Animas County, together with their comrades from Huerfano and most of the Fremont miners.[80]

A week after converging on Rouse, some 1,275 marchers arrived in Trinidad. There they marched through the streets to a large clearing, "when a circle was formed around a platform" near a brickyard, so that the miners could listen to a series of rousing speeches from supportive local politicians and labor leaders. Speaker after speaker celebrated the miners' movement as a patriotic struggle in which workingmen of many nations and races had joined together to defend fundamental American rights—to earn a living wage, to move about freely, to assemble peaceably—against oppressive corporations and the "private armies" of deputies and guards who did their bidding. "More than one hundred years ago, gentlemen," one orator intoned,

> when there was not a white man in all this land, when these mountains which pass through this state were a theory, so far as human knowledge went, the people of England attempted to oppress those colonies over on the Atlantic coast; patriots assembled on the Boston Commons, and in other places, and dared those men to oppress them longer, and I say to you that they were men from every civilized land, men who claimed as their mother tongue that of every civilized nation of Europe, and they raised that flag and said "under that flag we will be free men or under that flag you may bury our dead bodies." That flag, gentlemen, waves still. In this valley, under the shadow of the grandest mountain that traverses the United States, preserved to us by those men, the cradle of liberty is being rocked by men speaking almost every tongue. Men have assembled to state their grievances, and from different sources the resistance comes. These men demand a right, and they will express their views.

Another speaker reminded the miners that when "the Red Coats called upon the Minute Men upon the field to 'desperse [*sic*], you rebels, or we will fire upon you' . . . America, with her little 13 colonies, came out victorious in that great struggle. And I predict, gentlemen, that the miners of Las Animas county and Southern Colorado will come out victorious in this struggle against the oppression that has been brought against them."[81]

Having drunk deeply from the well of republicanism, the marchers proceeded from camp to camp, enjoying a great deal of public support and some success in persuading those who were still at work in the mines to join the struggle. Colorado Fuel and Iron and its competitors fought back with injunctions. Sheriffs' deputies also did the companies' bidding, "interfering with individuals on public highways," blocking the marchers' movements, and allegedly "insulting [their] wives." When "a couple of hundred men and women" trekked to Sopris, they were "met at the company's grounds by 300 deputies." A day after the strikers were turned away, the Sopris colliers voted to remain at work, and similar defeats ensued.[82]

By mid-June, the marchers seemed unable to reach their fellow miners except through deception. "While ostensibly holding a meeting at Sopris," the *Pueblo Daily Chieftain* reported of the strikers, "many were slipping away, and last night at quitting time several hundred appeared ten miles away in Gray Creek with no deputies to oppose them, and as a consequence that camp has joined the strikers in a body." The ruse was carried out "so quietly . . . that the band playing in front of the company's store was the first intimation the company had that strikers were within ten miles." Whenever the marchers moved openly to confront colliers laboring in company-owned camps, however, they ran up against court orders and officers of the law.[83]

In the end, strikers failed to secure the "unanimity" on which their movement depended, for their marches stalled at the borders of closed camps. In Fremont County, union miners made sure that "not a pound of coal [was] produced." Farther south, though, the operators replaced strikers with "anybody that [would] work, whether he [had] ever been in a coal mine or not," including a "well known one-armed deputy of Sopris." Strikebreakers ensured that Colorado's "coal supply," as the *Colorado Springs Gazette* reported, "continue[d] ample in spite of the troubles throughout the state." John Osgood bragged, "'There is no possibility of a coal famine and the strike leaders are deceiving their followers in leading them to suppose that the employers will be forced to accede to their demands to avoid such an unfortunate condition of affairs.'" In many other parts of the nation, by contrast, striking coal miners proved much more successful at shutting off the flow of fossil fuel. Reports from Chicago declared that "never was there a time in the history of the city where the coal bins were so nearly cleaned up of bituminous coal as at present."[84]

As mineworkers in most of the Northeast and Midwest managed to secure a compromise settlement with the operators, their counterparts in Colorado faced a less certain future. Yet even as many marchers returned home, the strike endured and, for a time, grew more intense. Crested Butte colliers joined in, and the Trinidad Coal and Coke Company posted notices at Starkville permanently discharging all strikers. In late June a state convention of the United Mine Workers issued the so-called Pueblo Manifesto. Blaming the strike on "the greed and selfishness of employers to become richer and make the poor, but honest workingmen poorer," the striking miners demanded uniform weights and rates, semimonthly pay in cash, elected checkweighmen, "the abolishment of the scrip and truck store system," the restoration of prestrike wages to New Castle's colliers, the creation of pit committees to prevent discrimination against union miners, and "recogni[tion] by our employers as an organized body of craftsmen brought together with the object of mutual protection for social comfort and education."[85]

Following the convention, the miners gathered in a vacant lot in downtown Pueblo. After Frank Lloyd expatiated on his "hope and belief that the negro miners of the south would refuse to come here and take the places of the Colorado men," William Howells, state organizer for the United Mine Workers, rebuked the operators for "having taken from [the colliers] their best blood and their American privilege of earning an honest livelihood. . . . They were human beings and stood by the Declaration of Independence" and its guarantee of "life, liberty, and the pursuit of happiness." He implored the operators "to confer with us that uneven conditions may be made right. . . . We ask to be a party to the deal that affects our very existence. The 340,000 miners ask to have equal rights with the 7,000 men who invest their money."[86]

A month later, the miners held a second and more desperate convention in Pueblo. Any hope of precipitating a fuel famine was shattered, the fall rush of coal orders was looming, and hunger was spreading through the camps. Many strikers were anxious to settle. Union leaders met with several large coal operators to work out a truce. On August 3, 1894, four hundred Fremont County colliers congregated one last time at McDonald's Grove to vote "on the question of returning to work at the same basis they were working on when they quit." By a slim majority, they decided to go back to work at the rates before the strike, provided that the companies promise to pay their employees regularly and in cash. Miners elsewhere in southern Colorado and northern New Mexico also approved the settlement. A few days later, local union officials announced, "The great strike of the western United Mine workers . . . has been declared off by the executive board."[87]

In retrospect, the marching strike of 1894 foreshadowed both the collective might that unionization promised and the growing importance of spatial and social control in the efforts of Colorado Fuel and Iron and its competitors to cut labor costs and prevent labor organization. The operators had successfully repulsed the miners' mobilization, without granting the United Mine Workers any of its demands. Yet they were hardly sitting pretty. Defeating a sympathetic movement launched during the slackest season of a deep regional depression had cost the companies tens of thousands of dollars in deputies' wages, and hundreds of thousands more in lost revenue. John C. Osgood and his counterparts realized that they might easily have lost the strike. No less important, they noted the decisive role that closed camps had played in the companies' victory. When the marchers could move freely and talk openly, after all, they succeeded. But when they tried to take Rouse, Sopris, and other closed camps, the miners' mobilization stalled, and the strike was denied the critical mass it needed to prevail. Thus it was that Colorado mine operators came to embrace industrial paternalism during the same summer that a fierce nationwide strike by Eugene Debs's American Railway Union was discrediting George Pullman's grand experiment in paternalistic town-building on the industrial outskirts of Chicago.[88]

Yet still opposition flourished in the depths below and in the increasingly circumscribed vernacular landscapes above, awaiting only the right conditions to erupt. "'Liberty crushed to earth,'" an orator had declared to the marchers in Trinidad back in early June, "'will rise again.'" And indeed, the next time so many miners took up the march through these same foothills, they would carry high-powered rifles instead of shotguns, and they would use them not to hunt game but to wage war.[89]

6

The Quest for Containment

The marching strike demonstrated the potential of company towns to stop miners' protests in their tracks. In the process, it inspired southern Colorado's largest coal corporations to depart from the ambivalent paternalism of early decades. Company leaders surmised that the vernacular landscape— the open, informal arrangements of space and power that took shape outside the mines in the 1870s and '80s—had played a crucial role in the 1894 conflict, by giving the militancy engendered in the mine workscape room to surface and spread. The best way to contain union activism, executives and managers decided, was to transform the coalfield landscape. First Colorado Fuel and Iron, then the other large operators, built paternalistic company towns whose every feature was carefully designed to inculcate subservience and loyalty in an increasingly diverse, persistently militant workforce.

With the return of economic prosperity to the Mountain West during the mid-1890s, demand for fossil fuels skyrocketed; as the coal industry expanded and intensified production, mine operators enlisted a range of experts—doctors, engineers, architects, educators, and sociologists—to replace the vernacular landscapes of southern Colorado with company-controlled landscapes. Like their counterparts who were spearheading the contemporaneous campaigns to assimilate Native Americans and "new" immigrants from southern and eastern Europe and tightening Jim Crow's grasp on the South, builders of company towns in Colorado sought to control the threats that workers and ethnic "others" posed. Drawing on a long tradition in Anglo-American reform, mine bosses attributed the record of labor unrest in the southern fields neither to the inferiority of mineworkers nor to the irrepressibility of class conflict. Instead, the operators drew an analogy between unionism and the spread of contagious disease. "The line of education we have selected," Dr. Richard Corwin of Colorado Fuel and Iron explained, "has been that of prophylaxis—prophylaxis as it pertains to the health and good of our people." Corwin, like many other company town builders, thought of human society as an organism besieged by threats. In the thinking of Corwin and his counterparts, unions and strikes loomed large, joining typhoid, squalor, and hunger as ills jeopardizing the "good of our people." By eradicating environments in which the militancy fostered down in the mines could gain ground on the surface, and then quarantining coal camps against infection from without, advocates of company towns thought they could bring lasting peace to the coalfields. Yet in their zeal to contain the independence and craft pride, the solidarity and pugnacious masculinity, that periodically united miners of many backgrounds, coal companies were producing a landscape of woe destined to become both a cause and a setting for the deadly coalfield war of 1913–1914.[1]

Starting at least a century earlier, European coal mine operators had pioneered exploitative company towns in which mineowners held the title to all the houses, compensated colliers in scrip, and forced mining families to trade at a company store. This system then crossed the Atlantic, to take hold in Pennsylvania and elsewhere, alongside the customary relations of production that shaped coal mine workscapes and colliery work cultures. Operators in the Colorado southern fields had seldom adopted this system during the 1870s and '80s. In the wake of the marching strike of 1894, however, the coal companies' quest for containment intersected with the emergence of a movement known to contemporaries as social welfare work, and to historians as welfare capitalism or industrial paternalism. Manufacturers such as the National Cash Register Company, International Harvester, and the H. W. Heinz Company were the first to embrace this "business of benevolence"; coal companies in many parts of the nation followed suit in the 1890s and 1900s. John Osgood's Colorado Fuel and Iron Company proved particularly recep-

tive, going so far as to establish a Sociological Department under Dr. Corwin's direction in the spring of 1901, to coordinate its paternalist project.
Other large operators in the southern fields, particularly Victor-American
(which had come under Osgood's control by 1901) and the American Smelting and Refining Company, also adopted elements of welfare capitalism,
though their efforts generated little public scrutiny and remain virtually un-
documented.[2]

Welfare capitalists, despite the spectacular failure of George Pullman's
model company town outside Chicago to contain labor unrest among railroad car makers, remained insistent that company towns could serve as a
beacon of enlightened modernity; such expertly planned environments, Dr.
Corwin and others believed, could turn disgruntled migrants from all over
the world into "better citizens" who were "more contented with their work."
By the 1900s the new company town campaign undoubtedly provided many
workers and their families with houses that were larger, cleaner, and more
modern than most other coalfield dwellings; at a monthly rent of two dollars
per room, even a large six-room house cost an average mining family less
than a quarter of its monthly income. Medical facilities also improved. An
esteemed professor from Northwestern University Medical School declared
Colorado Fuel and Iron's new Minnequa Hospital "the most perfect in the
world," and a multipronged public health campaign in the camps resulted in
cleaner coal camp environments and healthier workers. Perhaps most important of all were educational advancements that created possibilities beyond
those company executives had anticipated. Night classes imparted the English language skills some mineworkers used to become union organizers or
leave the coalfields for better work; camp schools enabled some colliers' sons
to avoid a life of labor in the mines, and a few coal miners' daughters to escape the drudgery that had been their mothers' lot.[3]

Company towns were hardly an unmitigated evil, yet they utterly failed
to contain militancy or suppress unionism. Far from making mining families
more contented, company stores, camp guards, the corruption exercised on
local political and legal systems, company housing, and other elements of the
new paternalism further fanned the flames of unrest. In the process, the company town system armed mining families and their union with a powerful
rhetoric of opposition in which the republican idiom of opportunity, liberty,

and justice reinforced the craft arcana of turns, damps, and dead work. Even before the cement had set or the paint had dried on the new closed camps, colliers began to attack these places as un-American, despotic throwbacks to old-world feudalism that were entirely out of place in a New West that promised opportunity and upward mobility for all. Because of the companies' efforts to reform space and society, working people increasingly made common cause with regard not only to workscape travails, but also to the trials of life outside the mines. Thus did a landscape designed to contain conflict in the mines sow the seeds of its own destruction.[4]

Lord Osgood's Domain

Aspen is today synonymous with glamour, wealth, and serenity, but this twenty-first-century haven for the global glitterati was once a smoking, churning hub of coal-powered industrialism. In its late nineteenth-century heyday Aspen was a silver camp. As elsewhere, though, coal provided the energy that powered mining, smelting, and much else in town. Suppose we take a trip to retrace the route along which some of this fuel traveled. Heading north through the Roaring Fork Valley, we turn west and up the valley of the Crystal River. After passing Carbondale, we notice ochre cliffs begin to narrow into miles of zigzagging canyon walls, which eventually part to reveal a bank of ruined beehive ovens. Veering left, we find ourselves on the boutique-lined main street of Redstone, a model industrial community once designed to embody the spirit of progressive paternalism.

Coal baron John C. Osgood, the callous archindustrialist who engineered the merger of Colorado Fuel and Iron and gained a well-deserved reputation as one of the most determined union busters in the Rockies, envisaged Redstone as a showplace. Here Osgood and his inner circle could retreat from the busyness and grime of the Front Range cities that served as headquarters to Colorado Fuel and Iron's far-flung industrial empire; here they would demonstrate their success at reconciling the ostensibly incompatible imperatives of coal extraction and labor concord. The marching strike of 1894 had prompted Osgood and his allies to rethink their longstanding ambivalence toward company towns, company stores, scrip payment, and similar policies of labor control long used in European and eastern American coalfields.

Reform-minded businessmen on both sides of the Atlantic increasingly believed that they could achieve labor peace by assuming greater responsibility for the conditions in which their employees lived and labored. The welfare capitalists who inspired Osgood blended humanitarian, "almost utopian" concern for their workers with a selfish desire to avoid costly labor disputes.[5]

Redstone was Colorado Fuel and Iron's most elaborate and expensive effort to eliminate labor unrest through planning and social control. Holding vernacular landscapes responsible for giving unionism and strikes room to flourish, Osgood and his subordinates set about creating new living spaces intended to foster allegiance to home, country, and company. Yet these paternalists, even as they looked ahead to a progressive future in which contented mining families would abandon their militancy to advance the mutual interests of the laboring classes and their employers, also looked back fondly to an imagined feudal past. Redstone, designed by Theodore Davis Boal, an Iowa-born architect trained at the École des Beaux Arts in Paris, became the material embodiment of this double vision. The town's layout, landscape, and architecture turned a stretch of riparian ranchland into a modern fiefdom for Lord Osgood. On this stage Osgood hoped to enact a grand drama of transformation.[6]

Tucked into the western end of this domain, Osgood built Cleveholm, a forty-two-room Tudor manor house whose name compounded the first syllable of the executive's middle name, Cleveland, with a suffix suggesting genteel domesticity. Osgood lavished $2.5 million—a sum equivalent to the yearly earnings of four thousand to six thousand coal miners—on this twenty-four-thousand-square-foot manse. As Italian and Austrian stonemasons crafted the building's exterior, other tradesmen were busy fitting the rooms out with all sorts of regal flourishes imported by steamship and rail from around the world: "ruby red velvet" for the dining room, Honduran mahogany for the tea room, hand-stenciled linen in the reception room, "green Spanish leather" below the library's inlaid ceiling of gold and silver, and the pièce de resistance, an ensemble of two "huge" Tiffany chandeliers that cast their gemlike reflections the length of the immense living room. A worthy riposte to Andrew Carnegie's castle in Scotland, George Vanderbilt's Biltmore estate in western North Carolina, and Jay Gould's Lyndhurst in the

Hudson Valley, Cleveholm affirmed the orphan industrialist's ascension to the upper echelons of American society.[7]

Osgood's luxurious manor house lay nestled in a forty-two-hundred-acre estate described by one journalist as "a great natural park made more attractive by the landscape gardener's art." Known as Crystal Park, the tract was enclosed by fences and guarded by a gamekeeper. Elk, bighorn sheep, antelope, and deer soon sought refuge there, and the stretch of the Crystal River flowing through the estate teemed with trout, "thanks to the addition to its waters from the hatcheries and the watchfulness that has been exerted over" it. Closer to the manor, Osgood built a sort of hobby ranch to house fancy breeds of livestock. Prize-winning Polanjus bulls and "the finest horses" grazed in Crystal Park's lush pastures; nearby, a barn and eighteen other outbuildings sheltered common cattle, horses, and poultry. With its manor house, game park, manicured lawn, and stable of prize cattle and thoroughbreds, Cleveholm lacked only a local peasantry to complete Osgood's neofeudal domain. And so the company laid out a large "village garden" downstream from Osgood's ranch, on bottomlands cleared of the "huts" erected to provide shelter for the workers who had built Redstone. The irrigated garden plots and buildings for stock and poultry, paternalists hoped, would encourage coke plant workers to spend their off-work hours laboring on the land.[8]

As for the workers' town, Osgood wanted its eighty-five cottages to reconcile past and present, employer and employee. Boasting a unique floor plan, a pseudo-Swiss facade, and Arts and Crafts elements, each dwelling celebrated artisanship and individuality. "Beauty," *Camp and Plant* crowed, "has been the guiding principle in the building up of our little town. We do not have monotonous rows of box-car houses . . . but tasteful little cottages in different styles, prettily ornamented, . . . and painted in every variety of restful color." Each of these structures was "finished with good wood work" inside, with "lath and plaster walls, proper provision for good draught in chimneys and opportunities for baths. Many of the houses are papered, have curtains on the windows as well as roller shades and are fitted up with substantial furniture."[9]

Redstone's laborers, once they were assigned to houses by the mine superintendent, enjoyed homes that a craftsman or clerk in Denver or New York might have envied; an array of services would sweeten the deal. Osgood

6.1. Redstone. Photograph by L. C. McClure. Denver Public Library, Western History Collection, MCC-2507.

wanted his householders to enjoy the same urban comforts enjoyed by middle- and upper-class residents of Front Range cities and larger mining towns. The construction of two reservoirs and a small hydroelectric plant to supply Redstone with power and clean water prompted one journalist to announce that the town was "assuming metropolitan airs." To one observer, it all "seem[ed] simply wonderful—the transformation. On this spot but a few short years ago the wolf howled and the coyote skulked. . . . Now . . . all is activity, and the modern electric light turns night into day." The company also built a well-stocked store, a model school building, and a clubhouse, the last of which featured rooms for billiards, games, and reading, as well as "a commodious lounging and drinking room" equipped with "a large Regina music box and a graphophone," not to mention a theater "provided with a full set of stage scenery, electric stage lights and other up-to-date features." These venues for diversion, education, and consumption were intended to create what

Camp and Plant called "an ideal community"—a place where "the temptations of life are reduced to a minimum" and every inhabitant, "from the humblest unskilled workman upwards," were "all . . . afforded opportunity for pleasant and comfortable homes, and an ideal livelihood."[10]

Osgood expected that workers would repay the company's largesse by exchanging worker solidarity and militancy for company loyalty and industrial harmony. And that is more or less how it turned out: the scene shaped the drama, or so the praise that Redstone garnered from social-reform periodicals would suggest. "The sense of responsibility . . . shown by this Western mining company in seeking to ameliorate the condition of its employees and to beautify their surroundings," the *Outlook* declared, "furnishes an example which Eastern operators might well emulate." Though "some stockholders might criticise the using of company funds for humanizing purposes," Osgood averred that he was "simply carrying out good business principles in promoting the welfare of his employees."[11]

Fighting organized labor had proved expensive, but giving in to it threatened to be costlier still. Colorado Fuel and Iron thus saw new company towns as a promising investment. And indeed, Osgood's neofeudal experiment paid dividends in the summer of 1903, when workers at Redstone and Coalbasin, the mining camp that supplied coal to Redstone's ovens, were among the few groups of Colorado mineworkers refusing to join a United Mine Workers strike. "Business is moving along here and at the basin," a source reported at the height of this nasty conflict, "as if there were no strike at all in the State." If Redstone had tamed the union, however, it could not ride herd on the industrial economy. Though Osgood continued to retreat to Cleveholm until his death in the 1920s, his model workers' town remained fully operational for less than a decade. High mining costs, excessive freight rates, and the continuing decline of silver mining together forced Colorado Fuel and Iron to shut down its Redstone operations in 1909.[12]

Expansion and Erosion

Only a small percentage of the hundreds of coal cars rolling along the rail corridors of the mountains and plains hauled fuel from Osgood's feudal utopia along the Crystal River. The southern fields, not Redstone, yielded most of the coal and coke on which consumers throughout this energy-hungry region were growing to depend. Coal companies simultaneously whetted this appetite and struggled to satisfy existing demand by extending their hold over labor, resources, and markets in Fremont, Huerfano, and Las Animas counties.

As Redstone generated positive attention as a model of industrial benevolence, new towns of quite a different character were taking shape along the main salients of coal industry expansion in the southern fields. Generally envisioned as mineworker enclaves, not mineowner retreats, set amid semiarid scrub instead of high-country splendor, planned by engineers instead of architects, built by contractors instead of craftsmen, and intended to promote efficiency instead of beauty, the new company towns of the southern fields bore scant resemblance to Redstone.

Osgood sought to transform the languishing, technologically obsolete steel mills he had inherited from William Palmer's Colorado Coal and Iron Company into paragons of modern efficiency. But for the renamed Minnequa Mills to succeed, Osgood's firm needed to secure both a better supply of iron ore and more extensive reserves of coking coal. The immense agglomeration of fixed capital at the steelworks could perform economically only if it ran continuously. Since colliers held the power to shut the works down, preventing militancy among mineworkers became more important than ever.

By the late 1890s, Colorado Fuel and Iron had purchased or leased 20,000 acres of additional coal lands in Colorado and New Mexico from subsidiaries of two railroads, the Colorado Midland and the Atchison, Topeka, & Santa Fe. Dwarfing these transactions, however, was the $750,000 purchase of the Colorado portion of the Maxwell Land Grant. Hundreds of Hispano and Anglo farmers and ranchers had settled on the grant in the preceding decades. The absentee Maxwell Land Grant Company called them squatters, and made this label stick through the so-called Stonewall Valley War of 1888 and a succession of legal wrangles that culminated in an 1894 court decision declaring the company to be sole owner of the entire grant. Despite these bitter disputes, Colorado Fuel and Iron had long coveted the coal beds beneath this 258,000-acre tract stretching south from the Purgatoire to the New Mexico border. Osgood's radical expansion of the Pueblo steelworks revived this old dream. As a consequence, a community of small farmers and truck gardeners living along a bend in the Purgatoire, like many farmers and herders on the grant itself, faced a fight they could not win. [13]

The Colorado & Wyoming Railway, built to transport the energy trapped beneath the Maxwell tract to furnaces, boilers, stoves, hearths, and generating stations throughout the region, hugged the banks of the Purgatoire. The river, like the railroad, though, followed its own logic. In the first years of the twentieth century track and stream collided with especially unfortunate consequences near a fertile stretch of bottomland cultivated by dozens of star-crossed Italian, Hispano, and Anglo agriculturists.

Court records document the variety and value of the bounty these small-holders had harvested from the bottomland soil. One family, the Cesarios, grew "corn, beans, pepper, turnips, celery, pumpkins, squashes, lettuce, parsnips, cabbage and other plants." Another, the Gagliardis, submitted this accounting of what the expansion of King Coal had cost them:

3,565 plants of celery at 3c per plant

One acre of Cabbages, 3000 plants injured at 5c each

1/4 acre Beets, 25 sacks, 50c per sack

1/8 acre Turnips, 22 sacks, 75c per sack

50 square feet Parsnips, 15 sacks at $1.00 each

1/2 acre Sugar Corn, 250 doz. at 10c

1/2 acre winter onions, 40 sacks at $1.00 per sack

355 Plants of Tomatoes, 10c each

175 hills of Hubbard Squash, 25c each

75 hills Pumpkins at 25c per hill

200 hills of Cucumbers at 25c[14]

Mine work often offered an industrial means to an agricultural end, and coal had surely lured at least some of the plaintiffs to southern Colorado. Read in this light, the Gagliardis' inventory was not just a tally of lost produce, but a catalogue of dashed hope.

The farmers' troubles began around 1900, when Colorado Fuel and Iron's railway subsidiary started the first of several efforts to "cut a new channel across a bend or curve made by the natural bed" of the river. This action, claimed the Cesarios, "changed the course" of the river, so that it was "continually caving" off large chunks of their best land. A freshet caused by a misguided effort by railroad engineers to shore up the river bank "destroyed a

cutting of Alfalfa . . . standing in shocks or small stacks," as well as "the vegetables at that time growing." The railway had forced "incanculable [*sic*], irreparable and continuing" losses, Manuelita Abeyta alleged, in a suit seeking
to enjoin the Colorado & Wyoming (C&W) from further damaging her crops
and those of twenty-three other families along the Lopez ditch.[15]

Abeyta's complaint charged the railroad with denying her and her neighbors "a bountiful harvest," an injustice that had legal, ecological, and moral
dimensions. Company counsel acknowledged the damage but attributed it to
forces beyond the company's control. The "unprecedented and extraordinary floods and freshets" that destroyed the crops of Abeyta, the Cesarios,
and others, they declared, "were the acts of God and inevitable accidents
which no human foresight could guard against or prevent."[16]

This argument may have swayed the pliant local jury that heard the case,
but there was nothing inevitable about the Purgatoire farmers' predicament.
John Osgood, not the Almighty, had set in motion the chain of events that
had caused the river to inundate the plaintiffs' land. To sell more steel, Osgood had to unearth more coal. If in the course of bridging the gap between
mine and mill, the tomatoes and Hubbard squashes planted by "Mexicans"
and Italians got in the way, then that was just too bad.[17]

Such dislocations came with the territory as Colorado Fuel and Iron expanded its operations on the Maxwell Grant. Soon after the company purchased the grant, CF&I lawyers initiated ejectment proceedings against the
remaining settlers. Many, though, proved reluctant to abandon their homes.
Dozens of Hispanos from El Valle de los Rancheros, for example, relocated
to a company farm, where they grew feed for mine mules on shares. Others
served not as tenants on the company domain, but as coke oven laborers and
coal miners in the new workscapes rising along the Purgatoire. A third group,
extending older patterns of migration and mobility, supplemented work in
the ovens and mines by cutting mine timbers, farming, gardening, or herd-
ing, in some cases as contract laborers, in others as proprietors.[18]

The Menace of the Open Camp

As coal companies expanded, they also sought to increase production at
many of their existing properties. The work culture and vernacular land-

scape that had developed over the previous decades in the open camps of the southern fields threatened this effort. As a consequence, companies sought to rationalize these messy spaces by attacking independent stores, saloons, and worker-owned housing.

Companies had long tolerated the colliers' hard-drinking ways; they even collected license fees from saloons on company land. By the 1900s, though, Colorado Fuel and Iron proclaimed alcohol the "greatest shortcoming" of its employees. In addition to sparking violence, the company claimed, drinking sapped the miners' productivity, squandered their wages, and gave them a safe place in which to air their grievances. The company therefore declared its intention to make its camps, or at least those parts "under the control of the management, as orderly and decent a place for men, women and children to live as can be found in the United States." Some working people surely benefited from the company's prohibition campaign; miners' wives, for example, lost little love on an addictive depressant that encouraged profligacy, illness, and abuse. Yet saloon closures also curtailed opportunities for interethnic socializing and labor organizing.[19]

Independent stores were also facing elimination. Colorado Fuel and Iron and Victor Coal and Coke, having refused to renew a batch of store contracts in the 1890s and 1900s, concentrated the retail trade in their camps under the Colorado Supply Company, which Osgood had initially organized in 1888 to operate boardinghouses and general stores. Although stock in both Colorado Fuel and Iron and Victor floundered in those years, the tight clique of majority stockholders enjoyed a compensatory perquisite that made up for the poor performance of their coal company shares: exclusive control over stock in the store company, which paid dividends of 20–27 percent *annually* during the early 1900s. As the store company mushroomed into one of the largest retail and wholesale establishments in southern Colorado, Osgood and his insiders profited handsomely, while reducing the risk that independent merchants would extend credit to strikers during labor disputes.[20]

Companies attacked worker-built structures still more zealously. Many of the shacks and adobes that mineworkers had built in years previous suffered the same fate as saloons, independent merchants, and Purgatoire Valley farmsteads, all casualties of the coal companies' twin goals of expanding production and neutralizing mineworker militancy. On occasion, companies simply bought miners out. Many coalfield families, though, turned a cold shoulder to company agents bearing cash. When a 1907 fire destroyed a neighborhood in the open camp of Coal Creek, the birthplace of the marching strike of 1894 as well as a more successful miners' strike in 1901, Colorado Fuel and Iron offered to buy up lots from all whose houses had been destroyed. Not a single family would sell. Through their refusal, the people of Coal Creek blocked the company's attempt to take over this crucial incubator for labor organization and mass mobilization.[21]

Corporations exercised greater leverage in camps where local mine managers had previously tolerated or even encouraged workers to build homes on company land. Executives bent on erasing vernacular landscapes from the face of the coalfields worked with company counsel to enact new procedures that presented householders with a Hobson's choice: Sign a ground lease or suffer dismissal and ejectment. These leases, while enabling alleged squatters to remain in their homes for a nominal rent, often a dollar a year, also allowed companies to revoke the contracts on just three days' notice. Disobey the mine boss? Join the union? Then take out your pay, head back over the threshold of the home you built or bought with the sweat of your brow. Tell family and friends what you've done, then pack up and begone. In this manner the coal companies turned leases into instruments of control.[22]

On other occasions the operators employed even nastier tactics. In Victor's Chandler camp, for instance, the company ordered miners who had built homes on land purchased from the company "to move or leave their houses." In its infinite generosity, Osgood's firm "offer[ed] to liquidate the purchase price." Several miners asked that the company also reimburse the taxes they had paid on "their" property. Victor refused the request and even fired several of the men who made it. "Being out of work," the *Cripple Creek Times* lamented, "they were either compelled to leave their families and seek employment elsewhere, or remain there and starve." In this manner Chandler changed from a workers' community into a company town.[23]

Colorado Fuel and Iron executives were sensitive to the damage that its enclosure movement might inflict on the already questionable public image of the company. They determined to use *Camp and Plant*—which was published by the company twice a month and circulated to an extensive list of managers, clerks, steelworkers, mineworkers, progressive reformers, and

One of the Recently Constructed Company Houses at Rouse.

A House in the Mexican Plaza, Rouse.

6.2a and b. Company Housing as Progress. "Rouse and Hezron: Two Picturesque Coal Camps in Huerfano County," *Camp and Plant* 1 (March 8, 1902): 198–199, Denver Public Library, Western History Collection.

journalists—to depict worker-built homes as uniformly primitive, crowded, and unclean. One of the many photographs published in the course of the company efforts to redirect public opinion contrasted a neat frame structure—"The Style of House That the Company Builds"—with a decrepit adobe cellar improbably twisted around a tree trunk—"The House a Mexican Laborer Built for Himself." Another contrasted a large white Victorian dwelling "recently constructed" by the company at Rouse with an aging adobe "House in the Mexican Plaza" adjoining the same camp. "There are but few 'shacks,' 'dug-outs,' 'shanties' or 'adobes' left in [Primero]," another article boasted, "and these the company is having demolished as rapidly as the owners' consent can be obtained. Such as remain," *Camp and Plant* reasoned, "serve but to mark the violent contrast in point of healthfulness and comfort between the dwellings erected by the former residents of this region and those put up by The Colorado Fuel and Iron Company for its men." The moral of such stories was clear: The onward march of progress and benevolence demanded that operators replace the older arrangements of space and property responsible for incubating disease and disorder with tidy towns composed of modern American workmen's homes.[24]

Putting Paternalism into Place

Whether new company towns took shape on land freshly incorporated into the company's domain or atop earlier mining camps, the purpose of these new places was to increase the efficiency of mining and coke making, restrict worker mobility, and eradicate the labor militancy that had erupted with such force in the marching strike of 1894. Whereas early coal camps had developed gradually and without any central plan, the closed camps built from the mid-1890s onward took shape with startling dispatch. "Little more than two years ago," a *Camp and Plant* article on one of the new Maxwell Grant camps exclaimed,

the solitude of Smith Canon was unbroken except by the straying ranch horse, the coyote and the wandering goat-herder and his charges. Today, nestling among the hills, is Primero, an exceedingly pretty and thrifty village of about 1,500 inhabitants, and instead of the ranch horse we see the mine mule, we hear the locomotive whistle instead of the howl of the wolf, and where the goat-herder, wrapped in his many scarfs, slumbered, the electric motor is moving thousands of tons of coal. Solitude is displaced by the hum of industry.[25]

Effecting so complete a metamorphosis, of course, required imagination, organization, resources, and a great deal of work.

Coal companies subordinated all else to the "hum of industry"; town planning was no exception. The engineering departments that supervised new mine development also designed most of the towns. One of their first challenges involved locating rail facilities, mine tunnels, surface structures, and various technological systems to streamline the way in which air, mules, men, timber, and of course coal moved between the subterranean workscape and the surface. Engineers also tried to secure a steady, sanitary supply of water for the camps by devising an extensive system of dams, tanks, pumps, pipes, and hydrants. Self-consciously "modern" camps such as Colorado Fuel and Iron's Primero and the American Smelting and Refining Company's Cokedale even featured electric streetlights, "an invaluable ally to morality" in the coalfields, just as in the Front Range cities they fueled.[26]

Pipes and power lines ran along streets generally laid out on gently sloping sites in rectilinear grids, an uncommonly efficient and economical way to order space. After surveying and staking out the town site, engineers began to fill the cells of the grid with structures. They often chose high ground near the mine mouth as a site for the town's central political and economic institutions: mine offices, the company store, and housing for the superintendent and other mine officials.[27]

Engineers laid out workers' housing on the surrounding tracts. Company houses, as *Camp and Plant* spilled a lot of ink in pointing out, were indeed more commodious than most of the shacks, shanties, and adobes they superseded. Adapted from common patterns and built of cement and wood, the three-to-six-room dwellings were often laid out in homogeneous rows, each house replicating its neighbor, though in a few new towns built to model the benefits of industrial paternalism, the operators added some variety by mixing shapes and finishes. Segundo had been "laid out in regular streets," for instance, but its houses featured "porches and projecting eaves . . . painted in

6.3. New Rouse: A Political Landscape. Copyright Colorado Historical Society, 20004310.

different pleasing colors." At a time when "monotonous uniformity" prevailed in many coal camps, Colorado Fuel and Iron dreamed that Segundo would evoke "the streets of a village of freeholders." Company aspirations to put up such facades, of course, did little to change the fact that mining families differed from freeholders in two fundamental ways: they neither owned their own dwellings nor governed their own communities.[28]

Mineworkers and their families began to migrate to the new towns even before contractors, tradesmen, and laborers had translated the blueprints into physical reality. First on the scene were the development workers who would drill tunnels and sink mine shafts. Once these practical miners had established the basic features of the mine workscape, other workers began to arrive. There was an unmistakably Western American cast to the mix of inhabitants: Hispano families displaced from the Maxwell Grant; Welshmen tempted by rumors of beautiful coal; Pennsylvanians whose restless energy impelled them to abandon overcrowded coal patches for wide-open spaces; African Americans seeking refuge from Jim Crow laws; wives and children rejoining their menfolk—these and other migrants began to find jobs and make new homes in the new company towns.

The companies knew that this ragtag gathering in an age-old borderland presented both a problem and a possibility. Two decades of industrial struggle in the southern fields had revealed the power of mine workscapes and work cultures to inculcate a strong sense of shared grievance among mining families of disparate backgrounds. The future, by contrast, still held the promise of harmony, but only if companies could compel coalfield migrants to join together as loyal employees and tractable "Americans" instead of as militant unionists. The deliberate destruction that striker-soldiers would unleash on the company town landscape during the Ten Days' War of 1914 would thus represent a reaction not merely to the killings at Ludlow, but also to the campaign Colorado Fuel and Iron and its competitors had embarked on to impose spatial and social order after the marching strike of 1894.

Commanding Space

C. E. Smith was neither a unionist nor a striker, yet he would experience the companies' quest for control just the same. Smith worked as a physician at Colorado Fuel and Iron's Minnequa Hospital, built in the late 1890s to accommodate the company's lengthening roster of steelworkers and miners. Smith's boss, Richard Corwin, was a busy man—director of the hospital, head of Colorado Fuel and Iron's Medical and Sociological Departments, an amateur Egyptologist and occasional member of the American School of Archaeology. Corwin expected the physicians under his command to take an active role in what he called prophylaxis—in both the literal and figurative meanings of the word. And so in January 1904 C. E. Smith set out on a southbound train from Pueblo at the height of the first coalfield-wide strike since 1894. After transferring to the Colorado & Wyoming in Trinidad, Smith traveled up the Purgatoire. Passing what remained of the truck farms planted by the Cesarios, the Abeytas, and their neighbors, he soon came to Primero. Spanish for "first," the town's name, like those of other camps—Segundo, Tercio, Cuarto, Quinto, and Sexto—belied the efforts of Colorado Fuel and Iron's leaders to shroud an empire based on numbers in Spanish romance.

C. E. Smith had a different sort of number on his mind, however, as his train pulled into Primero's new frame depot. The doctor had come to perform in the clubroom of the A. C. Cass School, named for a "close business associate and intimate friend" of Osgood. "Several of the Japanese miners" the company had imported to break the strike would later upstage Smith by appearing "in costume and graphically illustrat[ing] the sword dance and war songs . . . as danced and sung during the late Japanese-Chinese war." But the good doctor's troubles began the moment he "alighted from his train." Something about "his appearance excited the suspicions" of the camp guards entrusted with executing Colorado Fuel and Iron's quarantine campaign. After seizing the doctor, they "escorted him down the track," *Camp and Plant* reported with perverse amusement, and began "to search him for concealed weapons and for the purpose of conducting a quiet little general investigation as to his fitness to enter Primero." Had it not been "for the opportune appearance of one of the doctor's old patients matters would have gone hard with him."[29]

The company magazine found Smith's predicament humorous, but Colorado Fuel and Iron and its counterparts were deadly serious in their efforts to erect and enforce cordons sanitaires at Primero and other new company towns. Miners called such bounded and tightly supervised spaces closed camps, and for good reason. Designed to isolate workers from the ills of colliery work culture and the United Mine Workers, these camps were usually encircled by barbed wire fences. Camp marshals and mine guards patrolled the periphery, manned the gates that coal companies placed on public highways, and monitored the railroad tracks that connected the coal towns of southern Colorado with the outside world. Migrants who had traveled thousands of miles and crossed many national frontiers seeking work now had to cross one final border. Those allowed inside soon learned about "a rule observed in all the camps": any " 'undesirable citizen' [was] eliminated as soon as possible." The companies' expansive definition of "undesirable" types included union agitators, suspected union members, editors of labor-friendly newspapers and journals, peddlers, politicians of the wrong persuasion (Republicans and Populists in the 1890s, Democrats in the 1900s), state labor officials, and, on one occasion, even the governor of Colorado himself. And should colliers ever strike again, closed camps could be militarized, just as they had been in 1894, when guards and deputies stopped marchers in their tracks and kept fossil fuel flowing into Western markets.[30]

The coal companies' campaign to enclose and police space extended from highway and hillside to courtroom and polling place. Such political and legal machinations dated back to William Palmer's day, but the operators' interference in local government reached new heights in the early twentieth century, as the egregious general election of 1906 showed. Horton Pope of Osgood's Victor-American Fuel later confessed that he and the Colorado Fuel and Iron attorney, Cass Herrington, had conspired to secure a U.S. Senate seat for Simon Guggenheim, scion of the smelter-monopolists who had recently built a model coal-mining and coke-making town at Cokedale, a few miles west of Trinidad. Company executives were seeking not simply to place a friend in high office, but also to solidify and extend their control over underground and surface space by corrupting local governments. Since the state legislature still chose Colorado's senators, coal company lawyers were interested not in "bribing individual voters directly," Pope explained, "so much as in controlling every situation and position." Spending half a million dollars, and focusing their efforts on Huerfano and Las Animas counties, "they began with the county judge, the district attorney, the sheriffs and county officers."[31]

Guggenheim prevailed in his Senate bid; no less important, the friendly officials and unscrupulous jurists elected in this and other races proved important allies in the new company town campaign. Such men enabled operators to escape liability for mine accidents. Civil courts and coroners' juries in the southern fields earned a reputation for exonerating the coal companies, even in clear-cut instances of negligence. Corruption also made it easier for companies to evade responsibility for the damage their expansion inflicted. The Purgatoire truck farmer Cesario Abeyta, for instance, complained to no avail about the empanelment of a mine guard on the jury trying his wife's case. Coal companies "could get convictions where they wanted them," as Pope put it, "and exemptions from convictions where they wanted them." As "far as law" in the camps was concerned, recalled one old miner, "the company was law."[32]

As the companies solidified their control over "every situation and position," they co-opted public power and used it to advance private ambition. In the process, they essentially guaranteed that they "could readily free themselves" of virtually anyone "they wished to get rid of because he was an organizer or for any other reason." The Huerfano County sheriff Jefferson Farr, a former "stock man and Butcher," became the most feared enforcer of the operators' will. "I am the king of this county," Farr allegedly proclaimed to the union organizer Mike Livoda. So aggressive was Farr that the state legislator Casimiro Barela portrayed Farr's long tenure as a "reign of terror," and indeed Livoda, John Lawson, and other union men complained about the charges Farr trumped up and the beatings the sheriff ordered his lackeys to dispense.[33]

Coal companies pulled few punches in their campaign to contain militancy and halt the spread of unionization. The main challenge to their efforts came, not surprisingly, from the United Mine Workers. When the union tried to return to the southern fields in 1907 following a crushing defeat in the 1903–1904 miners' strike, Las Animas County sheriffs' deputies raided the union's Trinidad office and arrested union activists. The organizers were eventually released with a parting threat: "If he would leave Trinidad," one organizer was told, "he would not in future be molested." If he stayed in King Coal's growing dominion, however, he was taking his life into his hands.[34]

The prophylactic campaign, however, involved much more than asserting control over vernacular landscapes. If coal camps functioned like organisms, then their well-being depended not simply on isolation from sources of infection, but also on the strengthening of their ability to fight contagion. Colorado Fuel and Iron and its competitors thus extended their energies from the quest for expansion and enclosure to the reengineering of all the communities under company control. Store, school, home, and club each had its own role to play in the operators' efforts to eradicate the underlying causes of industrial conflict.

Consuming Designs

By the early twentieth century, Osgood's Colorado Supply Company had begun to launch new stores with lavish opening galas that drew hundreds, even thousands, of shoppers. The 1909 debut of the Morley store, just north of the New Mexico line in the rugged Raton Mesa country, presented a particularly arresting sight. Swastikas—a common motif in Southwestern Indian art—graced "yellow wagons, the paper bags, wrapping paper, stationary and every other representative portion of the store's paraphanalia [*sic*]." Why

6.4. Colorado Supply Company Store, Primero, 1916. Copyright Colorado Historical Society, 10038066.

would a company whose stores served coal miners and steelworkers appropriate a symbol from Native Americans? Why would it build the Morley store and other structures in Mission Revival styles? And why would it stock newly opened company stores with Navajo blankets, "Zuni bows and arrows, Zuni blankets, Navajo rings, bracelets, breastpins, buttons, spoons, belts and sashines," and other Indian handicrafts? Such questions hint at some of the complexities of the retail business in King Coal's expanding realm.[35]

Colorado Fuel and Iron had displaced Hispanic and Italian truck farms along the Purgatoire bottomlands, leveled adobes throughout older coal camps, and enclosed the Maxwell Grant and other Hispano homelands. Its store company added insult to injury when it borrowed a page from the Santa Fe Railroad and the other Southwestern corporations responsible for creating what Carey McWilliams, perhaps the most perceptive social critic of the Western scene during the mid-twentieth century, denounced as a "Spanish fantasy past." Company officials described Morley's architecture as "really very appropriate to this region," an "artistic reproduction of an old Spanish fort," but local Hispanos probably saw little honor in the reference. In southern Colorado as in other parts of the Southwest, cultural appropriation reinforced material dispossession.[36]

Once customers passed beyond the pseudo-Spanish facade of the Morley store, they found displays of plenty that called to mind not colonial Santa Fe or the Hopi mesas but rather the commercial districts of Denver or Chicago. "There is scarcely an article that could be thought of that is not found in their stores," one Colorado Supply Company booster proclaimed. And indeed, photographs of Supply Company stores show surprisingly large and varied stocks of branded consumer products. Larger facilities had departments not only for meat, groceries, and dry goods, but also for furniture, Italian foodstuffs, Indian arts and crafts, and other items.[37]

That company stores generally did not look much different from mercantile establishments beyond the coal barons' purview—and tried so hard to forge an image out of imagined Southwestern yesterdays—seems odd, given the accusations leveled against the Colorado Supply Company and its competitors. "For a miner to escape being plucked by one of the Company's stores," a typical lament began, "is equal to subjecting himself to every mean, little, annoying, discrimination that the management can inflict upon him. It may not at once result in his dismissal from the mine if he buys anything outside of the store, but there will be a number of small, sneaking, underhanded ways"—short weights, bad room assignments—"in which he will be made to feel that he is being discriminated against." Should these tactics fail "to convince him that he must not buy his goods where he can buy them the cheapest then he is told by the superintendent that he is no longer needed in the company's service." Such grievances ensured that the eradication of company stores would figure among the demands that southern Colorado's colliers made whenever they went out on strike.[38]

Yet beneath the "pluck-me store" stereotype was a more complex reality. Coalfield migrants exercised considerable autonomy as shoppers. LaMont Montgomery Bowers, the crotchety executive dispatched by the Rockefeller interests to represent the family at Colorado Fuel and Iron, expressed a determination "to prevent our employees being swindled by unscrupulous Jews, Italians and other cut-throat dealers who would control the business if we should withdraw and leave the field open," yet peddlers continued to tout their wares throughout the camps of the southern coalfields. Sears, Montgomery Ward's, and other firms also did "an immense amount of mail order business in the camps." John Osgood, who claimed that "from one to a half dozen traders wagons" traveled from Trinidad to nearby coal-mining communities "delivering goods," admitted that these traders could "do on some things better than we owing to the assortment that they can get." Lest one doubt the coal king's word, a letter from a Sopris miner to the *United Mine Workers' Journal* on the eve of the marching strike took pains to point out that the Colorado Supply Company store was "not a pluck-me any more than the private dealer's store. In many instances it is cheapest," and in others "not any higher in price than private stores." Trinidad and Walsenburg bustled on Saturday evenings with men, women, and children who poured down from the surrounding camps to socialize and shop; after mine paydays, the towns even took on a "circus day appearance." Miners, one old collier remembered, "traded at the company store although it was their privilege to buy elsewhere." Even people with no connection to coal mining sometimes traded at the Supply Company. All told, company stores treated mining camp residents not as captive customers who could be forced into buying a limited stock of overpriced necessities, but rather as consumers who could be tempted into purchasing items ranging from the essential to the frivolous.[39]

In the competition for mining family custom, company stores possessed many advantages. With more than a dozen locations, the Colorado Supply Company wielded immense wholesale purchasing power. Company stores also profited from their close association with mining companies. Certainly claims that superintendents and mine bosses harassed miners into trading at company stores are too widespread to dismiss. The companies' efforts to enclose town space both excluded many rival retailers and peddlers from the camps and made it easier for company officials to monitor the purchases of mining families.

The scrip system reinforced these advantages. Payday came to most coal camps just once a month. Many households had difficulty making ends meet from pay envelope to pay envelope. Companies therefore offered employees scrip, paper certificates deducted from the next month's pay envelope. These certificates offered miners what one called "just an advanced payment"—or, in other words, a credit against future earnings. Not only did scrip run miners into debt, but it could be redeemed only for its full value at company stores. Mining families who wished to use scrip at other retailers' could still do so—they could even try to hawk it for cash—but only at a discount, which eroded their purchasing power. Moreover, the vicissitudes of mine workscapes and coal markets made it impossible for families to predict future wages in advance. A bad room assignment, an early spring, a falling roof, or any number of other common occurrences could transform short-term credit into long-term debt, leaving a worker little recourse but to remain on his current job.[40]

Ultimately, legalized debt peonage and other forms of coercion worked in tandem with shining storerooms to strengthen the power that mining companies exercised over their employees. As superintendents leaned on mineworkers to shop only at company stores, storekeepers were marketing an inclusive American identity based on consumption of "the newest and latest of everything," so that coalfield migrants would spend their earnings—and perhaps a little more—on a "constantly changing" array of stock. When mining families found they could not afford the bill of goods the companies had sold them, they lashed out at the employers, whom they blamed for tempting the migrants with consumer desires few miners could fulfill—and hence into the emasculating trap of debt and dependence.[41]

Helping the Foreigner Help Himself

Though stores and company houses might help breed loyalty, industrial paternalists largely entrusted the cultivation of citizenship and contentment among current and future employees to institutions whose charter was more explicitly educational. "The work done in co-operation with the schools in the several camps," *Camp and Plant* declared, "has been by far the most important and has consumed by far the largest proportion of the very considerable sums which The Colorado Fuel and Iron Company has spent for the betterment of its men." Companies devoted these "considerable sums" not to property taxes, which they shirked shamelessly, but instead to initiatives they could control more closely: school construction, adult education, and kindergartens.[42]

The schools that Colorado Fuel and Iron built reflected romantic commonplaces about native peoples and their inevitable corollary, nature. Dr. Richard Corwin credited an *Indian School Journal* article with the inspiration for naming a new camp Katcina. The word, he explained, "comes to us from the Hopi Indians. It is the title of a song sung by the lonely night traveler to drive away the evil spirits that are supposed to be abroad in the darkness, and something of a prayer to the Great Spirit to shield one from harm and danger." Corwin found it "fitting that in this new and model town, whose very name implies the banishment of the spirits of darkness, the newest and most modern type of school house is to stand as the white man's 'Katcina,' driving away the spirits of ignorance and shielding the young from harm and danger."[43]

Though the company soon renamed this camp Morley after the nearest rail stop, it continued to perceive schools as a crucial shield against unions and other "spirits of darkness." And so while many American children learned their ABC's inside buildings named after national heroes, the corporate patriarchy that ruled the southern fields eschewed the usual short list of school namesakes—George Washington, Abraham Lincoln, Horace Mann— in favor of John C. Osgood, Richard Corwin, A. C. Cass, and other company fathers. Conceiving of schools as "real social centers for the young and old," company educators also made these facilities available for church and club meetings and adult education.[44]

"We truly help the foreigner to help himself," the company asserted. As part of this self-help campaign, male teachers gave English lessons to miners for a monthly fee of three to five dollars. A company bulletin explained, "In enabling [the foreigner] to understand our language by opening to him our schools, our settlements, and kindred institutions, we pave the way to good American citizenship." The oppositional Americanism that miners had celebrated during the marching strike of 1894 with republican orations and American flags was, of course, precisely what the coal companies sought to contain in their quest to reconstitute William J. Palmer's vision of Colorado as an "inner temple of Americanism." Adult education programs in the coal camps defined "good" citizenship in terms the general could have approved: respect for constituted authority, loyalty to the company, and compliance with white middle-class prescriptions regarding gender roles and consumer tastes. While men and boys learned English, coalfield women received instruction from female teachers in the hallowed duties of wifedom and motherhood. Domestic demonstrations on cooking, home decoration, sanitation, and other topics prepared migrant women to adapt the ways of middle-class white matrons in Pueblo and Peoria.[45]

Men and women in the new camps sometimes embraced domestic and linguistic instruction. Since they did so for their own reasons and on their own terms, though, welfare paternalists questioned the efficacy of adult education. "It is difficult to change the ways and manners of adults," as one reformer complained. "Their habits are formed and are not easily altered. With age comes indifference, a desire to be let alone and a loss of ambition." Company educators increasingly concentrated their efforts on children, in the belief that they were "tractable, easily managed and molded," lacking "set ways to correct and recast."[46]

Salvaging the innate potential of coal camp youth constituted an end in itself for industrial paternalists, but it also promised further rewards. By checking the spread of deviance and militancy from one generation to the next, companies aspired to eliminate these ills from the new company towns, and thus to inoculate these spaces against the contagion of unionism. Hoping that kindergartens would make potential strikers into loyal worker-citizens, Colorado Fuel and Iron executives invested a great deal of money and hope in these programs. Camp children, unlike their refractory parents, afforded "excellent material on which to work," one reformer declared, "and it is marvelous how soon the spirit of Americanism is imbibed." The walls of Palmer's "inner temple of Americanism" may have crumbled, but paternalist educators felt confident that they could enlist the children of the coal camps to put them back together again.[47]

Welfare reformers endeavored to assimilate the polyglot children of the coalfields into the American nation and the company family through a combination of methods. Since most coalfield children began kindergarten unable to understand English, the curriculum steered away from academic work and toward "physical culture," "construction work," and "rhythm work." Nature study and school gardens were particularly popular. Company educators believed that by silently "watching germinating seeds and growing plants," students would absorb "an effective sermon teaching the miracles of nature and the wisdom of practicing what nature teaches"—hardly a neutral lesson, given welfare reformers' habit of seeing labor militancy as a horrible mutation of the natural order.[48]

Once they had learned enough English to begin reading, "the children are surrounded by the best influences," explained the Colorado Fuel and Iron kindergarten head Mrs. M. G. Grabill. From this beginning, they could be "brought in touch with the best literature, and taught to spend their leisure hours in useful reading or harmless amusement, instead of wasting their time idly on the streets. The result undoubtedly will be higher citizenship." To Grabill and other educators, "the streets" embodied the hazards of the vernacular landscape. Such heterogeneous and public spaces facilitated the sociability, mobility, and disorder that seemed to define "lower" citizenship. In the process, they offered conduits for the spread of opposition and labor unrest.

Carefully supervised kindergartens offered an antidote to the unruly thoroughfares outside. Children reared in spaces of domestic order and restraint, welfare capitalists believed, would become dutiful citizens schooled to live out the rest of their lives in productive labor and "harmless amusement." Kindergartens, like other elements of the company schools, thus reflected the combined spatial and social power to which the coal company attorney Horton Pope had referred when he spoke of "controlling every situation and position."[49]

Home Safe Home

Social welfare reformers trusted schools not simply with molding the next coalfield generation, but also with wedging company paternalism into the ostensibly private space of workers' homes. As one kindergarten advocate explained, the company "recognized that this institution not only takes the child in hand at its most impressionable period, but that it furnishes a center from which to radiate influences that affect the whole social betterment situation." Another declared, "The kindergarten is not only a link between the home and the school, but it is also a very simple and persuasive interpreter of the school to the home and of the teaching function of the home to mothers and fathers." In this context, a kindergarten teacher could be "more than an instructor of children.... She is a social settlement worker co-operating with and seeking to stimulate every broadly educational work in the community in which she lives."[50]

Welfare reformers in the coalfields, like their progressive colleagues in industrial cities and on Indian reservations, sought to enlist the "restraining and refining influences" of the home as a prophylactic against actual and figurative contagion. In this campaign, miners' cottages were not just dwellings: they were also repositories of moral virtue. Through exterior landscaping and interior design, welfare capitalists sought to turn company houses into sanctuaries where mining families could lead orderly middle-class lives, protected from the temptations of street, saloon, and workscape.[51]

An ideal company home, like the closed camp that contained it, began with a fence to delimit the private realm within. Welfare reformers urged coalfield families to plant the ground between picket fence and cottage wall. "Give to a house a few vines," one reformer effused, "surround it with a yard of green grass in which are a few beds of flowers and two or three trees and you have transformed it entirely. You have changed it from a mere house and lot into a home, ... a spot whereon the eye rests with satisfaction and enjoyment and in which the whole family may take especial pride." Yards, gardens, and the pride they fostered, company officials hoped, might root a workforce of mobile migrants in company ground, while yielding food to fuel the miners' labors and blunt their demands for higher wages.[52]

As fences and gardens performed their magic outside the workers' homes, other tactics would cultivate respectability within. Attacking miner-built homes for offering "no inducement for anything above bare animal subsistance [sic]," *Camp and Plant* waxed eloquent on the subject of interior decorating. "A home must show the traces of sympathy and of love," an article dripping with middle-class values declared. "A true mother will strive earnestly to make her home not only as attractive and lovely as possible, but she will also try to combine comfort with beauty." Potted plants offered a simple start. Better still, though, were "vines, flowers, a canary bird and sunshine." Indulgent though such "luxuries" might have seemed to hard-pressed mining families, reformers blithely asserted that "nearly everyone can afford them. Indeed, a home cannot afford to be without them."[53]

Coalfield paternalists urged workers to complement the introduction of plants and pets with touches of cultural refinement. *Camp and Plant* published full-page reproductions of great artworks. One issue featured Van Dyck's *Baby Stuart,* Millet's *Angelus,* and "a list of good frescoes and paintings, reproductions of which may safely be recommended for household decoration." Another included Raphael's *Sistine Madonna* above a caption that urged mothers to take advantage of the "wonderful reproducing processes" that made it possible to "beautify and dignify" homes by hanging "noble pictures which our children will learn to love and understand, and by which their lives and characters may be enobled [*sic*] *and* refined." Once "photographed on the sensitive nature of childhood," these wholesome images could "never be lost or eradicated."[54]

The emphasis *Camp and Plant* placed on mechanical reproductions echoed a deeper concern with the crucial role of camp homes in reproducing the mine workforce. Welfare paternalists endeavored to ease the difficult lives of coal camp women and improve the health of the mining population by making women's work more orderly, efficient, and scientific. "The time has passed," *Camp and Plant* warned, "when a cook can depend upon instinct, intuition and luck. No longer does one care to risk his life in the hands of a person who is ignorant of the chemical properties of food material and the chemical changes wrought by the processes of cooking." A spate of articles, lectures, and courses aimed to change women's drudgery into modern work. The sacred task of making company houses into homes, it seemed, was too important to entrust to amateurs.[55]

Through these efforts, mining companies endeavored to mold domestic environments, so that "harmful tendencies" would not inhibit the development of boys who would soon begin to work underground or of girls destined in most instances to become colliers' wives. Colorado Fuel and Iron assured housekeepers that "the results" of filling their homes with "good books" and "the best periodicals" would "show up in the making of a finer man or woman." The company's taste, of course, was decidedly conservative. Paternalists favored respectable newspapers, wholesome classics, and mainstream magazines. Redstone's clubhouse, for instance, subscribed to

Harper's, Scribner's, Youth's Companion, St. Nicholas, Outing, Ladies' Home Journal, and the *Craftsman;* while its library featured "full sets" of such authors as Washington Irving, James Fenimore Cooper, Rudyard Kipling, and Charles Dickens. The same arbiters of taste denounced detective, adventure, and Western stories as "unhealthful" and "abnormal." Such "yellow-backed" dime novels endangered "susceptible" young minds. More perilous still were "'Yellow' Periodicals" with their sensationalist critiques of corporate perfidy and capitalist excess. Industrialists saw the worker's home, in short, as at once a site of reproduction and an ideological space capable of "surround-[ing] these brothers"—and sisters—"of alien birth with an environment that shall represent all that is best in the political, intellectual and spiritual life of our state."[56]

Company Culture

Coalfield executives intended company clubs, like company houses, schools, and stores, to reorient the loyalties of mining families, from production to consumption, from mutualism at work to individualism in the market, from old-country chauvinism to what would later be called 100 percent American-ism. The belief that boredom begat drinking at best—and unionization at worst—had already inspired many companies to eliminate saloons from their property. To fill this gap, companies introduced clubs. These organizations met either in the multiple-use rooms of the new schoolhouses or in dedi-cated clubhouses featuring a large room for meetings, as well as in smaller reading rooms and parlors equipped with billiards and card tables. John Osgood, a whiskey connoisseur, declared, "My own opinions are not such that I want to prevent anyone from drinking." Instead, Osgood introduced the idea of serving alcohol in company clubs under "certain well-defined regulations" enacted to prevent the "rioting and disorder" that so troubled executives. Colorado Fuel and Iron banned women from club bars; it also limited the hours during which liquor could be served and forbade the work-ingmen's hallowed practice of "treating" fellow miners to rounds.[57]

Having eliminated or restricted drinking, coal companies proceeded to redirect their workers' attention to a range of programs intended to brighten the "serious and solemn" life of the camps, as David Griffiths—practical

miner, former state mine inspector, and Colorado Fuel and Iron official—
sympathetically described it. In addition to musical programs such as Dr.
C. E. Smith's performance at Primero, clubs offered lectures on topics such
as European art, the discovery of America, and public health. Speakers
brought in by the company educated workers about germ theory and disease
transmission and also sought to indoctrinate them in bourgeois conceptions
of environmental and social order. In addition to entertaining audiences,
minstrelsy shows offered a crash course in American ideas of blackness and
whiteness. Film screenings also combined diversion and didacticism. Griffiths perceptively called film "the silent pedagogue of the age": it communi-
cated a range of powerful ideas about American social, economic, and cultural life in a visual medium easily understood by the many coal camp
residents who could neither read nor understand English.[58]

Through such activities, the companies hoped to counteract the solidarity
and militancy that had developed underground. At the dedication ceremony
for Starkville's Harmony Hall, men, women, and children crowded into every corner of a brand-new forty-foot by seventy-foot structure on a winter
evening in 1902. There they listened to a cleric implore them to remember
that "during these last twent[y]-five years of Starkville's history, 'harmony of
heart' has been on the whole the leading spirit of the place." This singular
force, he claimed, had "held the miners united among themselves and united
with their patrons. . . . It was to harmony, realized and persevered in," he asserted, "that Starkville owes the secret of her past success."[59]

The minister invoked the same dreams of classlessness and industrial
peace that had permeated William Jackson Palmer's visions three decades
before. Yet the very setting for his speech was a direct product of the turbu-
lent history of labor-management struggle in the southern fields. Colorado
Fuel and Iron had built Harmony Hall, after all, not to memorialize a preexisting condition of peace, but to contain the mobility and militancy that had
erupted with such force in 1894 and in previous conflicts.

Anyone who set foot in this carefully controlled space, the minister suggested, consented to join a united and contented corporate family protected
by vigilant company fathers from the scourges lurking outside. "Whenever
in the future you enter this hall," the minister admonished his audience,
"look upon it" and "let it remind you that it was harmony that wrought your

past success; let it convince you that in harmony lies the best guarantee of coming prosperity and finally let no one come in or go out of Harmony Hall without the clear consciousness that all his relations with his fellow men are friendly and harmonious."[60]

When the mining families of Starkville joined together some eighteen months later, they did so not in harmony with the company, but in solidarity with each other. In the process, they illustrated just how seriously the coal companies had misjudged the extent of workers' discontent. Stores, schools, homes, and clubhouses, like the militarization of camp perimeters, the corrupting of local governments, and the expansion of company control over vernacular landscapes, had failed to prevent solidarity and unionism from asserting themselves again. In truth, the new company towns left the southern coalfields more susceptible than ever to the ills they had been designed to eradicate.

What the Workers Wanted

Frank Hearne shared at least two traits with the minister who christened Harmony Hall in Starkville: a desire for harmony and a shocking ignorance of the contentious history of labor-management relations in the southern fields. After the Rockefellers acquired a controlling interest in Colorado Fuel and Iron in a series of transactions culminating in summer 1903, they offered Hearne, the former National Tube Company vice president, a five-year contract paying him fifty thousand dollars a year to replace Osgood at the helm of CF&I. Hearne arrived in Colorado in September 1903 to find the gold miners of Cripple Creek and Telluride, the silver miners of Lake City, the smelter workers of Colorado City and Durango, and the coal miners of the southern fields all up in arms. And though these disputes were spearheaded by different organizations—the more radical Western Federation of Miners in the hard-rock mines and smelters, the more moderate United Mine Workers in the collieries—all were part of a larger push by Colorado workers for an eight-hour day. Southern Colorado's coal miners also sought fair weights, better ventilation, a 20 percent increase in tonnage rates, twice-monthly paydays, and nondiscrimination against union members.[61]

In a published interview, Hearne complained: "This labor situation is puzzling. I don't know what grievances the men have. Why, I don't believe there is a corporation in the world that treats its employes as the Colorado Fuel and Iron company does. We have mighty near solved all the sociological problems in our towns in the southern part of the state. It is an object [lesson] just to see how things are handled down there. We have club rooms and public baths for the employes. They have the cleanest streets and the best sanitary arrangements of any town in Colorado." Mine workers, Hearne had been told, "get good pay, too, and they have short hours. I don't see what more they want."[62]

What had Hearne overlooked? He recognized that coal companies had spent large sums over the previous decade to reform the way they did business. The executives who had envisioned the new company towns saw them as showpieces for progressive paternalism. And yet if these experiments in welfare capitalism had in all likelihood improved the quality of housing, schooling, health care, and entertainment for many mining families, darker realities nonetheless lurked beneath the freshly painted facades of the new company towns. Mining companies had planned, designed, built, and operated closed camps because they believed that by refashioning coalfield environments, they could prevent rebellions like the marching strike of 1894. Rather than the physical manifestations of corporate omnipotence, new company towns were actually the embodiment of the long and still unfolding struggle between workers and companies.[63]

Even after the majority of miners and mining families in the southern coalfields inhabited closed camps, workers nonetheless retained more than enough power and autonomy to upset the companies' plans. Despite the company drive to destroy miner-built dwellings and vernacular landscapes, most open camps remained vital, and workers continued to occupy houses and settlements of their own even on the edge of new company towns such as Segundo. Despite the destruction of the Purgatoire truck gardens and the enclosure of the Maxwell Grant, connections between mining camps and the surrounding countryside remained strong. Despite the coal companies' temperance campaign, saloons beyond company control still did a brisk business by offering men space in which to vent, fight, and bond. Despite efforts to "Americanize" the mine workforce, old-country ties endured, as the rapid return of hundreds of Colorado miners to the Balkans following the outbreak of war there in 1912 attested. And despite the comprehensive campaign to remake the environments in which unionism flourished, the United Mine Workers remained intent on expanding into the southern fields. It waged a small but successful strike in Fremont County in 1901 and an all-out organization drive culminating in the 1903 declaration of a crippling strike (the very one Hearne found so difficult to understand).[64]

What Colorado Fuel and Iron's new leader failed to grasp, then, was that miners continued to want the same things they had always wanted: safety, fellowship, a higher quality of life, autonomy, dignity, and basic freedoms. The paradox of prophylaxis was that instead of confining the struggle over such issues to the workplace, closed camps actually exacerbated conflicts between miners and managers. By making home, community, and electoral politics the key battlefields in the struggle for control of the coalfields, companies unwittingly transformed disputes rooted in subterranean workscapes into an all-out struggle in which the very meaning and fate of America seemed to hang in the balance.

In "The Economic Struggle in Colorado," a treatise published serially by the reformist journal *Arena* in 1905–1906, the respected attorney and progressive gadfly J. Warner Mills advanced a passionate, systematic critique of Colorado's labor woes. A firm believer in "the supreme value of the economic measure in judging of men and of motives and of events and of institutions," Mills credited the industrial transformations of the previous decades with remaking an arid, isolated land into "a great empire" whose inhabitants held "the key to a vast vault, filled full and running over with precious treasures, and to a still vaster land, 'flowing with milk and honey.'" Evenly distributed, this bounty could have provided plenty for all. That was not the case, he wrote: "The stakes to fight for are so vast and extraordinary, that, under the present economy, it is unreasonable to expect there can be anything approaching an equitable division of the products of labor without dispute, turmoil and friction."

In the decades since William Palmer's hopeful visions, a clique of "throne-powers"—the railroads and the smelter trust, the gold and silver operators, Denver's public utility corporations and the large coal corporations—had managed to wrap "their distended maws" around "the choicest franchises, lands and opportunities . . . to be found in the West." Mills blamed "inequalities before the law" for reinforcing "inequalities in the enjoyment of special privileges, natural opportunities, and resources." The "barons of privilege" who controlled the mineral-intensive industrial economy did not simply usurp the people's patrimony by turning energy, ore, federal lands, urban space, and other public goods toward private gain; they also tried to disguise their ill-gotten privilege behind law-abiding respectability. The determination of right and wrong in the region, Mills lamented, had become "so grounded in the existing economy that it gives no word of condemnation for such inequality in the domain of force and violence."

Mills singled out the coal barons for particular scorn, assailing them for acting as if they had "acquired a right from God / To rule this coal and land and sod." And though he disparaged colliers as a mere "residuum"—"slow to comprehend the peonage" created by the new company town campaign of the previous decade, "and still slower to resort to the remedies of self-protection"—Mills surely knew that southern Colorado's mineworkers had already waged three general strikes and dozens of local disputes by the time "The Economic Struggle in Colorado" appeared in print. It would take seven long years for the working people of the coalfields to rise up again. When the next strike inevitably came, opposition to company towns and the "peonage" they represented would fan the flames first of resistance, then of rebellion.[65]

7

Shouting the Battle Cry of Union

Ten years after Frank Hearne expressed puzzlement over what the miners of the southern fields wanted, and almost two decades after the mass mobilizations of 1894, an even larger procession of mineworkers, women, and children was wending its way through the streets of Trinidad. The mood on this late-summer day in 1913 was tense, the mineworkers, in one observer's estimation, were "in a fighting mood, determined to wring the rights they [had] been denied so long from the Standard Oil–owned mine owners by force."[1]

Men, women, and children had traveled a long, winding road to reach this precipice; many years of struggle and suffering seemed to drive them toward the abyss before them. Nearly half a century earlier, William Jackson Palmer had ridden through these same streets before espying the coal seams in which many of the men and boys in this procession labored. The general dreamed of using the energy buried beneath the arid soil of this prematurely stagnant frontier to fulfill the region's latent promise. Palmer's enterprises and those of his competitors had indeed transformed these Western lands, but not in the manner the general had intended. They had failed to avoid the social and environmental destruction that the young American had witnessed on his tour of Britain in the 1850s; instead, the darker traits of industrialism had crossed the Atlantic and the Appalachians, the Mississippi and the Great Plains, intact. The classless utopia that Palmer had imagined was Colorado's destiny had yet to materialize. Instead, the Rocky Mountain region became an industrial society dependent on fossil fuel: exploitative, corrupt, unequal, rife with violence and excess.[2]

Those who marched through the streets of Trinidad on this September day had come from every corner of the earth to mine for coal, the humble rock without which this brave new world would not have come into being. Driven from their old homes by poverty or repression, drawn by the promise of good pay and safe conditions, and brought to Colorado by padrones, steam powered technology, and the migrant grapevine, they had left the worlds they had known to build this new one.

An Italian brass band led the procession of marchers. A Welsh choir trailed just behind, followed by more than 250 delegates and more than 3,000 "sympathizers" drawn from almost every camp in the southern fields. Signs of the work these men did would have been visible in the coal tattoos, missing fingers, and wooden limbs of many marchers. Also in evidence were the craft values of pride, solidarity, and militancy, reinforced by less-evident memories of the old country, workscape disasters, fallen partners or family members, and hopes forsaken.[3]

The roads the marchers followed to Trinidad not only stretched back to the subterranean natural world in which miners labored, but also led down from the company towns that coal corporations had constructed in response to the marching strike of 1894. The hundreds of women and children who joined in the 1913 procession, though they still marched behind an all-male group of delegates, far outnumbered the dozens directly involved in the 1894 marches—an indication of just how completely the new company towns had failed. The cause for which the marchers were fighting had changed, too, expanding from workplace grievances and economic issues to encompass demands for the eradication of the company town system and for the overthrow of company tyranny.

This procession built on a bedrock of grievance and struggle, but it had taken more than unrest to make a movement. The United Mine Workers had provided the impetus for the march; the union had also fixed the destination, Castle Hall, the venue for a state mineworkers' convention.

The United Mine Workers had returned to the southern fields in 1912. Already embroiled in a two-year-long strike in Colorado's northern fields, the union sought to shut off the flow of strikebreakers and strikebreaking coal from the southern fields. Using the so-called inside-outside technique, the UMW methodically set about organizing the mineworkers of Fremont, Huerfano, and Las Animas counties. One organizer—the outside man— sought work in a closed camp, where he secretly began to recruit potential union sympathizers, often through clandestine meetings underground or in the hills above the camps. The inside man, meanwhile, ingratiated himself with mine officials. Having won their trust, he then volunteered to help root out suspected unionists. Instead of turning in card-carrying United Mine Workers members, however, he handed over the names of nonunion men. Thanks to this method, credulous managers discharged and evicted hundreds of loyal workers, leaving behind a growing percentage of union members and sympathizers.[4]

The "big three" companies—Colorado Fuel and Iron, Victor-American, and Rocky Mountain Fuel—responded by stepping up their repression and refusing to meet with union leaders. By late summer 1913, the companies' intransigence left little hope for a peaceable settlement, and the mid-August murder of union organizer Gerald Lippiatt in the streets of Trinidad by two agents of the Baldwin-Felts Detective Agency had set everyone on edge. The people of the coalfields now steeled themselves for a showdown that had been nearly half a century in the making.[5]

The workers entered this battle as many had entered past conflicts: joined in song. In the long, bloody fight to come, the song they sang would serve as a dirge and a lament. For now, though, they roared out "The Colorado Strike Song." The "great parade" of people all "took up the swelling chorus of the song," more than three thousand voices joining together to defy servitude by belting out lyrics of liberation penned by the youthful Frank Hayes, the UMW's Socialist vice president, and set to the rousing Civil War tune "The Battle Cry of Freedom."

> We will win the fight today, boys,
> We'll win the fight today,
> Shouting the battle cry of union;
> We will rally from the coal mines,
> We'll battle to the end,

Shouting the battle cry of union.
The union forever, Hurrah! boys, hurrah!
Down with the Baldwins, up with the law;
For we're coming, Colorado, we're coming all the way,
Shouting the battle cry of union.
We have fought them here for years, boys,
We'll fight them in the end,
Shouting the battle cry of union.
We have fought them in the North, now we'll fight them in the South,
Shouting the battle cry of union.
We are fighting for our rights, boys,
We're fighting for our homes,
Shouting the battle cry of union.
Men have died to win the struggle, they've died to set us free,
Shouting the battle cry of union.

As the men, women, and children of the coalfields voiced their readiness to fight for justice, freedom, and home, "all Trinidad throbbed with the song."[6]

When the parade reached its destination, the delegates peeled away from the brass band, choir, and "sympathizers" and filed into Castle Hall. Once inside, they again began singing "The Colorado Strike Song." Soon "the full-throated roar of it was taken up by the miners outside." For several minutes, "the thunder of strong men's voices" reverberated through the summer air, then died down as the Trinidad Convention was called to order.[7]

John McLennan, president of the Colorado State Federation of Labor and a United Mine Workers member, inaugurated this historic meeting by declaring: "'If a strike is called the strike will be carried on with all the characteristic vigor of the organization and every coal miner in America will be in back of us.'" After this promise of whole-hearted support from the four-hundred-thousand-member-strong mineworkers' union, the work of the convention began. "Reports of delegates concerning working conditions in their respective mines" dominated the program for the first two days. A succession of several dozen mineworkers took the podium, many accompanied by interpreters. Speaking of the workscapes in which they labored, the towns in which they lived, they recalled the state's horrible record of mine explosions and accidents; during 1913 alone, 104 men would die in Colorado's mines, and 6 in the mine workings on the surface, in accidents that widowed 51 and left 108 children fatherless. The speakers told of watching partners and friends die in falls of rock and coal—about bad air and short weights, pit bosses who demanded bribes for good places, incompetent superintendents, bullying mine guards, and rapacious company stores. They complained about government of the companies, by the companies, for the companies. "Every man," Tony Lamont of Cokedale complained, "is closely watched and if the guards suspect him of belonging to the organization, he is discharged." Charles Goold of Rockvale complained that he and his fellows were earning "a bare existence" only. "Every morning that I went into the mine," Joe Morzox of Tabasco declared, "I thought I would never come out alive."[8]

In "recitals of alleged wrongs dating back many years," the delegates told the history of the southern coalfields as they had experienced it. Fremont County delegate T. X. Evans, an irascible old collier whose voice of protest we will hear again, recalled the profound impact these speeches had on him:

> When I went to that convention, . . . I was never looking for a strike; I did not believe it would come to that; I thought we would be able to come together. . . . but the evidence that was given by the delegates representing the different camps was heart-breaking. . . . Men gave evidence of how they were treated; it was something fierce. There was one man there who spoke pretty fair English. He said he had a partner and the boss told him, "Now, you have got to take this mule to-day and drive." The fellow said, "I cannot drive; I never drove a mule in my life." The boss told him he had to do it and he went to take that mule and the mule balked on him and in fighting with the mule he was catched between the car and the ribs, and it squeezed him and broke something on his inside and he lay there, I guess, four hours, and he died. I thought that was fierce. I got that man's word for it. I did not see why it should occur. . . . It is a fact I never heard anything so heartbreaking as was said there that night.

The litany of death and suffering by colliers from throughout the southern fields extinguished any lingering doubts or misgivings among the delegates and convinced every last man in Castle Hall that a strike was necessary and just.[9]

After the last delegate had stepped down from the podium, "the closing hours of the convention," reported the *Trinidad Chronicle-News*, "were marked by dramatic scenes and by demonstrations of enthusiasm never witnessed before in this city." John Lawson, the United Mine Workers international board member from Colorado and one of the leading figures in the coalfield war that was about to commence, began by reading a report from the policy and scale committee that included the following strike demands:

> First—We demand recognition of the Union.
>
> Second—We demand a ten per cent advance in wages on the tonnage rates and the . . . day wage scale. . . . We also demand a ten per cent advance on the wages paid coke oven workers, and on all other classes of labor not specified herein.
>
> Third—We demand an eight-hour work day for all classes of labor in and around the coal mines and at coke ovens.
>
> Fourth—We demand pay for all narrow work and dead work, which includes brushing, timbering, removing falls, handling impurities, etc.
>
> Fifth—We demand checkweighmen at all mines to be elected by the miners without any interference by Company officials in said election.
>
> Sixth—We demand the right to trade in any store we please, and the right to choose our own boarding place and our own doctor.
>
> Seventh—We demand the enforcement of the Colorado Mining Laws and the abolition of the notorious and criminal guard system which has prevailed in the mining camps of Colorado for many years.

The delegates quickly and unanimously approved this program to reform mine workscapes and company town conditions and set September 23—just six days away—as the strike date.[10]

The announcement of the strike vote prompted "wild cheers." Then the irascible Mother Jones—the white-haired, foul-mouthed "angel of the miners" aptly described by one collier as a woman who "may not have done no dirty dishes, but she sure done a lot of good work for the union"—marched to the front of the hall and "threw down the gauntlet to the operators." As usual, she did not mince words. "'Rise up and strike,' she yelled. 'If you are too cowardly,'" she taunted the miners, "'there are enough women in this country to come in here and beat h— out of you.'" By impugning the miners' manhood, Jones brought the assembly inside Castle Hall to fever pitch. "'If it is to be slavery or strike,' Mother Jones exclaimed, 'then I say strike—strike— until the last one of you drop into your graves.'"[11]

Frank Hayes then took the platform to orchestrate "the psychological moment" of the convention. "'I know we cannot lose in this great industrial struggle,' he said, 'because our demands are just.'" The union had "'taken every honorable means to bring about an adjustment [but had] failed.'" With "'no other alternative left but to strike,'" Hayes reassured the delegates: "'When we strike, we strike to win.'" The union vice president stood ready to "'pledge . . . all the wealth and all the power of our great union.'" The United Mine Workers, he vowed, would "'never leave this field until [they had] stricken the shackles from every mine worker.'" The miners responded to Hayes's rhetoric of emancipation and his promise of victory with "wild demonstration."[12]

It took several minutes for delegates to absorb the seriousness of what they had done. "Suddenly, silence fell over the hall," the reporter for the *Denver Express* wrote. "The delegates realized they had said the word that would throw 9000 men out of work. They were awed by the greatness of the approaching struggle. Their faces became grave and stern." Fear and foreboding descended on the delegates, only to be pierced by "a man's voice from the rear of the hall . . . chanting the Colorado strike song." One row of hardpressed miners took up the song, then the next. Italians and Austrians, Welshmen and Hispanos, Swedes, Slovaks, and others all "rocked in their seats as they sang it. The thunder of it shook the hall. And so the convention adjourned." Within no time, news of the strike vote was "traveling like wildfire" up the hardscrabble canyons of the southern fields. The defiant lyrics and rousing melody of "The Colorado Strike Song," the "battle cry of union," echoed through every coal camp in the state.[13]

Prelude: The 1903–1904 Strike

The Trinidad Convention decreed that the strike would commence on September 23, thus giving mining families, mine operators, and coal consumers less than a week to prepare for the impending struggle. Though coal company managers declared themselves "'ready at any time to meet men actually in their employ, singly or in groups, to consider and adjust grievances,'" they refused to negotiate with the United Mine Workers. Instead, they laid plans for a fight that LaMont Bowers warned John D. Rockefeller, Jr., "would be serious indeed."[14]

These plans borrowed heavily from the victorious strategies the companies had pursued in the bitter colliers' strike of 1903–1904. The stark inequities and hazardous workscapes of the mineral-intensive industrial economy, its erosion of such crafts as hard-rock mining through the introduction of machines, and the ongoing recruitment of new migrants in the effort to lower wages and combat solidarity—all these factors had ensured that the bitter class conflict that had erupted in the Cripple Creek and Pullman strikes and in the colliers' marching strike of 1894 would continue to fester. The Leadville mine war of 1896–1897, the Front Range smelter dispute of 1899, and dozens of other strikes had turned Colorado into what one contemporary regarded as "a storm-center in labor troubles." Serious as Colorado's "troubles" of the 1890s had been, however, they paled in comparison to the industrial wars of 1903–1904. First, the Western Federation of Miners declared another strike at Cripple Creek, in sympathy with the smelter workers of Colorado City, Denver, Durango, and Pueblo; hard-rock miners at Idaho Springs and Telluride then joined the struggle. "Everything seems to be on Strike in Colorado," griped William Jackson Palmer from a summer camping trip in the mountains; "Big" Bill Haywood declared that "the entire state was in conflagration"; and the progressive *Outlook* ominously declared of Colorado, "Class lines are now drawn with a more dangerous sharpness in that commonwealth than in any other."[15]

Coal mine workers throughout Colorado walked off the job in the fall of 1903. Operators in northern Colorado hastened to confer with the union and offered to grant the miners every demand but the eight-hour day, which they claimed would make it impossible for them to compete with the southern operators. The northern colliers walked off the job anyway, steadfast in their support for the eight-hour day and wary about betraying their southern brethren by signing a separate peace. After the miners rejected further operator concessions, however, the United Mine Workers' accommodationist president John Mitchell took the unusual step of calling for a second vote. By a margin of 228 to 165, the northern colliers elected to return to work.[16]

Mitchell's machinations undercut the southern Colorado miners' chances of success and reinforced the operators' resolve to crush the union. John C. Osgood, the mastermind behind the new company town system, devised a strategy comprising four components: dirty tricks, co-optation of state power for private purposes, neutralization of strikers' mobility, and control of information. When miners went out on strike a decade later, the operators would dust off the array of tactics that had carried them to victory in 1903–1904.

Dirty tricks, the first of the tactics operators used in the 1903–1904 dispute, encompassed bribes, espionage, and violence. Companies lured turncoats and stool pigeons with large payouts. They also retained detective agencies to keep tabs on union organizers and officials, as well as to recruit gunslingers for jobs as mine guards. A report from one of private detective William Reno's men shows how coal company hirelings used violence to combat the strike. "Nic Oddo refused to vacate" one of Victor-American's camps, the goon R. L. Martel claimed, "so I told Thompson to arrest him on the charge of vagrancy." Then he ordered four men to "wait for [Oddo] down by the bridge and they 'Kangarooded' [beat] him and the last I heard of him he was in the hospital, and he will not attempt to come back to Hastings. It seems that the only way to get these agitators out of the camp," the agent mused, "is to 'Kangaroo' them and when they are all gone, I am satisfied the boys will go to work." Meanwhile, in the western coalfields, John Lawson and his family narrowly escaped death when the henchmen of a mineowner, Perry Coryell, dynamited their home.[17]

When such tactics failed to produce the desired result, the companies brought in National Guardsmen to reinforce the detectives. Four hundred militiamen, fresh from battling the Western Federation of Miners in Telluride, marched into Trinidad on March 24, 1904, bearing orders from the conservative Governor James Peabody. As it happened, union miners from throughout the southern fields were convening in Trinidad at that very moment. And though reports claimed that the colliers had entered the meeting intending to call off the strike, the delegates "were so incensed at the unwarranted and uncalled for action of the governor," John Mitchell later claimed, "that instead of calmly considering the status of the strike and declaring it off, as they undoubtedly would have done had the troops not been there, they decided that while the civil laws had been suspended, a resumption of work would be regarded not as a recognition of their defeat by the coal companies, but as a cowardly surrender to Peabody." Major Zeph Hill's forces, bankrolled largely by mineowners and the reactionary "citizens' alliances" formed by conservative elites in response to more than a decade of labor insurgency, disarmed strikers but not mine guards. They further outraged union miners by stationing themselves between strikers and strikebreakers, a move that turned any attempt to prevent the importation of scabs into an act of "insurrection and rebellion against the state."[18]

By enlisting detectives and the state militia to do their dirty work, coal companies intensified the campaign of control over workers' living space and movement so fundamental to the company town system. They closed coal camp saloons, forced strikers to register with military authorities, and forbade union men to drive on public roads or enter the new company towns. Operators also evicted miners from many of the remaining dwellings they had built on company land, some of which were subsequently demolished. The militia even used public health as a pretext for relocating tent colonies away from railroad tracks and depots, thus making it much harder for strikers to confront strikebreakers. Most troubling of all to coalfield migrants, though, was the use of militia to deport strikers. Governor Peabody, interpreting union sympathies as a priori evidence of nonresident status, ordered guardsmen to round up and deport all "nonresident" strike leaders from Las Animas County. By June 1904, more than 180 strikers had been jailed, often without formal charges' having been filed. State troops subsequently forced 97 men, as well as Mother Jones, to leave the state. Some they dumped on the high plains of Kansas, others in the New Mexico desert. Many deportees never returned to the southern coalfields, but at least one contingent straggled back on foot, sustaining themselves on their homeward journey by hunting jackrabbits.[19]

The final component of the operators' 1903–1904 strike strategy consisted of a far-reaching effort to keep the sordid story of repression in the southern coalfields from reaching the general public. Major Hill began to censor the press the instant he arrived in southern Colorado, threatened to expel from the strike zone reporters who filed negative stories about the militia, concealed the deportation of sixteen men, and effectively shut down the union's Italian-language newspaper, *Il Lavatore Italiano,* by arresting the editor and a contributor. Hill even ordered his signal corps to monitor every telegraph message and telephone call out of Trinidad; communications that were deemed suspicious were diverted to Hill's headquarters. As the militia did everything it could to prevent damaging information from leaking out of the southern coalfields, the coal companies were doing all they could to cultivate a positive public image: offering sympathetic reporters privileged access to their company towns, providing newspapers with spurious articles supposedly written by nonunion colliers, and issuing detailed press releases presenting their spin on events to copy-hungry newspapers.[20]

Whatever the medium, the companies stuck to the same message: Before union agitators had whipped Colorado's mineworkers into a frenzy, miners had been laboring contentedly, enjoying high wages, good working conditions, and prosperous home lives in progressive company towns. But then, silver-tongued careerists and demagogues—men whom the Colorado Fuel and Iron counsel D. C. Beaman caricatured as agitators "who flourish in controversy and starve in peace"—incited ignorant foreigners to wage an all-out war against private property, the rule of law, and other hallowed American institutions. A letter attributed to a "Trinidad District Miner," but almost certainly written by a company apologist, proclaimed scrip "one of the greatest blessings the miners enjoy, for it carries with it many conveniences which none but the miner can appreciate.... Had it not been for the men Mr. Mitchell sent out here to talk to the poor unfortunate[s] who could not understand and yet who control the vote because of their number," he continued, "I dare say no one working in the south would have talked strike, let along come out." But once these "men drawing fancy salaries for agitating worked upon the men who could not understand," the benighted migrants came out. Soon, "the rest followed, believing it would be wrong for Americans to stay at work and let the poor foreigner fight for him [*sic*]." Through such false or tendentious interpretations, coal companies denied the long history of struggle boiling up from the mines and erupting from the new company towns. In their eyes, the union bore sole responsibility for the strike.[21]

The strategies of dirty war, state co-optation, restriction of movement, imposition of surveillance, and propaganda proved effective—so effective, in fact, that by summer 1904, the companies were shipping coal at 80 percent of prestrike capacity. Mitchell and other union leaders, as critics would point out in the months and years to come, deserved some of the blame for the strikers' increasingly untenable position. By cajoling northern Colorado colliers into signing a separate peace, Mitchell neutralized the miners' greatest advantage: the fossil-fuel dependency of Western consumers. Once the economic lifeblood of the region was again flowing freely, John Mitchell urged the southern colliers to call off the strike. When the rank and file defied the union leadership in June 1904 by voting to prolong the strike—a move that directly contradicted the companies' portrayal of the strike as rooted in United Mine Workers demagoguery, not southern colliers' militancy—the international board retaliated by cutting off the relief payments on which strikers depended for food and other necessities. Delegates, facing penury and starvation, called off the strike soon thereafter. Some returned to work by late summer. Many others, however, found themselves blacklisted, and hence forced either to leave Colorado or enter another line of work.[22]

Nine years later, with the United Mine Workers again bent on organizing the southern fields and rumors of a strike on every tongue, coal company executives trotted out the same formula that had served them so well in 1903–1904. They stepped up assaults against union organizers, in the process killing at least one man; planted moles within the United Mine Workers; and expelled hundreds, even thousands, of suspected union miners from the camps (many of whom turned out to be antiunionists targeted by the "inside-outside" system). Once the Trinidad Convention had voted to strike, W. H. Reno, now head of Colorado Fuel and Iron's in-house detective service, and Albert Felts, whose Baldwin-Felts Detective Agency had recently played an instrumental role in defeating United Mine Workers strikes in West Virginia, began in the summer of 1913 to hire dozens of thugs from Cripple Creek, Denver, Salt Lake City, Kansas City, Chicago, and beyond. The companies also proceeded to enlist sympathetic newspapers willing to portray the strikers by using the same rhetoric perfected a decade earlier, as well as to lay the groundwork for National Guard intervention. In the meantime, private armies and law officers from local governments beholden to King Coal would do their best to hold the miners at bay.[23]

Meanwhile, in New York, one of the richest families in the world embarked on a course identical to the one it had charted without reproach in 1903–1904. In that strike, John D. Rockefeller, Jr., whose father had recently acquired a controlling interest in Colorado Fuel and Iron, had expressed unqualified faith in Frank Hearne, the Rockefeller family's man in Colorado.

> We agree fully with the attitude which you have taken regarding the labor situation and with your statement as to general policy. We are prepared to stand by [you] in this fight and see the thing out, not yielding an inch. Recognition of any kind of either the labor leaders or union, much more a conference such as they request, would be a sign of evident weakness on our part. We have dealt fairly and generously with our men up to date and intend to do so in the future, and we do not believe it is for their interests, as we know it is not for the interests of the company to allow any interference on the part of the union.

Ten years later, staff members at the Rockefeller headquarters at 26 Broadway ignored initial reports of impending labor strife. Beside a passage in a letter warning that a strike was about to erupt in the southern fields, John Junior penciled the word "irrelevant." More concerned with financial results than labor relations, he deferred to the crotchety LaMont Bowers, Hearne's successor as the Rockefellers' man at Colorado Fuel and Iron. Bowers, meanwhile, fed the family just-so stories of the sort operators had long used to explain away their workers' militancy. The Trinidad Convention, Bowers informed Rockefeller's office, "was made up principally of union men brought into Trinidad . . . together with paid healers." Bowers implausibly declared, "There was none from any of our mines who had been sent there as a representative of the miners. The five or six of our men who were there, dropped in as men drop into a political convention, not as delegates, with one or two exceptions. . . . We mention this," Bowers concluded, "to show you to what extremes these men will go in order to carry their point." Bowers elaborated on similar themes in another letter. "We have the good will of our men and are perfectly satisfied," he stated. "Not more than 10 percent belong to unions." Many of the rest, particularly "these foreigners," were afraid that United Mine Workers members would intimidate and even assault them. Though Bowers "hope[d] to be able to keep a large number of our men," he predicted, "Many of those who do go out will, after a few days when they find we are able to protect them, return to their work."[24]

When John D. Rockefeller, Jr., first acknowledged the strike two weeks after it commenced, he expressed unqualified support for Bowers and his lieutenants. "You gentlemen cannot be more earnest in your desire for the best interests of the employes of your Company than we are," Rockefeller assured Bowers. "We feel that what you have done is right and fair. . . . Whatever the outcome may be," John Jr. promised, "we will stand by you to the end."[25]

To the denizens of boardrooms and clubhouses in New York and Denver alike, the causes of the strike remained all too clear: outside agitators had invaded Colorado, then alternately intimidated and misled the state's previously contented and well-paid miners. Having inflamed these gullible foreigners to the point of savage rage, the union stood poised to unleash a reign of anarchy that threatened both the rights of capital and the workers' true self-interest.[26]

Thus with singing and storytelling did miners and mineowners steel themselves for battle.

Exodus

September mornings in southern Colorado ordinarily dawn crisp and bright. Imagine the miners' dismay, then, when they and their families awoke to near-freezing temperatures and driving rains on the morning slated for the strike's commencement. The dirt roads of the southern coalfields quickly turned to mud; "a driving, searching wind" added to the strikers' woes, confronting the thousands of men, women, and children evicted from company housing with an exodus of the most trying sort.[27]

Over the preceding days, miners and mining families had been busy preparing for the coming fight. Meanwhile, John D. Rockefeller, Jr., ignored the news from Colorado, and LaMont Bowers joined John C. Osgood and other executives to set in motion a plan similar to the one that had delivered the operators from the last major colliers' strike. Union rules permitted engineers, boilermen, and pumpmen to stay on the job during labor conflicts, thus protecting mine workscapes from irreparable harm. Rock would continue to fall, water and gas to flow, but miners, superintendents, and company men did what they could to minimize the damage. While other workmen shored up haulageway roofs, inspected ventilation circuits, and led mules out of the pits to pasture outside, colliers took care to leave their rooms in good order, hoping, after all, soon to return victorious to their old places. Once miners had prepared their places, they "drew," or "took out," their tools. This vernacular expression for going out on strike reflected the miners' status as craftsmen who owned the tools of their trade—as free men empowered to deny employers access to these tools, as well as to the skills and energies needed to wield them effectively.[28]

Leaving work even before the Trinidad Convention had authorized the strike, the miners of Delagua and Valdez drew their tools first. Next to come out were the Huerfano County colliers, perhaps 70 percent of whom had left the mines by Saturday, September 21. Two days later, virtually every mineworker in Fremont County—and an estimated 80 to 90 percent of the mine labor force in Las Animas and Huerfano counties—had joined the struggle, as had most of Crested Butte's workforce, a few hundred colliers from the outskirts of Colorado Springs, four hundred miners from the newly opened Routt County collieries near Steamboat Springs, and over a thousand nonunion miners in northern Colorado, where hundreds of union miners had been on strike since 1910.[29]

The coalfield war involved women and children, too, of course. A second tributary of the September exodus began with them. "Preparations for a long siege," one account reported, "led to busy scenes of household migrations." Coal camp homes often comprised women's workscapes. As women in the closed camps packed up and prepared to leave, they, too, were taking out their tools, but with one crucial difference: their work would hardly cease once male family members walked off the job.[30]

Few strikers had as much time to move as they would have liked. After the strike began at Tabasco, one account alleged, "mine guards hastened to the little huts where miners lived and threw their families and furniture into the street. Little children so ejected were hurt and several fights resulted."

Fearing the knock of company thugs on their door, mining families gathered up the things they had carried to the coalfields as well as the scanty possessions they had acquired since their arrival. Once they had packed, many coalfield migrants took to the road again (in fact, many hundreds had already left the coalfields in advance of the strike). Hundreds, perhaps even thousands, of miners returned to their old countries; recent arrivals were particularly likely to head home. At least a few thousand other Colorado colliers took jobs offered by the union in Wyoming, Pennsylvania, or West Virginia; others secured work through relatives, compatriots, and padrones, while a few melted back into the army of tramps riding rails.[31]

The strike prompted thousands to elaborate on and accelerate the patterns of migration they had established over the decades, but more than twenty thousand men, women, and children chose to stay in Colorado. Some undoubtedly expected the strike to end soon; others had no place else to go. The simplest explanation for why so many stayed behind, however, might also be the most powerful: as "The Colorado Strike Song" declared, strikers were "fighting for [their] homes." Despite the dangers of the mines, despite the repression and indignity imposed on them by company towns, tens of thousands of migrants from all around the world had come to feel that they belonged to the southern Colorado coalfields, and the coalfields to them. They had hacked productive mines out of lifeless earth, contributed to the transformation of the Mountain West from an arid, isolated frontier periphery into an industrial core, and made homes for themselves in the gritty coal camps.[32]

The fortunate minority who owned their homes or who rented accommodations from someone other than the mining companies generally stayed put. The rest found themselves homeless when companies evicted them from closed-camp dwellings. Some joined relatives, compatriots, and friends on ranches, farms, and truck gardens established by fellow migrants over the preceding decades. Several Tyrolean miners and ex-miners, to give just one example, had homesteaded in Huerfano County. Though Emma Pazar's father owned his own house at Rouse, Colorado Fuel and Iron guards forced him to leave when the strike began. So the Pazars loaded their belongings into a covered wagon and headed for the Bernelli Ranch on Bear Creek, then filed a homestead claim on a 160-acre farm on the other side of the river.

7.1. Strikers in Ludlow. Denver Public Library, Western History Collection, X-60461.

Strikers also "swarmed into" open camps and independent towns, such as Trinidad, where "small vacant houses" were reportedly "filling up." Still others rented land in the countryside and moved onto plots outside Segundo and Valdez for the duration of the dispute. One resourceful contingent even reoccupied the abandoned camp of Engleville.[33]

Probably the largest contingent, however, moved into union tent colonies located at Aguilar, Rugby, Piedmont, Sopris, Old Segundo, Tercio, Walsenburg, Forbes, Pictou, and of course Ludlow. Don McGregor of the *Denver Express* provided the most vivid reporting on "the exodus" from closed camps to tent colonies. "Miners and wives and children crouched pitifully on top of high-piled little wagons, bending low in futile effort to avoid the rain. The faces of the men were set heavy with foreboding; the faces of the women stolid with the memory of suffering that had gone before and the sure knowledge of more to come; the faces of the children were twisted in misery." Each of the fifty-seven wagons McGregor passed on his drive from Trinidad to Ludlow carried a bewildered, woebegone family perched atop its worldly belongings. "What a mockery of the state's boasted riches!" McGregor lamented. "What a commentary on the prosperity of the miners of Colorado! Prosperity! Little piles of rickety chairs! Little piles of miserable looking straw bedding! Little piles of kitchen utensils! And all so worn and badly used they would have been the scorn of any second-hand dealer." McGregor could find not "a single article even approaching luxury, save, once in a score of wagons, a cheap, gaily painted gramophone! With never a bookcase! With never a book! With never a single article that even the owners thought worth while trying to protect from the driving rain! And these were the contents of the homes of the miners whom the mine owners have called prosperous and contented!"[34]

Only those who had witnessed the evacuation, McGregor claimed, could "imagine its pathos. The exodus from Egypt was a triumph, the going forth of a people set free." The mass departure of strikers, by contrast, winding "its bowed, weary way between the coal hills on the one side and the far-stretching prairie on the other . . . was an exodus of woe, of people leaving fears for new terrors, a hopeless people seeking new hope, a people born suffering going forth to certain new suffering."[35]

Tent Colony Community

Union tent colonies, despite considerable differences in their population and layout, had in common the arrangement of tents around a central communal space. Ludlow, the largest of the camps, featured a large parade ground on which strikers assembled almost every day to listen to speeches. The adjacent "Big Tent" served as the local union headquarters as well as a workplace, where women (and some children and men) together did the work required to sustain the colony. These communal spaces also hosted dances, festivities on national holidays, religious festivals, and parades. For the sake of sanitation and economy, the union laid out camps on well-drained grids with privies at a safe remove from water sources and tents. Drinking water from wells or barrels, coal for heating and cooking, lumber to frame floors and walls—the union supplied these, too. As for housing, the union supplemented a large order of canvas wall tents from a Pueblo dealer with hundreds of tents vacated after the union's recent defeat in the West Virginia coalfields.[36]

Tent colony living left much to be desired. The bad weather that attended the exodus from the company towns kicked off one of the worst winters in living memory. Union-supplied coal helped mining families cook food and keep warm, but canvas offered scant protection against wind and precipitation; some tents even collapsed in blizzards, such as the early-December storm that dumped several feet of snow on the colonies, while setting records throughout Colorado.[37]

As for food, strikers had little luck bagging any game other than jackrabbits, which they hunted with guns, picks, shovels, and wire snares. Fish from the few streams in the area provided some additional protein, as did the chickens and other domesticated animals that women kept in and around the colonies. Far and away the largest source of food, however, was groceries purchased with weekly union relief payments, disbursed according to a formula based on the male-breadwinner ideal: three dollars per man, one dollar per woman, and fifty cents per child. Strikers patronized stores in adjacent towns, or tent colony commissaries whose business was contracted out to independent merchants; families also purchased eggs, dairy products, and meat from farmwives and ranchwomen, as well as vegetables from truck-garden peddlers. Through a combination of frugality, resourcefulness, and grit, strikers managed to ward off hunger—no mean achievement, when a family of six received just six dollars a week, less than half what an average miner might have made in the same period.[38]

Despite these physical hardships—and perhaps because of them, too—colonies sometimes took on an almost utopian cast. Loosely organized, thoroughly egalitarian, committed not to containing mineworkers' militancy but rather to channeling it toward the union's purposes, Ludlow and its counterparts presented a stark contrast with the new company towns. In time, the strikers grew "real close," one participant recalled, "just like a big family."[39]

This family, like the households that composed it, remained rigidly patriarchal. Women and girls experienced little liberation from their labors, though they now worked collectively in the Big Tent and other communal spaces instead of isolated within their own homes. Nationalism and ethnic ties also retained their salience. Men such as the Greek martyr of Ludlow, Louis Tikas, served as "captains," mediating between British American union leaders and the more than twenty nationalities represented in the colony. On the whole, though, strikers upheld a vision of Americanism best summarized by the old republican motto, *E pluribus unum.* "We had everything there," former driver Alex Bisulco recalled of Ludlow, "Greeks, Italians, Slavs and all, the League of Nations was there, you might say." In the camps, these diverse peoples "all stuck together," in Bisulco's words, forging a whole that transcended the sum of its parts.[40]

One visitor proclaimed Ludlow "the true melting pot," and indeed tent colonies reinforced the interethnic sociability facilitated by mine workscapes and vernacular landscapes. In the process, they buttressed the growing sense of conviction that led migrants from radically different backgrounds to embrace a common identity and a common interest in the success of the strike. "In the evening," the union organizer Mike Livoda later recalled, "I used to get out there a little ways from the camp, you know, and listen to music in those camps. They'd be singing in every language in the world in that tent colony, how those miners were unified together and stuck together." This concordance of diverse lyrics, instruments, and musical styles offered an apt metaphor for the solidarity that generally prevailed in the camps.[41]

Tent colonies functioned as military encampments as well as refugee camps and incubators of group identity. From the start, Ludlow was undoubtedly the most martial of the camps. Strategically located, like many of the other colonies, the camp was protected by rifle pits and guarded by sentries. On the central parade ground strikers held rallies and planned picket lines against incoming trains carrying scabs; there they sang "The Colorado Strike Song" pretty much every night, sometimes belting out the lines, one

7.2. Lending a Hand at the Ludlow Commissary. Denver Public Library, Western History Collection, Z-215.

miner recalled, until their "tonsils hurt"; there they steeled themselves for the coming storm, for it seemed likely from the time the union set up the Ludlow camp that this stretch of ground, like Rouse two decades before, would become the fulcrum on which the strike of 1913–1914 would pivot.[42]

Bringing the State Back In

The Trinidad Convention called the strike, the 1903–1904 prelude had supplied the script that the companies would follow, and the exodus created the tent colonies. A little over a month after the strike began, on October 28, the Colorado National Guard would enter the strike zone. Some were already predicting, though, that what started as a peacekeeping mission would end in what Don McGregor of the *Express* called "civil war, red and bloody."[43]

Governor Elias Ammons had entered the statehouse the same way Woodrow Wilson reached the White House: through a side door opened when Progressives split off from the Republican Party in 1912. Though many Colorado labor leaders had supported the Progressive candidate for governor, Edward Costigan, a contingent led by the United Mine Workers' John Lawson put its considerable weight behind Ammons. Not only had the ranchman's Democratic predecessor appointed staunch unionists as secretary of state and deputy labor commissioner, but he had refused to dispatch the militia to put down the colliers' strike in the northern fields. Sealing many union miners' support for the Democrats was a party platform calling for "legislation empowering the governor, the attorney general and the courts to destroy" the coal companies' dominion over Huerfano and Las Animas counties "and restore to the people of these counties their right of self-government."[44]

Like so many politicians, though, Ammons changed his tune once he took his office. He might have responded to the strike of the southern miners as Theodore Roosevelt had to the Pennsylvania anthracite miners' strike of 1902: by forcing employers and employees to arbitrate. Instead, Ammons—a man elected in no small part thanks to the support of labor—stuck his head in the sand, extracting it only to utter bland pronouncements urging both sides to comply with state laws addressing twice-monthly paydays, the importation of strikebreakers, and other points of contention. The governor's noninterventionist stance frustrated the operators' plan to enlist the state militia to suppress the strike. "We have here a pin-head governor," Bowers carped, "who could put the troops into the territory and end the strike in twenty-four hours."[45]

The reassurances of key elected officials in the coalfields gave the governor the pretext he needed to keep the militia in its barracks. Assaults, murders, and gun battles had marred the strike even before its formal declaration. Even so, Trinidad's Democratic mayor M. T. Dunlavy assured the governor, "'We can handle the situation as far as Trinidad is concerned.'"[46]

Dunlavy's confidence, however, did not extend to Ludlow. There, "where the strikers [were] gathering in a great camp," Dunlavy warned Ammons just a week after the strike began, "I fear there may be trouble." And indeed, it was the volatility and violence that centered on Ludlow that finally forced the governor's hand. "There is probably no camp in the district affected by the strike," the *Walsenburg Independent* claimed, "where stronger animosity is displayed between the company employees and the miners." A federal investigator concurred, reporting: "The strikers at the Ludlow tents are in a highly nervous condition." The miners, he alleged on October 9, "expect trouble and are apparently ready to create a very grave situation on slight provocation." Mine guards proved even more eager to fight. After numerous gun battles erupted around the colony in late October, Ammons made the fateful decision to bring state troops back into Colorado's labor wars for the first time since Peabody's ignominious tenure.[47]

The Colorado National Guard received deployment orders from the governor on October 28, after the strike had already claimed more than two dozen lives, including those of several strikers, strikebreakers, mine guards, and innocent bystanders around Ludlow. Ammons ordered the militia "to obtain a speedy return of law and order in the disturbed districts." In hopes of preventing further bloodshed, the governor "directed" National Guard commandant John Chase:

To disarm everybody, unless authorized to bear arms,

To close up saloons wherever there is any disturbance.

To require that all persons employed as guards in the protection of property shall stay on the property guarded.

To see that no deputy sheriffs or constables be employed, except citizens of the county they serve, and only such numbers as may be deemed necessary for the conduct of public business.

To see that all persons desiring to return to work shall be permitted to do so and come when they will without molestation or interference of any kind whatsoever; and during the restoration of order or until further orders no strike-breakers shall be shipped in.[48]

Ammons's move worried many Coloradans. "The whole state," the *Florence Daily Citizen* explained, "trembled in the thought of armed conflict and consequent bloodshed, of terrors to humanity, suffering and heavy expense. . . . The people of Colorado," the *Citizen* believed, "have not yet recovered, or rather their state hasn't, from the strike troubles during the Peabody administration." Some strikers also expressed alarm at the return of the militia. "The wildest excitement prevailed in the tent colonies of the striking miners," the *Citizen* reported. "The hot heads among the strikers, principally

7.3. Striking Mining Families in Front of the Zanetell Tent, Forbes Colony. Denver Public Library, Western History Collection, X-60448.

Greeks, were uncontrollable. They suggested to their countrymen that the troops be fired upon and offered to lead a mob to blow up the mines."[49]

Many strikers, however, welcomed the National Guard, reasoning that it would provide a neutral buffer that would protect them from mine guards and company detectives. Moreover, Ammons's order that "no strike-breakers shall be shipped in" assuaged fears that state troops would intervene to sabotage the strikers' efforts to orchestrate a fuel famine. Paradoxically, militiamen may have received their warmest greeting at Ludlow. As troops paraded around the tent colony, "'little children in white'" burst out singing "The Colorado Strike Song," while waving the Stars and Stripes in an impromptu parade. Even the irascible General Chase found the scene "memorable." Captain Nickerson seconded the guardsmen's commander, by observing that "every diplomatic profession of good faith" attended this initial encounter between strikers and militiamen in the camp that guardsmen would destroy six months later.[50]

Whatever "good faith" Nickerson detected, however, soon began to dissipate. The National Guard enforced the governor's disarmament order unevenly. Militiamen confiscated all the weapons they could find in the tent colonies, even as company guards retained most of their arsenal. The guardsmen soon shifted from neutrality to partisanship in other ways, too. Militia officers drawn largely from the state's professional class naturally gravitated toward coal company executives who shared their WASP heritage, bourgeois manners, and conservative worldview—and away from coalfield migrants and union leaders. Institutional connections reinforced such private sympathies. The state auditor, Roady Kenehan, a staunch union supporter, sought to hamstring the militia by delaying or refusing to pay the National Guard's mounting bills. The auditor's well-intentioned move qualifies as perhaps the most misguided maneuver in the Great Coalfield War, for coal companies and their store subsidiaries astutely stepped in to fill the financial vacuum that Kenehan had left. Working with Denver's largest bankers, Colorado Fuel and Iron and its allies arranged to foot the bill for the troops' food, fuel, and other supplies. In time, they even paid the guardsmen's salaries.[51]

When Chase issued new orders in early November that replaced company guards at several mines with militiamen, he set in motion the most ominous trend of all: the growing practice of mustering former sheriff's deputies, mine guards, and detectives into the National Guard. Thereafter, a militia composed of troops possessing little or no direct connection with the strike was transmuted into a force of men boasting a checkered history as criminals, counterinsurgents, and union busters. As company rule and the armed power of the state became more and more difficult to disentangle, the strikers' attitude toward the militia changed from welcome to wariness to outright hostility.[52]

The guardsmen's shifting sympathies undercut the peace their arrival in the strike zone had temporarily instituted. Petty violence resumed in November, renewing widespread fears that the strike might erupt into all-out war. Yet still Ammons grasped at the naive hope that peace lay just a simple conversation away.[53]

Kenneling the Dogs of Industrial War

It must have been a curious sight: three striking miners—Archie Allison, David Hamman, and T. X. Evans—arrived at Colorado's gold-domed capitol building shortly before 10 A.M., probably clothed in their Sunday best. A few minutes later, three coal company executives—Jesse Welborn of CF&I, John Osgood of Victor-American, and David Brown of Rocky Mountain Fuel—strode in, dressed in business suits. Ammons, fed up with the withering criticism that operators, strikers, and the public were heaping on him, ushered the six men into a conference room and forbade reporters to enter. The governor was trying against all odds, after all, to resolve perhaps the biggest strike in Colorado history by staging a "man-to-man talk."[54]

The executives spoke for their particular companies, while Evans, Allison, and Hamman ostensibly represented not the United Mine Workers, but the strikers of Fremont, Huerfano, and Las Animas counties, respectively. This odd conceit signaled the governor's uncritical acceptance of the pledge Colorado Fuel and Iron president Jesse Welborn had made in a letter of November 5, which declared the companies' willingness to uphold state laws guaranteeing six of the seven demands of the Trinidad Convention if the strikers agreed to drop the seventh demand, recognition of the UMW.

The "joint conference" held in late November 1913 constituted the last, best hope for settling the strike. Ammons expected that by studiously avoiding any discussion of union recognition, miners and operators could make peace in less than twenty-four hours. Instead, the fundamental differences in experience, perspective, and goals that leap out from the previously unstudied transcripts of these proceedings—oddly overlooked by every previous historian of the coalfield war—reveal that miners and operators found it impossible to agree on even the most minor points. The gulf between operators and strikers illustrated the depth of the rupture between them; meanwhile, the impasse that resulted from the joint conference provided the coal companies with the leverage they needed to trick Elias Ammons into shifting his stance, thus placing the weight of the state of Colorado behind the operators.[55]

Denver's *Rocky Mountain News* implored the conferees to remember "that the eyes of Colorado [were] set hungrily" on the proceedings: "It should be no secret to them that from every angle and corner of this sorely-tried commonwealth hope waits for the word of their deliberations that will tell them the story of promise or defeat. . . . Do not disappoint this people," the paper pleaded. "Forget the passions, the bitterness and the promptings of retaliation that have disfigured this splended [*sic*] state since the first raucous note of class warfare went hurtling through the chain of coal-seamed hills of the south.... Send the dogs of industrial war back to their kennels, and 800,000 people will bless and thank you with their most expressive gratitude."[56]

Only by forgetting, it seemed, could the two sides settle their differences. The three miners, however, had no intention of denying the histories that had brought them into battle with their employers. Evans had migrated from Wales by way of Iowa, Allison seems to have been English, and Hamman was probably American-born. All three were practical miners whose superior skills enabled them to earn much more than the state average. None was a stranger to labor conflict; Allison, to give the most illuminating example, had petitioned Governor Peabody during the 1903–1904 strike, beseeching him to "line out a measure of free speech, to guide the Law Officers and peoples leaders, directing the Mayor of Walsenburg to advise the law officers as to what freedom of speach the people are intitled to." He was particularly keen that strikers be permitted to "meet on the public highways and public grounds and exchange views with our fellow creatures without being interfered with by the law Officers." Allison closed his protest against the companies' enclosure of public spaces with verse that might have been taken straight from a broadside in Revolutionary Boston or William Palmer's Philadelphia:

> In the spirit of truth we'l put our trust,
> Our laws t'ween man and man be just,
> And let our National moto be
> Emblem of truth and liberty.
> Then should power threaten to invade,
> To spoil our homesteads law or trade,
> We'l hurl them from our land and sea
> With Arms of truth and liberty.[57]

Before Allison and his fellows could resuscitate such working-class republican worldviews at the governor's conference in 1913, however, Osgood nearly derailed the talks. The old union-buster suggested that the conferees could "save a lot of time" by tackling union recognition first. The "meat of the whole thing is right there," he claimed. "The strike would not have been called—at least not at this time—if there had not been a desire on the part of the United Mine Workers of America officials to organize the state." The governor rejoined: "It may not be necessary to discuss that feature at all." Yet despite Ammons's best efforts, the governor could not divert the conversation from the divisive issue of unionization. "We have very strong opinions in regard to this organization," Osgood explained. "We insist on the right of men to join a Union if they so desire; we recognize that they have the same right that we have to join capital in corporations in order to put business in shape." Osgood claimed to have no quarrel with unionization in *principle;* what he opposed was the United Mine Workers' *practice.* "There are unions and unions," he intoned, "just as there are men and men, and corporations and corporations." The United Mine Workers had "called this strike and attempted to force us to do business, and we do not care [to] continue meeting these officials. . . . They have no business with us nor we with them. . . . The day will come," Osgood foresaw, "when there will be Unions that we would be mighty glad to see you join, but their purposes would be to build men up and not break them down, as is the case today. A man who can make more money in mining coal," the owner claimed, "is quietly told not to exert himself, as by his superior skill he will injure some other fellow, and that the cause of one is the cause of all, and that he should hold himself back a little."[58]

The colliers' mutualism troubled Osgood no end. "We will never be able to build up the civilization that we want," he declared, "until those ideals are abolished." "The Union . . . is the thing that is checking [the miners' advancement]," he announced. "The biggest men in the United States," he claimed, "worked their way up from the ranks" instead of "by joining organizations where they could not, by their merit or skill, advance." Osgood knew; "I started as poor as you," he reminded the miners; "I had to leave school and earn my own living at fourteen years of age." Osgood's main critique of the United Mine Workers boiled down to this: the union institutionalized a mutualism that challenged company authority over the mine workscape and thwarted honest workmen in their efforts to exercise their sacrosanct right to upward mobility.

Osgood's tirade placed the miners on the defensive. Adding to their discomfort was the peculiarity of sitting across the table from some of the richest, mightiest men in the state. "You understand gentlemen," Allison stammered, "that we are just simple miners. We are bit a bit [*sic*] awkward and we have not got the same expression and we would like a little consideration on account of that." After Allison's initial gesture of humility, though, the colliers proceeded to mount a case that was neither awkward nor simple. For more than twelve remarkable hours, three colliers drawn from the strikers' ranks spoke their truth to the assembled representatives of King Coal and the state of Colorado.

The miners derived this truth from experience—their own and that of their fellow strikers. Largely avoiding ideological abstractions and legal technicalities, the colliers returned time and again to the subject they knew best: mining coal. The operators could talk until they were blue in the face about "outside agitators" fomenting trouble among "contented" miners, but they could not convince Evans, Allison, and Hamman that the miners' strike had started with the union instead of the mine workscape. Only through the reform of working conditions underground, the miners believed, could any meaningful agreement emerge.

The colliers repeatedly brought the discussion back to their home ground. Evans proudly claimed that he did "not have to bow [his] head to any man in Colorado as far as mining [was] concerned." He and his mates did not hesitate to tell the operators how they should be running their mines. Hamman asked Osgood if he had a blueprint of one of his company's mines. "What is the point about that?" Osgood wondered. "That the mine is drove wrong," Hamman replied. All three colliers related numerous conversations in which they had challenged the judgment of their superiors, and several in which they had pointedly confronted bosses and superintendents.

Such assertions of craft pride and independence echoed three broad complaints miners had with the management of the collieries. First, the miners attributed Colorado's horrible record of accidents and disasters to company negligence. Evans, the best storyteller among the three, interrupted Osgood's opening antiunion diatribe to recount the tale of the 1896 Vulcan Mine disaster. "I went to New Castle," he began—"thought it was the only place on earth; such a beautiful coal field." But once Evans started working in this gassy property, his admiration was eclipsed by anxiety. Managers asked Evans for safety advice but ignored his recommendations. "The condition did not improve." One morning, a peculiar fog hung low over the mine. "'So . . . I told the woman I said, "that mine is going to go up today, I do not think I ought to go to work" and she said, "no you are not going to go to work, if she is going to go up."'" Evans walked to the mine mouth and told the shaft man that "I would not go down. He said, 'ain't you going down?' I said, 'No she is going to go up.' . . . He said, 'They watered the place good Saturday night' I said, 'They might have thought so, but when I left the place Saturday night they had not watered it.'" As Evans predicted, the mine exploded. "It would not have gone up," Evans concluded, "if they had watered it."

Because of the Colorado coal industry's grim safety record—the worst of any major coal-mining state—Evans believed that "it would be to the best interests [of the miners] to have an organization." Brown retorted, "When we have an explosion we pay dearly for it." "Yes, and we pay dear too," Evans shot back, *"with our lives."*

The miners also voiced discontent with so-called dead, or deficiency, work: essential but uncompensated tasks like timbering, laying track, and brushing down loose roof. "There is a good deal of advantage taken on deficiency work," Evans complained. "If a boss takes exception to a man, don't want him, he will put him up against deficient places, and it will cripple him probably a dollar or two dollars a day and he has no way in the world to get out of it only to quit and get out, and if he quits the same thing will happen somewhere else."

Beyond complaining about dead work and unsafe conditions, the miners challenged the tyranny of bosses and the companies that employed them. The colliers complained of short weights and corrupt mine officials who expected miners to "pay taxes" (bribes) in exchange for good places. Evans claimed that he had worked in New Castle with a man "abler than I was in body and he would lie down and I would get after this fellow time and time again. I would say to him, 'You are paid as much as I am paid; get a move on you' and he told me plainly he did not have to, that . . . 'I pay so much a month for my job.'" When Evans complained to the mine superintendent (the recipient of this man's "taxes"), he "put me on the bum. I was not wanted and for ten years," Evans claimed, "I travelled the state. . . . Simply because I was declaring myself and tried to show them where they were lacking." Allison went further, to draw intriguing connections between work relations underground and company corruption above. "We all know," he boldly asserted, "that politics have been very unsatisfactory in the country as well as in the mines. The conditions that prevailed here for the last twenty years . . . have got the youth, the young rising generation, into a state of corruption," the ardent republican declared in an argument reminiscent of his letter to Governor Peabody, "and they have thought they could not get along unless they fell in with the way. . . . The result was that there were a good many people getting connected with the mines that were unscrupulous."

The operators replied that they hired bosses and superintendents from the ranks of practical colliers. Hamman retorted that such "men who were raised up from the mine, they have changed a whole lot since they were working; since they got in this position it seems that they do not take interest . . . in the *work,* just take an interest in the *job.*" To value the work, Hamman implied, was to uphold the colliers' craft; to value the job, by contrast, was to become a company toady. Honest practical miners, Allison claimed, "always come in the way of the boss. . . . The supers get jealous of a good man or intelligent men and what we think is that you people have not got that; *you don't really know what is going on.*" Here Allison hit on the core of the colliers' critique. "You people don't know what is going on," Hamman seconded, "and if you people were in closer touch with what is going on at these mines I believe you would change your minds yourself."

The striking colliers criticized company misrule, but they also offered a program of reform. Replace corporate hierarchy, they urged, with workers' democracy. To Ammons's chagrin, the three miners proved incapable of discussing strike demands, the workscape environment, or work relations underground without constantly returning to the subject of unionization.

The colliers attributed two primary benefits to the union. The first was educational. Evans believed that the United Mine Workers could provide the operators with "a better class of people"—better not because of their race or nationality, but because of the mechanism that unionization proposed to put in place for practical miners to train green men. "This foreign element," Allison complained, "are illiterate and do not understand the customs very well and down in the mines . . . the intelligent miner has a great deal to contend with from them." But instead of arguing that inexperienced miners should be excluded from the pits, Allison instead believed that new migrants "have to be educated, not only to read and write, but to do their work; they have to be taught that . . . they must do it right."

The union also afforded protection to "pit committees"—the representative but essentially ad hoc bodies that British American colliers had traditionally formed to present their grievances and demands to operators. William Palmer had been put off by the talk of striking he had overheard when visiting one such committee back during his British tour in 1855. Such committees and their Colorado offshoots embodied deep-seated traditions of local power and workers' control. "We used to have a committee without an organization in years gone by," Evans claimed. "The people would pull together and they would even elect an organization, locally, in the mines." Such committees, the miners believed, could "settle any grievance that may arise in the mine." To Evans and his comrades, the United Mine Workers constituted an extension of these bodies. Far from placing the collieries under the command of a massive international labor organization directed by demagogues and careerists, unionization would actually give colliers and their employers a way to settle grievances quickly and equitably without enlisting distant corporate and union hierarchies. "Suppose that he was boss and I had some deficiency," Evans postulated. "If you were reasonable and I was reasonable we could settle the question between us both; but if I was unreasonable and as a rule an old, experienced miner is very unreasonable, they would have to call the committee and . . . they would step in between the two parties."[59]

Pit committees, Evans believed, could counterbalance the power of corrupt local officials and ill-informed executives; in the process, they could protect what the colliers intriguingly called "the miners' law." Asked by Brown whether he believed that "the Union can enforce the law better than the Governor or the officials in power," Allison replied, "It is the law of the mines that I am speaking about, not the State laws; *the laws that the mines ought to be ruled by.*" When Osgood inquired, "What is the nature of the laws of the miners outside of the State laws?" Hamman replied simply: "To have the mines safe." Here, again, the miners equated workscape safety and workers' control, self-governance and craft autonomy, thus predicating their cause on the same dynamics that had underpinned coalfield conflict since the inception of the industry.[60]

The operators, like Palmer before them, categorically refused to accept the miners' vision of industrial democracy. "It is human nature that you would want to settle your own grievances," Osgood granted, "and the next thing to doing it yourself would be to have some one who may have the same grievance the next day; but," he pleaded, "is that just to the operators? It does not seem to me that it is . . . and I think we might as well fight this proposition out, with the consent of the Governor, right now. That the proper man to settle grievances is the superintendent of the mines and not a committee of the men."

Ammons chose instead to direct the conversation back toward the enforcement of state law. He even asked the operators to guarantee striking miners their old places unless they had been convicted of a crime. But it was all for naught. Both miners and operators resolutely returned to the intractable issue of union recognition, with the operators restating their opposition to the United Mine Workers and the colliers reiterating their belief that only through a union could they educate green men, settle grievances, and uphold the miners' self-determined laws of safety and mutualism.

As the talks dragged on past midnight, the governor foolishly convinced himself that he had brokered a settlement on every count but union recognition. Late in the talks, Ammons asked the three colliers what they would advise their fellow strikers back in the southern fields to do. "In going back to the mine," Allison responded, "we, as the men, want the Union to begin with, the pit committees, and the recognition of the Union, *you may call it the United Mine Workers of America,* but we want the recognition of the Union." Brown's instant, unequivocal response summed up the sentiments of every major mining corporation in the southern field: "And that you will never get."[61]

Evans was loath to let the matter rest there. "You gentlemen seem to be so fair and, if you are sincere, what objection would you have to drawing a contract so we could go on in peace?" "You have had ten years of peace," Welborn shot back, "at very good wages." The miners surely disagreed on both counts: their wages were certainly competitive, but hardly "very good." As for Welborn's "ten years of peace," most mining families had probably experienced it as a decade of almost ceaseless worry, danger, and repression. "We are in no position without an organization to defend ourselves," Evans tried to explain to the governor. "We are at the mercy of them."

With the talks once again nearing collapse, Ammons desperately tried to save the day. "After listening to this conference," the governor declared, "there are still less differences than I imagined; there appears to be only one question apparently insurmountable." The governor's optimistic declaration betrayed his utter inability to grasp why this "one question" of unionization mattered to mineworkers. "Let's forget that there has been a past," the uncomprehending governor had pleaded earlier in the day, "and say that you have a lot of mines that you want to operate and here are some men that want to work in them; now, then on what terms can we make an arrangement to take up that work?" The strikers, however, refused to forget the histories that had carried them into this conflict, nor would they forsake unionism, which offered a counterweight to danger and disaster belowground and the operators' campaign of prophylaxis on the surface.

The joint conference represented the first and last time strikers and mine operators would face each other across the negotiating table. The colliers had articulated their discontent and traced its roots to decades of pent-up frustration. The operators, though conceding many of the facts and some of the logic on which the strikers' case rested, still refused to give a single inch. Ammons, meanwhile, seemed to have ignored or misunderstood practically every point the miners had tried to make. Following the talks, he drafted a settlement proposal taken almost entirely from Welborn's letter of November 5—a proposal that obligated the coal companies only to follow existing state laws.

When miners at mass meetings in the southern fields refused to approve the governor's settlement, the real tragedy of the joint conference became apparent. In a letter to the Rockefellers, Welborn revealed the operators' ruse. "We reached no direct understanding," Welborn wrote of the conference. "In fact we wanted none. . . . Nevertheless, the conference accomplished a great deal of good as it convinced the Governor that the grievance [*sic*] of the men were of a trivial character and that we had already granted, even before demanded and before the strike was called, everything that the men had a right to ask or strike for."[62]

The companies had fooled the gullible governor. Ammons, vexed by the miners' rejection of his proposed settlement, issued new orders to the National Guard. At the governor's behest, General Chase stepped up arrests of strike leaders and held most without formal civil charges until special military tribunals could interrogate and try them. He also issued a new directive, General Order 17, that made it easier for coal companies to import strikebreakers. "Those acquainted with inside conditions in the strike zone," the *Denver Post* reported, "say that many of the soldiers sympathize with the strikers. For this reason, in some districts, it is said, the strikers have been given material assistance in the way of keeping non-union men out of the mines. In other districts, it is equally certain that the mine owners have been favored to the extent that men who desired to go to the mines to work were afforded protection." Ammons's order "clarified the military atmosphere materially." "All men who desire to work in the mines," it directed, "shall be afforded protection provided they have knowledge that a strike is in progress and are familiar with working conditions."[63]

The new policy proved decisive. Back in September, a Denver newspaper had carried a headline that must have sent a chill down many readers' spines: "COAL FAMINE IS NEAR BECAUSE OF STRIKE." Yet despite the crucial winter upsurge in demand for domestic coal, no fuel famine developed. Railroads hauled in supplies from other coalfields in Colorado and neighboring states, as well as from a few unionized mines in the southern fields; coal companies and railroads also diverted shipments from industrial users to domestic consumers. Far more ominously for the strikers, Ammons's new orders to the militia brought an influx of strikebreakers into the mines. In a portent of things to come, National Guardsmen at Ludlow enacted the new policy by dispersing "a crowd of more than 100 women and children, armed with clubs and stones gathered at the station" to attack a trainload of scabs. As state troops helped coal companies escape the labor shortage—and hence the fuel blockade—on which the strikers' cause turned, the operators gained the upper hand. By early December, U.S. courts were indicting union leaders for conspiracy to restrain trade, while Welborn was reporting that Colorado Fuel and Iron had "fair forces" at work in some mines and "all of the men that they can now employ" in others. Later that month, Bowers informed Rockefeller in New York: "We now have in the southern fields all the miners that we can use to supply the mills, coke ovens, railroads and the probable limited demand for domestic and other purposes from now on."[64]

The operators may not have known "what was going on" in the mines they owned. But they were astute enough to take advantage of a governor who had ridden the labor vote to the statehouse. And so far from answering the *Rocky Mountain News*'s plea to return the dogs of industrial war to their kennels, the joint conference instead unleashed them.

In Dubious Battle

The strikers felt the tide turning against them—felt it pulling them back out from the hopeful shore into a sea of despair. If the ebb of events seemed to have them in its grip, however, this did not necessarily foreclose the possibility that things might turn again. The mood of defiance in the tent colonies and open towns dissipated as winter descended.

The cautious welcome extended to state militiamen in late October had become but a faint memory; hostility now governed virtually any encounter between guardsmen and strikers. Especially outrageous in the eyes of miners and their many sympathizers around the nation was Chase's order in early January that Mother Jones, now in her eighties, be escorted past the state line. The militia also arrested dozens of other strikers and union leaders and held them without trial or even formal charges until a special military commission could hear their cases. No pretense of neutrality remained. Colorado Fuel and Iron automobiles were frequently seen parked outside the adjutant general's headquarters at the Columbian Hotel in Trinidad. Company officials openly participated in the militia's interrogations of strikers, while elsewhere in the strike zone regular militiamen, who were more interested in returning home than in serving as the mailed fist of corporate power, elected to muster out of the National Guard, only to be replaced by company gunmen.[65]

Once capital and the state had joined forces against them, union leaders lost faith that they could win the strike without carrying the fight beyond Colorado. Sympathetic congressmen such as Colorado's Edward Keating, a stanch supporter of organized labor, and Maryland's David Lewis, a Welsh-born former collier whose moving oration on the miners' "privations" silenced all opposition, authorized a federal investigation. The resulting inquiry, which was conducted by the House Subcommittee on Mines and Mining and entailed four weeks of hearings in Denver, Walsenburg, and

7.4. Speakers at Ludlow. Denver Public Library, Western History Collection, X-60372.

Trinidad between February and March 1914, was widely covered in the national press, as was the testimony by John D. Rockefeller, Jr., before the subcommittee in Washington, D.C., in early April. His ability to express "the views which I entertain, and which have been drilled into him from his earliest childhood," said John D. Rockefeller, Sr., so pleased him that he promptly gave his son ten thousand shares in Colorado Fuel and Iron. In truth, though, neither the union nor the operators emerged from the hearings looking very good. The complexity and violence of the conflict, combined with the subcommittee's lack of real power, stymied the union's efforts to enlist federal authority to intervene on the strikers' behalf.[66]

As the investigations unfolded, peace, strangely enough, seemed to be in the ascendant. Militiamen and strikers had engaged in many heated exchanges in December and January. After Chase and his men attacked a women's march in Trinidad, however, the violence began to abate. By late February, the budget-conscious Governor Ammons tried to stanch the hemorrhaging of funds from the state treasury by withdrawing all but two hundred militiamen from the strike zone. A few weeks later, the governor announced that the state would soon pull out of the coalfields altogether and return authority to civil officials.[67]

In retrospect, of course, these outward signs of calm portended a storm—the open warfare so long feared. The first sign of renewed trouble occurred at the union tent colony erected outside Forbes. Chase reported to Woodrow Wilson that on March 8, "a non-union miner was atrociously murdered near" there. Two days later, Chase's men rode through the colony, rounding up and imprisoning all sixteen men in the camp and destroying every tent, "to forestall further outlawry." Emma Zanetell, whose home had been dynamited by antiunion men in 1894 after her father joined the men marching from Sopris to Rouse, was turned out of her tent-home into the sleet and snow, where her newborn twin babies sickened and died. In response to such outrages, the president of the Globe Detective Agency informed the governor, union men were assembling revolvers, rifles, and ammunition, while many "Baldwin-Felts men [had] been recruited into the [militia] service." He reckoned, "Unless all signs fail, a reign of terror can be expected." By early April, a militia officer reported from the strike zone, "Things are in an awful mess here." As Kenehan blocked funds and the coal companies scrambled to pay the militia's tab, soldiers were left "ragged, dirty an[d] with only a few nickels left after paying their bills, or as much of them as they could. It is a terrible disgrace to the state of Colorado."[68]

Hardly one to notice which way the wind was blowing, Governor Ammons ignored all evidence of the impending crisis and withdrew most of the remaining militiamen from the strike zone. By April 17 the only troops remaining on active duty in the southern fields comprised thirty-four members of Lieutenant Karl Linderfelt's Company B (organized just three days earlier and heavily manned by "mine guards, pit bosses, clerks, engineers, and foremen employed by the CFI and Victor-American"), along with Company E (a somewhat larger contingent from Walsenburg whose members were virtually all "employed in and about the mines").[69]

While Bowers assured the Rockefellers that the strike was "wearing itself out," strikers in the tent colonies and open towns were growing restive. Many strikers interpreted the withdrawal of the regular militia and the mustering in of mine guards as ominous. They had long dreaded a concerted campaign by companies and the state to wipe Ludlow and its fellow tent colonies from the southern Colorado landscape. Meanwhile, company officials and the skeleton force of state troops that remained in the strike zone looked to the future with a corresponding and equally intense fear that the strikers would soon try to capitalize on the withdrawal of the National Guard. The strikers not only vastly outnumbered the militiamen but were widely known to count among them many combat veterans. If they launched an all-out offensive, it could leave both the collieries and the closed camps in ruins.[70]

It was a formula for disaster: two armies preparing for a battle that both had come to perceive as inevitable. In this context of pervasive paranoia, threat and counterthreat, any enemy movement seemed to presage a full-blown assault. Both sides had carried out beatings and murders over the previous seven months and exchanged tit for tat in the frequent skirmishing around Ludlow, Forbes, and other colonies. By mid-April the death toll for the strike had edged toward thirty. As the spring sun dawned at Ludlow on April 20, the actions of the Colorado National Guard and the strikers' armies alike triggered mutual suspicion. The day of reckoning was at hand, virtually everyone concluded. All it took was one gunshot to ignite the powder keg.[71]

The details of what happened next are in dispute. The confusion that characterizes any battle, the irregular makeup of both fighting contingents, the weak chain of command in each, the absence of neutral witnesses, the partisan worldviews of two sides staring past each other, the yawning gulf of hatred and misunderstanding that separated them—these and other complications make it foolish to think that we can know with any certainty what actually occurred on April 20.

This admission does not imply, however, that all stories about Ludlow deserve equal credence. Few major events in American history seem so shrouded in misconceptions, harbored not only by the general public but even by esteemed scholars. And so the lack of clarity in the historical record notwithstanding, it behooves us to review the broad outlines of the fighting. Militia officers met with Louis Tikas in the morning. In John Lawson's absence, Tikas was in command of the colony; the National Guard turned to him when a woman made the claim that her husband was being held against his will in the colony. As Tikas talked with Major Patrick Hamrock, strikers began to mill about in a manner that Hamrock found worrisome. At the same juncture, other militiamen were moving into positions that raised the strikers' fears. A single mysterious shot then sent the entire southern fields into chaos.[72]

Within an instant, a morning that had begun like many others dissolved into disaster. Several hours of fighting ensued, during which both sides brought in reinforcements. Male strikers headed down the arroyo leading away from the colony, seeking to draw the guardsmen's fire away from Ludlow. This tragically ill-conceived effort to protect the women and children still remaining in the colony instead left the camp at the National Guard's mercy.[73]

Miners alleged that their opponents were using exploding bullets; whatever the ammunition, state troops raked the colony with machine-gun and rifle fire. Militiamen claimed that John Lawson had unloaded cases of weapons when he reached the colony by automobile around eleven in the morning; wherever they had procured their guns, the strikers certainly brought plenty of firepower to bear—more than might have been expected, given the repeated complaints unionists had made over the preceding months regarding the National Guard's uneven application of the governor's disarmament order.[74]

Several men and boys died over the course of the day: Frank Snyder, the twelve-year-old who emerged from his family's hiding place; Private Alfred Martin, the sole militiaman to die that day, whose body strikers allegedly mutilated; Primo Larese, an unfortunate onlooker; and a few others. But there is little reason Ludlow would have achieved such infamy if not for a turn of events no one could have anticipated. As militiamen descended on the colony in the late afternoon, the tent city erupted in flames. The cause of the fire, like the identity of the first shooter, remains a matter of speculation. In one story, militiamen descended upon Ludlow and put it to the torch; in another, bullets—in some versions, the strikers', in others the guardsmen's—ignited stores of ammunition and explosives that union leaders had cached in the colony. There is little doubt, though, about the culpability of Karl Linderfelt and other militiamen in the death of Louis Tikas: they shot him in the back after Linderfelt smashed a rifle butt over his head.[75]

With the colony in ruins, Ludlow's leader slain, its inhabitants driven from their homes for the second time in seven months, and the dead on the strikers' side outnumbering those of their foes eighteen to one, it appeared to be a decisive victory for the state and its corporate allies. But it was hardly the end of the road for the strikers. They had an immense advantage in numbers and superior knowledge of both the coalfield landscape and guerrilla tactics. Most important of all, the desire for revenge now burned as fearsomely as the flames that had reduced the tent colony to ash. Ludlow was a massacre, but it was also a battle—the opening battle in a war the strikers had every intention of winning.

The Power of the Match

The designation "massacre" would appear to refer to a horrible but finite act of violence, yet the fighting at Ludlow unleashed further fusillades of words and weapons. "The flame of war which was lighted at Ludlow," a *Rocky Mountain News* editorial lamented, "has not stopped there." A journalist, Clara Ruth Mozzer, reported from the coalfields five days after the outbreak of fighting at Ludlow, "In this country, where the grim spirit of death stalks and prowls, there is nothing unbiased, nothing impartial. Everyone is sitting on one side of the fence or the other, there is no straddling."[76]

Company executives and militia officers explained Ludlow's destruction in time-tested rhetoric: a small group of National Guardsmen, they claimed, had occupied a vulnerable position, surrounded by a much larger force. Overwhelmingly composed of "ignorant foreigners," particularly Greek veterans of the Balkan Wars, this bloodthirsty throng had set out on the morning of April 20 to launch a full-fledged union offensive. Guardsmen had returned fire to protect their own lives and those of their fellows, killing some of the attackers and a few unfortunate bystanders. After many hours of shooting, a guardsman's bullet had accidentally ignited ammunition that strikers were keeping in the colony against the governor's order (another version of the story maintained that a stove had exploded). After the dry canvas tents of Ludlow had gone up in flames, the valiant men of the National Guard risked their lives to save any strikers who remained in the colony. As for the dead women and children later found lying in what journalists melodramatically

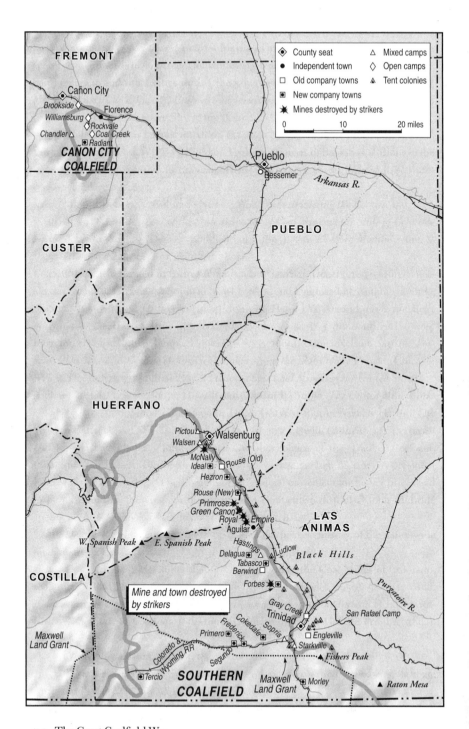

FREMONT

◈ Cañon City
Brookside ◇
Williamsburg ◇ ● Florence
◇ Rockvale
Chandler △ ◇ Coal Creek
⊡ Radiant
**CAÑON CITY
COALFIELD**

CUSTER

PUEBLO

◈ Pueblo
◇ Bessemer
Arkansas R.

HUERFANO

Pictou △ ◈ Walsenburg
Walsen ✸
McNally ⊡
Ideal ⊡ □ Rouse (Old)
Hezron ⊡ ▲

Rouse (New) ⊡
Primrose ✸
Green Cañon ✸ ▲
Royal ✸ ● Empire
Aguilar ●

LAS
ANIMAS

W. Spanish Peak ▲ ▲ E. Spanish Peak

Hastings ✸
Delagua ⊡ △ Ludlow
Tabasco ⊡ *Black Hills*
Berwind □

COSTILLA

Forbes ✸ ⊡ ▲

┌─────────────────────────┐
│ Mine and town destroyed │
│ by strikers   │
└─────────────────────────┘

Purgatoire R.

Gray Creek ▲
Cokedale ⊡ Trinidad ◈ ▲▲ San Rafael Camp
Sopris ⊡ ▲
Primero ⊡ Frederick ⊡ □ Engleville
Colorado & Segundo ⊡ ▲ Starkville ▲
Wyoming RR
Maxwell
Land Grant →

⊡ Tercio
Segundo Maxwell ⊡ Morley ▲ Fishers Peak
SOUTHERN Land Grant
COALFIELD ▲ Raton Mesa

7.1. The Great Coalfield War.

called the Black Hole of Ludlow, they had died well before the fire began, victims of the careless miners responsible for packing them into a tiny, unventilated cellar.[77]

Major Edward Boughton, a Cripple Creek mining attorney and counsel for the Colorado National Guard, become the most ardent proponent of such stories. With the Rockefeller family's assistance, Boughton—whom strikers described as "insane" and his fellow officers as "incompetent and dead beat"—embarked on a speaking tour that took him to Boston, Chicago, New York, and elsewhere. The major summarized the view from his side of the fence before the U.S. Commission on Industrial Relations on May 27: "There was no such thing as the Ludlow massacre," he declared. "Nobody was massacred at Ludlow. Nobody was killed at Ludlow in the tent colony or burned, with the one exception of a small child by the name of Snyder, who during the day . . . had faced toward the arroyo for a private purpose, and was shot in the forehead from the direction of the position of the tent colonist combatants."[78]

The miners and their allies saw the attack on Ludlow from a very different perspective. In their eyes, it represented the outcome of a deliberate plan to strike at the heart of their movement, the colony that John C. Osgood had termed "the center of devilment." It was many days before the strikers could come up with an accurate body count, for the militia cordoned off the site and forbade unauthorized people to survey the scene. Through their field glasses, though, strikers believed they could make out several contorted bodies among the ruins of the colony. Union officials estimated that the militia had killed between forty-five and sixty-six strikers; union leaders even accused militiamen of incinerating dozens of bodies on pyres at the tent colony as well as in the coke ovens of Tabasco, Hastings, and other closed camps in the canyons above Ludlow.[79]

A gunfight that strikers might have perceived as a battle became something altogether different: "'the most terrible massacre in American industrial history,'" as a United Mine Workers circular dated April 22 proclaimed. The *Denver Times* asserted: "The entire state, sympathizers and non-sympathizers alike, is aroused as never before at the slaughter of innocent children and defenseless women."[80]

For many colliers, the striking miners' failure to protect the women and children of the Ludlow colony called into question their masculinity. "The fact that women and children were killed in the Ludlow tent colony," declared the *Florence Daily Citizen*, "has caused the greatest indignity." The deaths of fellow workmen in mine accidents and strike-related violence had already done much to fuel the miners' ire; that a still-unknown number of "women and children were made the targets," as a Denver journalist phrased it, "of modern warfare" only deepened the miners' need to reclaim their sense of manhood.[81]

Strike leaders and tent colony captains sought to channel the mood among the rank and file of mourning, anger, and injured masculinity into a concerted military response. The result was a campaign of retributive violence, in which seven months of civil unrest and almost half a century of labor-management tumult at last came to a head. For ten days, the mineworkers of southern Colorado engaged in the fiercest, deadliest labor uprising since the Civil War.

From the moment the fighting began, the guerrillas' first priority was to safeguard the women and children in the homes of sympathetic ranch families and townspeople, at Camp San Rafael (a tent colony founded for Ludlow refugees), and in other places of refuge. Despite the significant role that women and children had assumed throughout the strike—attacking scabs, marching in union parades, and so forth—the miners now viewed the strike as a man-to-man struggle to be waged in a combat zone where women and children no longer had any place. The strikers, reinforced by local men from "all walks of life . . . : bartenders, saloonkeepers, storekeepers, businessmen, carpenters," organized themselves into battalions of between one hundred and five hundred men, then used their superior knowledge of the southern Colorado landscape to launch swift, stealthy, effective attacks.[82]

By the morning after the massacre, striking miners were already wreaking havoc throughout the strike zone. "The hills in every direction suddenly seemed to be alive with men," one witness reported. In the days ahead, miners besieged Hastings, Tabasco, Delagua, Berwind, and other camps, destroyed mine buildings and tunnels at the Empire, Royal, Green Cañon, and Primrose mines, blew up several railroad bridges, and even dynamited the retaining dam that impounded drinking water for the company towns above Ludlow. As small forces waged guerrilla war, other contingents secured arms and ammunition by breaking into company stores. One twenty-man brigade even captured a D&RG locomotive at El Moro and took it to a junction one mile east of Ludlow, where they unloaded troops and ammunition for tent colony refugees hiding in the Black Hills. Three days after the Ludlow Massacre, the *Denver Times* proclaimed the miners to be "engaged in a war to death." As a result, "ruin lay on every hand." Clara Ruth Mozzer wrote: "Many of the strikers are in the hills without knowing whether all or some of their family are among the dead. Like animals at bay they are wild with dread."[83]

In Denver, meanwhile, a fierce debate was raging among labor leaders. A coal company spy who had infiltrated United Mine Workers headquarters reportedly overheard one Western Federation of Miners leader threatening: "These employers will be made to feel [the] potent power of the match unless they come through clean and recognize the Union, as we intend to win even if we have to reduce this State to ashes." "They fully expect," the detective alleged, "that there will be a prolonged war with Mexico [President Wilson had launched an attack on Veracruz, Mexico, on April 21, 1914] and that organized labor will make itself felt in a way never experienced before in the United States. . . . The Unions in this country will be practically united in one body and no time is to be lost in solidifying the ranks of labor." Whether such reports were apocryphal or not, the "Call to Arms" issued by the federation, the United Mine Workers, and the Colorado State Federation of Labor suggested that revolution was in the air. There is no telling what might have happened had moderate unionists failed in urging restraint.[84]

Even after United Mine Workers attorney Horace Hawkins worked out a truce with state officials, however, telegrams, telephone calls, and even personal visits from union leaders to the fighting miners failed to bring peace to the strike zone. "'We made every effort to send word to every district in Colorado that a truce was on,'" John McLennan of the Colorado State Federation of Labor told reporters shortly after his release from jail on April 25, "'and I am at a loss to understand the reported outbreaks.'" McLennan and his counterparts underestimated the challenges of communicating with scattered, highly mobile brigades without any apparent central command structure that were engaging in guerrilla campaigns, nor did strikers have any reason to believe that the militia would keep to its side of the peace agreement. Far more important, however, was the fact that the miners' armies were em-

7.5. Colorado National Guardsmen Mustering for Inspection, Las Animas County.
Denver Public Library, Western History Collection, X-60565.

phatically not waging war for either the abstract principle of unionism or the
United Mine Workers. Instead, they were fighting for themselves and for
their families, for one another and for the dead. No agreement made in Denver could convince the strikers to lay down their arms before they had redeemed themselves and reclaimed the coalfields.[85]

"'Remember Ludlow,'" a journalist discovered, served as "the battle cry of
the men who lost wives and children in Monday's slaughter of the innocents,
and of their fellows whose sympathies have been stirred and who are fearful for the safety of their own loved ones. These men declare they are fighting
for liberty, for freedom from oppression, and not for revenge alone." Waging
what they considered the good fight, fearing with ample reason that they
might be arrested, deported, or even massacred if they laid down their arms,
the strikers tore through the coalfields. Rumors located improbable numbers
of them seemingly everywhere, but the devastation they wrought was real
enough. By the time the fighting stopped after the destruction of the closed
camp at Forbes and other skirmishes in several parts of the strike zone, the
strikers had killed more than thirty strikebreakers, mine guards, and militia-

7.6. Funeral Procession for Louis Tikas, April 27, 1914. Photograph by Lewis R. Dold. Denver Public Library, Western History Collection, X-60441.

men, destroyed six mines, and laid Forbes and parts of other company properties to waste, all while suffering only a handful of casualties.[86]

Let Us Forget for Once That We Are Ladies

Peace came only because of the intercession of two outside forces. The first, a "silent army of 1,000 women"—"women with babes in arms, white haired women whose eyes were dimmed by age, working women, women from Capitol hill, women of all classes and all ages"—marched on the Colorado capitol on April 25, beseeching the governor, "as mothers and citizens of the state, that he end the warfare raging in the southern coal fields before more innocent blood is shed." March organizer and Denver socialite Dora Phelps Buell explained the women's strategy to a reporter. "This is not a time to be ladylike. For heaven's sake, let us forget for once that we are ladies. Let us be women. If militancy is needed to compel the governor to accede to our demands, let us then resort to militancy. Women should not be ashamed to be militant if that is the only way they can stop so uncivilized a condition of affairs as that which prevails in the strike district." Buell planned to compel the governor to "remember the women and children of Ludlow." She added, "Remember that the people of the state are aroused. Remember you are their servant and they have the power to command you to do their will." She intended to warn Ammons: "Unless the morning's gathering of women receive satisfactory assurances . . . his office may be crowded night and day with women who will constantly repeat their demands to him. They will pester him to death and defy him or anyone else to remove them."[87]

Once Buell and the others had reached the capitol, Alma Lafferty, president of the Women's Peace Organization, "mounted the stairway and called the meeting to order. 'We are here on a very serious business,' she shouted above the commotion which came from the shuffling of feet. 'We will wait on the governor and see that he put a stop to this warfare.'" Lafferty proclaimed: "'We are not going to abuse the governor, but we do not want civil war in Colorado. . . . Be dignified and quiet and show the people of this country that we are in earnest.'" Ammons sent his doorman to inform the women that the governor could not meet with them because his chambers were not sufficiently spacious to accommodate them all. Shrugging off his lame excuse, the women decided that if Ammons's rooms would not fit them, the house legislative chambers certainly could. Then they "turned and began to surge up the stairway toward the house."[88]

The governor tried to ignore and outlast the women. Far from losing heart, though, they "kept their vigil," launching into " 'the Battle Hymn of the Republic,' 'John Brown's Body,' 'Onward Christian Soldiers' and 'Nearer, My God, to Thee'" whenever their resolve began to flag. Speeches by march leaders did even more to rally the crowd's spirits. "'Women, we are making history,'" Buell declared, "'Stay on.' 'We will!' they cried back." The entire day passed. Nonplussed, Lafferty's committee remained "on the job, tired-eyed but cheerful. All day it had followed [Ammons] like a Nemesis." In response to Lieutenant Governor Fitzgarrald's efforts to persuade the women that they would do better to leave Ammons alone, Evangeline Heartz, another prominent member of the committee, "pointed her finger at Fitzgarrald" and implored him to remember that "'the women of Denver are gathered upstairs. They want to see Governor Ammons and they will see him. Do you hear?"[89]

What happened next, one newspaper proclaimed, would surely "go down in history as one of the most remarkable demonstrations by women which ever took place in this country." In "an assemblage that gave equal suffrage a new meaning," a delegation of marchers led by Lafferty met with Ammons in his office and "demanded" that he "at once dictate a telegram to President Wilson calling for federal intervention in Colorado's industrial strife." Ammons then entered the assembly chambers, to the applause of the women gathered there. Lafferty assured him, "We, representing the women of Denver, are here today on a peaceful mission. We do not intend to take sides in this terrible strife in Colorado. All we want is for this warfare in our state to cease, and we are here in the name of the women and children to demand that you end it."[90]

Ammons, his face "drawn and haggard from worry and loss of sleep" and "every muscle in his body twitch[ing]," spoke next. The governor said that he had been in touch with Washington. But the White House, he claimed, was preoccupied with Mexican affairs: Wilson's attack on Veracruz earlier in the week had prompted a diplomatic crisis. Spurred on by the women's entreaties, though, Ammons decided to send another plea to Wilson. "Where men had failed," the *Denver Times* approvingly concluded, women "succeeded," a triumph that "did more to prove the worth of women as voters and as citizens—did more to prove their right to equal suffrage with men— than any movement heretofore chronicled in history. . . . They, the women, decided to act and to let their actions speak for themselves. The women wanted something and, quite after the fashion of women, they ACTED and GOT WHAT THEY DEMANDED."[91]

The president responded on April 28 by dispatching a second major agent of peace, the U.S. Army. As federal troops rushed to the coalfields in compliance with Wilson's orders, the final spasms of unrest shook the region. The deadliest attack was the assault on Forbes (with which this book began), but the strikers' battalions were busy elsewhere, too, trying to inflict as much damage as they could before the U.S. Army interceded. Why the miners balked at taking on federal troops is not entirely clear—indeed, army officers remained watchful for signs of further trouble—but war weariness and the commonsense calculation that they had nothing to gain and everything to lose by fighting the regular army were probably the decisive factors. And so nine days after gunfire erupted at Ludlow, dispatches from the strike zone at last reported, "Everything quiet."[92]

Requiem

Most strikers probably welcomed the peace. Yet as a war of annihilation turned into a war of attrition, the miners watched their prospect of victory slip away. Already out of work for eight months and barely scraping by on strike relief, mineworkers lacked the financial wherewithal to outlast deep-pocketed coal companies. Colorado Fuel and Iron alone could boast that it had $5.6 million cash on hand, massive reserves that it had skimmed from the bounty of the earth and the sweat of miners' brows.[93]

Secretary of War Lindley Garrison explained the army's approach: "What we wish to do is to preserve as nearly as we possibly can an impartial attitude." When compared with the Colorado militia, the army did indeed remain largely neutral—with one big exception: they paved the way for hundreds, then thousands, of nonunion men to enter the mines, and therefore to break the strike. "Of course, our first duty is to maintain public order," Garrison declared. "Our second purpose should be to restore conditions as nearly as possible to those of normality"—in other words, to the prestrike situation of corporate control over mine workscapes and the new company towns. Federal troops prohibited the importation of strikebreakers, but they refused to intervene when men arrived at the mines seeking work. To exploit this enormous loophole, the operators not only began in mid-May to place want ads listing job openings in the mines, but probably offered prospective mineworkers train fare to the collieries. Though army officers refused to permit hundreds of workers secured in this manner to start working, production figures nonetheless demonstrate the companies' ability to reman most of their mines. By July, output at Colorado Fuel and Iron pits had returned to roughly 70 percent of their prestrike levels.[94]

Meanwhile, out-of-work miners and their families began to feel the pinch of poverty. "The strikers are about out of money," one officer wrote from Williamsburg, "and cannot much longer maintain the present status. They want to go to work. If any way could be opened to them, of letting them down easy, they might possibly take advantage of it." Jesse Welborn informed Rockefeller headquarters in August, "All of the reports that have come to us from confidential sources during the past few weeks indicate a growing dissatisfaction on the part of all the strikers, and threats have been made by many (some of which have been put into execution) to return to work." He believed it "not improbable" that strike benefits would be "withdrawn or materially reduced," a move that would leave most mining families with little choice but to abandon the strike. As the executive suspected, the union's finances were faltering. Increasingly skeptical that the Colorado strike had any prospect of success, the United Mine Workers' national leadership sought an honorable conclusion to the conflict. But the operators, unyielding to the end, remained as insistent as ever that they would not negotiate with the union.[95]

With the strike in shambles and the strikers in despair, Colorado's coal mine workers held another convention in early December 1914. This time, no brass band or chorus preceded the delegates into the hall; no army of "sympathizers" marched behind. Instead, two hundred representatives, exhausted from fifteen months on strike, straggled into a Denver meeting place. After brief speeches by Frank Hayes, Mother Jones, John Lawson, and others, they considered a proposal from the international board. The proposal emphasized the hardships the strikers were enduring, the sacrifices they had made, and the organization's conviction that Woodrow Wilson's labor-friendly administration would use federal power to force the operators to settle the dispute fairly.

The president's plan to appoint a commission charged with resolving the Colorado coalfield war had precipitated the Pueblo convention and gave the United Mine Workers leadership the opening it needed to seek an end to a costly struggle it could no longer win. "'In view of this urgent request,'" read the union's recommendation to the Denver delegates, "'we deem it the part of wisdom to accept his suggestion and to terminate the strike.'" In a carefully worded statement, the union declared that it was

> doing the best thing possible for the men on strike who have suffered so long in order that justice might be done. We have spent an enormous

amount of money in waging this struggle for justice and fair play in the mining fields of Colorado, but have felt that it was spent in as noble a cause as it was ever given to man to espouse. We are not unmindful of the heroic struggle waged by the miners of Colorado since the strike began. It is with feelings of pain and sorrow that we recall the massacre of our men, women and children at Ludlow.

Making no mention of the Ten Days' War that followed, the union pronounced "the sacrifices made, the privations endured" over the past fifteen months "without a parallel in the history of the labor struggles of America. Only those who have suffered grievous wrongs," the proposal concluded, "could endure such a prolonged conflict. All lovers of liberty and believers in fair play between man and man must admire the heroic struggle of the Colorado miners against the great wealth and influence of Rockefeller and his associations." Union leaders asserted their own belief: "Our people have not died in vain and . . . the battle they have waged against such tremendous odds has aroused the conscience of the nation." They also made a prediction: "Out of the martyrdom of our people will come the dawn of a better day for the suffering miners and their families in the coal fields of Colorado."

Studiously avoiding any mention of the forty or so lives the strikers had taken in the course of the coalfield war, the union asserted that it had made "every overture for peace since the beginning of this conflict . . . only to be ridiculed, and in the end thirty-five of our men, women and children were murdered before the people of the nation came to understand that the coal strike in Colorado was not a local or a state issue, but a national issue of vital importance, involving civic as well as industrial rights." President Wilson's "appointment of a permanent presidential commission of fair-minded men" would ensure a new order:

> that the old-time oppression and tyranny will be no more and that public opinion will compel the large operators of Colorado to deal justly with our people. We recognize no surrender and shall continue to propagate the principles of our humanitarian movement thruout the coal fields of Colorado. We advise all men to seek their former places in the mines and those who are refused employment we shall render as-

sistance to the best of our ability, and shall provide every legal protection to those of our members who are being persecuted by the hirelings of organized greed.[96]

With this proposal to call off the strike, the debate began. Miners from the northern fields favored continuing the struggle; those from the south "were a unit in standing by the executive board which had made the startling and unlooked-for proposition to call off the fight." After twelve hours of discussion, the northern delegates decided to relent. Like the vote that had authorized the southern colliers' strike fifteen months earlier, this vote was unanimous.[97]

"The first intimation the outside world had of the settlement of this most titanic of labor struggles," the *Denver News* reported, "came when a burst of song floated thru the closed door of the convention hall." The newspaper correspondents waiting outside "straightened up and listened. The music was 'Shouting the Battle Cry of Freedom.'" The words, of course, were those of "The Colorado Strike Song." The very tune that had fortified the miners' resolve at Castle Hall back in September 1913 now echoed mournfully. "The delegates were all singing lustily. Men from the northern and southern fields stood up and joined hands and sang, and the tears rolled down the faces of some of them. Verse after verse of the song, with words written by miners themselves, peeled [*sic*] forth." From the dais, "the officers of the executive board and of the district union joined in the song, tho plainly they were almost breaking under the nervous strain." The strike was over.[98]

The fifteen-month struggle had proved costly, by any measure. In addition to the property destroyed in the course of Ludlow and the Ten Days' War and the dozens of lives lost, the principal adversaries had poured huge sums into the conflict. The Associated Press estimated the total financial toll of the strike as "approximately $18,000,000," and though this figure seems inflated, Colorado Fuel and Iron had lost over $1.6 million in the course of the strike, the United Mine Workers had spent $870,000, and many millions more were lost by other coal companies, the state and federal governments, striking mining families, and steelworkers laid off at the Pueblo mills because of a lack of fuel. Other losses defy easy accounting. The strike and massacre had sullied reputations, displaced thousands from their longtime homes, bitterly divided coal-mining communities, shut hundreds of miners out of the hard jobs they nonetheless cherished, and created gaping voids in the lives of all those who had lost loved ones.[99]

All these losses notwithstanding, the workers' movement that momentarily threatened to assume revolutionary dimensions had failed to reform either the mine workscapes or the company towns, which together bore responsibility for fomenting decades of industrial struggle in the southern coalfields. The Rockefeller Plan, a company union subsequently created by William Lyon Mackenzie King at the behest of John D. Rockefeller, Jr., enabled Colorado Fuel and Iron mineworkers to present grievances to local officials. The Rockefellers also tried to rectify some of the worst excesses of the closed camps. Yet like John Osgood and William Palmer before them, the Rockefellers held to a vision of Western industrialism that left workers no real place on the land.[100]

Epilogue

When the southern Colorado colliers went on strike in 1919, 1921, and 1922 under the United Mine Workers, and again in 1927 in a dispute involving the more radical Industrial Workers of the World, they ensured that the Great Coalfield War would mark not the endpoint of class conflict in the region, but rather the most dramatic moment in an ongoing history of struggle that carried on through the New Deal. Memories of the massacre continued to loom large, informing the Rockefeller Plan, inspiring the state to create a board of labor arbitration, and steeling the American labor movement in its fight to secure the rights for which the martyrs of Ludlow had given their lives. In different ways and to varying degrees, each of these uses of the past—enlisting the history of the coalfield war in the politics that corporations, unions, and the state adopted to champion their respective interests—cut the events of April 20, 1914, off both from their deep context of nearly half a century of contentious relationships between workers, capitalists, and the natural world and from the ensuing workers' uprising, which still remains the most violent American labor rebellion of the postemancipation era.[1]

As acts of remembering and forgetting were continually reshaping the meaning of Ludlow, the mineral-intensive energy economy was changing in ways that would have ominous consequences for mining families and mining companies alike. Coal production peaked during World War I, then went into a steep, steady decline because of the introduction of gasoline-powered automobiles, trucks, and farm machinery, as well as the continuing falloff in hard-rock mining and smelting. Colliery employment plummeted during the 1920s, as diesel fuel supplanted coal on Western railroads, and as pipelines linked the Front Range cities and even Colorado Fuel and Iron's own steelworks to natural gas fields on the High Plains. Petroleum and natural gas became the main drivers of a Western economy more dependent than ever on fossil fuel–burning technologies that initiated wide-ranging transformations in production processes, consumer aspirations, physical structure and the fabric of daily life in cities and suburbs, and much else. As a consequence, several major coal mines closed down by the 1930s. Most of the rest ceased operations by the 1950s, at which point only a few high-grade metallurgical coking-coal mines remained open; but these then shut down too, as cheap foreign steel forced severe cutbacks at the Pueblo steelworks during the 1970s and 1980s.[2]

Coalfield migrants and the families they raised in southern Colorado, meanwhile, were experiencing the highs and lows of the changing energy economy. Automobiles, whose use during the coalfield wars had been restricted to company officials, militia officers, and labor leaders, became more widely available in the late 1910s. Many miners began to commute to the pits from independent towns, adjacent camps, and even ranches and farms out in the countryside, thus gaining a further measure of freedom from company paternalism. The near-total mechanization of cutting and loading after the 1920s fundamentally transformed the relation between human labor and natural processes in the mine workscape. The increasing obsolescence of craft traditions, the scarcity of work, and miners' continuing need and desire to move around to seek out better opportunities—these factors together led most coalfield migrants to set out on the road once again. Returning to the strategy of mobility that had brought them and their forebears to the mining camps, they moved on—to Montana and Utah, California, and most of all the Front Range cities of Denver and Pueblo, where many thousands of their descendants make their homes today.[3]

The decline of coal mining changed the landscape almost as significantly as the rise of the industry had. The subterranean workscapes that colliers hewed from the earth have continued to evolve long after the abandonment of the mines. Deep within these no-longer-peopled places, rock and coal have fallen, mine timbers have decayed, poisonous gases have accumulated, and groundwater has poured in.

Mine closures not only unmade mine workscapes but also undercut the raison d'être of the southern Colorado coal camps. Despite chronic economic woes, open camps and independent towns largely toughed it out. Their populations aging, their young people mostly forced to look for opportunity elsewhere, they have entered the long senescence that set in across much of rural America during the twentieth century. If Trinidad, Walsenburg, Aguilar, and other communities are mere shadows of their former selves, virtually all the closed camps have disappeared entirely. Coal companies, instead of paying the higher property taxes levied on improved land, dismantled the places they had so carefully designed and built to contain the colliers' militancy. Generally speaking, it takes a good map to locate the scattered concrete foundations, tunnel openings, and heaps of mine waste that make up the physical remnants of southern Colorado's clanking, smoking mines and the densely populated communities that supported them.

A few of the open camps have gone through different but equally problematic metamorphoses. Crested Butte has become a bustling ski resort where renovated colliers' cottages fetch millions of dollars, while in the Cucharas Valley near La Veta and the Purgatoire Valley west of Trinidad, outdoor recreation and second-home developments have attracted many newcomers. Deeper continuities underlie the apparent contrast between present-day growth in these areas—booms driven by the supposedly benign enjoyment of nature—and the nineteenth-century booms premised on the extraction of natural resources. Paradoxically, the leisure landscapes taking shape on top of former coalfields depend even more than their extractive predecessors on the fossil-fuel industrial economy. Few Americans would be willing to live in such places without cars or the food, building supplies, and consumer goods produced by mineral-powered industries across the world, then hauled in to the Mountain West by diesel-powered container ships, trucks, and railroads. As for the light, heat, and electricity that lend comfort to faux-rustic cabins and the mushrooming McMansions of our New West, these forms of energy arrive, more often than not, via pipeline or transmission wire from gas wells and coal-burning power plants, gargantuan strip mines in the Powder River Basin of Wyoming. and heavily automated underground coal mines in western Colorado and eastern Utah.

The transformation of old coal-mining areas into vacation preserves has hardly reduced the need for labor in the Mountain West. The migration of overwhelmingly white and upper- and middle-class urbanites and suburbanites from the Front Range and other American urban regions to the former coal country has depended in no small part on new waves of working-class migrants who continue to bind the Mountain West to other places. Some source countries for workers in the "new" Western economy remain unchanged—Mexico and Russia, for instance. But others—Senegal and Jamaica—represent the further elaboration of the mass migrations that repeopled the southern coalfields a century ago. There is no sign that the exceptionally violent record of labor-management conflict in the coal industry will be repeated anytime soon, at least not in the United States. Yet in a region and a nation that continue to deny the significance or even the existence of class and class conflict, these forces continue to shape lives and landscapes. Almost a century and a half after William Jackson Palmer first embarked on his utopian empire-building scheme, this amnesia, this denial, obscures a Western past and present far more complicated—and far more troubled—than myth or memory would generally credit.[4]

Whether today's energy wars take place in corporate boardrooms or legislative chambers, in Nigeria or Venezuela, Bolivia or Iraq, and whether they take their toll on oil workers or on the retreating Arctic ice, they take place largely out of sight, if not always out of mind for most inhabitants of the developed world. The story of the Colorado coalfield wars should prompt us to ask more probing questions about our connection with these conflicts and our responsibility for the suffering and damage they are causing. In the process, it illustrates how a more holistic historical vision might help us understand the origins of the modern world's most pressing dilemmas. Poverty, disease, discrimination, inequality, global climate change, war, pollution—the environmental, social, political, and economic aspects of these problems are inextricably interconnected. Frederick Jackson Turner once pointed out that "in history, there are only artificial divisions." We will never see the past whole. Yet only by looking beyond the divisions can we learn this vital lesson: If our contemporary problems have resulted from interconnection—from the complex historical interactions this book has tried to trace between various elements of the natural world, different groups of people, and human institutions such as markets and states—then we must search for similarly intertwined solutions. On the eve of the transformation of the United States by fossil fuels, Henry David Thoreau declared that "in wildness is the preservation of the world." Today, the fate of our species and the future of the planet depends in no small degree on humankind's capacity to cope with the complexity and wild interconnectedness of a world that we have done much to shape but that nonetheless continues to elude our control in all sorts of marvelous and alarming ways.[5]

The past has forged the road along which we are traveling. Powerful forces vie to direct where we go from here, urging us in one direction or another. Yet the next step remains ours to take.

Abbreviations

AG File   Office of the Adjutant General, Document File 2154620, Record Group 94, Records of the Adjutant General's Office, National Archives and Records Administration (NARA), Washington, D.C.

AT&SF   Atchison, Topeka, & Santa Fe Railroad Papers, Kansas State Historical Society, Topeka

BHS   Bessemer Historical Society, Pueblo, Colo.

CC   Tutt Library, Colorado College, Colorado Springs

CC&I   Colorado Coal and Iron Company

CCMC   Subcommittee on Mines and Mining, *Conditions in the Coal Mines of Colorado: Hearings before a Subcommittee of the Committee on Mines and Mining*, 63d Cong, 2d sess. (Washington, D.C.: GPO, 1914), 1

CF&I   Colorado Fuel and Iron Company

CF&I-RAC   Business Interest Series, Record Group 2, Office of the Messieurs Rockefeller, Rockefeller Family Archives, Rockefeller Archive Center, Sleepy Hollow, N.Y.

CHS   Colorado Historical Society, Denver

CIR   Commission on Industrial Relations, *Final Report and Testimony*, 64th Cong., 2d sess. (Washington, D.C.: GPO, 1916), S. Doc. 415

CNG   Colorado National Guard

CNG Courts-Martial   Record of the General Court-Martial, Military District of Colorado, Charges of Arson in Relation to Ludlow Tent Colony 1914, box 10645, Colorado National Guard Records, Colorado State Archives, Denver

CSA   Colorado State Archives, Denver

CSF of L Colorado State Federation of Labor

CWA   Civil Works Administration Interviews, Colorado Historical Society, Denver

DPL   Western History and Genealogy Department, Denver Public Library

D&RG   Denver & Rio Grande Railroad Papers, Colorado Historical Society, Denver

EM   Eric Margolis Coal Project, Historical Collections, Archives, University of Colorado at Boulder Libraries

FF Frederick Farrar Papers, Denver Public Library

HCEHP Huerfano County Ethno-History Project, transcripts consulted at Pueblo Public Library and online at: www.spld.org

Hills Reports   R. C. Hills Reports on Coal Properties, CF&I Steel Corporation Papers, Colorado Historical Society, Denver

INS   Immigration and Naturalization Service, RG 85, NARA–Washington, D.C.

JFW Papers   Jesse Floyd Welborn Papers, Colorado Historical Society, Denver

LACC   Las Animas County Courthouse, Trinidad, Colo.

LADC   Las Animas County District Court Records, Las Animas County Courthouse, Trinidad, Colo.

LHC   Local History Center, Cañon City Public Library, Cañon City, Colo.

LMB Papers   LaMont Montgomery Bowers Papers, University of Binghamton Special Collections, Binghamton, N.Y.

OMR   Office of the Messieurs Rockefeller

RAC   Rockefeller Archive Center, Sleepy Hollow, N.Y.

RG   Record Group

UMWA   United Mine Workers of America

UU   Special Collections, Marriott Library, University of Utah, Salt Lake City

WJPP   William Jackson Palmer Papers (followed by location of repository)

YMCA Report   Peter Roberts, W. S. Hopkins, and John A. Goodell, "Report upon the Possible Service by the Young Men's Christian Association in the Mining Communities of the Colorado Fuel and Iron Company Based upon a Survey . . . ," folder 156, box 18, CF&I-RAC

Notes

Introduction

1. On the weather, see Ray Benedict testimony, in Edwin F. Carson Court-Martial, May 11, 1914, case no. 2, folder 6, Record of the General Court-Martial, Military District of Colorado, Charges of Arson in Relation to Ludlow Tent Colony, 1914, box 10645, Colorado National Guard Records, CSA (hereafter CNG Courts-Martial), p. 37. On troop numbers, see S. Julian Lamme testimony, ibid., p. 111; Edward J. Boughton testimony, Commission on Industrial Relations, *Final Report and Testimony*, 64th Cong., 2d sess., 1916, S. Doc. 415 (henceforth CIR), 7:6364. On mine guards as National Guardsmen, see the undated, unsigned report by Colorado National Guard (CNG) officers in folder 4, box 2, Frederick Farrar Papers, Western History and Genealogy Department, Denver Public Library (henceforth FF), p. 8.

2. Other types of uprisings by workers—particularly slave revolts—claimed more lives, but the Colorado coalfield war has no rival among postemancipation labor movements.

3. John R. Lawson testimony, May 28, 1914, in Karl E. Linderfelt Court-Martial, case no. 11, copy in box 2, FF. Boughton placed the colony's population at the time of the fighting at eight hundred; see Boughton testimony, CIR, 7:6371. For use of "White City" in relation to Ludlow, see Frank Fink and Theresa Fink, interview, n.d., in Huerfano County Ethno-History Project, www.spld.org (henceforth HCEHP), p. 1. The phrase may have been more commonly used to refer to the camp at Walsenburg; see Edward Verdeckberg, "Report of the District Commander Camp at Walsenburg from October

28, 1913, to May 5, 1914," box 1, John Chase Papers, Western History and Genealogy Department, Denver Public Library (henceforth DPL).

4. P. M. Cullon testimony, May 11, 1914, in Carson Court-Martial, p. 168; C. A. Conner testimony, May 11, 1914, in Maurice Bigelow Court-Martial, case no. 6, folder 8, CNG Courts-Martial, pp. 111–112.

5. S. Julian Lamme testimony, in Carson Court-Martial, p. 101; Maurice Bigelow testimony, May 11, 1914, in Garry S. Lawrence Court-Martial, case no. 4, folder 7, CNG Courts-Martial, p. 48; Mother Jones, *The Autobiography of Mother Jones,* 3rd rev. ed. (Chicago: Kerr for Illinois Labor History Society, 1977), 191–193.

6. *Denver Express,* Sept. 22, 1913. Secondary sources enumerate the dead in a variety of ways; the figure of twenty—Private Martin, eighteen strikers, and an onlooker named Primo Larese—seems authoritative. See Carson Court-Martial, pp. 6–28; and Scott Martelle, *Blood Passion: The Ludlow Massacre and Class War in the American West* (New Brunswick, N.J.: Rutgers University Press, 2007), 222–223.

7. Jones, *Autobiography,* 191–192. Still more powerful than the articles that began appearing on April 21 were the photographs that the *Rocky Mountain News* and other publications started carrying on April 22. For book-length treatments of Ludlow, see Martelle, *Blood Passion;* Priscilla Long, *Where the Sun Never Shines: A History of America's Bloody Coal Industry* (New York: Paragon House, 1989), 272–297; George McGovern and Leonard Guttridge, *The Great Coalfield War* (Boston: Houghton Mifflin, 1972); Barron B. Beshoar, *Out of the Depths: The Story of John R. Lawson, a Labor Leader* (Denver: Colorado Historical Commission and Denver Trades and Labor Assembly, 1957); and Zeese Papanikolas, *Buried Unsung: Louis Tikas and the Ludlow Massacre* (Salt Lake City: University of Utah Press, 1982).

8. I define the frontier as a zone of intercultural contact and conflict, not, with Frederick Jackson Turner, as the dividing line between civilization and savagery.

9. LaMont Montgomery Bowers to John D. Rockefeller, Jr., folder 211, box 23, Business Interest Series, Record Group 2, Office of the Messieurs Rockefeller, Rockefeller Family Archives, Rockefeller Archive Center, Sleepy Hollow, N.Y. (henceforth CF&I-RAC); Ed Doyle to John P. White, Apr. 21, 1914, env. 4, Edward S. Doyle Papers, DPL; Doyle interview in the *Rocky Mountain News,* Apr. 22, 1914.

10. Constance Doyle Jackson to Jack Foster, Oct. 16, 1958, folder 17, box 3, John R. Lawson Papers, DPL; Upton Sinclair, *King Coal: A Novel* (New York: Macmillan, 1917), and Sinclair, *The Coal War: A Sequel to "King Coal,"* intro. John Graham (Boulder: Associated Press of Colorado, 1976); Woody Guthrie, "Ludlow Massacre," in *Struggle,* Smithsonian/Folkways SF, album 40025; Howard Zinn, "The Colorado Fuel and Iron Strike, 1913–1914" (M.A. thesis, Columbia University, 1952); Howard Zinn, "The Colorado Coal Strike, 1913–14," in Howard Zinn, Dana Frank, and Robin D. G. Kelley, eds., *Three Strikes: Miners, Musicians, Salesgirls, and the Fighting Spirit of Labor's Last Century* (Boston: Beacon, 2002); McGovern and Guttridge, *Great Coalfield War;* George

McGovern, "The Colorado Coal Strike, 1913–1914" (Ph.D. diss., Northwestern University, 1953); Beshoar, *Out of the Depths.*

11. Jerome Greene to J. M. Glenn, July 12, 1914, folder 146, box 20, Industrial Relations—Colorado Fuel and Iron Co., 1914–1915, Administration, Program and Policy Files, Rockefeller Foundation Papers, RG 3, Rockefeller Archive Center (henceforth RAC); Raymond B. Fosdick, *John D. Rockefeller, Jr.: A Portrait* (New York: Harper, 1956). An early articulation of this story was an official statement by the operators: see *Rocky Mountain News,* Apr. 25, 1914.

12. Charles Wayland Towne to John D. Rockefeller, Jr., May 2, 1914, folder 173, box 20, CF&I-RAC; Jerome Greene to John D. Rockefeller, Jr., July 6, 1914; folder 176, ibid.; "Ivy Lee, New York's Door Opener," *New York Herald,* Feb. 25, 1917; John D. Rockefeller, Jr., to Jesse Floyd Welborn, June 8, 1914, folder 2, Jesse Floyd Welborn Papers (henceforth JFW Papers); "Railway Officers," *Railway Gazette* (1914): 1104, folder 568, box 74, RG 2, Office of the Messieurs Rockefeller, Friends and Services III 2H, RAC. Lee's work constituted a milestone in the emergence of public relations. Stuart Ewen, *PR! A Social History of Spin* (New York: Basic, 1996), 78–83. In these efforts Rockefeller had plenty of help; millions of Americans, including more than a few workers, harbored virulent antiunion sentiments. See Newell Dwight Hillis, *A Straight Sermon to Young Men: A Remarkable Statement Showing the Real Issue of the War in Colorado* (Detroit: n.p., 1914?); and Stephen H. Norwood, *Strike-Breaking and Intimidation: Mercenaries and Masculinity in Twentieth-Century America* (Chapel Hill: University of North Carolina Press, 2002), 114–170.

13. *Colorado: A Guide to the Highest State,* comp. Writers' Program of the Works Projects Administration in the State of Colorado (New York: Hastings House, 1941), 375. For more on the politics of Ludlow in the WPA guide, see Susan Schulten, "How to See Colorado: The Federal Writers' Project, American Regionalism, and the 'Old New Western History,'" *Western Historical Quarterly* (Spring 2005): 49–70. See also Colorado Bar Association, "Historical Foreword and Bibliography," 2003 Mock Trial Competition, Colorado Bar Association, http://www.cobar.org (accessed Apr. 1, 2008); "Fitting Reminder of Ludlow," *Denver Post,* July 9, 2005.

14. Several recent attempts to incorporate Ludlow into a synthetic treatment of the Progressive Era address the Ten Days' War superficially if at all. Alan Dawley, *Changing the World: American Progressives in War and Revolution* (Princeton, N.J.: Princeton University Press, 2003), 27–33, 266; Shelton Stromquist, *Reinventing "The People": The Progressive Movement, the Class Problem, and the Origins of Modern Liberalism* (Champaign: University of Illinois Press, 2006), 176; Maureen A. Flanagan, *America Reformed: Progressives and Progressivisms 1890s–1920s* (New York: Oxford University Press, 2007), 218–220. Another study overlooks the Colorado coalfield war entirely: Michael McGerr, *A Fierce Discontent: The Rise and Fall of the Progressive Movement in America, 1870–1920* (New York: Oxford University Press, 2003).

15. *Denver Times,* Apr. 21 and 22, 1914. On the initial fights, see anonymous telegrams, Apr. 20, 1914, folder 144, box 7, CF&I-CHS.

16. "Call to Arms," Apr. 22, 1914, published in *Florence Citizen* and *Rocky Mountain News,* Apr. 23, 1914; *Denver Times,* Apr. 22–24 and Apr. 27, 1914; *Rocky Mountain News,* Apr. 25 and 27, 1914.

17. "Detection Rept.," enclosed in LaMont Montgomery Bowers to John D. Rockefeller, Jr., May 9, 1914, folder 203, box 22, CF&I-RAC. The report attributed the most incendiary comments to "O'Neill," probably John O'Neil, editor of the WFM organ, the *Miners' Magazine.* His speech at the capitol was excerpted in *Denver Times,* Apr. 27, 1914. See also Martelle, *Blood Passion,* 183–190.

18. Telegraphic dispatches by coal company officials during the fighting referred to strikers as rednecks, as did militia court-martials. Anonymous to anonymous, Apr. 20, 23, and 28, folder 144, box 7, CF&I Papers–CHS; Maurice Bigelow and C. A. Connor Courts-Martial, cases nos. 6 and 7, folders 7 and 8, CNG Courts-Martial. On the fights that the labels "redneck" and "scab" caused among Walsenburg schoolchildren, see Francis Nelson interview by Elaine Baker, Oct. 17, 1979, in HCEHP, n.p. On efforts by Lawson and other leaders to inform strikers of the truce by driving around making the announcement from a motorcar, see *Rocky Mountain News,* Apr. 25 and 26, 1914. By the 28th, union leaders admitted "they had no firm sense of what had really happened" in the previous days' attacks by strikers. *Rocky Mountain News,* Apr. 28, 1914.

19. Patrick Hamrock testimony, in Carson Court-Martial, pp. 229, 237–238; Andrew E. Riddle interview, n.d., transcript in Mesa County Oral History Project, Museum of Western Colorado, Grand Junction, Colorado, p. 5 (quoted); Anast Chipian interview, July 1, 1974, folder 6, box 6, Greek Oral History Collection, Special Collections, Marriott Library, University of Utah, Salt Lake City (henceforth UU), p. 14; Dan DeSantis, interview, Jan. 19, 1978, transcript in box 9, Eric Margolis Coal Project Papers, Historical Collections, University of Colorado, Boulder (henceforth EM), p. 2; Bill Lloyd interview, transcript in box 10, ibid., p. 17; Memorandum, S. J. Donleavy, Mar. 10, 1915, in John D. Rockefeller, Jr., to Jesse Floyd Welborn, Apr. 3, 1915, folder 17, JFW Papers; *Rocky Mountain News,* Apr. 29, 1914; W. A. Holbrook to U.S. Adjutant General, May 3, 1915, box 1, AG File; *Rocky Mountain News,* Apr. 26, 1914. Among the Colorado National Guard, few were more experienced than Karl E. Linderfelt, who bragged that he had "handled men pretty much all my life in different commands, in different places in the world." Karl Linderfelt testimony, in C. E. Taylor, P. M. Cullom, T. J. Casey, Charles Patton, G. G. Osborne, F. M. Mason, Dan Pacheco, H. B. Faulks, E. J. Welsh, and D. C. Campbell Court-Martial, May 11, 1914, CNG Courts-Martial, p. 361.

20. J. S. Grisham to Elias Ammons, Apr. 22, 1914, folder 1, box 26751, Governor Elias Ammons Papers, Colorado State Archives (henceforth CSA); S. F. Fitzgarald and John Chase to Ammons, ibid.; *Rocky Mountain News,* Apr. 24, 1914. Contemporaries commonly defined the southern fields to include Las Animas and Huerfano counties. I in-

clude Fremont County, despite the geological discontinuity, because of the close links both labor and capital forged between the mines around Cañon City and those farther south.

21. "Coroner's Inquest over the Bodies of Deceased: Edward Kessler, Jacob Smith, Joseph Upson, K. Itow, Geohey Murakami, M. Niwa, Toni Hino, George Hall, S. A. Newman, and Steve Dtoraka," Las Animas County Courthouse, Trinidad, Colorado (hereafter Forbes inquest); E. K. Cowdrey testimony, Las Animas County Grand Jury Proceedings, June 24, 1914, folder 5, box 2, FF, pp. 73–75. On the strikers' marching out, see *Rocky Mountain News,* Apr. 24, 1914; on Camp San Rafael as refugee encampment, see *Rocky Mountain News,* Apr. 27, 1914, and the unidentified clipping dated Sept. 24, 1914, in John Lawson Scrapbook, John R. Lawson Papers, DPL.

22. Forbes inquest, 23–26, 36–41.

23. Ibid., 2–3, 22; *Denver Times,* Apr. 30, 1914. A reactionary journal later made unsubstantiated accusations that strikers had tortured and killed "three little Japs" and an "old negro." [Jim Jam Junior], "The Truth About Colorado's Civil War," *Jim Jam Jems* (July 1914): 39–40.

24. *Rocky Mountain News,* Apr. 23, 1914; *Denver Times,* Apr. 24, 1914; Dan DeSantis interview; *Rocky Mountain News,* Apr. 29, 1914. Major Holbrook of the U.S. Army also believed that bad "weather conditions [might] account for some lack of activity on part [of] strikers." W. A. Holbrook to J. C. McReynolds, May 1, 1914, box 1, AG File.

25. W. A. Holbrook to J. C. McReynolds, Apr. 30, 1914, box 1, AG File. The fullest accounting of the dead is in Martelle, *Blood Passion,* 222–224, appendix B. On the financial costs of the strike, see "J. K. T." to Jesse Floyd Welborn, and Welborn to John D. Rockefeller, Jr., Apr. 2, 1915, folder 16, JFW Papers. Several reports alleged that strikers planned to resume fighting if federal troops let down their guard; particularly credible were allegations that strikers were planning to concentrate their forces in the western coalfields near Crested Butte, Baldwin, Glenwood Springs, and Oak Creek in Routt County. See copy of report from Inspector D-139, conveyed in Cimic to E. L. Prentiss, Apr. 29, 1914, folder 5, box 26751, Gov. Ammons Papers; Holbrook to Lindley Garrison, May 3, 1914, box 1, AG File; CF&I to Garrison, May 7, ibid.; and James Lockett to Garrison, May 9, ibid.

26. *Denver Times,* Apr. 23, 1914; Donald Joseph McClurg, "Labor Organization in the Coal Mines of Colorado, 1878–1933" (Ph.D. diss., University of California, Los Angeles, 1959), 364; George P. West, *Report on the Colorado Strike* (Washington, D.C.: U.S. Commission on Industrial Relations, 1915), reprinted in Leon Stein and Philip Taft, eds., *Massacre at Ludlow: Four Reports* (New York: Arno and New York Times, 1971), 23; *San Francisco Chronicle,* May 4, 1915.

27. On the suppression of memory following uprisings from below, see James C. Scott, *Domination and the Arts of Resistance: Hidden Transcripts* (New Haven, Conn.: Yale University Press, 1992), 86.

28. Zinn, in contrast to many interpreters of Ludlow, celebrates "the undeterred spirit of rebellion among working people" that the Colorado coalfield war epitomized. Howard Zinn, *The Twentieth Century: A People's History*, rev. ed. (New York: HarperCollins, 1998). See also Melvyn Dubofsky, *The State and Labor in Modern America* (Chapel Hill: University of North Carolina Press, 1994).

29. For a critique of the fragmented nature of recent scholarship in labor history, see Dubofsky, *State and Labor*. On work and the environment, see Arthur F. McEvoy, "Working Environments: An Ecological Approach to Industrial Health and Safety," *Technology and Culture* 36 (supplement 1995): S145–S172; Richard White, "Are You an Environmentalist or Do You Work for a Living? Work and Nature," in William Cronon, ed., *Uncommon Ground: Toward Reinventing Nature* (New York: Norton, 1995), 171–185. On occupational health, see Mark Wyman, *Hard Rock Epic: Western Miners and the Industrial Revolution, 1860–1910* (Berkeley: University of California Press, 1979); Alan Derickson, *Workers' Health, Workers' Democracy: The Western Miners' Struggle, 1891–1925* (Ithaca, N.Y.: Cornell University Press, 1988); Derickson, *Black Lung: Anatomy of a Public Health Disaster* (Ithaca, N.Y.: Cornell University Press, 1998; David Rosner and Gerald Markowitz, *Deadly Dust: Silicosis and the Politics of Occupational Disease in Twentieth-Century America* (Princeton, N.J.: Princeton University Press, 1991); Claudia Clark, *Radium Girls: Women and Industrial Health Reform, 1910–1935* (Chapel Hill: University of North Carolina Press, 1997); Christopher C. Sellers, *Hazards of the Job: From Industrial Disease to Environmental Health Science* (Chapel Hill: University of North Carolina Press, 1997); and Mark Aldrich, *Safety First: Technology, Labor, and Business in the Building of American Work Safety, 1870–1939* (Baltimore: Johns Hopkins University Press, 1997). On working-class environmental history, see Louis S. Warren, *The Hunter's Game: Poachers and Conservationists in Twentieth-Century America* (New Haven, Conn.: Yale University Press, 1997); Karl Jacoby, *Crimes against Nature: Squatters, Poachers, Thieves, and the Hidden History of American Conservation* (Berkeley: University of California Press, 2001); Andrew Hurley, *Environmental Inequalities: Class, Race, and Industrial Pollution in Gary, Indiana, 1945–1980* (Chapel Hill: University of North Carolina Press, 1995); "Environmental Justice in the City," special edition of *Environmental History* 5 (2000); Ellen Stroud, "Troubled Waters in Ecotopia: Environmental Racism in Portland, Oregon," *Radical History Review* 74 (1999): 65–95; Nancy Quam-Wickham, "'Cities Sacrificed on the Altar of Oil': Popular Opposition to Oil Development in 1920s Los Angeles," *Environmental History* 3 (1998): 189–209; Chad Montrie, *To Save the Land and People: A History of Opposition to Surface Coal Mining in Appalachia* (Chapel Hill: University of North Carolina Press, 2003); Chad Montrie, "'I Think Less of the Factory Than of My Native Dell': Labor, Nature, and the Lowell 'Mill Girls,'" *Environmental History* 9 (2004): 275–295; John Soluri, *Banana Cultures: Agriculture, Consumption, and Environmental Change in Honduras and the United States*

(Austin: University of Texas Press, 2005); Gunther Peck, "The Nature of Labor: Fault Lines and Common Ground in Environmental and Labor History," *Environmental History* 11 (2006): 212–238; Lissa Wadewitz, "Pirates of the Salish Sea: Labor, Mobility, and Environment in the Transnational West," *Pacific Historical Review* 75 (2006): 587–627; Linda Nash, *Inescapable Ecologies: A History of Environment, Disease, and Knowledge* (Berkeley: University of California Press, 2006).

30. Mining nomenclature varies from place to place and time to time, so some clarifications are in order. I use "collier" and "coal miner" interchangeably; I typically use both terms to refer to men who worked at the mine face extracting coal, but occasionally I use the term more generally. "Mineworker" always connotes a broader range of workers—the colliers at the face who constituted the overwhelming majority of the labor force at any Colorado colliery, as well as trapper boys, drivers, and other so-called company men who worked in and around the mines. I use "Hispana," "Hispano" or the more specific *nuevomexicana* and *nuevomexicano* to refer to people with Spanish surnames who were born in New Mexico, Texas, Arizona, California, or Colorado during the Spanish and Mexican periods, as well as their descendants. I use "Mexican" to refer to Mexican nationals; "Mexican American" to refer to naturalized immigrants from Mexico and their descendants; and "Mexican" to evoke the manner in which Anglo Coloradans collapsed the important distinctions between Hispanos, Mexicans, and Mexican Americans.

31. "British American," for our purposes, comprises migrants from England, Wales, Scotland, and Ireland, as well as "white" miners born in the United States who descended from colonial and early national immigrants from Germany and other parts of Northern and Western Europe. While including Irish and non-British native-born Americans in this category is admittedly problematic, it is nonetheless preferable to using "Anglo-American," because it better encompasses Scots and Welshmen and more fully recognizes the continuities between the work cultures of Britain and the United States.

32. On the industrial West, see Melvin Dubofsky, *We Shall Be All: A History of the Industrial Workers of the World* (Chicago: Quadrangle, 1969). Wyman, *Hard Rock Epic;* Arthur F. McEvoy, "Law, Public Policy, and Industrialization in the California Fisheries, 1900–1925," *Business History Review* 57 (1983): 494–521; William G. Robbins, "In Pursuit of Historical Explanation: Capitalism as a Conceptual Tool for Knowing the American West," *Western Historical Quarterly* 30 (1999): 277–293; David Igler, *Industrial Cowboys: Miller and Lux and the Transformation of the Far West, 1850–1920* (Berkeley: University of California Press, 2001); Igler, "The Industrial Far West: Region and Nation in the Late Nineteenth Century," *Pacific Historical Review* 69 (2000): 159–192; and Andrew Isenberg, *Mining California: An Ecological History* (New York: Hill and Wang, 2005).

33. It is a very rare survey text or historiographical synthesis on U.S. history, for instance, that devotes more than a page or two to coal, coal miners, coal-mining strikes, and

related topics. This oversight is particularly tragic, given the availability of such fine works as David Nye, *Consuming Power: A Social History of American Energies* (Cambridge, Mass.: MIT Press, 1999); Barbara Freese, *Coal: A Human History* (Cambridge, Mass.: Perseus, 2003); Alfred Crosby, *Children of the Sun: A History of Humanity's Insatiable Appetite for Energy* (New York: Norton, 2006); and the several dozen fine studies on coal, coal miners, and coal strikes that are cited in the following pages. One danger of the academic habit of pasting the prefix "post-" onto key words is the implication of eclipse, of complete transformation, rather than accretion. A postindustrial economy remains impossible without an industrial base, even if most industrial activities are now performed beyond the borders of the United States, Japan, and Western Europe.

34. Lest this statement seem hyperbolic, several well-posted contemporary observers believed that revolution was in the air. One Trinidad resident, for instance, maintained that if the army had "pursued a vigorous policy and started to disarm the strikers first. . . a revolution would have broken out which would extend to all corners of the nation." "J. C. H." to Mr. Thatcher, May 3, 1914, folder 173, box 20, CF&I-RAC.

1. A Dream of Coal-Fired Benevolence

1. William Jackson Palmer passport, Oct. 22, 1870, folder 19, box 1, WJPP-CHS.

2. Career details from "Data Desired for Biographies: America's Successful Men," June 10, 1896, folder 1, ibid. On Palmer's experiences with the Hempfield, see William Jackson Palmer to Isaac Clothier, June 23, 1853, in Isaac Clothier, comp., *Letters, 1853–1868, Gen'l Wm. J. Palmer* (Philadelphia: [privately printed], 1906). For young Palmer's fondness for trout fishing and his plans for a trip up the Hudson Valley, see R. H. Lamborn to William Jackson Palmer, Sept. 2, 1852, and May 1, 1853, folder 506, box 7, WJPP-CHS. Biographies of Palmer include John S. Fisher, *A Builder of the West: The Life of William Jackson Palmer* (Caldwell, Ida.: Caxton, 1939); Brit Allan Storey, "William Jackson Palmer: A Biography" (Ph.D. diss., University of Kentucky, 1968); and George L. Anderson, "General William Jackson Palmer: Man of Vision," *Colorado College Studies* 4 (1960).

3. George S. Emerson, *Engineering Education: A Social History* (Newton Abbot, U.K.: David and Charles; New York: Crane and Russak, 1973); *The Making of an Engineer: An Illustrated History of Engineering Education in the United States and Canada* (New York: Wiley, 1993). Perhaps the greatest American engineer of the day, Charles Ellett, Jr., on the basis of his own youthful grand tour, advised Palmer to go to Europe. Charles Ellett, Jr., to William Jackson Palmer, June 16, 1855, folder 454, box 6, WJPP-CHS.

4. Palmer names the ship in William Jackson Palmer to parents, Oct. 17, 1862, folder 185, box 3, WJPP-CHS. He purchased the knapsack in Liverpool. William Jackson Palmer to parents, July 5, 1855, folder 696, box 9, ibid. For letters of introduction, see

Lucretia Mott to William Smeal, May 13, 1855, folders 2–7, box 2, WJPP, Colorado Springs Pioneers Museum.

5. Frank Jackson to William Jackson Palmer, May 23, 1855, folder 480, box 7, WJPP-CHS; Gerard Ralston to William Jackson Palmer, Sept. 11, 20, and 28, 1855, folder 559, box 7, and Feb. 13, 1856, folder 560, ibid.; William Jackson Palmer to Frank Jackson, June 29 and July 13, 1855, folder 689, box 9, ibid.; Benjamin Bannan to William Jackson Palmer, Sept. 18, 1855, folder 216, box 3, ibid.; J. Edgar Thomson to William Jackson Palmer, Sept. 7, 1855, folder 606, box 8, ibid. An undated clipped advertisement for "letters from our attentive Foreign Mining Correspondent" is in folder 236, box 3, ibid.

6. William Jackson Palmer to Frank Palmer, July 5, 1855, folder 694, box 9, WJPP-CHS; William Jackson Palmer to parents, July 8, 1855, folder 696, ibid.; W. J. P. [William Jackson Palmer], "Underground Walks in England, No. 5," *Miners' Journal,* Oct. 13, 1855.

7. William Jackson Palmer to Frank Jackson, July 16, 1855, folder 689, box 9, WJPP-CHS.

8. Ibid.; William Jackson Palmer to Frank Jackson, July 17, 1855, ibid. George Orwell would later describe experiencing still-greater discomfort while visiting these same mines: George Orwell, *The Road to Wigan Pier* (London: Gollancz, 1937).

9. W. J. P., "Underground Walks in England: 'The Black Country,' No. 7," *Miners' Journal,* Nov. 10, 1855; W. J. P., "Underground Walks in England: 'The Black Country,' No. 8," *Miners' Journal,* Nov. 28, 1855; and W. J. P., "Underground Walks in England: 'The Black Country,' No. 9," *Miners' Journal,* Dec. 8, 1855.

10. W. J. P., "Underground Walks in England, No. 5"; Carbon, "Underground Walks in England, No. 2," *Miners' Journal,* Aug. 18, 1855; and W. J. P., "Underground Walks in England, No. 3," *Miners' Journal,* Sept. 1, 1855.

11. W. J. P., "Underground Walks in England, No. 5,"; W. J. P., "Underground Walks in England: 'The Black Country,' No. 7"; Carbon, "Underground Walks in England, No. 2"; "Our Foreign Mining Correspondence," *Miners' Journal,* Aug. 11, 1855.

12. W. J. P., "Underground Walks in England, No. 6," *Miners' Journal,* Oct. 27, 1855.

13. W. J. P., "Underground Walks in England: 'The Black Country,' No. 9."

14. J. Thomas Scharf and Thompson Westcott, *History of Philadelphia, 1609–1884,* 3 vols. (Philadelphia: Everts, 1884), 3:2191 (quotation); William Jackson Palmer to J. Edgar Thomson, Sept. 3, 1855, folder 200, box 3, WJP-CHS, and June 19, 1856, folder 224, ibid.; J. Edgar Thomson to William Jackson Palmer, Sept. 7, 1855, folder 606, box 7, ibid.; Gerard Ralston to William Jackson Palmer, Sept. 11, 1855, folder 559, ibid.; diary entries for Jan. 14–22, May 22, and Nov. [n.d.], 1857, folder 223, box 3, ibid.; [William Jackson Palmer], "Report on the Coal Valley Mines and the Rock Island & Peoria Railroad, of Illinois," Nov. 10, 1857, folder 269, box 4, ibid.; notice of election to Franklin Institute, Aug. 18, 1859, folder 12, box 1, ibid.; [William Jackson Palmer], *Report of Experiments with Coal-Burning Locomotives, Made on the Pennsylvania Railroad, April–August,*

1859 (Philadelphia: Crissy and Markley, 1860). On the Franklin Institute's long-standing support for commercial uses of anthracite, see Sean Patrick Adams, *Old Dominion, Industrial Commonwealth: Coal, Politics, and Economy in Antebellum America* (Baltimore: Johns Hopkins University Press, 2004), 60–61.

15. William Jackson Palmer, "Plan: The Anderson Troop," Sept. 1, 1861, copy in Clothier, *Letters,* 91; William Jackson Palmer to Queen Mellen, Apr. 3, 1869, quoted in Fisher, *Builder of the West,* 153–154; "The General's Story," *Harper's New Monthly Magazine* 35 (June 1867): 60–74. On William Jackson Palmer's military career, see Fisher, *Builder of the West,* 68–125.

16. William Jackson Palmer to father, Feb. 19, 1863, folder 186, box 3, WJPP-CHS; William Jackson Palmer to Mellen, Apr. 3, 1869; William Jackson Palmer to Harry Lamborn, Sept. 6, 1861, folder 183, box 3, WJPP-CHS; William Jackson Palmer to C. Lamborn, Oct. 4, 1861, WJPP, Beinecke Rare Book and Manuscript Library, Yale University, New Haven, Conn.; William Jackson Palmer to Lamborn, n.d. [1864?] folder 1, ibid.

17. William Jackson Palmer to Emma Taylor Lamborn, Sept. 25, 1865, folder 4, WJPP, Beinecke.

18. Quotations from William Jackson Palmer to John Perry, Aug. 5, 1867, copy in General William J. Palmer Correspondence from Colorado to New Mexico, DPL (henceforth WJPP-DPL); Charles S. Hinchman to Palmer, Aug. 26, 1867, folder 474, box 6, WJPP-CHS. On the survey generally, see William A. Bell, *New Tracks in North America: A Journal of Travel and Adventure Whilst Engaged in the Survey for a Southern Railroad to the Pacific Ocean during 1867–68* (London: Chapman and Hall, 1869), and William J. Palmer, *Report of Surveys across the Continent in 1867–'68, on the Thirty-Fifty and Thirty-Second Parallels, for a Route Extending the Kansas Pacific Railway to the Pacific Ocean at San Francisco and San Diego* (Philadelphia: Selheimer, 1869).

19. On stone coal, see entry for Sept. 14, 1842, in Rufus Sage, *His Letters and Papers, 1836–1847,* ed. LeRoy R. Hafen and Ann W. Hafen (Glendale, Calif.: Clark, 1956), 1:73. Quotations are in William Jackson Palmer to John Perry, Aug. 11, 1867, and n.d., WJPP-DPL.

20. I draw overwhelmingly on recent scientific studies in the following paragraphs, but this basic scenario was clear to Palmer and his contemporaries. William Jackson Palmer, *The Denver & Rio Grande Railway of Colorado and New Mexico* (London: Norman, 1871), 5; James T. Hodge, "On the Tertiary Coals of Colorado," in F. V. Hayden, *Preliminary Report of the United States Geological Survey of Wyoming, and Portions of Contiguous Territories . . .* (Washington, D.C.: GPO, 1871); Persifor Frazier, Jr., "The Coals of the Rocky Mountains," ibid.; and especially A. Lakes, "The Trinidad Coal Region of Southern Colorado," in *Colorado State School of Mines Annual Report of Field Work and Analyses Relating to the Economic Geology of Colorado* (Denver: Rocky Mountain News, 1886), 92.

21. L. N. R. Roberts and M. A. Kirschbaum, "Paleogeography of the Western Interior of Middle North America: Coal Distribution and Sediment Accumulation," U.S. Geological Survey Professional Paper 1561; Kirk R. Johnson and Robert G. Raynolds, *Ancient Denvers: Scenes from the Past 300 Million Years of the Colorado Front Range* (Denver: Denver Museum of Nature and Science, 2003), 15–20; George Irving Finlay, *Colorado Springs: A Guide Book Describing the Rock Formations in the Vicinity of Colorado Springs* (Colorado Springs: Out West, 1906), 41.

22. Ogden Tweto, "Laramide (Late Cretaceous–Early Tertiary) Orogeny in the Southern Rocky Mountains," in B. F. Curtis, ed., *Cenozoic History of the Southern Rocky Mountains,* Geological Society of America Memoir 144 (Boulder, Colo.: Geological Society of America, 1975), 1–44; Odgen Tweto, "Summary of Laramide Orogeny in Colorado," in Harry C. Kent and Karen W. Porter, eds., *Colorado Geology* (Denver: Rocky Mountain Association of Geologists, 1980), 129–134; John McPhee, *Rising from the Plains,* in *Annals of the Former World* (New York: Farrar, Straus and Giroux: 1998), 294–427; Joseph M. English and Stephen T. Johnston, "The Laramide Orogeny: What Were the Driving Forces?" *International Geology Review* 46 (2004): 833–838.

23. On climate, see Garland R. Upchurch, Jr., "Dispersed Angiosperm Cuticles: Their History, Preparation, and Application to the Rise of Angiosperms in Cretaceous and Paleocene Coals, Southwestern Interior of North America," *International Journal of Coal Geology* 28 (1995): 177; Alan Graham, *Late Cretaceous and Cenozoic History of North American Vegetation, North of Mexico* (Oxford: Oxford University Press, 1999), 155; Johnson and Raynolds, *Ancient Denvers,* 22; Willis T. Lee and F. H. Knowlton, *Geology and Paleontology of the Raton Mesa and Other Regions in Colorado and New Mexico,* United States Geological Survey Professional Paper 101 (Washington, D.C.: GPO, 1917), 234–235. On present-day analogues, see Romeo Flores, "Geologic and Geomorphic Controls of Coal Development in Some Tertiary Rocky Mountain Basins, USA," *International Journal of Coal Geology* 23 (1993): 43–73. See also the articles in R. A. Rahmani and R. M. Flores, eds., *Sedimentology of Coal and Coal-Bearing Sequences,* International Association of Sedimentologists Special Publication 7 (Oxford: Blackwell Scientific, 1984); and James C. Cobb and C. Blaine Cecil, eds., *Modern and Ancient Coal-Forming Environments,* Geological Society of America Special Paper 286 (Boulder, Colo.: Geological Society of America, 1993).

24. Harold H. Schobert, *Coal: The Energy Source of the Past and Future* (Washington, D.C.: American Chemical Society, 1987), 19–42; Peter Joseph Adams, *The Origin and Evolution of Coal* (London: Her Majesty's Stationery Office, 1960); Rahmani and Flores, *Sedimentology of Coal and Coal-Bearing Sequences;* Claus F. K. Diessel, *Coal-Bearing Depositional Systems* (Berlin: Springer-Verlag, 1992), 5–40; and Andrew C. Scott, ed., *Coal and Coal-Bearing Strata: Recent Advances,* Geological Society Special Publication 32 (Oxford: Blackwell Scientific, 1987).

25. Schobert, *Coal*, 32.

26. Larry Thomas, *Coal Geology* (Chichester, U.K.: Wiley, 2002), 95; M. L. Jeremic, *Strata Mechanics in Coal Mining* (Boston: Balkema, 1985), 75.

27. The term "mineral-intensive industrialization," like much of the analysis that follows, builds on the work of E. A. Wrigley.

28. Key works on these transitions include E. A. Wrigley, *Continuity, Chance and Change: The Character of the Industrial Revolution in England* (Cambridge: Cambridge University Press, 1988); Vaclav Smil, *Energy in World History* (Boulder, Colo.: Westview, 1994); Rolf Peter Sieferle, *The Subterranean Forest: Energy Systems and the Industrial Revolution* (Cambridge, U.K.: White Horse, 2001); Kenneth Pomeranz, *The Great Divergence: China, Europe, and the Making of a Modern World Economy* (Princeton, N.J.: Princeton University Press, 2000); Alfred Crosby, *Children of the Sun: A History of Humanity's Insatiable Appetite for Energy* (New York: Norton, 2006). For a highly accessible treatment of the basic concepts, see Vaclav Smil, *Energies: An Illustrated Guide to the Biosphere and Civilization* (Cambridge, Mass.: MIT Press, 1999).

29. William Jackson Palmer to Jackson, July 17, 1855; Wrigley, *Continuity, Chance, and Change*, 68–81.

30. Wrigley, *Continuity, Chance, and Change*, 29–30; E. A. Wrigley, "Two Kinds of Capitalism, Two Kinds of Growth," in *Poverty, Progress, and Population* (Cambridge: Cambridge University Press, 2004), 75.

31. Wrigley, *Continuity, Chance, and Change*, 28, 51.

32. Ibid., 28, 126–129; E. A. Wrigley, "Poverty in Traditional Societies," in *Poverty, Progress, and Population*, 213–220.

33. Wrigley, *Continuity, Chance, and Change*, 29; Ricardo quoted in Wrigley, "The Quest for the Industrial Revolution," in *Poverty, Progress, and Population*, 29. See also Wrigley, "The Divergence of England: The Growth of the English Economy in the Seventeenth and Eighteenth Centuries," ibid., 48.

34. Wrigley, *Continuity, Chance, and Change*, 29.

35. On the failure of gold mines to pay, see Elliott West, *The Contested Plains: Indians, Goldseekers, and the Rush to Colorado* (Lawrence: University Press of Kansas, 1998), 225–227. On grasshoppers, see Frank Hall, *History of the State of Colorado . . .* (Chicago: Blakely, 1889–1895), 1:449; R. Schiffmann to William Jackson Palmer, Aug. 25, 1868, folder 239, box 4, WJP-CHS; Cyrus Thomas, "Agriculture of Colorado," in F. V. Hayden, *Third Annual Report of the United States Geological Survey of the Territories, Embracing Colorado and New Mexico . . .* (Washington, D.C.: GPO, 1873), 248–249. On the locust problem in the West more generally, see Jeffrey A. Lockwood, *Locust: The Devastating Rise and Mysterious Disappearance of the Insect That Shaped the American Frontier* (New York: Basic, 2004). LeRoy Hafen accurately termed the mid-1860s the "days of discouragement." Hafen, *Colorado and Its People: A Narrative and Topical History of the Centennial State* (New York: Lewis, 1948), 1:290.

36. William H. Brewer to wife, July 29, 1869, in Edmund B. Rogers, ed., *Rocky Mountain Letters 1869: A Journal of an Early Geological Expedition to the Colorado Rockies* (Denver: Colorado Mountain Club, 1930), 14. For earlier grim prognostications of the territory's future, see *Rocky Mountain News,* June 17 and 26, 1867, and July 31, 1867.

37. On water transport and the frontier, see Oscar Winther, *The Transportation Frontier: The Trans-Mississippi West, 1865–1890* (New York: Holt, Rinehart and Winston, 1964); Ari Kelman, *A River and Its City: The Nature of Landscape in New Orleans* (Berkeley: University of California Press, 2003), 50–86; and Annalies Corbin, *The Life and Times of the Steamboat Red Cloud, or, How Merchants, Mounties, and the Missouri Transformed the West* (College Station: Texas A&M University Press, 2006).

38. Despite Palmer's profession that the Arkansas River offered "an unlimited amount of water power, fully equal to the best in New England," the historian Wilbur Stone argues that only in the early twentieth century was "the use of streams of Colorado for power purposes . . . undertaken on what may well be called a gigantic scale." Palmer, *Report of Surveys,* 149; Wilbur Stone, *History of Colorado* (Chicago: Clarke, 1918–1919). Even today, hydropower generates only 3 percent of Colorado's annual electric production, compared to much larger percentages in other Western states. "Colorado State Electricity Profile," 2006, at www.eia.doe.gov (accessed Mar. 30, 2008). On waterpower, see Ellen Wohl, *Virtual Rivers: Lessons from the Mountain Rivers of the Colorado Front Range* (New Haven, Conn.: Yale University Press, 2001).

39. Thomas, "Agriculture of Colorado," 247; L. H. Eicholtz Diary, June 10, 1867, L. H. Eicholtz Diaries, microfilm, CHS; Palmer, *Report of Surveys,* 8; Charles R. Green to parents, June 11, 1867, Charles R. Green Papers, DPL; National Atlas, *Precipitation Map for Colorado* (Reston, Va.: USGS, 2005), at http://www.nationalatlas.gov (accessed Mar. 30, 2008).

40. On these adaptations and abandonments, see E. Steve Cassells, *The Archaeology of Colorado,* rev. ed. (Boulder, Colo.: Johnson, 1997), 145–146, 171, 181–182; and Tammy Stone, *The Prehistory of Colorado and Adjacent Areas* (Salt Lake City: University of Utah Press, 1999), 74, 89–91, 94, 127. There is much uncertainty about the presence of corn horticulture on the northeastern plains of what is now Colorado during the Woodland and Central Plains Tradition periods, but firmer evidence for southeastern Colorado during the same period. Ann Mary Johnson and Alfred E. Johnson, "The Plains Woodland," Terry L. Steinacher and Gayle F. Carlson, "The Central Plains Tradition," and Richard R. Drass, "The Southern Plains Villagers," all in W. Raymond Wood, ed., *Archaeology on the Great Plains* (Lawrence: University of Kansas Press, 1998), 213, 247, and 424. On comparative population densities, see Russell Thornton, *American Indian Holocaust and Survival: A Population History since 1492* (Norman: University of Oklahoma Press, 1987).

41. Momaday, quoted in West, *Contested Plains,* 54; see, more broadly, ibid., 48–58; Frank Gilbert Roe, *The Indian and the Horse* (Norman: University of Oklahoma Press,

1955); Pekka Hamalainen, "The Rise and Fall of Plains Indian Horse Cultures," *Journal of American History* 90 (Dec. 2003): 833–862. On plants and animals as biotechnologies, see Philip Scranton and Susan R. Schrepfer, eds., *Industrializing Organisms: Introducing Evolutionary History* (New York: Routledge, 2004).

42. Charles R. Green Diary, July 8, 1867, Charles R. Green Papers, DPL; *Philadelphia Press,* June 29, 1867; Bell, *New Tracks in North America,* 45. On the decline of the bison, see West, *Contested Plains;* Elliott West, "Animals," in *The Way to the West: Essays on the Central Plains* (Albuquerque: University of New Mexico Press, 1995); Thomas G. Andrews, "Tata Atanasio's Unlikely Tale of Utes, Nuevo Mexicanos, and the Settling of Colorado's San Luis Valley," *New Mexico Historical Review* 75 (2000): 4–41; Andrew C. Isenberg, *The Destruction of the Bison: An Environmental History, 1750–1920* (New York: Cambridge University Press, 2000); Dan Flores, "Bison Ecology and Bison Diplomacy: The Southern Plains from 1800 to 1850," *Journal of American History* 78 (1991): 465–485, and Flores, "Bison Ecology and Bison Diplomacy Redux: Another Look at the Southern Plains from 1800 to 1850," in *The Natural West: Environmental History in the Great Plains and Rocky Mountains* (Norman: University of Oklahoma Press, 2001), 50–70.

43. Donald W. Meinig, *Southwest: Three Peoples in Geographical Change, 1600–1970* (New York: Oxford University Press, 1971), 27–35; Thomas G. Andrews, "Settling the San Luis Valley: Ecology, Society, and 'Beautiful Roads' in the Hispanic Colonization of Conejos and Costilla Counties, Colorado" (M.A. thesis, University of Wisconsin-Madison, 1997); Janet Lecompte, *Pueblo, Hardscrabble, Greenhorn: The Upper Arkansas, 1832–1856* (Norman: University of Oklahoma Press, 1978); and Alvin T. Steinel, *History of Agriculture in Colorado: A Record of Progress in the Development of General Farming, Livestock Production and Agricultural Education and Investigation, on the Western Border of the Great Plains and in the Mountains of Colorado, 1858–1926* (Fort Collins, Colo.: State Agricultural College, 1926).

44. Charles R. Green to parents, July 28 and 31, 1867, Charles R. Green Papers; Charles R. Green, letter published in *Daily Missouri Democrat* (St. Louis), Sept. 30, 1867.

45. Green letter in *Daily Missouri Democrat,* Sept. 30, 1867; *Philadelphia Press,* Aug. 22, 1867. See also Charles R. Green to parents, July 31 and Aug. 11, 1867, in Charles R. Green Papers.

46. Ned Blackhawk, *Violence over the Land: Indians and Empires in the Early American West* (Cambridge, Mass.: Harvard University Press, 2006), 176–225; West, *Contested Plains;* Andrews, "Tata Atanasio's Unlikely Tale."

47. Hall, *History of the State of Colorado,* 1:493. See also the famous letter of Horace Greeley, Albert Richardson, and Henry Villard from Gregory Gulch in 1859, quoted in Stone, *History of Colorado,* 1:244.

48. Quotation in letter from A. C. Hunt to unknown correspondent, Dec. 10, 1870,

box 2, Alexander Cameron Hunt Papers, CHS; Ingwal S. Horgen, comp. "History of Pike National Forest," 1923, typescript, doc. no. 25, Pike National Forest Historical File Microfilm, Local History Division, Penrose Public Library, Pikes Peak Library District, Colorado Springs, p. 31; A. W. Hoyt, "Over the Plains to Colorado," *Harper's New Monthly Magazine* 35 (June 1867): 5, 11; Bowles, *Across the Continent: A Summer's Journey to the Rocky Mountains, the Mormons, and the Pacific States, with Speaker Colfax* (Springfield, Mass.: Samuel Bowles; New York: Hurd and Houghton, 1866), 22; Henry Michelson, "The Present Condition of the Colorado Forest," n.d., folder 15, box 26949, Governor Charles S. Thomas Papers, CSA; Kathleen Brosnan, *Uniting Mountain and Plain: Cities, Law, and Environmental Change along the Front Range* (Albuquerque: University of New Mexico Press, 2002), 147–156; William Wyckoff, *Creating Colorado: The Making of a Western American Landscape, 1860–1940* (New Haven, Conn.: Yale University Press, 1999), 69–71.

49. Charles R. Green to "Heppie," Sept. 23, 1867, Charles R. Green Papers, DPL.

50. William Jackson Palmer, "Address of General William J. Palmer, Treasurer U.P.R.W.Co., E.D., Delivered before a Meeting of Citizens of New Mexico, at Santa Fe, September 21, 1867," in *Senatorial Excursion Party over the Union Pacific Railway, E.D. Speeches of Senators Yates, Cattell, Chandler, Howe and Trumbull; Hon. J. A. J. Creswell, Hon. John Covode, M.C., and Hon. Wm. M. McPherson, on the Pacific Railroad Question* . . . (St. Louis, Mo.: S. Levison, 1867). On the circumstances of this meeting, see William Jackson Palmer to John Perry, Sept. 17 and 26, 1867, WJPP-DPL; and circular enclosed with William Jackson Palmer to Perry, Sept. 28, 1867, ibid.; "Address of General William J. Palmer," 63–68.

51. William Jackson Palmer, "Address of General William J. Palmer," 68.

52. William Jackson Palmer to Queen Mellen, Jan. 30, 1870, folder 706, box 9, WJP-CHS.

53. Ibid.

54. These subjects have occupied the energies of too many historians to cite here. Two noteworthy efforts are Elliott West, "Reconstructing Race," *Western Historical Quarterly* 34 (Spring 2003): 7–26; and Heather Cox Richardson, *West from Appomattox: The Reconstruction of America after the Civil War* (New Haven, Conn.: Yale University Press, 2007).

55. William Jackson Palmer to Queen Mellen, Apr. 3, 1869; William Jackson Palmer to Mellen, June 11, 1869, folder 701, box 9, WJPP-CHS; Chase Mellen, "Address by Chase Mellen on the Occasion of the One Hundredth Anniversary of the Birth of General William J. Palmer," typescript of speech given Sept. 22, 1936, folder 66, box 1, ibid.; receipts from Charles Jackson, 12 month 4 [Quaker calendar], 1860, and from E. O. Thompson, Oct. 7 and Dec. 14, 1865, folder 24, ibid.

56. William Jackson Palmer to Queen Mellen, Jan. 17, 1870, folder 706, box 9, WJPP-CHS.

57. William Jackson Palmer to Queen Mellen, Aug. 7, 1869, folder 702, ibid.; and William Jackson Palmer to Mellen, Feb. 7, 1870, folder 706, ibid. For details on the purchase, see Irving Howbert, "Part of Address by Irving Howbert," Kiwanis Club of Colorado Springs, Sept. 19, 1921, folder 69, box 1, ibid. The place-name Bijou was already being used several miles to the east, for a creek coming off the Monument Divide as well as for a KP station.

58. William Jackson Palmer to Mellen, Aug. 7, 1869.

59. Ibid.; Renato Rosaldo, "Imperialist Nostalgia," in *Culture and Truth: The Remaking of Social Analysis* (Boston: Beacon, 1989), 68–90. In the same vein, see William Jackson Palmer to Queen Mellen, Nov. 15, 1869, folder 704, box 9, WJP-CHS.

60. William Jackson Palmer to Mellen, Aug. 7, 1869.

61. William Jackson Palmer to Queen Mellen, Mar. 28, 1869, folder 700, box 9, WJPP-CHS; William Jackson Palmer to Mellen, Jan. 17, 1870.

62. Palmer later articulated the protective power of the plains in Denver & Rio Grande Railway, *Second Annual Report of the Board of Directors of the Denver & Rio Grande Railway to the Stockholders, for the Year 1873* (Colorado Springs: Out West, 1874).

63. William Jackson Palmer to Mellen, Jan. 17, 1870.

64. Ibid.

65. Ibid.

66. These transactions are amply documented in WJPP, the William A. Bell Papers, and the Alexander Hunt Papers, all at CHS; Herbert O. Brayer, *A Case Study in the Economic Development of the West,* vol. 2 of *William Blackmore: Early Financing of the Denver & Rio Grande Railway and Ancillary Land Companies, 1871–1878* (Denver: Bradford-Robinson, 1949); and H. Lee Scamehorn, *Pioneer Steelmaker in the West: The Colorado Fuel and Iron Company, 1872–1903* (Boulder, Colo.: Pruett, 1976).

67. William Jackson Palmer to Queen Mellen, July 24, 1871, folder 708, box 9, WJPP-CHS.

2. The Reek of the New Industrialism

The title for this chapter is paraphrased from Lewis Mumford, *Technics and Civilization* (New York: Harcourt, Brace, 1936), 169.

1. *Colorado Miner* (Georgetown), June 30, 1870.

2. Rolf Peter Sieferle, *The Subterranean Forest: Energy Systems and the Industrial Revolution* (Cambridge, U.K.: White Horse, 2001), 126–133; Vaclav Smil, *Energy in World History* (Boulder, Colo.: Westview, 1994), 160–164; Samuel Smiles, *The Life of George Stephenson, Railway Engineer,* 5th ed. (London: John Murray, 1858); Barbara Freese, *Coal: A Human History* (New York: Penguin, 2003), 89–92.

3. Seymour Dunbar, *A History of Travel in America* (Indianapolis, Ind.: Bobbs-Merrill, 1915), 3:872–975; Michael Williams, *Americans and Their Forests: A Historical*

Geography (Cambridge: Cambridge University Press, 1989); James A. Ward, *J. Edgar Thomson: Master of the Pennsylvania* (Westport, Conn.: Greenwood, 1980), 100–101, 171–174. For an excellent work that uses the political economy of coal to explain the divergent fortunes of Pennsylvania, Virginia, and West Virginia through the 1870s, see Sean Patrick Adams, *Old Dominion, Industrial Commonwealth: Coal, Politics, and Economy in Antebellum America* (Baltimore: Johns Hopkins University Press, 2004).

4. On route locations, see F. V. Hayden, *Annual Report of the United States Geological and Geographical Survey of the Territories Embracing Colorado and Parts of Adjacent Territories: Being a Report of Progress of the Exploration for the Year 1874* (Washington, D.C.: GPO, 1876), 33; *Fourth Annual Report of the Board of Directors of the Kansas Pacific Railway Company to the Stockholders* (St. Louis: Levison and Blythe, 1871), 8; Clyde King, *The History of the Government of Denver with Special Reference to Its Relations with Public Service Corporations* (Denver: Fisher, 1911), 69; E. O. Davis, *The First Five Years of the Railroad Era in Colorado* (Golden: Sage, 1948), 128–133; Robert Athearn, *Rebel of the Rockies: A History of the Denver and Rio Grande Railroad* (New Haven, Conn.: Yale University Press, 1962); H. Lee Scamehorn, *Pioneer Steelmaker in the West: The Colorado Fuel and Iron Company, 1872–1903* (Boulder, Colo.: Pruett, 1976); Arthur Ridgway, "Denver & Rio Grande Development of Physical Property in Chronological Narrative," typescript dated Jan. 1921, folder 71, box 2, D&RG, p. 57; "The Colorado and Wyoming Railway," *Camp and Plant* 3 (Feb. 18, 1903): 145–149; Francis B. Rizzari, "Railroads of the Crystal River Valley," *Denver Westerners Brand Book* 20 (1964): 369–405. On the AT&SF's precocious choice to divest of coal operations, see E. P. Ripley to Aldace F. Walker, Jan. 20, 1896, FF 19–2, RR box 36, New York Executive Department Files, AT&SF.

5. *Eleventh Biennial Report of the Inspector of Coal Mines of the State of Colorado, 1903–1904* (Denver: Smith-Brooks, 1905), 130; Arthur Lakes, "The Coal Fields of Colorado," *Colorado School of Mines Technical and Engineering Society Bulletin* 2 (Jan. 1904): 11–23; R. C. Hills, "Colorado Coal Fields," and "Report on the Lands of the Colorado Fuel Company and the Denver Fuel Company: With a Supplementary Report on the Lands of the Grand River Coal & Coke Co.," in Hills Reports; H. Lee Scamehorn, *High Altitude Energy: A History of Fossil Fuels in Colorado* (Boulder: University Press of Colorado, 2002); David A. Wolff, *Industrializing the Rockies: Growth, Competition, and Turmoil in the Coalfields of Colorado and Wyoming, 1868–1914* (Boulder: University Press of Colorado, 2003).

6. One noteworthy illustration of this point is the much greater extent and density of Colorado's rail network when compared with those of states such as Nevada, Arizona, or Idaho that largely lacked workable coal deposits.

7. William Jackson Palmer to Queen Mellen, July 24, 1871, folder 708, box 9, WJPP-CHS; Thomas G. Andrews, "'Made by Toile'? Tourism, Landscape, and Labor in Colorado, 1858–1917," *Journal of American History* 92 (2005): 847; William Cronon, *Nature's Metropolis: Chicago and the Great West* (New York: Norton, 1991), 74–81.

8. Unattributed source, Feb. 16, 1871, quoted in Davis, *First Five Years of the Railroad Era*, 133. See also Cronon, *Nature's Metropolis*, 74–80.

9. M. C. Ihlseng, "Review of the Mining Interests of the San Juan Region," in Colorado State School of Mines, *Annual Report of Field Work and Analyses Relating to the Economic Geology of Colorado* (Denver: Rocky Mountain News, 1886), 41; *Report of the Durango Trust to the Subscribers* (Colorado Springs: Gazette Publishing, 1884), 9; Joe B. Warner to David Wood, Feb. 4, 1884, folder 2, David Wood Papers, Beinecke Rare Book & Manuscript Library, Yale University, New Haven, Conn.; James Gillespie to David Wood, May 11, 1885, ibid.; A. M. Woodruff to Wood, Apr. 20, 1890, folder 3, ibid.; Rose Kingsley, *South by West: Or Winter in the Rocky Mountains and Spring in Mexico* (London: Isbister, 1874), 70; *Camp and Plant* 3 (Jan. 3, 1903): 11; "Snowed Under," *Harper's Weekly,* Jan. 24, 1885, 52, 55; Cronon, *Nature's Metropolis,* 74–76, 79–80; Wolfgang Schivelbusch, *The Railway Journey: The Industrialization of Time and Space in the Nineteenth Century* (Berkeley: University of California Press, 1986), 42–44.

10. Samuel Bowles, *Across the Continent: A Summer's Journey to the Rocky Mountains, the Mormons, and the Pacific States, with Speaker Colfax* (Springfield, Mass.: Bowles; New York: Hurd and Houghton, 1866), 62; unattributed source, Nov. 25, 1870, quoted in Davis, *First Five Years of the Railroad Era,* 124; "The Evolution of Power on the Denver & Rio Grande Railroad," 1913, folder 2948, box 57, D&RG; Wilbur Stone, *History of Colorado* (Chicago: Clarke, 1918–1919), 1:333, 341–342; LeRoy Hafen, *Colorado and Its People: A Narrative and Topical History of the Centennial State* (New York: Lewis, 1948), 1:370; C. F. Ray to unknown, Jan. 23, 1889, folder 16, box 1, CF&I-CHS. Curiously, Hafen goes on to provide some exact figures drawn from operating routes that suggest that prices were actually closer to $2–3 per ton-mile.

11. *Cañon City Record,* Sept. 4, 1913. The D&RG's 1888 annual report suggests the significance of mineral freights for earnings; coal, coke, and ore together accounted for 45.99 percent of the railroad's revenue during a year characterized by warm weather and depressed coal traffic. *Third Annual Report of the Denver and Rio Grande R. R. Co. for the Year Ending December 31, 1888* (Denver: News Printing, 1889), 4, 24.

12. Statistics from U.S. Census, "Table 20: Colorado—Race and Hispanic Origin, 1860–1990," online at www.census.gov (accessed Mar. 30, 2008).

13. William Cronon, "Kennecott Journey: The Paths out of Town," in William Cronon, George Miles, and Jay Gitlin, eds., *Under an Open Sky: Rethinking America's Western Past* (New York: Norton, 1992).

14. *Second Annual Report of the Board of Directors of the Denver & Rio Grande Railway to the Stockholders, for the Year 1873* (Colorado Springs: Out West, 1874), 14.

15. Reproductions can be found in National Irrigation Congress, *Colorado as an Agricultural State: The Progress of Irrigation* (Denver: Kelly, 1894), n.p., and on the cover of Colorado & Southern Railway, *What to See in Colorado: National Education Association Convention, Denver, Colorado, July 5–9, 1909* (n.p.: n.p., n.d.). For a modern

reprint, see "Denver: Central Area, 1892–1894," in John Fielder, *Colorado 1870–2000* (Englewood, Colo.: Westcliffe, 2000), 12–13. The analysis that follows builds on the wonderful treatment of urban-hinterland relations in Cronon's *Nature's Metropolis,* a work that unfortunately overlooks the centrality of coal to the rise of Chicago and the transformation of the Great West.

16. For general treatments of urban growth, see Kathleen Brosnan, *Uniting Mountain and Plain: Cities, Law, and Environmental Change along the Front Range* (Albuquerque: University of New Mexico Press, 2002); William Wyckoff, *Creating Colorado: The Making of a Western American Landscape, 1860–1940* (New Haven, Conn.: Yale University Press), 1999; and Stephen J. Leonard and Thomas J. Noel, *Denver: Mining Camp to Metropolis* (Niwot: University Press of Colorado, 1990). On coal markets, see Wolff, *Industrializing the Rockies.* On pooling, see C. M. Higginson to E. P. Ripley, June 18, 1896, folder 19–2, RR box 36, New York Executive Department Files, AT&SF Papers. On the significance of railroad "breaking points" for urban growth in the West, see Cronon, *Nature's Metropolis,* 83–91.

17. Palmer to Mellen, July 24, 1871; decennial figures from U.S. Census data; other figures from *Third Annual Report of the Denver Board of Trade for the Year Ending Jan. 1, 1872* (Denver: Denver Tribune Association Print, 1872), 21.

18. Jerome Smiley, *History of Denver* (1901; repr. Denver: Old Americana, 1978), 871–98; Frank E. Shepard, "Industrial Development in Colorado," in James H. Baker and LeRoy R. Hafen, eds., *History of Colorado* (Denver: Linderman, 1927), 2:714–716; Rodman W. Paul, *The Far West and Great Plains in Transition, 1859–1900* (New York: Harper and Row, 1988), 104; C[larence] K[ing], "Colorado Industries," *Iron Age* 49 (May 12, 1892): 923–924 and "Colorado Industries—II," *Iron Age* 49 (May 19, 1892): 962–964. Contrast this with Cronon's emphasis on current flows of solar energy in fueling the Western economy: Cronon, *Nature's Metropolis,* 149–150.

19. "A New Rocky Mountain Industry," *New York Daily Graphic,* Nov. 18, 1881, p. 135; Herbert N. Casson, *The Romance of Steel: The Story of a Thousand Millionaires* (New York: Barnes, 1907), 309. The best works on the travails of the Pueblo plant are H. Lee Scamehorn, *Pioneer Steelmaker of the West,* and Scamehorn, *Mill and Mine: The CF&I in the Twentieth Century* (Lincoln: University of Nebraska Press, 1992). See also "The Colorado Discrimination Suit," *Iron Age* 62 (Nov. 10, 1898): 16; Alfred C. Cass testimony, Feb. 23, 1899, *CF&I vs. Southern Pacific et al.,* case 3807 U.S. District Court for Colorado, copy in box 11, CF&I-CHS; and A. C. Cass letterpress book, 1898, folder 98, box 6, ibid.

20. "More and More Iron," *Pueblo Chieftain,* Feb. 20, 1903; "Pueblo Steel Works," *Denver Republican,* Jan. 23, 1882; F. A. Delano to J. C. Osgood, May 27, 1892, folder 90, box 5, CF&I-CHS; *Fourteenth Annual Report of the Colorado Fuel and Iron Co. for the Year Ending June 30, 1906* (Denver: n.p., 1906), 6; John Birkinbine, *Report on the Water Supply of Minnequa Works at Pueblo, Colo.* (Denver: Smith-Brooks, [1906]); A. H. Hel-

ander, "The Engineering Department at the Minnequa Works, Pueblo," *Camp and Plant* 3 (June 6, 1903): 511–515.

21. Quotation from H. A. Deuel, untitled speech, n.d. [1901 or 1911], folder 130, box 6, CF&I-CHS. See also *Pueblo Courier,* Sept. 2, 1898; F. E. Parks to LaMont Bowers, Feb. 27, 1911, folder 190, box 21, CF&I-RAC; H. A. Deuel, "The Shops and Their Functions: How Repairs Are Carried On at the Minnequa Works, Told by the Assistant Superintendent of Shops," *Camp and Plant* 3 (Mar. 28, 1903): 267–274. *Camp and Plant* reported on accidents in many issues; see also "Hospital Report of the Colorado Fuel and Iron Company for 1898–1899," July 1, 1899, folder 107, box 6, CF&I-CHS, p. 16; and John A. Fitch, *The Steelworkers* (New York: Russell Sage Foundation, 1910).

22. *Report of the Denver Board of Trade Showing the Business of Denver and the Industrial Product of Colorado for 1877* (Denver: Daily Times, 1878), 10; Trevor Corry, comp., *Beautiful Colorado: An Interesting and Instructive Journey over Mountains and through Dales; Deep into the Bowels of the Earth, through Fertile Valleys and Orchard-Covered Plains* (Denver: Carson-Harper, 1901); *Mining Investor,* Nov. 30, 1903, quoted in Michael Neuschatz, *The Golden Sword: The Coming of Capitalism to the Colorado Mining Frontier* (New York: Greenwood, 1986), 44–45. The best work on Colorado smelting remains James E. Fell, Jr., *Ores to Metals: The Rocky Mountain Smelting Industry* (Lincoln: University of Nebraska Press, 1979). See also Paul, *Far West and Great Plains in Transition,* 265–269; Shepard, "Industrial Development in Colorado," 701–707; C. K., "Colorado Industries," 923–924; Denver Society of Civil Engineers, *Some Answers to Questions Likely to Be Asked by the Members of the American Society of Civil Engineers during Their Visit to Denver, on the Occasion of Their Annual Convention, July 2, 1886* ([Denver]: C. J. Kelly, [1886]), 93; and Robert Guilford Taylor, *Cripple Creek Mining District* (Palmer Lake, Colo.: Filter, 1973), 50–51. For reactions to the smelter trust, see *Littleton Independent,* May 31, 1901; *Longmont Ledger,* July 4, 1902; and *Colorado Transcript* (Golden), Apr. 5, 1905.

23. Jane Edelstein oral history, in Pueblo Mosaic Transcripts, Western History Room, Pueblo Public Library, vol. 1, pp. 2–6; Anna Fasula oral history, ibid., pp. 2–9; Mary Hrusovsky and Mary Baltazar oral history, ibid., p. 1; "Hundred Thousand Club against Scrip System," unidentified clipping, Jan. 25, 1906, box 12, CF&I-CHS; *Pueblo Chieftain,* Jan. 26, 1906; United States Immigration Commission, *Immigrants in Industries,* pt. 25, *Japanese and Other Immigrant Races in the Pacific Coast and Rocky Mountain States,* 61st Cong., 3d sess., S. Doc 747, vol. 3 (Washington, D.C.: GPO, 1911); Joanne West Dodds, *They All Came to Pueblo: A Social History* (Virginia Beach, Va.: Donning, 1994), 148; Leonard and Noel, *Denver,* 185; Larry Betz, *Globeville: Part of Colorado's History* (Denver: Larry Betz, 1972).

24. "'Mexico' or 'Mexican Town': Picturesque Settlement of Smelter Laborers in the Heart of Pueblo," *Camp and Plant* 4 (Sept. 26, 1903): 245–250.

25. *Annual Report of the State Board of Horticulture and the State Beekeepers' Associa-*

tion of the State of Colorado for the Year 1902 (Denver: Smith-Brooks, 1903), 236; "80216: City's Dumping Ground," *Denver Post,* May 2, 2004; Jeffrey Leib, "Neighbors of Ex-Asarco Plant to Join Mandated Cleanup of Toxic Metals," *Denver Post,* Oct. 10, 2004; Todd Hartman, "10-Year Soil Cleanup Completed," *Rocky Mountain News,* Oct. 25, 2006.

26. "Picturesque and Beautiful Places in and about Pueblo," *Camp and Plant* 4 (July 11, 1903): 16; *Denver Times,* Aug. 14, 1899, p. 1. On attitudes toward smoke more generally during this period, see David Stradling, *Smokestacks and Progressives: Environmentalists, Engineers, and Air Quality in America, 1881–1951* (Baltimore: Johns Hopkins University Press, 1999).

27. Quoted in Leonard and Noel, *Denver,* 61. See also Wyckoff, *Creating Colorado,* 119–120; Dodds, *They All Came to Pueblo,* 77–79.

28. Smiley, *History of Denver,* 870; Richard Harding Davis, *The West from a Car-Window* (New York: Harper and Brothers, 1892), 219; *Camp and Plant* 2 (Oct. 11, 1902): 359; *Camp and Plant* 4 (July 25, 1904): 34; George W. Hilton, *The Cable Car in America: A New Treatise upon Cable or Rope Traction as Applied to the Working of Street and Other Railways* (Berkeley, Calif.: Howell-North, 1971), 131; Don Robertson, Morris Cafky, and E. J. Haley, *1871–1900, Not an Automobile in Sight,* vol. 1 of *Denver's Street Railways* (Denver: Sundance, 1999), 120–121, 147–149, 195; Sam Bass Warner, *Streetcar Suburbs: The Process of Growth in Boston, 1870–1900* (Cambridge, Mass.: Harvard University Press, 1962); Kenneth T. Jackson, *Crabgrass Frontier: The Suburbanization of the United States* (New York: Oxford University Press, 1985); Denver Planning Commission, *A Study for Mass Transportation,* vol. 3 of *The Denver Plan* (Denver: Publishers, 1931), 14–16. Streetcar lines also connected industrial and working-class suburbs to the center city, as many scholars have recently emphasized; my argument about environmental and social inequalities does not depend on an industrial core city encircled by bucolic suburbs; instead, I emphasize a distinction between the heavily industrial, working-class communities in the Platte River Valley—some within Denver's city limits, others beyond them—and affluent suburbs farther afield. Richard Harris and Robert Lewis, "The Geography of North American Cities and Suburbs, 1900–1950: A New Synthesis," *Journal of Urban History* 27 (2001): 262–293.

29. On the variety of coal qualities and coal prices available in the Denver market, see J. J. Thomas to B. S. Fitch, Oct. 26, 1887, folder 64, box 4, CF&I-CHS. Other prices based on Ben Chase, *The Richest Region of the Rockies: A Guide to Colorado and the Rocky Mountains* (Denver: National and International Bureau of Information, 1884), 25; James Gardiner to O. Metcalf, May 31, 1889, folder 35, box 2, CF&I-CHS; entries in Daybook, Nov. 1, 1892, through Jan. 18, 1895, Queen City Wood and Coal Yard Papers, CHS, *Denver Post,* Apr. 2, 1913; case no. 521, Denver & Rio Grande Railroad Accident Reports, vol. 3, DPL; Ruth Schwartz Cowan, *More Work for Mother: The Ironies of Household Technology from the Open Hearth to the Microwave* (New York: Basic, 1983), 61–62, 96, 163–164;

Susan Strasser, *Never Done: A History of American Housework* (New York: Pantheon, 1982), 55–58; Priscilla J. Brewer, *From Fireplace to Cookstove: Technology and the Domestic Ideal in America* (Syracuse, N.Y.: Syracuse University Press, 2000), 175–177, 236–238; Freese, *Coal,* 142–147. As an illustration of the confusion some elite suburbanites felt in the face of furnaces and other new coal-burning household technologies, see the H. J. Taylor drawing reprinted as "Suburban Men and Furnace, 1896," in Becky M. Nicolaides and Andrew Wiese, eds., *The Suburb Reader* (New York: Routledge, 2006), 79.

30. Mary Pattison, *Principles of Domestic Engineering: Or the What, Why and How of a Home* (New York: Trow, 1915), 114. Here as throughout this chapter, my analysis is informed by David Nye, *Consuming Power: A Social History of American Energies* (Cambridge, Mass.: MIT Press, 1999).

31. Unattributed source, Apr. 4, 1871, quoted in Davis, *First Five Years of the Railroad Era,* 140; Scamehorn, *High Altitude Energy,* 72–85.

32. *Denver: "Queen City of the Plains"* (n.p.: n.p., n.d.); *Denver Souvenir, Issued for Distribution at the National Turnfest . . .* (Denver: Colorado Herold Job Print, [1909]); Thomas J. Noel, *Buildings of Colorado* (New York: Oxford University Press, 1997), 60. See also John Jakle, *City Lights: Illuminating the American Night* (Baltimore: Johns Hopkins University Press, 2001), esp. 133–137.

33. James Bretz, *Mansions of Denver: The Vintage Years, 1870–1938* (Boulder, Colo.: Pruett, 2005), 52; Geraldine B. Bean, *Charles Boettcher: A Study in Pioneer Western Enterprise* (Boulder, Colo.: Westview, 1976), 127–128; Mark Rose, *Cities of Light and Heat: Domesticating Gas and Electricity in Urban America* (University Park: Pennsylvania State University Press, 1995), 72–73; Nye, *Consuming Power,* 96.

34. Davis, *The West from a Car-Window,* 215; "Famous Denver Gas and Electric Building by Night" (postcard) (Denver: Sanborn Souvenir Co., n.d.), at www.cardcow.com (accessed Apr. 9, 2008).

35. Denver Foundation for Architecture, *Guide to Denver Architecture: With Regional Highlights* (Englewood, Colo.: Westcliffe, 2001), 17; *Report of the Denver Board of Trade,* 19, 93; "Brick Manufacture," clipping from *Colorado Exchange Journal* (Oct. 1889); Frances Melrose, "Building a 'City of Bricks,'" *Rocky Mountain News "Now,"* Aug. 9, 1981, p. 10; Thomas Tonge, "Bricks and Their Manufacture in Denver," *Western Architect and Building News* 2 (Dec. 1890): 155; Diane Wilk, *A Guide to Denver's Architectural Styles and Terms* (Denver: Historic Denver, 1995), 60; Richard R. Brettell, *Historic Denver: The Architects and the Architecture, 1858–1893* (Denver: Historic Denver, 1973), 2; *Rocky Mountain News,* June 4, 1977; Noel, *Buildings of Colorado,* 348; contract with Portland Cement Company, Feb. 3, 1905, *Secretary's Record F. Contracts & Leases,* CF&I-CHS.

36. Western Slope Congress of Colorado, *Western Colorado: A Glimpse into Nature's Richest Treasury Vaults . . .* (Grand Junction, Colo.: Grand Junction "News" Book and Job Print, 1893), 7.

37. *Leadville Weekly Democrat,* Dec. 31, 1881; Smith quoted in Stone, *History of Colorado,* 1:342; *Fourth Annual Report of the Colorado Coal and Iron Co.* (Colorado Springs: Daily Gazette Publishing Company, 1883), 12.

38. *Gunnison Democrat,* Dec. 15, 1880; Charles Stokes Wayne, "The New Cripple Creek," *Harper's Weekly,* Feb. 13, 1897, p. 162. Yearly consumption of coal in Aspen in 1889 exceeded 24,000 tons, roughly 2.5 tons per capita; James Gardiner to O. Metcalf, May 31, 1889, folder 35, box 2, CF&I-CHS. On consumption patterns, see John Harvey, business journal, July 28, 1880, through July 31, 1883, John Harvey Collection, CHS. Coal was so useful that customers were willing to pay high prices resulting from the added expense of packing it in via donkey to Creede. See photograph *Packing Coal to the Mines of Creede—1893,* in Nolie Mumey, *Creede: History of a Colorado Silver Mining Town* (Denver: Artcraft, 1949), 61.

39. Mark Wyman, *Hard-Rock Epic: Western Miners and the Industrial Revolution, 1860–1910* (Berkeley: University of California Press, 1979); Elliott West, "Worlds of Work," in Rodman Wilson Paul, *Mining Frontiers of the Far West, 1849–1880,* rev. ed. (Albuquerque: University of New Mexico Press, 2001); Frank Fossett, *Colorado: A Historical, Descriptive and Statistical Work on the Rocky Mountain Gold and Silver Mining Region* (Denver: Daily Tribune Steam Printing House, 1876), 37.

40. Wyman, *Hard-Rock Epic,* 85–89; John Codman, *The Round Trip by Way of Panama through California, Oregon, Nevada, Utah, Idaho, and Colorado with Notes on Railroads, Commerce, Agriculture, Mining, Scenery, and People* (New York: Putnam, 1879), 314–315; Rock Island Lines, *Colorado: Under the Turquoise Sky* (n.p.: Allen, 1912), n.p.; Fossett, *Colorado,* 159–160.

41. Quoted in Wyman, *Hard-Rock Epic,* 92. Wayne, "The New Cripple Creek," even compared that camp to a New England manufacturing city. On organized responses to these problems, see Alan Derickson, *Workers' Health, Workers' Democracy: The Western Miners' Struggle, 1891–1925* (Ithaca, N.Y.: Cornell University Press, 1988); Melvin Dubofsky, *We Shall Be All: A History of the Industrial Workers of the World* (Chicago: Quadrangle, 1969); and John Enyeart, *"By Laws of Their Own Making": Rocky Mountain Workers and American Social Democracy, 1870–1924* (Palo Alto, Calif.: Stanford University Press, forthcoming).

42. W. B. Vickers, "History of Colorado," in *History of Clear Creek and Boulder Valleys, Colorado, Containing a Brief History of the State of Colorado from Its Earliest Settlement to the Present Time, Embracing Its Geological, Physical and Climatic Features . . .* (Chicago: Baskin, Historical Publishers, 1880), 24; Rodman Paul, "Colorado as a Pioneer of Science in the Mining West," *Mississippi Valley Historical Review* 47 (1960): 34–50.

43. C. K. Holliday to Thomas Nickerson, n.d., folder 578.4, box 578, Historical Files, AT&SF; Edward Blair, *Leadville: Colorado's Magic City* (Boulder, Colo.: Pruett, 1980),

104; Ingwal S. Horgen, comp., "History of Pike National Forest," 1923, typescript, document 25, Pike National Forest Historical File Microfilm, Local History Division, Penrose Public Library, Pikes Peak Library District, Colorado Springs, 44; Caroline H. Dall, *My First Holiday; or, Letters Home from Colorado, Utah, and California* (Boston: Roberts Brothers, 1881), 40. For coal's role in the various stages of processing, see John Harvey, business journal, 316–317; modification of contract between CF&I and Sunshine Coal Company, 1888, folder 66, box 4, CF&I-CHS; Fossett, *Colorado,* 159, 162.

44. James T. Hodge, "On the Tertiary Coals of Colorado," in F. V. Hayden, *Preliminary Report of the United States Geological Survey of Wyoming, and Portions of Contiguous Territories . . .* (Washington, D.C.: GPO, 1871), 318; Holliday to Nickerson, n.d., folder 578.4, box 578, Historical Files, AT&SF; Vickers, "History of Colorado," 72; C. M. Chase, *The Editor's Run in New Mexico and Colorado* (Montpelier, Vt.: "Argus and Patriot" Steam Book and Job Printing, 1882), 182; Blair, *Leadville,* 98; William Willard Howard, "The Modern Leadville," *Harper's Weekly* supplement, Dec. 1, 1888, 928. Even when Western coke had to be transported large distances, it squeezed out charcoal; for estimates that Arizona copper production realized a 75 percent savings once coke making commenced at Raton, see A. A. Robinson to Morley, Nov. 16, 1878, conveyed in Robinson to William B. Strong, Nov. 28, 1878, folder 578.4, box 578, Historical Files, AT&SF.

45. Union Pacific Passenger Department, *Colorado: A Complete and Comprehensive Description of the Agricultural, Stock Raising and Mineral Resources of Colorado,* 5th ed. (St. Louis: Woodward and Tiernan, 1892), 35. Here I build on Elizabeth Jameson, *All That Glitters: Class, Conflict, and Community in Cripple Creek* (Champaign: University of Illinois Press, 1998).

46. *History and Description of the Cripple Creek Mining District: Mining and Business Directory, City of Cripple Creek and Adjacent Towns* (Cripple Creek: Hazeltine, 1894), 24; *Twelfth Biennial Report of the Bureau of Labor Statistics of the State of Colorado, 1909–1910* (Denver: Smith-Brooks, 1911), 16, 339; Franklin Guiterman, "Status of Mining and Smelting in Colorado," *Engineering and Mining Journal* 90 (Nov. 19, 1910): 1009–1010; U.S. Census, "Historic Population Counts, 1900 to 1990, for All Counties in Colorado," online at www.census.gov (accessed Mar. 30, 2008).

47. "Prospectus: The Colorado Fuel and Iron Company, General Mortgage (50 Years) 5% Sinking Fund Gold Bonds," Feb. 1893, folder 92, box 5, CF&I-CHS, 12 (emphasis added); Scamehorn, *Mill and Mine,* 201–202; *Annual Report of the Colorado Fuel Company, for the Year Ending June 30th, 1889* (New York: n.p., 1889), 9; *Denver Times,* Nov. 16, 1901; and "Secretary's Record F. Contracts & Leases. CF&I," CF&I-CHS.

48. Rupert Norval Richardson and Carl Coke Rister, *The Greater Southwest: The Economic, Social, and Cultural Development of Kansas, Oklahoma, Texas, Utah, Colorado, Nevada, New Mexico, Arizona, and California from the Spanish Conquest to the Twentieth Century* (Glendale, Calif.: Arthur C. Clark, 1934), 423; *Twelfth Biennial Re-*

port of the Bureau of Labor Statistics, 339; Donald Worster, *Dust Bowl: The Southern Plains in the 1930s* (New York: Oxford University Press, 1979); U.S. Census, "Historic Population Counts, 1900 to 1990."

49. Alvin Steinel, *History of Agriculture in Colorado: A Record of Progress in the Development of General Farming, Livestock Production and Agricultural Education and Investigation, on the Western Border of the Great Plains and in the Mountains of Colorado, 1858–1926* (Fort Collins, Colo.: State Agricultural College, 1926), 258–259; Hal Borland, *High, Wide and Lonesome* (Philadelphia: Lippincott, 1956), 70; *Eleventh Biennial Report of the Inspector,* 130.

50. George R. Caldwell, "Marvelous Growth of the Grand Valley," *Sixteenth National Irrigation Congress, Official Southwestern Souvenir* (Denver: Smith-Brooks, 1908), 157; Worster, *Dust Bowl,* 90; "Brief" [1906], folder 190, box 9, CF&I-CHS, 31; Clarence A. Lyman, *The Grand River Valley in Colorado: Its Orchards Ranches and Varied Resources* (n.p., 1908); Steinel, *History of Agriculture in Colorado,* 259; John Opie, *Ogallala: Water for a Dry Land,* 2nd ed. (Lincoln: University of Nebraska Press, 2000), 75–76.

51. E. P. Ripley to Victor Morawetz, Oct. 17, 1903, box RR 138, New York Executive Department Files, AT&SF; contracts between CF&I and American Beet Sugar Co., Oct. 1, 1900, May 31, 1901, and U.S. Sugar and Land Co., Apr. 19, 1906, *Secretary's Record F. Contracts & Leases,* CF&I-CHS; Steinel, *History of Agriculture in Colorado,* 284, 304, 306–307; *Biennial Report of the Bureau of Labor Statistics of the State of Colorado, 1907–1908* (Denver: Smith-Brooks, 1908), 28. On industrial food systems and the organic, see Michael Pollan, *The Omnivore's Dilemma: A Natural History of Four Meals* (New York: Penguin, 2006).

52. On rail-coal combines, see contract between the Grand River Coal & Coke Company and the Kansas & Colorado Coal Company, Mar. 12, 1889, folder 66, box 4, CF&I-CHS; contract with Missouri Pacific Railroad, May 19, 1896, *Secretary's Record F. Contracts & Leases,* "Report of Denver Bureau of Coal Statistics," folder 329, box 137, SG 2, series 1, President's Office 1884, Incoming Correspondence, Union Pacific Railroad Archives, Nebraska State Historical Society, Lincoln; D. O. Clark to H. G. Burt, Jan. 17, 1903, folder 341, box 39, ibid. Dealers on the plains earned less than their counterparts in Denver, $1, as compared with $1.65. *Denver Times,* Sept. 14, 1907. On "exports" to neighboring states, see *Third Biennial Report of the State Inspector of Coal Mines of the State of Colorado: For the Years of 1887–88* (Denver: Collier and Cleaveland, 1889), 6; *Fifth Biennial Report of the State Inspector of Coal Mines of the State of Colorado for the Years 1891 and 1892* (Denver: Smith-Brooks, 1893), 7; *Sixth Biennial Report of the State Inspector of Coal Mines of the State of Colorado for the Years of 1893–94* (Denver: Smith-Brooks, 1895), 3; *Wilkes-Barre News,* Apr. 5, 1906; Stone, *History of Colorado,* 1:454. An enormous historiography focuses on the Grange movement, populism, and other movements through which farmers took on the railroads, but few of these works address how coal exacerbated these conflicts.

53. Borland, *High, Wide and Lonesome,* 73–75. On homesteads as elements of a high-energy society, see Nye, *Consuming Power,* 113.

54. On the relation between the calories contained in coal and in the food that coal-burning implements helped produce, see Nye, *Consuming Power,* 103.

55. For contemporary country and state statistics, see www.nationmaster.com and www.statemaster.com, accessed Mar. 30, 2008. For historic figures on Britain, see Sidney Pollard, "A New Estimate of British Coal Production, 1750–1850," *Economic History Review* 33 (1980): 212–235. Conversions come from interview with Dan Binkley, Colorado Forest Restoration Institute and Warner College of Natural Resources, Colorado State University, Fort Collins, Colo., Nov. 7, 2007.

56. E. A. Wrigley, *Continuity, Chance, and Change: The Character of the Industrial Revolution in England* (Cambridge: Cambridge University Press, 1988), 75.

57. *Denver Post,* Oct. 4, 1907. Railroad archives document the arrangements that railroads made to reallocate the nation's coal resources during strikes. See D. O. Clark to H. G. Burt, Sept. 6, 1902, folder 339, box 39, SG 2, series 1, UP Papers; E. P. Ripley to Walker D. Hines, Sept. 5, 1910, file 25–1, box RR 45, New York Executive Department Files, AT&SF.

58. "The Coal Question," *Pueblo Chieftain* [1872?]. For negative accounts of coal dealings, see *Denver News,* Apr. 11 and May 16, 1902, July 17, 1903, Apr. 21 and May 20, 1905; *Florence Citizen,* Apr. 18, 1902; *Denver Post,* Feb. 17, Apr. 4 and 5, May 12, and Nov. 8, 1905; *Pueblo Star-Journal,* Mar. 22, 1903; *Denver News,* July 17, 1903; *Denver Times,* Jan. 11, 1905; and *Clay's Denver Review,* Feb. 27, 1904. LaMont Bowers later investigated land frauds during the Osgood era and confirmed that the company had obtained some two thousand acres at ten dollars an acre, when the actual value of these lands was at least two hundred dollars an acre; LaMont Montgomery Bowers to C. O. Heydt, folder 211, box 23, CF&I-RAC.

59. Haralambos Kambouris, "Separation," in "Pages of My Life and Various Poems: My Leaving Greece for America and My Sojourn in America," translated typescript, folder 8, box 2, Greek Archive, UU. The centrality of coal mining to the industrial world was frequently asserted in the pages of union publications. See J. Connel, "A Miners' Life," *United Mine Workers Journal,* Mar. 21, 1895.

3. Riding the Wave to Survive an Earth Transformed

1. Donald Mitchell interview, Feb. 5, 1978, transcript in box 11, EM, p. 2.

2. *El Moro Monitor,* July 21, 1893.

3. Mary Thomas testimony, CIR, 7: 6356–6357.

4. Bessie Eccher interview, Jan. 16, 1980, transcript in HCEHP, p. 1.

5. For one mention of a gun from the old country, see Victor Bazanele interview, n.d., box 7, EM, n.p.

6. Lucy Salyer, *Laws Harsh as Tigers: Chinese Immigrants and the Shaping of Modern American Immigration Law* (Chapel Hill: University of North Carolina Press, 1995). On migrants' coming with addresses, see John Skerl interview, Jan. 12, 1973, folder 8, box 1, South Slavs Oral History Collection, UU, p. 19.

7. Studies of race, color, and whiteness are too numerous to cite. Particularly relevant here, though, are David R. Roediger, *The Wages of Whiteness: Race and the Making of the American Working Class* (New York: Verso, 1991); Matthew Frye Jacobson, *Whiteness of a Different Color: European Immigrants and the Alchemy of Race* (Cambridge, Mass.: Harvard University Press, 1998); and Thomas A. Guglielmo, *White on Arrival: Italians, Race, Color, and Power in Chicago, 1890–1945* (New York: Oxford University Press, 2004). For a thoughtful critique, see Peter Kolchin, "Whiteness Studies: The New History of Race in America," *Journal of American History* 89 (2002): 154–173. See also Jim Dimante interview, Apr. 21 and 24, 1978, transcript in box 9, EM, p. 51.

8. On the bodily markings of McBride and others, see Fremont County and Huerfano County Naturalization Records, CSA.

9. For a mention of a "beautiful mine," see T. X. Evans in "Proceedings of Joint Conference," Nov. 26, 1913, typescript in box 26, CF&I-RAC, 17.

10. Mike Livoda interview, Nov. 8, 15, and 30, 1968, and Sept. 20, 1980, transcripts in box 10, EM; Stephen Burnett Brier, " 'The Most Persistent Unionists': Class Formation and Class Conflict in the Coal Fields and the Emergence of Interracial and Interethnic Unionism, 1880–1904" (Ph.D. diss., University of California at Los Angeles, 1992), 265.

11. Zeese Papanikolas, *Buried Unsung: Louis Tikas and the Ludlow Massacre* (Salt Lake City: University of Utah Press, 1982), 7–8.

12. I use "old country" as a blanket term for the home regions of *all* coalfield migrants; in this formulation, the Hispano villages of southern Colorado and northern New Mexico, the soft coalfields of Pennsylvania, and the southern Italian countryside all figure as the "old country."

13. For an exemplary study that employs "transnational and diasporic approaches [to] remap migration patterns and experiences . . . in a global framework" that moves beyond immigration historians' traditional focus on the United States and Europe, see Mai Ngai, *Impossible Subjects: Illegal Aliens and the Making of Modern America* (Princeton, N.J.: Princeton University Press, 2004), 9.

14. On migrants' agency, see Leslie Page Moch, "Introduction," in Dirk Hoerder and Leslie Page Moch, eds., *European Migrants: Local and Global Perspectives* (Boston: Northeastern University Press, 1996); John Bodnar, *Transplanted: A History of Immigration in Urban America* (Bloomington: University of Indiana Press, 1985). My narrative approach here draws on Tim O'Brien, *The Things They Carried: A Work of Fiction* (New York: Penguin, 1990), and aspires to fulfill what Silvia Pedraza-Bailey calls "our need to do studies that link the micro and macro levels of analysis more tightly." Pedraza-Bailey

quoted in Moch, "Introduction," 3. At the same time, I attempt to update what Frank Thistlethwaite praised as Oscar Handlin's greatest accomplishment, "to convey the immigrant experience as tragic as well as epic." Frank Thistlethwaite, "Migration from Europe Overseas in the Nineteenth and Twentieth Centuries," in Rudolph J. Vecoli and Suzanne M. Sinke, eds., *A Century of European Migrations, 1830–1930* (Champaign: University of Illinois Press, 1991), 19.

15. Carter Goodrich, *The Miner's Freedom: A Study of the Working Life in a Changing Industry* (Boston: Marshall Jones, 1925); Keith Dix, *What's a Coal Miner to Do: The Mechanization of Coal Mining* (Pittsburgh: University of Pittsburgh Press, 1988); Jerry Wayne Napier, "Mines, Miners, and Machines: Coal Mine Mechanization and the Eastern Kentucky Coal Fields, 1890–1990" (Ph.D. diss., University of Kentucky, 1997); Joel Mokyr, *The Lever of Riches: Technological Creativity and Economic Progress* (New York: Oxford University Press, 1990), 294–296; David Greasley, "The Diffusion of Machine Cutting in the British Coal Industry, 1902–1938," *Explorations in Economic History* 19 (1982): 246–268; Jeff Hornibrook, "Local Elites and Mechanized Mining in China: The Case of the Wen Lineage in Pingxiang County, Jiangxi," *Modern China* 27 (2001): 202–228; Ian Phimister, "Lashers and Leviathan: The 1954 Coalminers' Strike in Colonial Zimbabwe," *International Review of Social History* 39 (1994): 165–196; and Alan Campbell, "Colliery Mechanisation and the Lanarkshire Miners," *Bulletin of the Society for the Study of Labour History* 49 (1984): 37–45.

16. *Fourth Annual Report of the Colorado Coal and Iron Co.* (Colorado Springs: Daily Gazette, 1883), 9. More generally, see David Montgomery, *Workers' Control in America: Studies in the History of Work, Technology, and Labor Struggles* (New York: Cambridge University Press, 1980).

17. E. S. McKinlay to Charles B. Lamborn, Mar. 28 and Apr. 13, 1881, folder 30, box 2, CF&I-CHS; George Engle, "Record of Coal Cutting Machinery," Apr. 1881, ibid.; Engle to Lamborn, Apr. 23, 1881, ibid.

18. Engle, "Report of Coal Cutting Machinery," week ending May 31, 1881, folder 30, box 2, CF&I-CHS. A funeral also silenced the machines; ibid., week ending Apr. 14, 1881. On Penitentes in the coalfields, see "El Cinico," and "Los Penitentes," *Camp and Plant* 3 (May 23, 1903): 461–464.

19. David J. Jones to E. S. McKinlay, Apr. 25, 1881, folder 30, box 2, CF&I-CHS; J. Imbrie Miller to T. Haskins DuPuy, Jan. 24, 1889, folder 28, box 1, ibid.; "Lechner Machines—Week Ending April 23rd 81," ibid.; George Engle to J. R. Cameron, May 18, 1881, ibid.; "Record of Coal Cutting Machinery," week ending May 7, 1881, ibid.; George Engle to Charles B. Lamborn, May 11, 1881, ibid.

20. [J. R. Cameron?] to A. H. Danforth, Dec. 31, 1885, folder 28, box 1, CF&I-CHS; *Fourth Annual Report of the Colorado Coal and Iron Co.,* 9–10; James Dalrymple, letter of Sept. 9, 1914, in *First Annual Report of the State Inspector of Coal Mines, 1913* (Denver: Smith-Brooks, 1914), n.p. For more on machines as "insurance against labor troubles,"

see anonymous letter to J. Van Houten, June 21, 1901, folder 18, box 32, Maxwell Land Grant Company Records, Center for Southwest Research, General Library, University of New Mexico, Albuquerque.

21. Wilbur Stone, *History of Colorado* (Chicago: S. J. Clarke, 1918–1919), 1:463–464. Labor productivity in American soft coal mines doubled during this period, to 751 tons per worker per year. Edward W. Parker, "The Coal Supplies and Coal Production of the United States," *Publications of the American Statistical Association* 13 (1912): 146.

22. Vaclav Smil, *Energy in World History* (Boulder, Colo.: Westview, 1994), 193. This irony seemed to have been lost on the Dillingham Commission, which presented a portrait of the coal industry as thoroughly mechanized. See Mark Wyman, *Round-Trip to America: The Immigrants Return to Europe, 1880–1930* (Ithaca, N.Y.: Cornell University Press, 1993), 46.

23. On the massacre, see folders in box 26694, Governor Jesse McIntyre Papers, CSA.

24. On inheritance, see Jim Dimante interview, transcript in box 9, EM, p. 50.

25. On land as "the heart of the peasant's desire," see Wyman, *Round-Trip to America,* 129–136.

26. Frances Burch, "The Life of Henry Johns," typescript in folder 1, Henry Johns Papers, DPL; Henry Johns "Rockvale," as told to H. C. Webster, CWA Interviews, vol. 366, doc. no. 5, p. 172. Johns probably spoke Welsh most of the time before emigrating, but he would surely have learned English at day school. On the Welsh education system, see Gareth Elwyn Jones, *Modern Wales: A Concise History, c. 1485–1979* (Cambridge: Cambridge University Press, 1984), 284–289. On British education and the advantages literacy provided to British immigrants, see Rowland Tappan Berthoff, *British Immigrants in Industrial America, 1790–1950* (Cambridge, Mass.: Harvard University Press, 1953), 127.

27. Burch, "Life of Henry Johns"; Johns "Rockvale"; "Employee's Service Record," folder 3, Henry Johns Papers. On the Welsh community, see William Jones, "History of the Welsh People of Colorado: An Essay on the History of the Welsh of Colorado from Its Earliest Settlement till Now," typescript translation dated 1937 of Evan Williams, *Traethawd Arhanes Cymru Colorado: O'i Sefydliad Boreuaf Hyd An Awr* (Denver: Evan Williams, 1889). See also Lewis Francis Joel to editor, *Seren Cymru,* July 14, 1873; E. Evans to unknown recipient, Feb. 16, 1880; Thomas Davies, Morgan M. Williams, and John Morgan to editor, *Tarian Y Gweithiwr,* Sept. 1, 1881; Cynfelin (R. Parry) to unknown recipient, Dec. 8, 1881—all in Alan Conway, ed., *The Welsh in America: Letters from the Immigrants* (Minneapolis: University of Minnesota Press, 1961), 269–277.

28. Jones, "History of the Welsh," 16, 35.

29. Burch, "Life of Henry Johns"; "Employee's Service Record"; International Correspondence School, "Instruction Papers," in Henry Johns Papers; Johns to E. H. Weitzel, Feb. 1, 1920, ibid.

30. Sam Vigil interview, May 1979, transcript in HCEHP, n.p.

31. Emilio and Gertrude Ferraro interview, May 22, 1978, transcript in box 9, EM, pp. 34–36; prefect quoted in Wyman, *Round-Trip to America,* 25. Aiello is discussed later.

32. George Pezell interview, Aug. 17, 1972, transcript in folder 2, box 1, South Slavs Oral History Collection, UU, pp. 1–2. Pezell claimed that his father had worked for CF&I at one point. Ibid., p. 10.

33. Louis Guigli interview, July 17, 1979, transcript in HCEHP, and box 10, EM, pp. 1–2.

34. Known officially as Victor Coal and Coke, then the Victor-American Fuel Company, the firm colloquially referred to simply as the Victor Company was the second-largest producer of coal and coke in the southern fields from the 1890s until the 1920s.

35. *Denver Republican,* Feb. 19 and 28, 1902; *Cripple Creek Times,* Feb. 14, 1902; *Walsenburg World,* Feb. 20, 1902. A Durango paper editorialized, "Every camp in Colorado should keep the Asiatics moving." *Durango Democrat,* Feb. 21, 1902.

36. 1880 manuscript census schedules, Huerfano County, Colorado; John H. M. Laslett, *Colliers across the Sea: A Comparative Study of Class Formation in Scotland and the American Midwest, 1830–1924* (Champaign: University of Illinois Press, 2000); Laslett, "British Immigrant Colliers, and the Origins and Early Development of the UMWA, 1870–1912," in John H. M. Laslett, ed., *The United Mine Workers of America: A Model of Industrial Solidarity?* (University Park: Pennsylvania State University Press, 1996), 33; Berthoff, *British Immigrants in Industrial America,* 51–55; W. Jett Lauck, "The Vanishing American Wage-Earner," *Atlantic* 110 (1912), 692; Charles Morgan testimony, Subcommittee on Mines and Mining, *Conditions in the Coal Mines of Colorado: Hearings before a Subcommittee of the Committee on Mines and Mining,* 63d Cong., 2d sess. (Washington, D.C.: GPO, 1914), 1:715–717. For exemplary studies of colliers outside the British Isles, see Marcel Gillet, *Les charbonnages du nord de la France au XIXe siècle* (Paris: Mouton, 1973); Roberto R. Calderón, *Mexican Coal Mining Labor in Texas and Coahuila, 1880–1930* (College Station: Texas A&M University Press, 2000); John J. Kulczycki, *The Foreign Worker and the German Labor Movement: Xenophobia and Solidarity in the Coal Fields of the Ruhr, 1871–1914* (Oxford: Berg, 1994); and Daniel Letwin, *The Challenge of Interracial Unionism: Alabama Coal Miners, 1878–1921* (Chapel Hill: University of North Carolina Press, 1998).

37. Laslett, *Colliers across the Sea.* "Newcomer-rebels" figured so prominently in coal mine labor forces around the world during this era because of staggering, hundredfold increases in global coal production, from ten million tons in 1810 to a billion tons in 1910. Smil, *Energy in World History,* 185. On Hispanos in the early Colorado mines, see *First Report of the Colorado Coal and Iron Co., Comprising the Sixth Report of the Central Colorado Improvement Co. and the Second Report of the Southern Colorado Coal and Town Co.* (Colorado Springs: Daily Gazette, 1880), 6; "Camp Engle or Engleville: One of

the Older Coal Camps Near Trinidad," *Camp and Plant* 1 (31 May 1902): 459–460. The railroad-colliery employment connection is discussed later in the chapter. On Chinese miners, see William Wei, "The Anti-Chinese Movement in Colorado: Interethnic Competition and Conflict on the Eve of Exclusion," *Chinese America: History and Perspectives* 1995 (1995), 179–197, and "Report of Coal Mine Accident, King, Park County, Colorado, Jan. 10, 1893," folder 14, box 26693, Governor Alva Adams Papers, CSA. The 1910 census showed just four Chinese in Huerfano and Las Animas counties. *Thirteenth Biennial Report of the Bureau of Labor Statistics of the State of Colorado, 1911–1912* (Denver: Smith-Brooks, 1913), 154. On African American miners, strikes, and "white" workers, see *First Biennial Report of the Bureau of Labor Statistics of the State of Colorado, 1887–1888* (Denver: Collier and Cleaveland, 1888), 140; *Pueblo Courier,* July 29, 1898; *Florence Daily Tribune,* May 13, 1902; *Denver Times,* May 14 and July 30, 1902; *Cañon City Record,* Sept. 20, 1904; "The Coal Camps of Fremont County," typescript, Local History Room, Cañon City Public Library; "Negro Churches in Cañon City," ibid.; *Cañon City Daily Record,* May 7, 1970; Alfred Owens interview, Feb. 2, 1978, transcript in box 12, EM, pp. 7, 34; Alfred Owens interview by Frances Daher, July 24, 1979, transcript in HCEHP, n.p. On twentieth-century migrant groups, see Lawrence Cardoso, *Mexican Emigration to the United States, 1897–1931: Socio-Economic Patterns* (Tucson: University of Arizona Press, 1980); Theodore Saloutos, *The Greeks in the United States* (Cambridge, Mass.: Harvard University Press, 1964); Henry Pratt Fairchild, *Greek Immigration to the United States* (New Haven, Conn.: Yale University Press, 1911). The 1912 report of the state labor commissioner showed 259 Japanese in Huerfano and Las Animas counties, the vast majority of whom were no doubt employed in coal mining. *Thirteenth Biennial Report of the Bureau of Labor Statistics,* 154.

38. A. E. Matthews. "Methods of Keeping Payrolls and Paying Employes," *Camp and Plant* 3 (Apr. 18, 1903): 341–345; Karen Mitchell, "Huerfano County, Colorado Miners' Page," at www.kmich.com.

39. Donna R. Gabaccia, "When the Migrants Are Men: Italy's Women and Transnationalism as a Working-Class Way of Life," in Donna R. Gabaccia and Vicki L. Ruiz, eds., *American Dreaming, Global Realities: Rethinking U.S. Immigration History* (Champaign: University of Illinois Press, 2006), 195. On migrant homemaking, see Yen Le Espiritu, *Home Bound: Filipino American Lives across Cultures, Communities, and Countries* (Berkeley: University of California Press, 2003), 2.

40. William Adamic interview by Frank Adamic, Jan. 15, 1985, transcript in LHC, pp. 64–65.

41. For a poetic expression of such regrets, see "In a Foreign Land," in Haralambos Kambouris, "Pages of My Life and Various Poems: My Leaving Greece for America and My Sojourn in America," translated typescript, folder 8, box 2, Greek Archive, UU.

42. On old-country wages, see Gabaccia, "When the Migrants Are Men," 196; Wyman, *Round-Trip to America,* 33–34. On the dual labor system in the Southwest, see Ma-

rio Barrera, *Race and Class in the Southwest: A Theory of Racial Inequality* (South Bend, Ind.: Notre Dame University Press, 1979); Linda Gordon, *The Great Arizona Orphan Abduction* (Cambridge, Mass.: Harvard University Press, 1999); Katherine Benton-Cohen, *Borderline Americans* (Cambridge, Mass.: Harvard University Press, forthcoming); Evelyn Nakano Glenn, "Race, Labor, and Citizenship in Hawaii," in Gabaccia and Ruiz, *American Dreaming, Global Realities*, 287–293. On Colorado wages, see David A. Wolff, *Industrializing the Rockies: Growth, Competition, and Turmoil in the Coalfields of Colorado and Wyoming, 1867–1914* (Boulder: University Press of Colorado), 41.

43. George J. Condas interview, n.d., transcript in folder 4, box 1, Interviews with Greeks in Utah, UU, p. 3; Ed Tomsic interview, Jan. 21, 1980, transcript in HCEHP, p. 1. On émigrés and conscription, see Mary Damash interview, May 28, 1978, transcript in Pueblo Mosaic Transcripts, Western History Room, Pueblo Public Library, vol. 1, p. 1; Yamato Ichihashi, "Emigration from Japan and Japanese Immigration into the State of California" (Ph.D. diss., Harvard University, 1913), 328; Adamic oral history, pp. 2–3. On Cretan migrants, see Helen Papanikolas interview, Aug. 6, 1982, transcript in folder 2, box 2, Interviews with Greeks in Utah, UU, p. 25.

44. Nick Halamandaris interview by Barron Beshoar, June 25, 1978, transcript in box 7, EM, p. 48; Dan DeSantis interview, Jan. 19, 1978, transcript in box 9, p. 1; Mickey Judiscak interview, May 22, 1980, in HCEHP, p. 1.

45. Mary Truden interview, July 19, 1974, transcript in folder 2, box 3, South Slavs Oral History Collection, UU, p. 5; "Report of Conditions Existing in Europe and Mexico Affecting Emigration and Immigration, Being a Compilation, in Digested Form, of Reports . . . ," folder 51411/1, General Subject Correspondence, Immigration and Naturalization Service, RG 85, NARA–Washington, D.C. (hereafter INS); John Foster Carr, "The Coming of the Italian," *Outlook* 82 (Feb. 24, 1906): 420.

46. Alfred Crosby makes an analogous argument regarding European imperialism in *Ecological Imperialism: The Biological Expansion of Europe, 900–1900* (New York: Cambridge University Press, 1986). I do not mean to suggest that the environment *determined* migration; rather, I insert the environment into Leslie Page Moch's argument that migration constituted "a socially mediated response to fundamental economic and demographic developments." Moch, "Introduction," 5.

47. Thomas J. Archdeacon, *Becoming American: An Ethnic History* (New York: Free Press, 1983), 30–31; Leslie Page Moch, "Dividing Time: An Analytic Framework for Migration History Periodization," in J. Lucassen and L. Lucassen, eds., *Migrations, Migration History, History: Old Paradigms and New Perspectives* (Bern: Peter Lang, 1997), 50; Carlo M. Cipolla, *The Economic History of World Population*, 6th ed. (Harmondsworth, U.K.: Penguin, 1974); William H. McNeill, *Population and Politics since 1750* (Charlottesville: University of Virginia Press, 1990), 1–21; Ichihashi, "Emigration from Japan," 345–372; D. V. Glass and E. Grebenik, "World Population, 1800–1950," in H. J. Habakkuk and M. Postan, eds., *The Industrial Revolutions and After: Incomes, Population and*

Technological Change, vol. 6 of *The Cambridge Economic History of Europe* (Cambridge: Cambridge University Press, 1965), 58, 65; Gustavo Cabrera, "Demographic Dynamics and Development: The Role of Population Policy in Mexico," *Population and Development Review* 20 suppl. (1994): 105–106. Japan's 1868 figure is extrapolated from these sources.

48. For a case study, see Ryan Johansson and Carl Mosk, "Exposure, Resistance and Life Expectancy: Disease and Death during the Economic Development of Japan, 1900–1960," *Population Studies* 41 (1987): 221. See also Walter T. K. Nugent, *Crossings: The Great Transatlantic Migrations, 1870–1914* (Bloomington: University of Indiana Press, 1992), 21–25; Glass and Grebenik, "World Population," 76; J. N. Hays, *Burdens of Disease: Epidemics and Human Response in Western History* (New Brunswick, N.J.: Rutgers University Press, 1998), 240–277; Gerald N. Grob, *The Deadly Truth: A History of Disease in America* (Cambridge, Mass.: Harvard University Press, 2002), 180–216.

49. Alfred W. Crosby, *The Columbian Exchange: Biological and Cultural Consequences of 1492* (Westport, Conn.: Greenwood, 1972).

50. Quotations ibid., 182–183; Leslie Page Moch, "European Perspective: Changing Conditions and Multiple Migrations, 1750–1914," in Hoerder and Moch, *European Migrants,* 123. This is not to portray old-country famines as purely "natural" disasters; the Irish potato famine and most other demographic catastrophes resulted from political and economic failure; often there was still adequate food for all, but mechanisms for compelling the wealthier classes to share their surpluses with the poor were inadequate.

51. Robert F. Foerster, *Italian Immigration of Our Times* (Cambridge, Mass.: Harvard University Press, 1919), 102. On rural resistance in regions that supplied emigrants to Colorado, the literature is too vast to survey adequately. Key foundations include E. J. Hobsbawm, *Primitive Rebels: Studies in Archaic Forms of Social Movement in the 19th and 20th Centuries* (New York: Norton, 1965); Charles Tilly, Louise Tilly, and Richard Tilly, *The Rebellious Century, 1830–1930* (Cambridge, Mass.: Harvard University Press, 1975); John Tutino, *From Insurrection to Revolution in Mexico: Social Bases of Agrarian Violence, 1750–1940* (Princeton, N.J.: Princeton University Press, 1986), 228–336; Ian Inkster, *Japanese Industrialisation: Historical and Cultural Perspectives* (London: Routledge, 2001), 74.

52. Moch, "Introduction," 7; Charles M. Sypolt, "Keepers of the Rocky Mountain Flocks: A History of the Sheep Industry in Colorado, New Mexico, Utah and Wyoming to 1900" (Ph.D. diss., University of Wyoming, 1974); Walter Nugent, *Into the West: The Story of Its People* (New York: Vintage, 1999), 166; Ronald Takaki, *Strangers from a Different Shore: A History of Asian Americans* (New York: Penguin, 1989), 193, 195; John W. Cole and Eric R. Wolf, *The Hidden Frontier: Ecology and Ethnicity in an Alpine Valley* (New York: Academic Press, 1974), 45, 82–83; Robert F. Foerster, "A Statistical Survey of Italian Emigration," *Quarterly Journal of Economics* 23 (1908): 75; Moch, "European Perspective," 119–121; George J. Sánchez, *Becoming Mexican American: Ethnicity, Cul-*

ture and Identity in Chicano Los Angeles, 1900–1945 (New York: Oxford University Press, 1993), 43–44.

53. Giovanni Federico, *Feeding the World: An Economic History of World Agriculture, 1800–2000* (Princeton, N.J.: Princeton University Press, 2005), 16–82.

54. On immigration to collieries, see A. G. Walker, "Migration into a South Yorkshire Colliery District, 1861–81," *Northern History* 29 (1993): 165–184; Norman J. G. Pounds, "The Spread of Mining in the Coal Basin of Upper Silesia and Northern Moravia," *Annals of the Association of American Geographers,* 48 (1958): 156–158; Norman J. G. Pounds, *The Ruhr: A Study in Historical and Economic Geography* (1952; repr. New York: Greenwood, 1968), 130; "Report of Conditions Existing in Europe and Mexico," 29–30; Ewa Morawska, "Shaping the Worlds of Labor: Labor Migrations of Poles in the Atlantic World Economy, 1880–1914," *Comparative Studies in Society and History* 31 (1989): 237–272. On Tyroleans, see Cole and Wolf, *Hidden Frontier,* 82. On Hispano labor patterns, see William A. Bell, *New Tracks in North America: A Journal of Travel and Adventure Whilst Engaged in the Survey for a Southern Railroad to the Pacific Ocean during 1867–8* (London: Chapman and Hall, 1869), 26; *Philadelphia Press,* Aug. 16, 1867; William Jackson Palmer to Queen Mellen, May 15, 1870, folder 707, box 9, WJPP-CHS. On "minorities" in collieries, see John J. Kulczycki, "Scapegoating the Foreign Worker: Job Turnover, Accidents, and Diseases among Polish Coal Miners in the German Ruhr, 1871–1914," in *Politics of Immigrant Workers: Labor Activism and Migration in the World Economy since 1830* (New York: Holmes and Meier, 1998); Kulczycki, *The Foreign Worker and the German Labor Movement;* Moch, "European Perspective," 127; Laslett, *Colliers across the Sea,* 21–22; Hoerder, "International Labor Markets and Community Building by Migrant Workers in the Atlantic Economies," in Vecoli and Sinke, *Century of European Migrations,* 83; and Foerster, *Italian Emigration of Our Time,* 157–158. On women and migrations, see Donna Gabaccia, "Women of Mass Migrations: From Minority to Majority, 1820–1930," in Hoerder and Moch, *European Migrants,* 90–111; and Walter T. K. Nugent, "Demographic Aspects of European Migration," ibid., 76–78.

55. Quotations from Wyman, *Round-Trip to America,* 22–25. See also Roger Daniels, *Coming to America: A History of Immigration and Ethnicity in American Life* (New York: HarperCollins, 1990), 185–186; J. Croil, *Steam Navigation* (Toronto: William Briggs, 1898); H. Fry, *The History of North Atlantic Steam Navigation* (London: Sampson, Low, Marston, 1896); D. Baines, *Emigration from Europe 1815–1930* (London: Macmillan, 1991); and Smil, *Energy in World History,* 196–197. On crossing times, see Commissioner General of Immigration to W. M. Rice, Apr. 24, 1898, folder 52705/1, INS. More generally, see Nugent, *Crossings,* 31–33, 98. On the influence of the railroad on Mexican immigration, see Sánchez, *Becoming Mexican American,* 17–37.

56. Quotation from Irishman in Wyman, *Round-Trip to America,* 23. On Greek toasts,

see Jim Dimante interview, p. 26; *Camp and Plant* 1 (Feb. 15, 1902): 157. Also, on return migration, see Morawska, "Shaping the Worlds of Labor," 254; Dino Cinel, *The National Integration of Italian Return Migration, 1870–1929* (New York: Cambridge University Press, 1991). Even in the 1850s, among occupations given by emigrants in statements to American immigration officials, "miner" ranked fifth. "Immigration into the United States," *Journal of the American Geographic and Statistical Society* 1 (1859): 91.

57. F. Bujak quoted in Morawska, "Shaping the Worlds of Labor," 256; James Pourtales, *Lessons Learned from Experience,* trans. Margaret Woodbridge Jackson (Colorado Springs: Colorado College, 1955), 1–3, 20. More generally, see Mokyr, *Lever of Riches,* 128–130; Croil, *Steam Navigation;* and Fry, *History of North Atlantic Steam Navigation.*

58. Investigators for the Dillingham Commission called it induced migration. John Gruenberg, "Abstract of a Report to the Immigration Commission by John Gruenberg, Immigrant Inspector," n.d., folder 52066, INS; Gruenberg to Daniel Keefe, Dec. 18, 1908, folder 52066A, ibid.

59. Gruenberg to Daniel Keefe, Dec. 18, 1908; "Report of Conditions Existing in Europe and Mexico," 38–40.

60. "Report of Conditions Existing in Europe and Mexico," 39; Gruenberg, "Abstract of a Report to the Immigration Commission," 21–22; exhibit, Rice Report, folder 52705/1, INS; H. H. Noth to secretary of the Treasury, Oct. 24, 1898, ibid.; Marcus Braun to Frank Sargent, June 3, 1905, folder 52011/B, ibid.; Deposition of Michael Dumbalakoff, Nov. 7, 1908, folder 52066/1, ibid.; translation of steamship company flier [1908], ibid.; F. Missler per Lanker to F. Missler, Apr. 5, 1907, ibid. For statistics and context, see Ichihashi, "Emigration from Japan," 313–315, 322–325; and Alan Taken Moriyama, *Imingaisha: Japanese Emigration Companies and Hawaii* (Honolulu: University of Hawaii Press, 1985).

61. Arthur Ridgway to Angelo Noce, May 22, 1922, quoted in Giovanni Perilli, *Colorado and the Italians in Colorado / Il Colorado e gl'Italiani nel Colorado* (Denver: n.p., c. 1922), 27–28; *Third Biennial Report of the State Inspector of Coal Mines of the State of Colorado: For the Years of 1887–88* (Denver: Collier and Cleaveland, 1889), 24.

62. *Pueblo Indicator,* Mar. 16, 1901; *First Biennial Report of the Bureau of Labor Statistics of the State of Colorado 1887–1888* (Denver: Collier and Cleaveland, 1888), 364–367; *Thirteenth Biennial Report of the Bureau of Labor Statistics,* 11–13; *Silver Plume Standard,* Mar. 16, 1901; translation of a broadside entitled "Compagni italiani," [1903 or 1904], folder 14, box 26716, Governor Peabody Papers, CSA; "Report of Conditions Existing in Europe and Mexico," 33–34; John J. D. Trenor to [commissioner of immigration], Apr. 18, 1908, folder 51960/1, INS; and, on Japan, K. Ueta to anon. [1898], folder 52705/1, ibid. On Skliris and padrones generally, see Gunther Peck, *Reinventing Free Labor: Padrones and Immigrant Workers in the North American West, 1880–1930* (New York: Cambridge University Press, 2000). On local contractors, see John Aiello and CF&I, June 26, 1893, in *Secretary's Record F. Contracts & Leases,* CF&I-CHS;

Robert A. Murray, *Las Animas, Huerfano, and Custer: Three Colorado Counties on a Cultural Frontier: A History of the Raton Basin,* BLM Cultural Resource Series no. 6 (Denver, 1979), 70. On resentment toward such entrepreneurs, see Zeph Hill to James H. Peabody, Mar. 25, 1904, folder 16, box 26716, Governor Peabody Papers, CSA; Brier, "'Most Persistent Unionists,'" 262. Federal investigations of the 1913–1914 strike revealed company recruiting practices; see, for example, Frank Ledrianowsky testimony, *CCMC,* 1:621–638. Unfortunately, I could not find any records documenting the existence of Mexican padrones in the pre-Ludlow period.

63. Emilio and Gertrude Ferraro interview; declarations of intention for Michael Anselmo, Giovanni Funaro, Michele Funoso, Felice Antonio, Fortunato Mauro, Salomone Antonio Mauro, Roff Pagnotta, and Joseph Reno, Huerfano County Naturalization Records, CSA; "Proceedings of Joint Conference," 181; "Synopsis of Compilation of Reports Submitted by Certain Immigration Officials Detailed to Europe and Mexico for the Investigation of Conditions Affecting Immigration to the United States," n.d., folder 51411/1, INS, 3.

64. For quotations about the effect of migrants' letters to the old country, see "Synopsis of Compilation of Reports," 3; "Report of Conditions Existing in Europe and Mexico," 46, 48–49; John Skerl interview, pp. 30–31; for Powderly quotation, see Gabaccia, "When the Migrants Are Men," 196; Ethelbert Stewart, "Money from Far Away," clipping from the *Daily News,* Apr. 18, 1907, reel 2, Ethelbert Stewart Papers, Southern Historical Collection, University of North Carolina Library, Chapel Hill (microfilm edition). See also Trenor to commissioner of immigration, Apr. 18, 1908; Victor Bazanele interview, n.p.; Merle Curti and Kendall Birr, "The Immigrant and the American Image in Europe, 1860–1914," *Mississippi Valley Historical Review* 37 (1950): 203–230; Wyman, *Round-Trip to America;* David Eltis, "Free and Coerced Transatlantic Migrations: Some Comparisons," *American Historical Review* 88 (1983): 258–260; and Morawska, "Shaping the Worlds of Labor," 260–262.

65. Ichihashi, "Emigration from Japan," 329–330; Mary Foote interview, transcript in HCEHP, p. 1; August Andreatta interview, Aug. 5, 1979, transcript ibid., p. 4; Anast Chipian interview, folder 6, box 6, Greek Oral Histories, UU, p. 3; "Report of Conditions," p. 44.

66. *Camp and Plant* 1 (Jan. 25, 1902): 98. On the coercive dimensions of free labor ideology, see Peck, *Reinventing Free Labor.*

67. John Brophy, *A Miner's Life: An Autobiography* (Madison: University of Wisconsin Press), 51. On routes out of coal mining, see "Interview with Charles E. Price by Ted James," July 10, 1985, LHC, 7; Deborah Frazier, "Sheep Ranching: Tough on the Body, Easy on the Spirit," *Los Angeles Times,* May 26, 1979; Demetrios Stathopulos, "The Greek Communities of Colorado: An Analysis of Life, Culture, and Traditions," typescript, n.d., folder 294, box 39, Theodore Saloutos Papers, Immigration History Research Center, University of Minnesota, Minneapolis.

4. Dying with Their Boots On

1. *Gunnison Review-Press,* Jan. 26, 1884.

2. Ibid.; *Dolores News,* Feb. 2, 1884; *New York Times,* Jan. 27, 1884; William Jones, "History of the Welsh People of Colorado: An Essay on the History of the Welsh of Colorado from Its Earliest Settlement till Now," typescript translation dated 1937 of Evan Williams, *Traethawd Arhanes Cymry Colorado O'i Sefydliad Boreuaf Hyd An Awr* (Denver: Evan Williams, 1889), 28.

3. *Denver Tribune,* Jan. 28, 1884.

4. For an exception, see Richard Maxwell Brown, "Western Violence: Structure, Values, Myth," *Western Historical Quarterly* 24 (1993): 4–20.

5. Many factors influence these interactions between work and environment; in the process, they widen the scope of the workscape well beyond the material world. First, people labor in nature and are part of the natural world—bodies, in other words. But human beings constitute their knowledge of both their own bodies and the rest of nature through culture, which is to say through epistemological and linguistic constructs; ideologies of race, class, and gender; and other socially constructed meaning-making processes ranging from the assessment of risk to the perception of pain. Moreover, most humans work within nature by wielding technologies such as tools, machines, and instruments of coercion over human and animal subordinates; these technologies extend and transcend the bodies of those who use them. People rarely labor under their own direction. Instead, they work as wage, contract, piece, or "unfree" laborers—and are thus cogs in the machinery of broader markets, larger organizational forms such as corporations, and wider technological networks such as energy systems. Finally, states through their political, legal, and military institutions structure interactions between and among workers, employers, and the natural world by defining and protecting property relationships, policing danger, facilitating or foreclosing reform, and executing or sanctioning some acts of violence while proscribing others.

6. George Orwell, *The Road to Wigan Pier* (London: Gollancz, 1937), 33. My approach to Colorado's mine workscapes is influenced in curious ways by June Nash, *We Eat the Mines and the Mines Eat Us: Dependency and Exploitation in Bolivian Tin Mines,* rev. ed. (New York: Columbia University Press, 1993); and Michael Taussig, *The Devil and Commodity Fetishism in South America* (Chapel Hill: University of North Carolina Press, 1983).

7. Gunnison county coroner's inquest, Jan. 30, 1884, manuscript in possession of Gunnison County Coroner, Gunnison, Colorado.

8. For examples of reconnaissance, see James Gardiner to W. B. Strong, Dec. 1 1881, folder 601.13, RR box 601, AT&SF Miscellaneous Files, AT&SF. One testimonial to the significance of such reports was their reproduction and preservation; reports by R. C. Hills, CF&I's geologist, filled several volumes; despite their length, the company pre-

served full sets at both its Denver and its Pueblo headquarters, even though they disposed of most of their other records. See Hills Reports.

9. On coal-mining methods, see the many practical and technical guides cited later in this chapter and the next, as well as Anthony F. C. Wallace, *St. Clair: A Nineteenth-Century Coal Town's Experience with a Disaster-Prone Industry* (Ithaca, N.Y.: Cornell University Press, 1987); Keith Dix, *Work Relations in the Coal Industry: The Hand-Loading Era, 1880–1930* (Morgantown: Institute for Labor Studies, University of West Virginia, 1977); George Korson, *Coal Dust on the Fiddle: Songs and Stories of the Bituminous Industry* (Philadelphia: University of Pennsylvania Press, 1943); and James Whiteside, *Regulating Danger: The Struggle for Mine Safety in the Rocky Mountain Coal Industry* (Lincoln: University of Nebraska Press, 1990).

10. Ibid. See also Chapter 5. On powder, see "In the Matter of the Explosion Which Occurred at the Sunshine Mine on the Evening of Sept. 3, 1897: Testimony of Witnesses Taken at Coroner's Inquest, Held Sept. 6 and 7, 1897," folder 13, box 26948, Governor Alva Adams Papers, CSA (henceforth Sunshine Mine inquest), p. 13; "Special Report on the Sunshine Coal Mine Explosion in Garfield County, Colorado, by Which Twelve Men Were Instantly Killed," typescript report, [1897], ibid., 11; *Rock Boring, Rock Drilling, Explosives and Blasting, Coal-Cutting Machinery, Timbering, Timber Trees, Trackwork*, International Library of Technology, vol. 86 (Scranton, Pa.: International Textbook, 1907).

11. Jack Dandrea, "Coal Mines I Worked In," Penrose Public Library, Pikes Peak Library District, Colorado Springs; Barron B. Beshoar, "Birds, Rats and Rattlesnakes Make Grimy Living in Coal Mines," *Rocky Mountain News*, Oct. 6, 1937 (despite the title, Beshoar makes no mention of rats in Colorado coal mines, nor does any other source); Samuel Nugent Townshend, *Colorado, Its Agriculture, Stockfeeding, Scenery, and Shooting* (London: "The Field" Office, 1879), 67.

12. Dandrea, "Coal Mines I Worked In"; Dan DeSantis interview, Jan. 19, 1978, transcript in box 9, EM, pp. 37–38.

13. Dan DeSantis interview, pp. 37–38.

14. Ibid. On the use of caged mice as a diagnostic tool, see International Correspondence Schools, *The Coal Miner's Handbook: A Handy Reference Book for Coal Miners, Pit Bosses, Fire Bosses, Foremen, Superintendents, Managers, Engineers, and All Persons Interested in the Subject of Coal Mining* (Scranton, Pa.: International Textbook, 1913); J. S. Haldane, "The Examination of Mine Air," in Clement Le Neve Foster and J. S. Haldane, eds., *The Investigation of Mine Air* (London: Charles Griffin; Philadelphia: Lippincott, 1905), 147; Walter S. Weeks, *Ventilation of Mines* (New York: McGraw-Hill, 1926), 151–153; and Max Ortega interview, Aug. 1975, transcript in box 12, EM, p. 6.

15. Juliet Clutton-Brock, *A Natural History of Domesticated Animals* (Austin: University of Texas Press, 1989), 95; Juliet Clutton-Brock, *Horse Power: A History of the*

Horse and the Donkey in Human Societies (Cambridge, Mass.: Harvard University Press, 1992), 43–44.

16. Bob Lloyd, "Mine Mules," *Western Horseman* 26 (1961): 58–59; Dan DeSantis interview, p. 18; "Humane Treatment of Colorado Fuel and Iron Company Mules," C&P 2 (Nov. 22, 1902): 510; Barron B. Beshoar, "Mules Safer in Gassy Mines Than Spark-Producing Motors," *Rocky Mountain News*, Oct. 5, 1937; *Twelfth Biennial Report of the Bureau of Labor Statistics of the State of Colorado, 1909–1910* (Denver: Smith-Brooks, 1911), 336–337; [John Cameron] to A. H. Danforth, Dec. 31, 1885, folder 28, box 1, CF&I-CHS; George S. Ramsay to E. M. Steck, Jan. 1, 1890, and Jan. 1, 1891, folder 28, ibid.; Feb. 23, Minutes of Executive Committee Meeting, folder 58, JFW Papers.

17. Ruth Curtis, Adolph and Jean Goemmer interview, Sept. 29, 1979, transcript in HCEHP, p. 17; Grace Chastain interview, n.d., ibid., p. 3; "Range and Forest: The Stone Wall Country," *CF&I Industrial Bulletin* 12 (1927): 3–5.

18. Dan DeSantis interview, p. 1; John R. Williams to William Thomas, Nov. 10, 1895, in Alan Conway, ed., *The Welsh in America: Letters from the Immigrants* (Minneapolis: University of Minnesota Press, 1961), 207; Executive Committee Minutes, Feb. 21, 1910, and Feb. 24, 1913, folder 58, JFW Papers; *Camp and Plant* 2 (Dec. 13, 1902): 584; *Camp and Plant* 3 (Jan. 10, 1903): 38; entry for Sept. 9, 1889, notebook 23, folder 30, box 2, Robert F. Weitbrec Papers, CHS; Lloyd, "Mine Mules," 58–59; Barron Beshoar, "Strong Arms and Stronger Words Aid Gentle Art of Mule Training," *Rocky Mountain News*, Oct. 4, 1937; Theodore H. Savory, *The Mule: A Historic Hybrid* (Shildon, U.K.: Meadowfield, 1979), 9–14, 22.

19. Alex Bisulco interview, June 27, 1978, box 8, EM, p. 60.

20. Ibid., p. 8.

21. Ibid., pp. 7–8; Dan DeSantis interview, p. 18.

22. Victor Bazanele interview, n.d., transcript in box 7, EM, n.p.; Alex Bisulco interview, June 27, 1978, transcript in box 8, EM, p. 8.

23. Alex Bisulco interview, p. 8.

24. Ibid.; *Rocco Moschetti, et al., v. Colorado Fuel and Iron Company,* civil case no. 2727, filed Apr. 3, 1908, Fremont County Court, Civil Cases, CSA.

25. Arthur Lakes, "The Trinidad Coal Region of Southern Colorado," in Colorado State School of Mines, *Annual Report of Field Work and Analyses Relating to the Economic Geology of Colorado* (Denver: Rocky Mountain News, 1886), 86; Alex Bisulco interview, pp. 20–21; Jim Dimante interview, Apr. 21 and 24, 1978, transcript in box 9, EM.

26. For mentions of these features, see R. C. Hills, "Prospectus Article on the Coal and Iron Lands of the Colorado Fuel & Iron Company," Aug. 20, 1892, in Hills Reports; and R. C. Hills to Paul Morton, June 15, 1896, ibid. More generally, see Colin R. Ward, ed., *Coal Geology and Coal Technology* (Melbourne: Blackwell Scientific, 1984), 152–154; Iain A. Williamson, *Coal Mining Geology* (London: Oxford University Press, 1967),

193–195, 198–200; Arthur Lakes, "Geology of Colorado Coal Deposits," in Colorado State School of Mines, *Annual Report of Field Work and Analyses* (Denver: News Printing, 1887), 69; R. C. Hills, "Coal Lands of the Colorado Coal and Iron Co. in Colorado," in Hills Reports, 80; "Report on the Lands of the Colorado Fuel Company and the Denver Fuel Company: With a Supplementary Report on the Lands of the Grand River Coal & Coke Co.," in Hills Reports, 114; *Florence Tribune,* Aug. 8, 1901.

27. "Coal Camps of Fremont County," clipping from Fremont-Custer Historical Society Newsletter, in LHC.

28. Alex Bisulco interview, p. 31.

29. A. Lakes, "Coal Field of Crested Butte, Gunnison County," in Colorado State School of Mines, *Annual Report of Field Work and Analyses Relating to the Economic Geology of Colorado,* 114; *Seventh Biennial Report of the Inspector of Coal Mines of the State of Colorado, 1895–1896* (Denver: Smith-Brooks, 1897), 35.

30. "Range and Forest," 4–6. See also the T. A. Schomburg Papers, CHS; Lewis A. Cummings, comp. and ed., "History of the Spanish Peaks Ranger District and Surrounding Country, San Isabel National Forest Region 2," Dec. 1947, typescript in Archaeology Office Files, San Isabel National Forest Headquarters, Pueblo, Colorado. On federal prosecutions against coal companies that trespassed on federal forest reserves, see *United States v. Frederick Crandall and the Colorado Fuel and Iron Company,* filed Jan. 16, 1901, box 60, Civil and Criminal Case Files 1867–1911, RG 21, Records of the District Courts of the United States, District of Colorado, NARA-Denver; *United States v. Archibald W. Alexander and the Colorado Fuel and Iron Company,* filed Jan. 16, 1901, ibid.; *United States v. Colorado Fuel & Iron Company,* cases nos. 1824 and 1826, filed June 22 and Aug. 1, 1903, box 67, ibid. Prop cutting rendered domestic water supplies in "Walsenburg and Trinidad . . . precarious." Henry Michelson, "The Present Condition of the Colorado Forest," typescript in "Forestry Association, Colorado Report on Conditions of Colorado Forests 1900," folder 15, box 26949, Governor Charles S. Thomas Papers, CSA, p. 4.

31. Victor Bazanele interview, n.p.; Whiteside, *Regulating Danger,* 74.

32. *Tenth Biennial Report of the Inspector of Coal Mines of the State of Colorado, 1901–1902* (Denver: Smith-Brooks, 1903), 78–9, 164, 168; *Ninth Biennial Report of the Inspector of Coal Mines of the State of Colorado, 1899–1900* (Denver: Smith-Brooks, 1901), 57, 136, 143–144; W. A. Easton testimony, coroner's inquest, body of Abel Silva, Jan. 31, 1914, Coroner's Inquests, LACC, Trinidad, 2–5; *Eighth Biennial Report of the Inspector of Coal Mines of the State of Colorado, 1897–1898* (Denver: Smith-Brooks, 1899), 123–124, 132; and *Seventh Biennial Report of the Inspector of Coal Mines,* 24, 27.

33. Union allegations notwithstanding, there is little evidence of companies' failing to supply miners with adequate timber. See *Eleventh Biennial Report of the Inspector of Coal Mines of the State of Colorado, 1903–1904* (Denver: Smith-Brooks, 1905), 6.

34. *Eighth Biennial Report of the Inspector of Coal Mines,* 53. For similar cases, see

Ninth Biennial Report of the Inspector of Coal Mines, 46, 49, 54–55, 59–60; and *Tenth Biennial Report of the Inspector of Coal Mines,* 151. See also Gunther Peck, "Manly Gambles: The Politics of Risk on the Comstock Lode, 1860–1880," *Journal of Social History* 26 (1993): 701–723.

35. John W. Brown, "Mining Royalties," *United Mine Workers Journal,* Feb. 6, 1913, reprinted in Korson, *Coal Dust on the Fiddle,* 128–129. It is unclear whether this is the same John W. Brown described as a "general" of the strike soldiers during the Ten Days' War.

36. Paraphrased from the song "Ballad of Spring Hill (Spring Hill Disaster)," written by Peggy Seeger and Ewan MacColl and popularized by the Peter, Paul, and Mary, album *A Song Will Rise* (Warner Bros., 1965).

37. *Thirteenth Biennial Report of the Inspector of Coal Mines of the State of Colorado, 1907–1908* (Denver: Smith-Brooks, 1909), 11, 37; *Eleventh Biennial Report of the Inspector of Coal Mines,* 112. On companies' failure to sprinkle, see ibid., 107; E. G. Coray testimony, *CCMC,* 1:174–184; *Seventh Biennial Report of the Inspector of Coal Mines,* 30; *Twelfth Biennial Report of the Bureau of Labor Statistics of the State of Colorado, 1909–1910* (Denver: Smith-Brooks, 1911), 32; George Engle, "Record of Coal Cutting Machinery," Apr. 1881, folder 30, box 2, CF&I-CHS; "Lechner Machines—Week Ending April 9th," ibid.; Engle, "Report Lechner Machines Week Ending Apr. 20th 81," ibid.; and William J. Cronon, "Landscapes of Abundance and Scarcity," in Clyde A. Milner II, Carol A. O'Connor, and Martha A. Sandweiss, eds., *The Oxford History of the American West* (New York: Oxford University Press, 1994).

38. William Jackson Palmer to R. F. Weitbrec, Apr. 23, 1877, folder 16, box 1, CF&I-CHS; J. Imbrie Miller to T. Haskins DuPuy, Jan. 24, 1889, folder 28, ibid.; *Denver Republican,* Aug. 2, 1904.

39. Thad McLaughlin, "Ground Water in Huerfano County Colorado," USGS Water-Supply Paper 1805 (Washington, D.C.: GPO, 1966); W. Brant Howard, "The Hydrogeology of the Raton Basin, Southcentral Colorado" (M.A. thesis, Indiana University, 1982), 26–48. George S. Ramsay to E. M. Steck, Jan. 1, 1890, folder 28, box 1, CF&I-CHS; *Seventh Biennial Report of the Inspector of Coal Mines,* 33; *Camp and Plant* 1 (Mar. 8, 1902): 194; *Camp and Plant* 1 (June 28, 1902): 572; *Camp and Plant* 2 (Sept. 13, 1902): 264; *Camp and Plant* 2 (Oct. 11, 1902): 364; Mickey Judiscak interview, May 22, 1980, in HCEHP, p. 8; E. C. Pielou, *Fresh Water* (Chicago: University of Chicago Press, 1998), 5; Michael Price, *Introducing Groundwater,* 2nd ed. (London: Chapman and Hall, 1996); Georg Matthess, *The Properties of Groundwater,* trans. John C. Harvey (New York: Wiley, 1982); and Paul F. Hudak, *Principles of Hydrogeology,* 2nd ed. (Boca Raton, Fla.: Lewis, 2000).

40. Quotation from *Camp and Plant* 1 (Dec. 20, 1901): 22; "Pictou Colorado: A Rich Mine of Domestic Coal," *Camp and Plant* 1 (June 21, 1902): 529–531; "Topography of Rouse 11," 1919, survey notebook in box K-2, Mining Department Records, Colorado

Fuel and Iron Company, BHS; file 68a, Old Land Records, ibid.; and CF&I Mining Department, "Report on Water Rights," Aug. 9, 1932, box 11, CF&I-CHS.

41. CF&I Mining Department, "Report on Water Rights"; George L. Kerr, *Elementary Coal-Mining: Designed to Meet the Requirements of Students Attending Classes on Coal-Mining, and of Miners and Others Engaged in Practical Work* (London: Charles Griffin; Philadelphia: Lippincott, 1902), 140; H. W. Hughes, *A Text-Book of Coal-Mining, for the Use of Colliery Managers and Others,* 5th ed. (London: Charles Griffin, 1904), 374; W. E. Lishman, "Pumping," in W. S. Boulton, ed., *Practical Coal-Mining, by Leading Experts in Mining and Engineering* (London: Gresham, n.d.), 3:172.

42. Mary Foote interview, n.d., in HCEHP, p. 12. See also Dandrea, "Coal Mines I Worked In."

43. *Thirteenth Biennial Report of the Inspector of Coal Mines,* 17.

44. Ibid., 8, 16; Jesse Floyd Welborn, "President's Remarks to Board of Directors at Meeting Held June 26th, 1907," folder 59, JFW Papers; *Seventh Biennial Report of the Inspector of Coal Mines,* 40; Emanuel Taperilli testimony, Sunshine Mine inquest, Sept. 6 and 7, 1897; David Griffiths, "How to Reduce Falls from Roof and Sides," in *Proceedings of the Rocky Mountain Coal-Mining Institute* (Denver: Smith-Brooks, 1913), 39.

45. "Damp," *Oxford English Dictionary,* 2nd ed., at http://www.oed.com.

46. *Fourth Biennial Report of the State Inspector of Coal Mines of the State of Colorado, for the Years of 1889–90* (Denver: Collier and Cleaveland, 1890), 75; Haldane, "The Examination of Mine Air," 134, and C. Neville Moss, *Gases, Dust and Heat in Mines* (London: Charles Griffin; Philadelphia: Lippincott, 1927), 60.

47. *Fourth Biennial Report of the State Inspector of Coal Mines,* 73–74; Stewart Herd to J. W. Brentlinger, May 30, 1893, folder 12, box 26692, Governor Davis Waite Papers, CSA; Alex Bisulco interview, p. 9a; *Thirteenth Biennial Report of the Inspector of Coal Mines,* 89–91; *Trinidad Advertiser,* May 20, 1907; Haldane, "Examination of Mine Air," 129–131, 143–144; Moss, *Gases, Dust and Heat in Mines,* 16–22; J. Barab, *Fumes Encountered in Mining Operations and Handling of Explosives* (Wilmington, Del.: Hercules Powder, 1922), 7–8, 18–20; and Malcolm J. McPherson, *Subsurface Ventilation and Environmental Engineering* (London: Chapman and Hall, 1993), 378.

48. *Twelfth Biennial Report of the Bureau of Labor Statistics,* 35–36; *Trinidad Advertiser,* Oct. 16, 1910; International Correspondence Schools, *The Coal Miner's Handbook,* 253; J. T. Beard, *Mine Gases and Explosions: Text-Book for Schools and Colleges and for General Reference* (New York: Wiley, 1908; London: Chapman and Hall, 1908), 129; William Fairley, *Mine Ventilation Made Easy, with an Appendix Containing Answers to 155 Questions, Selected from Various American Examinations for Mine Inspectors and Mine Foremen* (Scranton, Pa.: Colliery Engineer, 1894), 31.

49. Letter from Mac MCormac, M. Davis, and J. Prince, *Denver Post,* May 4, 1902. Sir Humphrey Davy also used the metaphor of methane as "monster" in this context; see

McPherson, *Subsurface Ventilation and Environmental Engineering*, 5. For various treatments of methane and firedamp, see "Explosives and Blasting," section 36, in *Rock Boring*, 29–30; International Correspondence Schools, *Coal Miner's Handbook*, 252, 258; Moss, *Gases, Dust and Heat in Mines*, 23–26; *Fourth Biennial Report of the State Inspector of Coal Mines*, 78; Fairley, *Mine Ventilation Made Easy*, 22; McPherson, *Subsurface Ventilation and Environmental Engineering*, 425–436. On blowers and outbursts, see Lakes, "Coal Field of Crested Butte," 114; *Tenth Biennial Report of the Inspector of Coal Mines*, 70; McPherson, *Subsurface Ventilation and Environmental Engineering*, 432–436; Moss, *Gases, Dust and Heat in Mines*, 26–28. Some authorities provided different definitions of firedamp. Moss, for instance, called it a mixture of methane, carbon dioxide, and nitrogen. *Gases, Dust and Heat in Mines*, 30–31.

50. Alan Derickson, *Black Lung: Anatomy of a Public Health Disaster* (Ithaca, N.Y.: Cornell University Press, 1998), 2, 4, 7–8, 14, 30–33. For language used by miners, see Foote interview, p. 6; Beatrice Nogare interview, n.d., in HCEHP, p. 4; and Minnie Ugolini and Arthur Bellotti interview, n.d., ibid., p. 3.

51. R. C. Hills, "Colorado Coal Fields, Including Notes on the Oil Shales of the Green River Group . . . ," in Hills Reports.

52. Fairley, *Mine Ventilation Made Easy*, 13–15; Thomas Bryson, *Theory and Practice of Mine Ventilation: A Text-Book for Students and a Book of Reference for Managers and Undermanagers* (London: Edward Arnold, 1924), 82–98; International Correspondence School, "Instruction Paper No. 7," in folder 7, Henry Johns Papers, DPL, 99–102; "Special Report on the Sunshine Coal Mine Explosion"; *Eleventh Biennial Report of the Inspector of Coal Mines*, 108; James T. Beard, *Mine Gases and Ventilation: Textbook for Students of Mining, Mining Engineers and Candidates Preparing for Mining Examinations Designed for Working Out the Various Problems That Arise in the Practice of Coal Mining, as They Relate to the Safe and Efficient Operation of Mines*, 2nd ed. (New York: McGraw-Hill, 1920), 164–166; Lakes, "Trinidad Coal Region," 95; *Twelfth Biennial Report of the Inspector of Coal Mines*, 108; *Fourth Biennial Report of the State Inspector of Coal Mines*, 76; R. C. Hills, "Report on the Lands of the Colorado Fuel Company and the Denver Fuel Company," in Hills Reports, 114; *Seventh Biennial Report of the Inspector of Coal Mines*, 30, 38, 40; "President's Remarks to Board of Directors at Meeting Held June 26th, 1907," box 59, JFW Papers, CHS; Minutes of Executive Committee Meetings, Dec. 2, 1910, Jan. 23, 1911, Jan. 25, and Oct. 17, 1912, and May 26, 1913, box 58, ibid.

53. Quotation from "Instruction Paper No. 7," 98. On distribution, see David Penman and J. S. Penman, *Principles and Practice of Mine Ventilation* (London: Charles Griffin, 1927), 192–206, Bryson, *Theory and Practice of Mine Ventilation*, 216–240, Walter S. Weeks, *Ventilation of Mines* (New York: McGraw-Hill, 1926), 183–199.

54. Whiteside, *Regulating Danger*, 74. The connection between ventilation and mili-

tancy was made by William Palmer in undated notes under heading "Coal Mining," c. 1856, folder 222, box 3, WJPP-CHS; and W. J. P., "Underground Walks in England, No. 6," *Miners' Journal,* Oct. 27, 1855.

55. *Trinidad Chronicle-News,* Jan. 15, 1910; unidentified clipping, Nov. 23, 1910, scrapbook 87, JFW Papers; *Denver Republican,* Nov. 25, 1910; *Third Biennial Report of the State Inspector of Coal Mines of the State of Colorado, for the Years of 1887–88* (Denver: Collier and Cleaveland, 1889), 43–56.

56. *Third Biennial Report of the State Inspector of Coal Mines,* 28–31.

57. *Eleventh Biennial Report of the Inspector of Coal Mines,* 108–109; Dr. L. G. Clark, testimony in Sunshine Mine inquest, 29; *Tenth Biennial Report of the Inspector of Coal Mines,* 66; 108; *Seventh Biennial Report of the Inspector of Coal Mines,* 57; *Twelfth Biennial Report of the Inspector of Coal Mines,* 10, 84–87, 109; *Thirteenth Biennial Report of the Inspector of Coal Mines,* 84–87.

58. Harry Bailey, testimony in Sunshine Mine inquest, 28; *Denver News,* May 21, 1907.

59. On rescue cars and crews, see *Report of the Medical & Sociological Departments of the Colorado Fuel & Iron Company 1909–1910* (n.p.: n.p., 1910); president's remarks, Dec. 2, 1910, Minutes of Executive Committee Meetings; *Report of the Medical & Sociological Departments of the Colorado Fuel & Iron Company 1913–1914* (Pueblo, Colo.: Franklin, 1914), 31, 33–35, 39.

60. *Eleventh Biennial Report of the Inspector of Coal Mines,* 108. On afterdamp and rescuers, see Feb. 15, 1911, "In the matter of the bodies of Joe Malich, Jon Freish, Ludwig Klapach, Karl Francis, Andy Kanovski, and eleven other miners," coroner's inquest, LACC; National Funeral Register, 1:578–579, Trinidad City Library, Trinidad, Colo.

61. Pete Gerglich interview, Feb. 7, 1978, transcript in box 10, EM, p. 17. Four weeks after the Primero disaster, only sixty-eight of seventy-five bodies had been recovered. *Denver Post,* Feb. 28, 1910. On another disaster in which one body was believed to have been buried in the mine, see *Denver Times,* Mar. 1, 1906.

62. Glen Aultman interview, June 26, 1978, transcript in box 7, EM, tape 2, p. 2.

63. For antiworker allegations, see LaMont Montgomery Bowers to Fred T. Gates, Feb. 1 and Oct. 10, 1910, folder 190, box 21, CF&I-RAC; LaMont Montgomery Bowers to Starr Murphy, Nov. 7. 1910, folder 84, box 27, LMB Papers, University of Binghamton Special Collections, Binghamton, N.Y. For union accusations, see *Denver Post,* Feb. 21 and 28, 1910, and Feb. 17, 1911; *Trinidad Chronicle-News,* Nov. 21, 1910. For a mixed decision, see *Eleventh Biennial Report of the Inspector of Coal Mines,* 112–113. For a finding of company neglect, see *Trinidad Chronicle-News,* Dec. 1, 1910. On assumption of risk, see *Thirteenth Biennial Report of the Inspector of Coal Mines,* 91.

64. *Seventh Biennial Report of the Inspector of Coal Mines,* 52–53; B. L. Davis testimony, Sunshine Mine inquest, 16 (emphasis added); *Thirteenth Biennial Report of the Inspector of Coal Mines,* 86.

65. Quoted in *Trinidad Chronicle-News,* Nov. 23, 1910. The jury remained unconvinced and found the company at fault for gross negligence. *Trinidad Chronicle-News,* Dec. 1, 1910. On New Castle, see *Third Biennial Report of the State Inspector of Coal Mines,* 32. By the 1880s William Galloway had demonstrated coal dust's explosive qualities through a series of experiments in Britain. The Colorado mine inspector in 1893 criticized those who still doubted these findings. A Western coal miner declared in 1901, "It has proven time and again that coal dust will explode without the aid of gas or carbonic hydrogen." Moss, *Gases, Dust and Heat in Mines,* 72–74; "Report of Coal Mine Accident, King, Park County, Colorado, Jan. 10, 1893," folder 14, box 26693, Governor Alva Adams Papers, CSA; "Black Diamond" (pseud.), "Coal Mining and Explosions in Mines of Western States," *United Mine Workers Journal,* Mar. 14, 1901. Officials of the CF&I might have turned to Beard's 1908 textbook, which shows that doubt persisted. Beard, *Mine Gases and Explosions,* 162–174.

66. *Denver Tribune,* Jan. 26, 1884, p. 1; *White Pine (Colo.) Cone,* Feb. 1, 1884, quoting the *Gunnison News-Democrat,* Jan. 27, 1884, extra ed.

67. *Denver Tribune,* Jan. 26 and 28, 1884; *Gunnison Review-Press,* Jan. 25, 1884.

68. *Gunnison Review-Press,* Jan. 25, 1884; *Denver Tribune,* Jan. 27 and 28, 1884; *Leadville Herald,* Jan. 29, 1884. For more, on other colliers seen as suspect, see *Denver Tribune,* Jan. 29, 1884.

69. *Leadville Herald,* Jan. 26, 1884; *Denver Tribune,* Jan. 27, 1884. Reporters took pains to point out that the Mollies' dispute with Gibson antedated the disaster. On the demise of the Mollies, see Kevin Kenny, *Making Sense of the Molly Maguires* (New York: Oxford University Press, 1998). David Wolff argues that Denver newspapers had started labeling strike violence Molly Maguirism in the 1870s because they were "unwilling to accept the notion that local miners could do such damage." David A. Wolff, *Industrializing the Rockies: Growth, Competition, and Turmoil in the Coalfields of Colorado and Wyoming, 1868–1914* (Boulder: University Press of Colorado, 2003), 43.

70. *Denver Tribune,* Jan. 26 and 28, 1884; *Leadville Herald,* Jan. 27, 1884; Gunnison County coroner's inquest.

71. *Gunnison Review-Press,* Jan. 26 and 29, 1884; *Denver Tribune,* Jan. 28 and 30, 1884; *Colorado Springs Weekly Gazette,* Feb. 2, 1884; *Leadville Herald,* Jan. 27 and 30, 1884. Though many of the dead were foreign-born, there is no record of any bodies being sent back across the Atlantic. A plaque erected in recent years at the Jokerville mass grave lists fifty-eight of the fifty-nine dead; the fifty-ninth and unlisted name is that of Peterson the Swede, the man judged responsible for causing the disaster.

5. Out of the Depths and on to the March

1. *Rocky Mountain News,* May 29, 1894.

2. Unidentified newspaper clipping, Feb. 25, 1871, in E. O. Davis, *The First Five*

Years of the Railroad Era in Colorado (Golden, Colo.: Sage, 1948), 135; *First Report of the Colorado Coal and Iron Co.: Comprising the Sixth Report of the Central Colorado Improvement Co. and the Second Report of the Southern Colorado Coal and Town Co.* (Colorado Springs: Daily Gazette, 1880), 5–6; *Fourth Annual Report of the Colorado Coal and Iron Co.* (Colorado Springs: Daily Gazette, 1883), 9–10; David A. Wolff, *Industrializing the Rockies: Growth, Competition, and Turmoil in the Coalfields of Colorado and Wyoming, 1868–1914* (Boulder: University Press of Colorado, 2003), 24–25.

3. Wolff, *Industrializing the Rockies*, 74, 88–95; *United Mine Workers Journal*, quoted ibid., 130; *Sixth Annual Report of the Colorado Coal and Iron Co. for the Year Ending December 31, 1884* (New York: Mann, [1885]), 8–11; *First Biennial Report of the Bureau of Labor Statistics of the State of Colorado, 1887–1888* (Denver: Collier and Cleaveland, 1888), 118–127, 139–140; Jacob Coxey, quoted in Shelton Stromquist, "The Crisis of 1894 and the Legacies of Producerism," in Richard Schneirov, Shelton Stromquist, and Nick Salvatore, eds., *The Pullman Strike and the Crisis of the 1890s: Essays on Labor and Politics* (Champaign: University of Illinois Press, 1999), 186.

4. Mentions of high wages during the 1850s and 1860s are legion; see Edward Bliss, *A Brief History of the New Gold Regions of Colorado Territory, together with Hints and Suggestions to Intending Emigrants* (New York: John W. Amerman, 1864), 18. For a nostalgic look back that implied that wages had subsequently dropped, see W. B. Vickers, "History of Colorado," in *History of Clear Creek and Boulder Valleys, Colorado . . .* (Chicago: O. L. Baskin, 1880).

5. Advertisement for J. G. Bearsley, *Colorado Miner* (Georgetown), Jan. 12, 1878; Wolff, *Industrializing the Rockies.*

6. *Fifth Annual Report of the Colorado Fuel and Iron Company for the Year Ending June 30, 1897* (Denver: n.p., 1897), 9. Jesse Floyd Welborn explained to stockholders one warm January, "The weather conditions have been unfavorable for a large consumption of coal." Overly severe winter weather, however, also posed problems because it halted the flow of empty railcars to the mines. Minutes of Executive Committee, Feb. 21, 1910, and Jan. 23, 1911, box 58, JFW Papers.

7. *Sixth Annual Report of the Colorado Coal and Iron Co.,* 8–9; Wolff, *Industrializing the Rockies*, 86, 149.

8. Wolff, *Industrializing the Rockies*, 86; *Annual Report of the Colorado Fuel Company, for the Year Ending June 30th, 1890* (New York: n.p., 1890), 4, 9. For a defense of wage cutting in depressed times, see *Sixth Annual Report of the Colorado Coal and Iron Co.,* 8–11. Railroad freight charges constituted another sizable chunk of the retail price of coal, but mining companies faced great difficulty in trying to reduce these charges.

9. Illustrative of this closing of ranks were the advertisements for railroads, banks, mining corporations, and ASARCO, which helped foot the bill for an antiunion history of the Cripple Creek strike published just weeks after the climax of the struggle: *The Story of the World's Greatest Gold Camp: The Labor Troubles of 1903–04, Told in Prose,*

Poetry and Pictures by the Cripple Creek Times (Denver: Smith-Brooks, 1904). On the railroad officials' concern over coal strikes, see [Victor Morawetz] to E. P. Ripley, Aug. 3, 1904, file 25–1, box RR 45, New York Executive Department Files, ATSF. Of John Osgood's antiunion stance, Ripley of the Santa Fe Railroad explained that though "his efforts . . . have cost us as well as him a great deal of money, . . . I am not yet prepared to say that it was not well spent." Ripley to A. F. Walker, Mar. 1, 1901, file 1–1, box RR 8.3, ibid. Labor leaders and progressives expressed harsh criticism of such collaborations; perhaps the fullest exposé is J. Warner Mills, "The Economic Struggle in Colorado," published serially in *Arena* 34 (1905), 1–10, 119–128, 248–264, 379–399, 485–495, 605–619; *Arena* 35 (1906), 150–158, 243–252, 467–476; and *Arena* 36 (1906), 375–390. For a relevant study of "bourgeois" class formation in opposition to labor, see Sven Beckert, *The Monied Metropolis: New York City and the Consolidation of the American Bourgeoisie, 1850–1896* (New York: Cambridge University Press, 2001).

10. Herbert Gutman, "The Negro and the United Mine Workers: The Career and Letters of Richard L. Davis and Something of Their Meaning, 1890–1900," in *Work, Culture, and Society in Industrializing America* (New York: Knopf, 1976), 173; John H. M. Laslett, *Nature's Noblemen: The Fortunes of the Independent Collier in Scotland and the American Midwest, 1855–1889* (Los Angeles: UCLA Institute of Industrial Relations, 1987). The literature on Western workers is vast; recent works that emphasize segmentation in hard-rock mining are Elizabeth Jameson, *All That Glitters: Class, Conflict, and Community in Cripple Creek* (Champaign: University of Illinois Press, 1998); Linda Gordon, *The Great Arizona Orphan Abduction* (Cambridge, Mass.: Harvard University Press, 1999); Susan Johnson, *Roaring Camp: The Social World of the California Gold Rush* (New York: Norton, 1999); Katherine A. Benton-Cohen, *Borderline Americans* (Cambridge, Mass.: Harvard University Press, forthcoming).

11. For more on "knowing nature through labor," see Richard White, "Are You an Environmentalist or Do You Work for a Living? Work and Nature," in William Cronon, ed., *Uncommon Ground: Toward Reinventing Nature* (New York: Norton, 1995), 171–185; and Richard White, *The Organic Machine* (New York: Hill and Wang, 1995). On workers and oral history, a relevant discussion is Warren D. Anderson, "Oral History and Migrant Wage Labor: Sources of Narrative Distortion," *Oral History Review* 28 (2001): 1–20. For more on the particular interviews I draw on later, see Eric Margolis, "Western Coal Mining as a Way of Life," *Journal of the West* 24 (1985): 1–115. I also use oral histories of mineworkers in eastern Utah, a region that was geologically and culturally similar to southern Colorado; moreover, mining families moved from one of these areas to the other with some frequency.

12. Bill Lloyd interview, May 18, 1978, transcript in box 10, EM; Walter Morgan Donaldson interview, July 18, 1993, transcript in folder 13, box 1, Carbon County Oral Histories, UU, p. 4. On boys entering mines, see Alex Bisulco interview, June 27, 1978, box 8, EM, pp. 30–31; Tally Evans interview, n.d., transcript in folder 15, box 1, Carbon County

Oral Histories, UU, p. 2; Frank and Caroline Tomsic interview, June 27, 1973, transcript in South Slavs Oral History Collection, ibid., p. 3; Irma Menghini interview, n.d., transcript in HCEHP, p. 6; and *Owen Conway v. Colorado Coal & Iron Company,* filed Feb. 23, 1888, case 1322, LADC. On colliers' entering the mines in their teens, see Claude and Laurence Amicarella interview, Feb. 21, 1978, box 7, EM, vol. 1, p. 113; Tom and Susie Somsky interview, box 13, Feb. 2, 1984, n.p. See also Robert McIntosh, *Boys in the Pits: Child Labour in Coal Mines* (Montreal: McGill-Queen's University Press, 2000).

13. On the turn, see Dan DeSantis interview, Jan. 19, 1978, EM, p. 20; Victor Bazanele interview, n.d., box 7, ibid., n.p.

14. Pete Aiello interview, Nov. 23, 1979, transcript in Carbon County Oral Histories, p. 6; White, "Are You an Environmentalist or Do You Work for a Living?" 179; Alex Bisulco interview, p. 10a; Don Mitchell interview, transcript in HCEHP, p. 4; International Correspondence Schools, *The Coal Miner's Handbook: A Handy Reference Book for Coal Miners, Pit Bosses, Fire Bosses, Foremen, Superintendents, Managers, Engineers, and All Persons Interested in the Subject of Coal Mining* (Scranton, Pa.: International Textbook, 1913), 203–204.

15. Walter Morgan Donaldson interview, p. 5; John Brophy, *A Miner's Life* (Madison: University of Wisconsin Press), 49; Marianne Fraser, "Warm Winters and White Rabbits: Folklore of Welsh and English Coal Miners," *Utah Historical Quarterly* 51 (1983): 246–258. See also George Korson's body of work: *Black Rock: Mining Folklore of the Pennsylvania Dutch* (Baltimore: Johns Hopkins University Press, 1960); *Coal Dust on the Fiddle: Songs and Stories of the Bituminous Industry* (Philadelphia: University of Pennsylvania Press, 1943); and *Minstrels of the Mine Patch: Songs and Stories of the Anthracite Industry* (Philadelphia: University of Pennsylvania Press, 1938).

16. John P. Thomas, for instance, "grew to young manhood in the mines." "To the Boys John P. and Old Dave of the Colorado Fuel & Iron Co.," Apr. 8, 1922, box 3, JFW Papers.

17. Henry "Welchie" Mathias interview, July 2, 1975, transcript in box 11, EM, p. 8; Claude and Laurence Amicarella interview, vol. 2, p. 15; Tony Hungaro interview, Mar. 8, 1978, transcript in box 10, EM, p. 11.

18. The state coal inspector stated, for instance, that the Italian Joseph Vietta and the Austrian F. F. Sippe were "experienced" and "practical" miners, respectively. *Seventh Biennial Report of the Inspector of Coal Mines of the State of Colorado, 1895–1896* (Denver: Smith-Brooks, 1897), 15; *Ninth Biennial Report of the Inspector of Coal Mines of the State of Colorado, 1897–1898* (Denver: Smith-Brooks, 1901), 61.

19. *Denver Times,* Jan. 19, 1906; John McNeil, "Address to Young Men Engaged in Coal Mining," in *Proceedings of the Rocky Mountain Coal Mining Institute Fifth Semi-Annual Meeting* (n.p.: [1916]), 92; "Alumni Personals," *Colorado School of Mines Technical and Engineering Society Bulletin* 2 (1904): 54–55; L. S. Bigelow, untitled typescript report [1915?], box 25, CF&I-RAC, 66–73.

20. Tony Hungaro interview, pp. 11–13; Brophy, *Miner's Life*, 40; Tim Ingold, *The Perception of the Environment: Essays on Livelihood, Dwelling and Skill* (London: Routledge, 2000).

21. E. P. Thompson, *The Making of the English Working Class* (New York: Vintage, 1966), 13; Claude and Laurence Amicarella interview, vol. 1, p. 83; Tony Hungaro interview, p. 17; Henry "Welchie" Mathias interview, p. 25; Joe Crump interview, n.d., transcript in HCEHP, p. 11; Pete Gerglich interview, Feb. 7, 1978, transcript in box 10, EM, pp. 14, 28.

22. Carter Goodrich, *The Miner's Freedom: A Study of the Working Life in a Changing Industry* (Boston: Marshall Jones, 1925); Claude and Laurence Amicarella interview, vol. 1, p. 84. For a critical assessment of the British industry, see Royden Harrison, *Independent Collier: The Coal Miner as Archetypal Proletarian* (New York: St. Martin's, 1978).

23. Victor Bazanele interview, n.p.; Dan DeSantis interview, p. 36; C. L. Baum testimony, *CCMC*, 579; *Camp and Plant* 3 (Apr. 18, 1903): 350; George Engle, "Record of Coal Cutting Machinery," Apr. 14, 1881, folder 30, box 2, CF&I-CHS. On miners' vacations, see *Camp and Plant* 4 (Aug. 1, 1903): 67. Perhaps the practice of miners' setting their hours explains why Jesse Floyd Welborn rightly anticipated little or no decrease in production when CF&I switched to an eight-hour day in 1913: Executive Committee Minutes, Feb. 24 and Apr. 21, 1913, folder 58, JFW Papers.

24. David Montgomery, *Workers' Control in America: Studies in the History of Work, Technology, and Labor Struggles* (New York: Cambridge University Press, 1980). On tool ownership, see Joe Perko testimony, "In the Matter of the Explosion Which Occurred at the Sunshine Mine on the Evening of Sept. 3, 1897: Testimony of Witnesses Taken at Coroner's Inquest, Held Sept. 6 and 7, 1897," folder 13, box 26948, Governor Alva Adams Papers, CSA, p. 31; *Tenth Biennial Report of the Inspector of Coal Mines of the State of Colorado, 1901–1902* (Denver: Smith-Brooks, 1903), 151.

25. Claude and Laurence Amicarella interview, vol. 1, p. 56; *Denver News*, Mar. 28, 1901; Fred Herrington to Ivy Lee, Sept. 26, 1914, folder 20, box 22, CF&I-RAC; Jesse Floyd Welborn to John D. Rockefeller, Jr., Apr. 10, 1915, folder 18, JFW Papers; Victor Bazanele interview, n.p.; Alex Bisulco interview, June 27, 1978, p. 31.

26. For one of many examples in which a miner who defied orders died, see *Ninth Biennial Report of the Inspector*, 52. Whereas dozens of photographs depict hard-rock miners posing with managers and engineers in their rooms, I have not identified a single photograph of a coal mine that shows a boss or superintendent with a miner underground.

27. Mark Wyman, *Hard Rock Epic: Western Miners and the Industrial Revolution, 1860–1910* (Berkeley: University of California Press, 1979), 90; Nancy Quam-Wickham, "Rereading Man's Conquest of Nature: Skill, Myths, and Historical Constructions of Masculinity in Western Extractive Industries," *Men and Masculinities* 2 (1999): 135–151.

28. Thomas Collier, "Longwall Coal Mining," *Proceedings of the Rocky Mountain Coal Mining Institute Thirteenth Semi-Annual Meeting* (n.p.: [1921?]), 163–164. See also John H. M. Laslett, *Colliers across the Sea: A Comparative Study of Class Formation in Scotland and the American Midwest, 1830–1924* (Champaign: University of Illinois Press, 2000).

29. Here I follow David Montgomery, who argues that "mutualism was the ethical seedbed for both the efforts of some workers to reform capitalism and the proposals of others to overthrow it." Montgomery, *Fall of the House of Labor: The Workplace, the State, and American Labor Activism, 1865–1925* (New York: Cambridge University Press, 1987), 4.

30. Dan DeSantis, interview, n.d., transcript in Black Lung Interviews, box 8, EM, p. 5; Alfred Owens interview, Feb. 2, 1978, transcript in box 12, EM, pp. 12–13. Brophy, *Miner's Life,* 48.

31. Dan DeSantis interview, p. 20.

32. Tony Hungaro interview, pp. 10–11; Peter Gerglich interview, p. 11.

33. Claude and Laurence Amicarella interview, vol. 1, p. 98; "Mutualism" and "Solidarity," *Oxford English Dictionary,* 2nd ed., at http://www.oed.com; "Solidarity," *Webster's Revised Unabridged Dictionary* (1913), online at http://machaut.uchicago.edu/websters (accessed Mar. 30, 2008).

34. Henry "Welchie" Mathias interview, p. 24.

35. John and Caroline Tomsic interview, n.d., box 13, EM, pp. 32–33. A "miner's life," one UMWA song began, "is like a sailor's." "The Miner's Lifeguard," in Alan Singer, "Using Songs to Teach Labor History," *OAH Magazine of History* 11 (1997): 13–16. See also Peter Linebaugh and Marcus Rediker, *The Many-Headed Hydra: Sailors, Slaves, Commoners, and the Hidden History of the Revolutionary Atlantic* (New York: Verso, 2001); and though problematic in many regards, Stephen E. Ambrose, *Band of Brothers: E Company, 506th Regiment, 101st Airborne from Normandy to Hitler's Eagle's Nest,* 2nd ed. (New York: Simon and Schuster, 2001), and other works by Ambrose. Neither oral histories nor contemporary documents address the possibility of male-male sexual encounters underground.

36. Davis is quoted in "A Look Back into History," *Cañon City Daily Record,* Apr. 5, 1971. "Loyalty to his fellow workers," according to Brophy, "required a very alert awareness of danger every minute that [a miner] spent in the mine. Careless or selfish actions that endangered lives were unthinkable, and any miner who broke the safety rules was quickly made aware of the other men's disapproval." Maintaining "good manners" involved considerable "policing" by miners of their fellow workers. Brophy, *Miner's Life,* 41–42. The importance of safety provisions in the strike demands for 1894, 1903–1904, and 1913–1914 will be discussed later.

37. Tony Hungaro interview, p. 17. On rough and respectable masculinities, see Steven Maynard, "Rough Work and Rugged Men: The Social Construction of Masculinity

in Working Class History," *Labour/Le Travail* 23 (Spring 1989): 159–169; and Steve Meyer, "Rough Manhood: The Aggressive and Confrontational Shop Culture of U.S. Auto Workers during World War II," *Journal of Social History* 36 (2002): 125–147. For an important argument linking the all-male environment underground with the embrace of interracial unionism in the Alabama collieries, see Daniel Letwin, *The Challenge of Interracial Unionism: Alabama Coal Miners, 1878–1921* (Chapel Hill: University of North Carolina Press, 1998).

38. Josephine Bazanele interview, Aug. 23, 1978, transcript in box 7, EM, p. 23.

39. Clare V. McKanna, Jr., *Homicide, Race, and Justice in the American West, 1880–1920* (Tucson: University of Arizona Press, 1997), 17, 23, 39, 41. For more on homicide rates, see Eric H. Monkkonen, *The Dangerous Class: Crime and Poverty in Columbus, Ohio, 1860–1885* (Cambridge, Mass.: Harvard University Press, 1975); Roger Lane, *Violent Death in the City: Suicide, Accident, and Murder in Nineteenth-Century Philadelphia* (Cambridge, Mass.: Harvard University Press, 1979); and Roger Land, *Murder in America: A History* (Columbus: Ohio State University Press, 1997).

40. Clare V. McKanna, Jr., "Alcohol, Handguns, and Homicide in the American West: A Tale of Three Counties, 1880–1920," *Western Historical Quarterly* 26 (1995): 470; McKanna, *Homicide, Race, and Justice in the American West*, 21; Emilio and Gertrude Ferraro interview, May 22, 1978, transcript in box 9, EM, p. 26; Isaac Williams is quoted in Eleanor Fry, "Large Operations and Half Dozen Major Camps Marked Peak Years of County's Coal Industry," clipping in Harold Smith Scrapbook, LHC; Norman Sams, Paul Butero, and Ernie Lira interview, Aug. 9, 1970, transcript in Penrose Public Library, Colorado Springs, p. 13; Lynn Abrams, *Workers' Culture in Imperial Germany: Leisure and Recreation in the Rhineland and Westphalia* (London: Routledge, 1992), 70; *Camp and Plant* 2 (July 19, 1902): 63; *Camp and Plant* 3 (Mar. 7, 1903): 213; Peter Roberts, W. S. Hopkins, and John A. Goodell, "Report upon the Possible Service by the Young Men's Christian Association in the Mining Communities of the Colorado Fuel and Iron Company Based upon a Survey, . . . " folder 156, box 18, CF&I-RAC (hereafter YMCA Report), 11, 32. Coal camp saloons in many ways resembled the urban drinking places analyzed in Madelon Powers, *Faces along the Bar: Lore and Order in the Workingman's Saloon, 1870–1920* (Chicago: University of Chicago Press, 1998).

41. See "Proceedings of Joint Conference: Held in the State Capitol, Denver, Colorado, at 10 o'clock A.M., November 26, 1913," box 23, CF&I-RAC, p. 77.

42. Claude and Laurence Amicarella interview, vol. 2, p. 32; Bill Lloyd interview, book 2, 1–8; John Skerl interview, Jan. 12, 1973, folder 8, box 1, South Slavs Oral History Collection, pp. 23–24.

43. Stephen Burnett Brier, " 'The Most Persistent Unionists': Class Formation and Class Conflict in the Coal Fields and the Emergence of Interracial and Interethnic Unionism, 1880–1904" (Ph.D. diss., University of California at Los Angeles, 1992), 235–238; "Bonne Bouche" (pseud.), "Colorado News," *United Mine Workers Journal*,

Mar. 1, 1894. Compare this persistence rate of around 30 percent over four years with the rates of around 30 percent *per decade* for Mexicans in Los Angeles in the early twentieth century, and upwards of 50 percent for white Angelenos and residents of Boston, Omaha, San Francisco, and other cities during the same period. George J. Sánchez, *Becoming Mexican American: Ethnicity, Culture and Identity in Chicano Los Angeles, 1900–1945* (New York: Oxford University Press, 1993), 70.

44. William Jackson Palmer to editor, *Colorado Springs Gazette* (not sent), Oct. 18, 1893, folder 724, box 9, WJPP-CHS; Mark Carlson, "Causes of Bank Suspensions in the Panic of 1893," *Explorations in Economic History* 42 (2005): 56–80; *United Mine Workers Journal*, Dec. 14, 1893.

45. "Bonne Bouche," "Colorado News"; Wolff, *Industrializing the Rockies*, 150.

46. *Sixth Biennial Report of the State Inspector of Coal Mines of the State of Colorado for the Years of 1893–94* (Denver: Smith-Brooks, 1895), 5–6; *El Moro Monitor,* Aug. 8, 1893; *Denver Republican,* Apr. 23, 1894.

47. Preamble reprinted in *United Mine Workers Journal,* Dec. 14, 1893. More generally, see Victor R. Greene, "A Study in Slavs, Strikes, and Unions: The Anthracite Strike of 1897," *Pennsylvania History* 31 (1964): 199–215; Harold W. Aurand, *From the Molly Maguires to the United Mine Workers: The Social Ecology of an Industrial Union, 1867–1897* (Philadelphia: Temple University Press, 1969); Daniel Nelson, *Shifting Fortunes: The Rise and Decline of American Labor, from the 1820s to the Present* (Chicago: Ivan R. Dee, 1997), 37; Andrew Roy, *A History of the Coal Miners of the United States . . .* (Columbus: J. L. Trauger, 1907); Maier B. Fox, *United We Stand: The United Mine Workers of America, 1890–1990* (Washington, D.C.: UMWA, 1990); William Hard, "The Western Federation of Miners," *Outlook* 83 (1906): 125; Letwin, *Challenge of Interracial Unionism;* Craig Phelan, "John Mitchell and the Politics of the Trade Agreement, 1898–1908," in Laslett, *United Mine Workers of America,* 72–103. As UMWA president John McBride phrased it: "The strength of our general movement for higher prices had to be measured by the strength of our weakest competitive districts." John McBride speech in *United Mine Workers Journal,* Feb. 14, 1895, p. 1.

48. *Denver Republican,* Apr. 22, 1894. No comprehensive history of the nationwide miners' strike of 1894 exists.

49. Donald Joseph McClurg, "Labor Organization in the Coal Mines of Colorado, 1878–1933" (Ph.D. diss., University of California, Los Angeles, 1959), 58–104; Wolff, *Industrializing the Rockies,* 137–138; *Third Biennial Report of the Bureau of Labor Statistics of the State of Colorado 1891–1892* (Colorado Springs: Gazette Printing, 1892), 59, 63.

50. *Denver Republican,* Apr. 24, 1894.

51. Ibid.; *Colorado Springs Gazette,* Apr. 25, 1894; *Rocky Mountain News,* Apr. 25, 1894; and *Pueblo Chieftain,* Apr. 25, 1894.

52. *Rocky Mountain News,* May 1, 1894; *Denver Republican,* May 1, 1894.

53. Interview with J. Kebler, *Rocky Mountain News,* Apr. 25, 1894.

54. CF&I seems a precocious example of Naomi Lamoreaux's portrait of mergers resulting from cutthroat competition after rapid expansion. Lamoreaux, *The Great Merger Movement in American Business, 1895–1904* (New York: Cambridge University Press, 1985); H. Lee Scamehorn, *Pioneer Steelmaker in the West: The Colorado Fuel and Iron Company, 1872–1903* (Boulder, Colo.: Pruett, 1976).

55. Sylvia Ruland, *Lion of Redstone* (Boulder, Colo: Johnson, 1981), 9–16; Scamehorn, *Pioneer Steelmaker,* 81–83; Pat R. Zollinger and Charles E. Osgood, *The Story of Redstone, Colorado* (Denver: Viking Enterprises, 1964); John L. Jerome, "Statement of Business and Personal Relations, John C. Osgood and John L. Jerome, August 1882 to August 1903," n.d., folder 2, John Lathrop Jerome Papers, CHS; Vaughn Mechau, "Redstone on the Crystal," paper read before the Denver Posse of Westerners, 1947, folder 133, CF&I Steel Corporation Papers, CHS.

56. Zollinger and Osgood, *The Story of Redstone;* Peter D. Vroom, "John Cleveland Osgood: Characteristics of the Dominant Colorado Financier," *New York Times,* Sept. 7, 1903.

57. Memorandum of agreement, Aug. 25, 1892, Minute Book, directors, Colorado Coal & Iron Company, folder 41, box 2, CF&I-CHS, 277–286. Of these coal lands, 68,187 were owned by the company and 3,670 were leased. *Prospectus: The Colorado Fuel and Iron Company, General Mortgage (50 Years) 5% Sinking Fund Gold Bonds,* Feb. 1, 1893, box 5, ibid., p. 2. By 1909, CF&I had become the seventeenth-largest industrial corporation in the United States, as measured by assets. Alfred Chandler, "The Beginnings of 'Big Business' in American Industry," in Thomas K. McCraw, ed., *The Essential Alfred Chandler: Essays toward a Historical Theory of Big Business* (Boston: Harvard Business School Press, 1988), 50.

58. See Osgood's claims before the Joint Conference of November, 1913, as quoted in Chapter 7.

59. *Rocky Mountain News,* May 1, 1894; *Denver Republican,* May 1, 1894; *Florence Oil Refiner,* May 3, 1894. The last source noted: "A great difficulty in getting at a true sentiment of the 600 miners was the necessity of interpreters for the Italians and Austrians, who numbered more than one-third of those present."

60. *Denver Republican,* May 1, 1894.

61. *Rocky Mountain News,* May 3 and 4, 1894; *Denver Republican,* May 3 and 4, 1894; Executive Committee, "New Mexico: In Line in the National Organization," *United Mine Workers Journal,* May 17, 1894, p. 2.

62. *Rocky Mountain News,* May 8, 1894; *Denver Republican,* May 8 and 10, 1894; *Pueblo Chieftain,* May 6 and 16, 1894.

63. *Victor Coal and Coke Company v. John Doe et al.,* May 18, 1894, case 2763, LADC; *Colorado Fuel & Iron Company vs. Chris Passevento et al.,* May 18, 1894, case 2764, ibid.; *Trinidad Advertiser,* May 17 and 24, 1894; *Rocky Mountain News,* May 20 and 26, 1894;

New Castle News, May 26, 1894; Emma Zanetell interview, June 27, 1978, transcript in box 14, EM, pp. 35–36. An interview with State Mine Inspector Reed suggested that the eviction order may have been rescinded: *Trinidad Advertiser,* May 31, 1894.

64. *Trinidad Advertiser,* May 24, 1894; *Rocky Mountain News,* May 20, 1894; *Pueblo Chieftain,* May 19 and 21, 1894.

65. *Pueblo Chieftain,* May 23 and 25, 1894; *New Castle News,* June 2, 1894.

66. *Rocky Mountain News,* May 21, 1894.

67. On the connection between mineworker militancy and the building of company towns, see Wolff, *Industrializing the Rockies,* 137; Thomas G. Andrews, "The Road to Ludlow: Work, Environment, and Industrialization in Southern Colorado, 1870–1915" (Ph.D. diss., University of Wisconsin-Madison, 2003), chap. 6.

68. "Proposition of Miners at Walsen, El Moro and Coal Creek," noted in *Secretary's Record G: Miscellaneous Papers,* 1985, CF&I-CHS, p. 82; agreement with A. H. Prescott, Apr. 3, 1882, in Minute Book, directors, Colorado Coal and Iron Company, folder 40, box 2, CF&I-CHS, 152; Contract with John Oiello [Aiello], Dec. 22, 1892, *Secretary's Record F: Contracts & Leases,* CF&I-CHS, p. 5; Wolff, *Industrializing the Rockies,* 63. On paternalism in Britain and Pennsylvania, see James Alan Jaffe, *The Struggle for Market Power: Industrial Relations in the British Coal Industry, 1800–1840* (New York: Cambridge University Press, 2003), 70–99; Gutman, *Work, Culture, and Society,* 327–328.

69. *Annual Report of the Colorado Fuel Company,* 6; Joseph Simons to H. E. Sprague, n.d. [1886?], folder 16, box 1, CF&I-CHS.

70. Simons to Sprague, n.d.; George Ramsay to E. M. Steck, folder 28, box 1, CF&I-CHS; minutes, May 9, 1888, Minute Book, directors, Colorado Coal and Iron Company, folder 41, box 2, ibid., 11; minutes, Apr. 3, 1889 in Minutes, Directors, Colorado Fuel Co., CF&I-CHS, p. 54. Wolff points out that Simons overlooked the main cause of low wages at Coal Creek: CC&I's success at crushing the 1884 miners' strike and the fury with which the company punished the miners' temerity. Wolff, *Industrializing the Rockies,* 97.

71. On vernacular architecture, see J. A. Kebler to J. C. Osgood, May 21, 1892, folder 66, box 4, CF&I-CHS; and Chapter 6.

72. John Brinckerhoff Jackson, *Discovering the Vernacular Landscape* (New Haven, Conn.: Yale University Press, 1984), xii, 150.

73. *Colorado Springs Gazette,* May 24, 1894; *Rocky Mountain News,* May 21 and 25, 1894; *Pueblo Chieftain,* May 23 and 25, 1894.

74. *Rocky Mountain News,* May 25, 1894; Powers, *Faces along the Bar,* 70, 228–236. The Italian Alex Bisulco remembered meeting Japanese miners in the saloon at Rugby and even learning some words in Japanese from them. On ethnic mixing in saloons, see Alex Bisulco interview, pp. 32–33; Dan DeSantis interview, pp. 62–63. Confirming these informative oral histories, McKanna found high rates of murders by blacks, whites, and Hispanos of members of other "racial" groups; since so many murders were committed

in saloons, we can infer that many saloons were interracial, as well as interethnic. Mc-Kanna, *Homicide, Race, and Justice in the American West,* 157. Women, though they were welcome in the front rooms of saloons, which were called wine rooms, were generally not allowed in the back barrooms. Mike Livoda interview, Nov. 8, 1968, transcript in box 10, EM, p. 22.

75. *Rocky Mountain News,* May 26, 1894; *New Castle News,* June 2, 1894.

76. *Pueblo Chieftain,* May 26 and 27, 1894; *Trinidad Advertiser,* May 31, 1894. The newspaper did not provide a first name, but see *United Mine Workers Journal,* May 31, 1894, p. 8.

77. *Rocky Mountain News,* May 29, 1894; *Trinidad Advertiser,* May 31, 1894.

78. *Trinidad Advertiser,* May 31, 1894; Emma Zanetell interview, pp. 34–36.

79. *Rocky Mountain News,* May 29, 1894.

80. The rest had returned home, "as there was such a long body of men and so many to feed . . . and they had traveled so far." *Pueblo Chieftain,* May 30, 1894; *Rocky Mountain News,* May 31, 1894; Emma Zanetell interview, p. 35; "R. B. Rile Bagging" (pseud.), "News from Colorado," *United Mine Workers Journal,* Sept. 6, 1894.

81. Bo Sweeney and J. J. Hendrick speeches, *Trinidad Advertiser,* June 7, 1894. Other speakers echoed much the same themes. Sweeney was listed elsewhere in the same source as a defense attorney in a habeas corpus case resulting from the strike.

82. *Pueblo Chieftain,* June 6 and 7, 1894; *Trinidad Advertiser,* June 14, 1894.

83. *Pueblo Chieftain,* June 9, 1894; *Trinidad Advertiser,* June 14, 1894. On the success of company tactics at Hastings, see, for instance, *New Castle News,* June 9, 1894. For a firsthand account, see Henry Long affidavit, June 14, 1894, folder 117, box 2, Michael Beshoar Papers, DPL. For CF&I's version of events, see *Second Annual Report of the Colorado Fuel and Iron Company for the Year Ending June 30, 1894* (Denver: n.p., 1894), 10–11.

84. *Trinidad Advertiser,* May 10 and 17, 1894; *Pueblo Chieftain,* June 7 and July 1, 1894; *Florence Oil Refiner,* June 12, 1894; *Colorado Springs Gazette,* June 14, 1894; Caroline Waldron Merithew and James R. Barret, " 'We Are Brothers in the Face of Starvation': Forging an Interethnic Working Class Movement in the 1894 Bituminous Coal Strike," *Mid-America* 83 (2001): 121–154. Smaller markets, such as Aspen, however, were more vulnerable. *New Castle News,* June 16, 1894.

85. *Pueblo Chieftain,* June 27 and 28, 1894; *United Mine Workers Journal,* June 14, 1894. "Striking miners" allegedly burned down a "forty-eight-foot trestle bridge" on the D&RG branch to Engleville. *Trinidad Advertiser,* Aug. 2, 1894. For a critical interpretation of the strike's resolution in one Pennsylvania district, see Mildred Allen Beik, *The Miners of Windber: The Struggles of New Immigrants for Unionization, 1890s–1930s* (University Park: Pennsylvania State University Press, 1996), 152–153.

86. *Pueblo Chieftain,* June 24, 1894.

87. *Pueblo Chieftain,* Aug. 3, 6, 8, and 10, 1894; *Colorado Springs Gazette,* Aug. 11, 1894; *Trinidad Advertiser,* Aug. 9, 1894.

88. For an example of the recriminations that followed the strike, see *New Castle News,* July 7, 1894. Wolff argues that the Pullman strike actually hurt the coal miners, because the cessation of train traffic destroyed whatever incentive the operators might have had to settle the dispute earlier. He also demonstrates that Osgood later conflated the marching strike with the Pullman strike. Wolff, *Industrializing the Rockies,* 153–154.

89. Bo Sweeney speech, *Trinidad Advertiser,* June 7, 1894.

6. The Quest for Containment

1. *Annual Report of the Sociological Department of the Colorado Fuel and Iron Company for 1907–1908* (Denver: Merchants, 1908), 7.

2. Kenneth Warren, *Wealth, Waste, and Alienation: Growth and Decline in the Connellsville Coke Industry* (Pittsburgh: University of Pittsburgh Press, 2001), 210; Stuart D. Brandes, *American Welfare Capitalism, 1880–1940* (Chicago: University of Chicago Press, 1976); Andrea Tone, *The Business of Benevolence: Industrial Paternalism in Progressive America* (Ithaca, N.Y.: Cornell University Press, 1997); Gerald Zahavi, *Workers, Managers, and Welfare Capitalism: The Shoeworkers and Tanners of Endicott Johnson, 1890–1950* (Champaign: University of Illinois Press, 1988); Howard Gitelman, "Welfare Capitalism Reconsidered," *Labor History* 33 (Winter 1992): 5–31; Gwendolyn Wright, *Building the Dream: A Social History of Housing in America* (New York: Pantheon, 1981), 184.

3. *Camp and Plant* 1 (Jan. 16, 1902): 80–81, 86; *Camp and Plant* 3 (Mar. 21): 262; *Camp and Plant* 3 (Apr. 25, 1903): 363–368.

4. "Involving as its major issue the demand of the miners for a voice in determining the conditions under which they worked," George P. West wrote in an influential report on the 1913–1914 coalfield war, "the Colorado conflict was also a struggle for a voice in determining political and social conditions in the communities where they and their families lived." The strike, West concluded, involved both "industrial rights" and "political rights." George P. West, *Report on the Colorado Strike* (Washington, D.C.: U.S. Commission on Industrial Relations, 1915), reprinted in Leon Stein and Philip Taft, eds., *Massacre at Ludlow: Four Reports* (New York: Arno and New York Times, 1971), 5–6.

5. Brandes, *American Welfare Capitalism,* 20–37; William H. Tolman, *Social Engineering: A Record of Things Done by American Industrialists Employing Upwards of One and One-Half Million of People* (New York: McGraw, 1909), 3; Tone, *Business of Benevolence;* Gwendolyn Wright, *Building the Dream: A Social History of Housing in America* (New York: Pantheon, 1981), 184. On the welfare provisions of European coal mining companies, see *The Housing of the Working People,* Eighth Special Report of the Commissioner of Labor (Washington, D.C.: GPO, 1895), 356.

6. For the best map of Redstone, see Colorado Fuel and Iron Co. Chief Engineer's Office, "The Colorado Fuel and Iron Company, Redstone," Nov. 10, 1903, roll 90, BHS.

7. Pat R. Zollinger and Charles E. Osgood, The Story of Redstone, Colorado (Denver: Viking Enterprises, 1964), 3, 6; Vaughn Mechau, "Redstone on the Crystal," paper read before the Denver Posse of Westerners, 1947, folder 133, CF&I Steel Corporation Papers, CHS, p. 10; "Historic Resources of Redstone, Colorado, and Vicinity," National Register of Historic Places Multiple Property Documentation Form, Mar. 1989, ibid.; Thomas J. Noel, Buildings of Colorado (New York: Oxford University Press, 1997), 499–500; and Catherine Clarke Fox, "Colorado Castle Seeks White Knight" (Mar. 4, 2005), online at http://www2.preservationnation.org/magazine/archives (updated Apr. 8, 2008). Surprisingly, scholars of welfare capitalism and model company towns have entirely overlooked Redstone.

8. *Denver Times,* May 18, 1902; Zollinger and Osgood, *Story of Redstone,* 6; *Camp and Plant* 1 (Apr. 5, 1902): 284; *Camp and Plant* 1 (May 3, 1902): 379; *Camp and Plant* 1 (June 14, 1902): 520; *Camp and Plant* 4 (July 25, 1903): 44; "Osgood Gamekeeper's Lodge," National Register of Historic Places registration form, Mar. 1989, folder 133, CF&I Steel Corporation Papers, CHS; *Carbondale Item,* Aug. 28, 1902; Mechau, "Redstone on the Crystal," 11, 16.

9. Mechau, "Redstone on the Crystal," 11; *Camp and Plant* 1 (Dec. 14, 1901): 8; Noel, *Buildings of Colorado,* 499–500; "Houses and Towns," *Camp and Plant* 5 (Dec. 26, 1904): 313; L. M. Bowers, "The Great Strike in Colorado," *Leslie's Illustrated Weekly Newspaper,* Feb. 5, 1914, p. 127; Tolman, *Social Engineering,* 247.

10. *Denver Times,* Feb. 2, 1901; Tolman, *Social Engineering,* 306; *Camp and Plant* 1 (June 28, 1902): 572.

11. "A Western Mining Company's Sociological Work," *Outlook* 72 (1902): 149–150.

12. *Camp and Plant* 5 (Jan. 16, 1904): 15; Francis B. Rizzari, "Railroads of the Crystal River Valley," *Denver Westerners Brand Book* 20 (1964), 389; Mechau, "Redstone on the Crystal," 17; Zollinger and Osbood, *Story of Redstone,* 7.

13. *Fourth Annual Report of the Colorado Fuel and Iron Company for the Year Ending June 30, 1896* (Denver: n.p., 1896), 8; Osgood to Cass, Aug. 20, 1896, folder 1, CF&I Steel Corporation Papers, CHS; and Julian Kennedy to Messrs. Blair & Company, Aug. 6, 1901, folder 35-9, microfilm roll E, ibid.; María E. Montoya, *Translating Property: The Maxwell Land Grant and the Conflict over Land in the American West, 1840–1900* (Berkeley: University of California Press, 2002).

14. *Dominic Cesario v. Colorado & Wyoming Railway Co.,* case 3970, LADC (filed May 9, 1903), in LACC; *Manuelita Abeyta v. The Colorado & Wyoming Railway Co.,* case 3736, LADC (filed Jan. 4, 1902), in LACC.

15. *Cesario v. Colorado & Wyoming; Abeyta v. Colorado & Wyoming; Thomas A. Thompson v. Colorado & Wyoming Railway Co.,* case 4091, LADC (filed Feb. 2, 1904).

16. *Cesario v. Colorado & Wyoming.*

17. Apparently the C&W "purchased the truck farms at Jansen and constructed the terminal yards," securing rights to the Lopez ditch in the process; it also acquired part of the Varros ditch near Segundo around the same time, eventually paying out a thousand dollars in damages to Leone Bonfadini, Elizabeth Thrower, Teresa Bianchi, and T. A. Thompson. J. M. Madrid, an old Las Animas Hispano settler, would later attribute the precipitate drop in agricultural productivity in the valley to the railroad's seizure of "valuable bottom land for its right of way," the coal companies' dumping of "refuse from the mines . . . in the valley and the river," and lumbering. "The water," claimed Madrid, which "no longer slowed down in its rush to the river, caused soil erosion at a very rapid rate." CF&I Mining Department, "Report on Water Rights," Aug. 9, 1932, box 11, CF&I-CHS, 13–15; "Interview with J. M. Madrid," by A. K. Richeson, CWA, Las Animas County, vol. 1, doc. no. 359/6, pp. 83–84.

18. Montoya, *Translating Property,* 205–208; José M. Romero, *El Valle de los Rancheros* (n.p.: José M. Romero, 1978); "Report of Ira B. Gale," folder 17, box 1, T. A. Schomburg Papers, CHS; "Saw Timber Cut on Vermejo Drainage from 1890 to April 1901," folder 16, ibid.

19. "The Nature and Scope of the Department's Work," *Camp and Plant* 2 (Aug. 23, 1902): 186; "Segundo, Colorado, and the Segundo Coke Ovens," *Camp and Plant* 3 (Apr. 25, 1903): 368; *Camp and Plant* 3 (Mar. 7, 1903): 213; *Annual Report of the Sociological Department of the Colorado Fuel and Iron Company for 1908–1909* (Denver: Merchants, 1909): 5, 21; Tolman, *Social Engineering,* 38.

20. Director's minutes, Aug. 18, 1897, and Oct. 7, 1903, folder 169, box 8, CF&I-CHS; entries for Aug. 21, 1895, Aug. 16, 1899, Aug. 19, 1903, and Sept. 27, 1906, Record Book A, Colorado Supply Co., ibid.; *Annual Report of the Colorado Supply Company for the Year Ending June 30, 1897* (Denver: n.p., 1897). On one effort to oppose this store monopoly, see *Dunlavy Bros. v. CF&I Co. et al.,* case 3696, LADC (filed Aug. 29, 1901), LACC. On dividends, see Bowers to Frederick Gates, Mar. 23, 1910, folder 188, box 21, CF&I-RAC. One insider placed CSC profits at 25–40 percent around 1900. "Statement of Business and Personal Relations, John C. Osgood and John L. Jerome, August 1882 to August 1903," n.d., section B, folder 14, John Lathrop Jerome Papers, CHS.

21. On outright purchases, see *Cripple Creek Times,* Feb. 14, 1902. On Coal Creek, see *Denver News,* July 7, 1907.

22. J. K. Brewster to J. A. Kebler, Nov. 12, 1895, file 19-9, tape E, CF&I Steel Corporation Papers, CHS; Carroll D. Wright, *A Report on Labor Disturbances in the State of Colorado, from 1880 to 1904, Inclusive, with Correspondence Relating Thereto* (Washington, D.C.: GPO, 1905), 337.

23. Cripple Creek Times, Feb. 14, 1902; J. T. Kebler to C. E. Herrington, Apr. 16, 1901, Old Land File 74, CF&I-BHS; and other correspondence in this file. Some squatters did manage to maintain their hold on their homes. YMCA Report, 12, 20.

24. "The New Mexico Camps," *Camp and Plant* 1 (Jan. 4, 1902): 49; "Rouse and

Hezron: Two Picturesque Coal Camps in Huerfano County," *Camp and Plant* 1 (Mar. 8, 1902): 193–198; "Primero, Colorado: One of the Three New Camps in the Valley of the Purgatoire," *Camp and Plant* 2 (Oct. 25, 1902): 397.

25. "New Church and Club House, Primero," *Camp and Plant* 4 (Aug. 22, 1903): 136.

26. YMCA Report, 43; *The Colorado Fuel and Iron Company's Tabasco Mine . . .* (n.p.: CF&I, Oct. 11, 1905), Map Collection, Colorado School of Mines, Golden; *The Colorado Fuel and Iron Company's Coal Basin Mine* (n.p.: CF&I, Jan. 1, 1909), ibid.; *The Colorado Fuel and Iron Company: Map of Spring Gulch Mine Pitkin Co. Colo.* (n.p.: CF&I, Oct. 19, 1916), ibid.

27. Frank Harenberg interview, May 21, 1978, box 10, EM, p. 30; John S. Garner, *The Model Company Town: Urban Design through Private Enterprise in Nineteenth-Century New England* (Amherst: University of Massachusetts Press, 1984), 78.

28. "Segundo, Colorado," 368; "Berwind and Tabasco," *Camp and Plant* 1 (Jan. 11, 1902): 58; *Trinidad Chronicle,* Mar. 27, 1907; *Florence Tribune,* Aug. 8, 1901.

29. *Camp and Plant* 5 (Jan. 16, 1904): 14; "The Late A. C. Cass," *Camp and Plant* 4 (Sept. 5, 1903): 186.

30. YMCA Report, 5; *Thirteenth Biennial Report of the Bureau of Labor Statistics of the State of Colorado, 1911–1912* (Denver: Smith-Brooks, 1913), 57–61; Claude W. Fairchild testimony, in *CCMC,* 1: 575; Memorandum, S. J. Donleavy, Mar. 10, 1915, in John D. Rockefeller, Jr., to Jesse Floyd Welborn, Apr. 3, 1915, folder 17, JFW Papers.

31. Horton Pope, quoted in Howard M. Gitelman, *The Legacy of the Ludlow Massacre: A Chapter in American Industrial Relations* (Philadelphia: University of Pennsylvania Press, 1988), 123–126. LaMont Bowers claimed that under the Rockefellers, CF&I abandoned such politicking. LaMont Montgomery Bowers to C. O. Heydt, May 11, 1913, folder 211, box 23, CF&I-RAC.

32. Quoted in Gitelman, *Legacy of the Ludlow Massacre,* 123–126; Appeal, in *Cesario v. Colorado & Wyoming;* Donald Mitchell interview, Feb. 5, 1978, transcript in box 11, EM, p. 12. Given the ready recourse of courts nationwide to common-law defenses against liability, such accusations could be confirmed only by statistical comparison of verdicts from Huerfano and Las Animas counties with those from coal-mining regions where the legal and political systems were not corrupted. Even the *perception* of manipulation, however, could take on its own reality if it prompted injured workers and survivors not to sue mining companies.

33. Gitelman, *Legacy of the Ludlow Massacre,* 123–126; Casimiro Barela to James H. Peabody, undated petition [1904?], folder 16, box 26716, Governor James H. Peabody Papers, CSA; Mike Livoda interview, June 20, 1973, folder 14, box 2, South Slavs Oral History Collection, UU, p. 16; Donald Joseph McClurg, "Labor Organization in the Coal Mines of Colorado, 1878–1933" (Ph.D. diss., University of California, Los Angeles, 1959),

149; Jefferson B. Farr testimony, Feb. 13, 1896, "In Re Italian Massacre Investigation Walsenburg Colo., Feb. 11, 12 and 13 1896," folder 6, box 26694, Governor Jesse McIntyre Papers, CSA. The Farr family benefited from grazing leases and water contracts with Colorado Fuel and Iron and its precursors. *Secretary's Record F, Contracts & Leases, CF&I,* May 15, 1891, Jan. 2, 1896, and Mar. 26, 1907, CF&I-CHS. It was only fitting that *Farr v. Neeley,* the 1915 Colorado Supreme Court case that struck down the company's political dominance of southern Colorado, bears the sheriff's name.

34. *Colorado Springs Gazette,* Sept. 13, 1907.

35. *Trinidad Chronicle-News,* Mar. 25, 1906; "The Colorado Supply Company Store at Minnequa," *Camp and Plant* 1 (June 7, 1902): 502.

36. Quotations from "Colorado Supply Co. Stores Have Grown to Present Size from Small Beginning," *CF&I Industrial Bulletin* 13 (Aug. 1928): 9; "The Colorado Supply Co.," *Denver Post,* Dec. 31, 1905; *Camp and Plant* 1 (Dec. 20, 1901): 17. On other store openings, see *Camp and Plant* 1 (Mar. 15, 1902): 218; and *Camp and Plant* 1 (June 21, 1902): 540. See also Charles H. Montgomery, *The Spanish Redemption: Heritage, Power, and Loss on New Mexico's Upper Rio Grande* (Berkeley: University of California Press, 2002); and William Deverell, *Whitewashed Adobe: The Rise of Los Angeles and the Remaking of Its Mexican Past* (Berkeley: University of California Press, 2004).

37. Trinidad Advertiser Sentinel Office, *Descriptive, Historical and Biographical Sketches Relative to Trinidad and Las Animas County . . .* (Trinidad, Colo.: Advertiser-Sentinel, 1899), n.p.; *Camp and Plant* 3 (June 6, 1903): 517; *Camp and Plant* 1 (Apr. 19, 1902): 330; and "Views of the Colorado Fuel & Iron Co.'s Steel Works Hospital and Mining Camps, July 1916," box 12, CF&I-CHS.

38. "How the Scrip System Is Used in Las Animas County," *Pueblo Sunday Opinion,* Jan. 20, 1906.

39. The quotations are drawn, in order of appearance, from LaMont Montgomery Bowers to J. B. McKennan, May 19, 1911, folder 98, box 28, LMB Papers; "Proceedings of Joint Conference," 196–200; "Bonne Bouche," "Colorado News," *United Mine Workers Journal,* Mar. 1, 1894; *Trinidad Advertiser-Sentinel* (Trinidad, Colo.), n.p.; Isaac Williams, quoted in Eleanor Fry, "Large Operations and Half Dozen Major Camps Marked Peak Years of County's Coal Industry," n.d., clipping in Harold Smith scrapbook, LHC. See also Weitzel to Bowers, Mar. 2, 1910, folder 96, box 28, CF&I-RAC; *Trinidad Chronicle,* July 25, 1906. More generally, see Price V. Fishback, "The Miner's Work Environment: Safety and Company Towns in the Early 1900s," in John H. M. Laslett, ed., *The United Mine Workers of America: A Model of Industrial Solidarity?* (University Park: Pennsylvania State University Press, 1996), 211; and Price V. Fishback, *Soft Coal, Hard Choices: The Economic Welfare of Bituminous Coal Miners, 1890–1930* (New York: Oxford University Press, 1992).

40. Frank Harenberg interview, p. 4; *Colorado Democrat,* Jan. 16, 1906; *Denver Times,* Nov. 17, 1902; *Pueblo Star-Journal,* Aug. 7, 1904; *Pueblo Courier,* Nov. 11, 1898. Scrip

dealers discounted the paper at 15–25 percent in Pueblo in 1902; three years later, though, saloons and stores in that city accepted it at face value, as did some stores in Trinidad. T. J. Donohue, letter to the editor, *Pueblo Chieftain,* Dec. 19, 1902; *Pueblo Star-Journal,* June 25, 1905; Victor Bazanele interview, n.d., box 7, EM, n.p. Some CF&I scrip even made it to New York City. *Denver Times,* June 3, 1903.

41. Quotation from *Trinidad Advertiser-Sentinel,* Souvenir Edition, n.p.; W. D. Gilbert, "Colorado Supply: Industrial Retail Stores," typescript dated Sept. 22, 1966, CF&I Steel Corporation Papers, p. 4. On consumption, citizenship, identity, and labor, see William Leach, *Land of Desire: Merchants, Power, and the Rise of an American Culture* (New York: Pantheon, 1993); Lawrence Glickman, "The Strike in the Temple of Consumption: Consumer Activism and Twentieth-Century Political Culture," *Journal of American History* 88 (2001): 99–128; and Lawrence B. Glickman, *A Living Wage: American Workers and the Making of Consumer Society* (Ithaca, N.Y.: Cornell University Press, 1997), 108–128.

42. "Excellent Public Schools," *Camp and Plant* 4 (Dec. 26, 1903): 557. On property taxes, see Claire C. French, *Rockefeller Welfare Plan in "Camp" Schools, a Farce: Startling Facts Disclosed by Searching Investigation of the Justice League Representative* (Denver: Eastwood-Elwell, 1916); *CF&I v. Board of County Commissioners, Las Animas County,* case no. 3506, LADC (filed Dec. 22, 1898), LACC. For the company justification, see *Annual Report of the Sociological Department of the Colorado Fuel and Iron Company for 1901–1902* (Denver: Merchants, [1902]), 6.

43. *Annual Report of the Sociological Department of the Colorado Fuel and Iron Company for 1906–1907* (Denver: Merchants, 1907), 24; *Trinidad Chronicle,* Mar. 25, 1907.

44. Quotation from *Report of the Medical and Sociological Departments of the Colorado Fuel & Iron Company 1912–1913* (n.p.: n.p., 1913), 41. See also *Annual Report of the Sociological Department of the Colorado Fuel and Iron Company for 1906–1907,* 24–25; *Camp and Plant* 1 (Mar. 8, 1902): 193–198; *Camp and Plant* 1 (June 21, 1902): 530; *Camp and Plant* 3 (Jan. 17, 1903): 69, 71; *Camp and Plant* 3 (Apr. 25, 1903): 367. Pueblo architect G. W. Roe designed the Katcina school, while Baird (first name unspecified) designed several other schools. On the tendency of operators to name "their newly founded company towns after themselves or after close relatives," see Mildred Allen Beik, *The Miners of Windber: The Struggles of New Immigrants for Unionization, 1890s–1930s* (University Park: Pennsylvania State University Press, 1996), xxiv.

45. Quotation from "Night Schools," *Bulletin, Sanitary and Sociological* 7 (Oct. 1909): n.p. See also *Annual Report of the Sociological Department of the Colorado Fuel and Iron Company for 1907–1908,* 23; *Annual Report of the Sociological Department of the Colorado Fuel and Iron Company for 1906–1907,* 16; "Sociological Work of the Colorado Fuel and Iron Company," *Camp and Plant* 2 (Aug. 30, 1902): 207; *Cañon City Clipper,* Aug. 22, 1902.

46. *Annual Report of the Sociological Department of the Colorado Fuel and Iron Com-*

pany for 1901–1902, 5–6. By 1909 CF&I again touted night schools because of worker interest, a change that suggests the continuing power camp residents exerted to shape paternalism.

47. "The Foreigner," *Bulletin, Sanitary and Sociological* 7 (Jan. 1910): n.p.

48. *Camp and Plant* 1 (March 8, 1902): 208; "Kindergartens in the Camps," *Camp and Plant* 5 (Feb. 6, 1904): 80–81; "Growing Things," *Bulletin, Sanitary and Sociological* 4 (Apr. 1907): n.p. This connection between nature and childhood reflected the influence of the suburbanizing middle class. Mary Corbin Sies, "'God's Very Kingdom on Earth': The Design Program for the American Suburban Home, 1877–1917," in Becky M. Nicolaides and Andrew Wiese, eds., *The Suburb Reader* (New York: Routledge, 2006), 189–190.

49. "Starkville, Colorado and the Starkville Mine," *Camp and Plant* 1 (Mar. 3, 1902): 364.

50. Tolman, *Social Engineering*, 259; "The Kindergarten in America," *Camp and Plant* 1 (May 17, 1902): 432; "Kindergartens in the Camps," 79.

51. "Social Science II," *Camp and Plant* 2 (July 12, 1902): 43.

52. "Social Science IV," *Camp and Plant* 2 (July 26, 1902): 86–7; *Report of the Medical & Sociological Departments of the Colorado Fuel & Iron Company, 1913–1914* (Pueblo, Colo.: Franklin, 1914), 36–38, 40; *Report of the Medical and Sociological Departments of the Colorado Fuel and Iron Company, 1914–1915* (Pueblo, Colo.: Franklin, 1915), 26.

53. YMCA Report, 42; "Social Science X: Interior Decoration of the Home," *Camp and Plant* 2 (Oct. 11, 1902): 348–349.

54. *Camp and Plant* 2 (Sept. 20, 1902): 286–287; "Social Science V," *Camp and Plant* 2 (Aug. 13, 1902): 141–142; "The Circulating Art Collection," *Camp and Plant* 1 (May 31, 1902): 469.

55. "Hospital Bureau of Information," *Camp and Plant* 2 (July 5, 1902): 7; Sarah Deutsch, *No Separate Refuge: Culture, Class, and Gender in the American Southwest, 1880–1940* (New York: Oxford University Press, 1987).

56. *Camp and Plant* 1 (Dec. 18, 1901): 18; *Camp and Plant* 1 (Jan. 16, 1902): 87; "Social Science XI: Good Books in the Home," *Camp and Plant* 2 (Dec. 13, 1902): 571; "Social Science XII: Good Periodicals in the Home," *Camp and Plant* 3 (Jan. 23, 1903): 91; "The Foreigner," n.p.

57. "Proceedings of Joint Conference," 221, 224 (quoted); Tolman, *Social Engineering*, 38–40. For an incisive analysis of the custom of "treating," see Madelon Powers, *Faces along the Bar: Lore and Order in the Workingman's Saloon, 1870–1920* (Chicago: University of Chicago Press, 1998), 93–118.

58. David Griffiths. "Advantages of Social Welfare," in *Proceedings of the Rocky Mountain Coal Mining Institute, Third Semi-Annual Meeting* (Denver: Wepf, n.d.), 46; "Hints

on Hygiene" series in *Camp and Plant:* "Doctors' Lectures," *Camp and Plant* 2 (Dec. 6, 1902): 550–551; *Camp and Plant* 1 (Dec. 14, 1901): 4; C&P 1 (Feb. 29, 1902): 1902. On minstrelsy, see *Camp and Plant* 2 (Oct. 11, 1902): 361; *Camp and Plant* 3 (Apr. 11, 1903): 330; *Camp and Plant* 3 (May 2, 1903): 403; and photo album, fall 1915, box 12, CF&I-CHS, which seems to show a lone African American player performing with a coal camp minstrel troop. On movies, see the photo "Moving Picture Audience," *Report of the Medical and Sociological Departments of the Colorado Fuel and Iron Company, 1913–1914;* YMCA Report, 5; and Steven Joseph Ross, *Working-Class Hollywood: Silent Film and the Shaping of Class in America* (Princeton, N.J.: Princeton University Press, 1998), 11–33.

59. *Camp and Plant* 1 (Mar. 8, 1902): 205–208.

60. Ibid., 208.

61. Herbert N. Casson, *The Romance of Steel: The Story of a Thousand Millionaires* (New York: A. S. Barnes, 1907), 315; Agreement, Sept. 2, 1903, folder 204, box 22, CF&I-RAC; "President Hearne of Fuel Company Has Passed Away," *Pueblo Star-Journal,* Feb. 26, 1907; Donald Joseph McClurg, "Labor Organization in the Coal Mines of Colorado, 1878–1933" (Ph.D. diss., University of California, Los Angeles, 1959), 107–108; Emma Langdon, *The Cripple Creek Strike: A History of Industrial Wars in Colorado, 1903–4–5* . . . (Denver: Great Western, 1904–1905); Wright, *Report on Labor Disturbances in Colorado,* 331.

62. *Denver News,* Sept. 12, 1903.

63. "Welfare capitalism," as Andrea Tone argues, "created an arena of negotiation—not just co-option—where workers made their voices heard." *Business of Benevolence,* 13.

64. Zeph Hill to James Peabody, Nov. 18, 1903, folder 8, box 26716, Peabody Papers, 4; YMCA Report; Minutes, CF&I Executive Committee, Jan. 27, 1913, folder 58, JFW Papers.

65. J. Warner Mills, "The Economic Struggle in Colorado," *Arena* 34 (1905): 1–10; 119–128, 248–264, 379–399, 485–495, 605–619; and *Arena* (1906), 150–158, 243–252, 375–390, 467–476.

7. Shouting the Battle Cry of Union

1. *Denver Express,* Sept. 15, 1913.

2. Intriguingly, an emphasis on energy systems instead of modes of production can perhaps help account for some of the common failings of capitalist and Communist regimes over the course of twentieth-century history.

3. *Denver Express,* Sept. 15, 1913; *Trinidad Chronicle-News,* Sept. 15, 1913; *Rocky Mountain News,* Sept. 16, 1913.

4. Barron B. Beshoar, *Out of the Depths: The Story of John R. Lawson* (Denver: Col-

orado Labor Historical Committee of the Denver Trades and Labor Assembly, 1942), 49–50; Mike Livoda interview, Nov. 30, 1968, transcript in box 10, EM, pp. 9–10.

5. Adolph Germer to Edgar Wallace, Aug. 18, 1913, box 1, Adolph Germer Papers, State Historical Society of Wisconsin.

6. *Denver Express,* Sept. 15, 1913. The official name of "The Colorado Strike Song" was "We're Coming, Colorado."

7. Ibid.

8. *Proceedings: Special Convention of District Fifteen United Mine Workers of America Held in Trinidad, Colorado, 16 September 1913,* env. 10, Edward S. Doyle Papers, DPL; *Trinidad Chronicle-News,* Sept. 15 and 16, 1913; *Denver Times,* Sept. 16, 1913; *First Annual Report of the State Inspector of Coal Mines, 1913* (Denver: Smith-Brooks, 1914), 1–7.

9. *Trinidad Chronicle-News,* Sept. 16, 1913; "Proceedings of Joint Conference, Held in the State Capitol, Denver, Colorado, at 10 o'clock A.M., November 26, 1913," box 23, CF&I-RAC, 159–160 (henceforth "Proceedings of Joint Conference").

10. *Trinidad Chronicle-News,* Sept. 17, 1913; *Denver Express,* Sept. 17, 1913.

11. *Trinidad Chronicle-News,* Sept. 17, 1913; *Rocky Mountain News,* Sept. 17, 1913; *Denver Times,* Sept. 17, 1913; *New York Times,* Sept. 18, 1913; Bill Lloyd interview, May 18, 1978, transcript in box 10, EM, p. 18.

12. *Trinidad Chronicle-News,* Sept. 17, 1913. Another account claimed that the delegates "shouted, danced about the room, vowed vengenace [*sic*] on the operators, and pledged themselves to stay with the strike until they won 'or dropped into their graves.'" *Walsenburg World,* Sept. 18, 1913.

13. *Denver Express,* Sept. 16 and 17, 1913; *Trinidad Chronicle-News,* Sept. 17, 1913; *Florence Citizen,* Sept. 17, 1913.

14. Statement in *Trinidad Chronicle-News,* Sept. 13, 1913; LaMont Montgomery Bowers to John D. Rockefeller, Jr., Sept. 4, 1913, folder 211, box 23, CF&I-RAC; Jesse Floyd Welborn to J. H. McClement, Sept. 6, 1913, ibid. On the 1903–1904 strike as a "prelude to Ludlow," see George G. Suggs, Jr., "The Colorado Coal Miners' Strike, 1903–1904: A Prelude to Ludlow?" *Journal of the West* 12 (1973): 36–53.

15. Quotations from William Jackson Palmer to Walter Hinchman, Aug. 31, 1903, folder 545, box 7, WJP-CHS; "The Colorado Coal Strike," *Outlook* 75 (Dec. 5 1903): 763*; William D. Haywood, *The Autobiography of Big Bill Haywood* (1929; repr. New York: International, 1974), 152. For context, see Carroll D. Wright, *A Report on Labor Disturbances in the State of Colorado, from 1880 to 1904, Inclusive, with Correspondence Relating Thereto* (Washington, D.C.: GPO, 1905); Elizabeth Jameson, *All That Glitters: Class, Conflict, and Community in Cripple Creek* (Champaign: University of Illinois Press, 1998); William Philpott, *The Lessons of Leadville,* Colorado Historical Society Monograph 10 (Denver: Colorado Historical Society, 1994); George G. Suggs, Jr., *Colorado's War on Militant Unionism: James H. Peabody and the Western Federation of Min-*

ers (Detroit: Wayne State University Press, 1972); Melvin Dubofsky, *We Shall Be All: A History of the Industrial Workers of the World* (Chicago: Quadrangle, 1969).

16. Donald Joseph McClurg, "Labor Organization in the Coal Mines of Colorado, 1878–1933" (Ph.D. diss., University of California, Los Angeles, 1959), 107–108; Emma Langdon, *The Cripple Creek Strike: A History of Industrial Wars in Colorado, 1903-4-5* . . . (Denver: Great Western, 1904–1905), 264; Wright, *Report on Labor Disturbances in Colorado,* 331, 335–336. Scrip payment and company stores also became issues during the course of the strike. *Denver Post,* Dec. 5, 1903.

17. R. L. Martel to W. H. Reno, Feb. 10, 1904, quoted without attribution in Winnifred Banner, manuscript biography of John Lawson, folder 21, box 3, John R. Lawson Papers, DPL; *New Castle Nonpareil,* Dec. 18, 1903. On Martel's role in other beatings, see Langdon, *Cripple Creek Strike,* 265–267. The use of "kangaroo" here seems unusual; perhaps Martel was drawing on the use of the term "kangaroo court," but clearly no proceedings of any sort were conducted before Oddo was beaten. Alternatively, Martel may have been referring to kangaroos' well-deserved reputation as fine boxers.

18. F. R. Woods to James Peabody, Dec. 2, 1903, folder 8, box 26716, Governor James Peabody Papers, CSA; Zeph Hill to Peabody, Mar. 27, 30, and 31 and Apr. 12, 17, and 19, folder 14, ibid.; Mitchell quoted in *Denver Republican,* Jan. 17, 1905; Suggs, *Colorado's War on Militant Unionism,* 95; *Pueblo Chieftain,* Nov. 14, 1903; "Colorado Coal Strike," 764*.

19. Wright, *Report on Labor Disturbances in Colorado,* 338, 341, 354–355; Alex Bisulco interview, June 27, 1978, transcript in box 8, EM, pp. 23–24; Langdon, *Cripple Creek Strike,* 265; McClurg, "Labor Organization in the Coal Mines of Colorado," 137–138; "List of Prisoners Deported from Camp Trinidad up to and Including April 2nd, 1904," folder 15, box 26716, Peabody Papers; Headquarters, First Provisional Battalion, National Guard of Colorado, Las Animas County Military District, Camp Trinidad, "Record of Prisoners Taken in Las Animas County Military District," folder 16, ibid.; Hill to Peabody, Apr. 11, 1904, folder 15, ibid.; Hill to Peabody, Apr. 27, May 7 and 23, and June 3, 1904, folder 14, ibid.; Victor Bazanele interview, n.d., box 7, EM, n.p. For a convoluted critique, see "The Issue in Colorado," *Outlook* 77 (1904): 395. More broadly, see Katherine Benton-Cohen, "Docile Children and Dangerous Revolutionaries: The Racial Hierarchy of Manliness and the Bisbee Deportation of 1917," *Frontiers: A Journal of Women Studies* 24 (2003): 30–50.

20. Stephen Burnett Brier, "'The Most Persistent Unionists'": Class Formation and Class Conflict in the Coal Fields and the Emergence of Interracial and Interethnic Unionism, 1880–1904" (Ph.D. diss., University of California at Los Angeles, 1992), 258–264; *U.S. v. John Simpson, William Howells, and Charles Demolli,* U.S. District Court, Pueblo, case 795 (filed Apr. 9, 1904), box 53, entry 75, Bankruptcy, Civil, and Criminal Case Files, 1879–1907, Records of the District Courts of the United States, RG 21, NARA-Denver; Hill to Peabody, May 7, 1904, folder 14, box 26716, Peabody Papers;

Wright, *Report on Labor Disturbances in Colorado,* 348, 350. When strikers nearly ambushed a car carrying company officials at Segundo, for instance, a reporter from Denver's *Polly Pry* weekly was in the car with them. *Trinidad Chronicle-News,* Dec. 9, 1903.

21. *Denver News,* Nov. 29, 1903; *Denver Republican,* Dec. 10, 1903. Contrast this suspicious document with a desperate antiunion letter from a miner's wife that bears every evidence of authenticity, [unknown writer] to Governor Peabody, Mar. 25, 1904, folder 16, box 26716, Peabody Papers, CSA.

22. *Eleventh Biennial Report of the Inspector of Coal Mines of the State of Colorado, 1903–1904* (Denver: Smith-Brooks, 1905), 66–92; *Minutes of the Sixteenth Annual Convention of the United Mine Workers of America* . . . (Indianapolis: Cheltenham, 1905), 177–180; *John Mitchell Exposed: His Autocratic and Traitorous Conduct in the Colorado-Utah Strike, and His Nefarious Connection with the National Civic Federation Laid Bare* (New York: New York Labor News, 1905); J. C. Sullivan to the Officers and Members of the CSF of L, July 1, 1904, book 37, CSF of L Papers, Western History Collections, University of Colorado at Boulder; *Trinidad Chronicle-News,* July 24, 1904. On the role of the Colorado strike as "a major turning point for Mitchell," see Craig Phelan, *Divided Loyalties: The Public and Private Life of Labor Leader John Mitchell* (Albany: State University of New York Press, 1994), 212–246.

23. Frank Wilson testimony, *CCMC,* 1:672–674; Albert C. Felts testimony, *CCMC,* 1:330–332, *Denver Express,* Sept. 18, 19, and 22; Mike Livoda interview, Nov. 8, 1968, transcript in box 10, EM, p. 21; unidentified clipping dated Sept. 20, 1913, folder 8, box 1, John R. Lawson Papers, DPL.

24. John D. Rockefeller, Jr., to Frank Hearne, Nov. 4 and 12, 1903, copy in box 116, Allan Nevins Papers, Rare Book and Manuscript Room, Butler Library, Columbia University, New York; Starr Murphy to LaMont Montgomery Bowers, Sept. 16, 1913, box 117, ibid.; handwritten note on LaMont Montgomery Bowers to John D. Rockefeller, Jr., Sept. 4, 1913, folder 211, box 23, CF&I-RAC; LaMont Montgomery Bowers to Murphy (two letters), Sept. 19, 1913, ibid.

25. John D. Rockefeller, Jr., to LaMont Montgomery Bowers, Oct. 6, 1913, folder 211, box 23, CF&I-RAC.

26. During and after the Ten Days' War, John D. Rockefeller, Jr., received dozens of letters articulating this interpretation. See box 20, CF&I-RAC. On such rhetoric more generally, see Carl Smith, *Urban Order and the Shape of Belief: The Great Chicago Fire, the Haymarket Bomb, and the Model Town of Pullman* (Chicago: University of Chicago Press, 1995), 238–246.

27. *Denver Express,* Sept. 24, 1913.

28. Ibid., Sept. 16, 1913; *Florence Citizen,* Sept. 22, 23, and 26, 1913; *Denver News,* Sept. 23, 1913; UMWA Policy Committee, "Special Strike Call to the Miners in the North," Sept. 24, 1913, folder 10, box 1, John R. Lawson Papers, DPL.

29. Of course, estimates of strike participation varied wildly. Operators initially claimed that only 45 percent of miners had taken out their tools, even though their own data showed this to be a lie. The union, meanwhile, declared that 95 percent of miners had joined the strike, a figure that was closer to the mark but nonetheless skewed. Such estimates served political purposes for both the union and the companies, and the public estimates of either should be considered with caution. I base the figure of 80–90 percent on Governor Ammons's estimate, which also tallies with the *Trinidad Chronicle-News* estimate of 85 percent strike participation, which seems surprisingly high, given that paper's allegiance to the operators. *Trinidad Chronicle-News,* Sept. 23, 1913; *Denver Express,* Sept. 23, 1913; *Florence Citizen,* Sept. 23, 1913; *Denver News,* Sept. 23, 1913; Jesse Floyd Welborn to McClement, Dec. 4, 1913, folder 211, box 23, CF&I-RAC.

30. *Rocky Mountain News,* Sept. 23, 1913; Priscilla Long, "The Women of the C. F. I. Strike, 1913–1914," in Ruth Milkman, ed., *Women, Work, and Protest: A Century of U.S. Women's Labor History* (London: Routledge and Kegan Paul, 1985).

31. *Denver Express,* Sept. 22 and 25, 1913; *Florence Citizen,* Aug. 28, 1913; journalist quoted in S. J. Dunlevy [or Donlevy] memorandum, Mar. 10, 1915, contained in John D. Rockefeller, Jr., to Jesse Floyd Welborn, Apr. 3, 1915, box 17, JFW Papers.

32. In March 1914 the union was supporting 21,000 people. Edward Doyle to William Green, Mar. 11, 1914, env. 4, Doyle Papers.

33. *Denver News,* Sept. 23, 1913; *Florence Citizen,* Sept. 26, 1913; Alber Pazar, Emma Pazar, Ernest Bellotti, and Virginia Bellotti interview, n.d., transcript in HCEHP, pp. 11–12; Minnie Ugolini and Arthur Bellotti interview, n.d., transcript ibid., pp. 1–3; Ben Marchiori interview, n.d., transcript ibid., p. 4; Dan DeSantis interview, Jan. 19, 1978, transcript in box 9, EM, p. 45; *Trinidad Chronicle-News,* Sept. 22 and 23, 1913.

34. *Denver Express,* Sept. 24, 1913. Many of these camps endured, yet a listing of tent colonies following the strike's conclusion would differ in several respects from the list just given. Jesse Floyd Welborn to John D. Rockefeller, Jr., Jan. 7, 1915, folder 7, JFW Papers; colony locations were also drawn on a copy of "Map of High Transmission Lines Operated by the Trinidad Electric Transmission Railway & Gas Co." (dated Nov. 6, 1913), in box 1, AG File.

35. *Denver Express,* Sept. 24, 1913.

36. Ed Doyle to William Green, Sept. 30, 1913, env. 4, Doyle Papers; Angeline Tonso interview, Oct. 12, 1983, transcript in box 13, EM, p. 41; Alex Bisulco interview, p. 27; Mike and Katie Livoda interview, Sept. 20, 1980, transcript in box 10, EM, p. 54; Beshoar, *Out of the Depths,* 74; Mary Thomas testimony, 7:6357; *Trinidad Chronicle-News,* Sept. 25, 1913.

37. "Even the good Lord," Mike Livoda recalled, "I think, possibly went against the poor miners." Mike Livoda interview, June 20, 1973, transcript in folder 14, box 2, South Slavs Oral History Collection, UU, p. 29. Welborn believed that the snows would "cause

a good many of the strikers who are living in the tents provided by the organization, to seek the comfortable houses and employment at the mines." Jesse Floyd Welborn to McClement, Dec. 4, 1914.

38. Ed Doyle to John White, Sept. 30 and Oct 6, 1913, env. 4, Doyle Papers; Emma Zanetell interview, June 27, 1978, transcript in box 14, EM, pp. 43–48; Steve Surisky interview, Feb. 7, 1978, transcript in box 13, EM, p. 7; Pearl Jolly testimony, CIR, 7:6351; Angeline Tonso interview, pp. 15–17.

39. John and Caroline Tomsic interview, n.d., box 13, EM, p. 14. See also Angeline Tonso interview, p. 36.

40. Alex Bisulco interview, p. 27; John Lawson testimony, May 28, 1914, Karl E. Linderfelt court-martial, case no. 11, box 2, FF, DPL, 50.

41. Sarah Deutsch, *No Separate Refuge: Culture, Class, and Gender on an Anglo-Hispanic Frontier in the American Southwest, 1880–1940* (New York: Oxford University Press, 1987), 105; Mike Livoda interview, Nov. 30, 1968, pp. 15–16.

42. Alex Bisulco interview, p. 35. Coal companies and army officers alike recognized the strategic value of Ludlow; see complaint in *CF&I v. John P. White, Frank J. Hayes, et al.*, case 6576, LADC (filed Mar. 20, 1914), LACC; James Lockett to Lindley Garrison, May 9, 1914, box 1, AG File.

43. *Denver Express*, Sept. 22, 1913.

44. Charles J. Bayard, "The Colorado Progressive-Republican Split of 1912," *Colorado Magazine* 45 (1968): 61–78; George McGovern and Leonard Guttridge, *The Great Coalfield War* (Boston: Houghton Mifflin, 1972), 76; Democratic State Central Committee, "Democratic State Platform: Progress in Every Plank" (n.p., 1912), in folder 168733, box 1581, entry 112, Department of Justice Central Files, Straight Numerical Files, 1908–1922, RG 60, U.S. Department of Justice Records, Archives II, NARA, College Park, Md. (henceforth Justice Dept. Files, Colorado Coal War).

45. LaMont Montgomery Bowers to M. B. Streeter, Oct. 10, 1913, copy in box 9, CF&I Steel Corporation Papers of original in LMB Papers; LaMont Montgomery Bowers to John D. Rockefeller, Jr., Oct. 21, 1913, folder 211, box 23, CF&I-RAC; *Trinidad Chronicle-News*, Sept. 30, 1913.

46. W. P. Dunlavy quoted in *Denver Express*, Sept. 30, 1913.

47. *Walsenburg Independent*, Oct. 4, 1913; Harry Kelly to James Clark McReynolds, Oct. 9, 1913, folder 168733, Justice Dept. Files, Colorado Coal War.

48. Ammons to Chase, Oct. 28, 1913, copy in folder 12, box 1, John R. Lawson Papers, DPL. The *Florence Citizen*, Oct. 28, 1913, estimated the toll at twenty-eight killed, eighteen "battles and skirmishes" fought, forty-one wounded and injured, eleven buildings and bridges wrecked, and $50,000 in property destroyed.

49. *Florence Citizen*, Oct. 28 and 31, 1913.

50. Beshoar, *Out of the Depths;* McGovern and Guttridge, *Great Coalfield War*, 139;

John Nankivell, *History of the Military Organizations of the State of Colorado, 1860–1935* (Denver: W. H. Kistler, 1935).

51. Trinidad Club membership card issued to Hildreth Frost, Oct. 30, 1913, env. 1, Hildreth Frost Papers, DPL; C. A. Conner to Frost, n.d. [Apr. 1914], ibid.; LaMont Montgomery Bowers to John D. Rockefeller, Jr., Nov. 18, 1913, folder 211, box 23, CF&I-RAC; *Denver Post,* Dec. 16, 1913.

52. Edward Verdeckberg, "Report of the District Commander Camp at Walsenburg from October 28, 1913, to May 5, 1914," box 1, John Chase Papers, DPL, p. 11.

53. *Trinidad Chronicle-News,* Nov. 8, 1913.

54. *Rocky Mountain News,* Nov. 26, 1913.

55. Ibid.

56. *Rocky Mountain News,* Nov. 25, 1913.

57. Draft of Resolution sent by Archibald Allison to Committee, UMWA, and then to James Peabody, Jan. 6, 1904, folder 6, box 26716, Governor James Peabody Papers, CSA (all misspellings appear in the original). For a similar formulation, see CSF of L to "The Unions throughout the State of Colorado," Dec. 30, 1903, book 37, Colorado State Federation of Labor Papers.

58. Unless otherwise noted, all quotations in the account are drawn from "Proceedings of Joint Conference."

59. On pit committees, see *Florence Oil Refiner,* June 3, 1892; *A Statement from the Operators of the Northern Coal Fields to Their Former Employees and Friends* (Denver: Smith-Brooks, 1910).

60. Emphasis added. Apparently, workers throughout the West were articulating their demands in similar terms. See John Enyeart, *By Laws of Their Own Making: Rocky Mountain Workers and American Social Democracy, 1870–1924* (Palo Alto, Calif.: Stanford University Press, forthcoming).

61. "Proceedings of Joint Conference," 247 (emphasis added).

62. Beshoar, *Out of the Depths,* 109; Welborn to McClement, Dec. 4, 1913, folder 211, box 23, CF&I-RAC. Five months later, after the Ludlow Massacre and the Ten Days' War had shocked the nation, John D. Rockefeller, Jr., "strongly advise[d]" his Colorado officers to remind union leaders, the public, and the chair of the House Subcommittee on Mines and Mining that "the operators had accepted Governor Ammons letter of Nov. 27 . . . but that the unions refused to permit the workers to accept the terms." Rockefeller believed that such a claim would place the operators "in a very strong position before the public in that it would be evident that all disorder since November 27 has been due to the refusal of the unions to accept the settlement." Welborn to McClement, Dec. 4, 1913, folder 211, box 23, CF&I-RAC; John D. Rockefeller, Jr. to LaMont Montgomery Bowers, Apr. 30, 1914, folder 211, box 23, CF&I-RAC, Starr Murphy to LaMont Montgomery Bowers, Apr. 30, 1914, copy in Nevins Papers. The operators did as John D. Rockefeller,

Jr., advised, to no effect, yet Rockefeller remained insistent on this strategy; Coal Operators to M. D. Foster, May 1, 1914, folder 211, box 23, CF&I-RAC; John D. Rockefeller., Jr., to Jesse Floyd Welborn and LaMont Montgomery Bowers, folder 211a, ibid.

63. *Denver Times,* Nov. 28, 1913; *Denver Post,* Nov. 28, 1913.

64. *Denver Express,* Sept. 16, 1913; *Florence Citizen,* Oct. 31, Nov. 2 and 7, and Dec. 1 and 9, 1913; Frank J. Hayes to Mother Jones, Nov. 28, 1913, in Mary Jones, *The Correspondence of Mother Jones,* ed. Edward M. Steel (Pittsburgh: University of Pittsburgh Press, 1985), 120. On resumption of production, see Jesse Floyd Welborn to McClement, Nov. 11, and Dec. 4 and 29, 1913, folder 211, box 23, CF&I-RAC; LaMont Montgomery Bowers to John D. Rockefeller, Jr., Nov. 22 and Dec. 22, 1913, ibid. John D. Rockefeller, Jr., responded to Bowers's news with delight: "I note with interest the fact that the miners are rapidly going to Colorado from the South and East. . . . It is most gratifying to feel that this struggle is so rapidly becoming a thing of the past." John D. Rockefeller, Jr., to LaMont Montgomery Bowers, Dec. 26, 1913, ibid.

65. McGovern and Guttridge, *Great Coalfield War,* 171. When Jones returned to Colorado in March, she was arrested and held incommunicado in a Trinidad jail. For her typically irascible letters from jail, see Mother to Terence Powderly, Mar. 22, 1914, and Jones to "the Public," Mar. 31, 1914, in Jones, *Correspondence of Mother Jones,* 122–126.

66. Edward Keating, *The Gentleman from Colorado: A Memoir* (Denver: Sage, 1964), 381–381; McGovern and Guttridge, *Great Coalfield War,* 177–205; Scott Martelle, *Blood Passion: The Ludlow Massacre and Class War in the American West* (New Brunswick, N.J.: Rutgers University Press, 2007), 155.

67. On the increasing violence in January, see Minutes of Executive Committee Meetings, Jan. 26, 1914, folder 58, JFW Papers; *Great Coalfield War,* 186.

68. John Chase to Woodrow Wilson, Mar. 12, 1914, folder 168733a, Justice Dept. Files, Colorado Coal War; Chase to Ammons, Mar. 11, 1914, folder 1, box 26751, Ammons Papers; Emma Zanetell interview, June 27, 1978, box 14, EM, pp. 41–45; Conner to Frost, n.d.

69. McGovern and Guttridge, *Great Coalfield War,* 205; *Walsenburg World,* Apr. 16, 1914.

70. LaMont Montgomery Bowers to John D. Rockefeller, Jr., Apr. 18, 1914, folder 211, box 23, CF&I-RAC; letter from president of Globe Inspection Co. [name illegible] to Ammons, Mar. 21, 1914, folder 5, box 26751, Ammons Papers. See also State Senator Helen Ring Robinson's retrospective claim, "'I knew this was going to occur,'" quoted in *Rocky Mountain News,* Apr. 22, 1914.

71. Martelle, *Blood Passion,* 222–223; "My men begged me to give the order to fire on these people," National Guard commander Karl Linderfelt later testified, "as they were getting into position and we were thoroughly convinced it was a fight." Karl Linderfelt testimony, May 11, 1914, in Edwin F. Carson Court-Martial, case no. 2, folder 6, CNG Courts-Martial, p. 144.

72. Pearl Jolly testimony, CIR, 7:6349–6350; Edward Boughton testimony, CIR, 7:6364–6366; Patrick Hamrock testimony, May 11, 1914, in Court-Martial of C. E. Taylor, P. M. Cullom, T. J. Casey, Charles Patton, G. G. Osborne, F. M. Mason, Dan Pacheco, H. B. Faulks, E. J. Welsh, D. C. Campbell [no case number], folder 14, CNG Courts-Martial, pp. 328–335. Typical of the confusion was C. E. Taylor's testimony: when asked "Who was it [who] fired the first shot?" he evasively replied, "They say it was the strikers." C. E. Taylor testimony, May 11, 1914, ibid., p. 374. Recent books have located Ludlow along the banks of the Purgatoire River (in fact, the camp lay near an arroyo some two dozen miles north of the river), called Ludlow a mining camp (a few small collieries operated intermittently across the canyon, but Ludlow itself was essentially a depot town), and minimized the extent of the conflict (colony residents were on strike not simply against Colorado Fuel and Iron, but against several other companies). Renowned scholars have even misplaced the year of the Ludlow Massacre (which took place in 1914, not 1917) and grossly exaggerated the number of strikers killed there (it was 18, not 60). It would seem risky to place much weight on interpretations built on such foundations. Richard White, *"It's Your Misfortune and None of My Own": A History of the American West* (Norman: University of Oklahoma Press, 1991), 349; Alan Dawley, *Changing the World: American Progressives in War and Revolution* (Princeton, N.J.: Princeton University Press, 2003), 27–33; Maureen A. Flanagan, *America Reformed: Progressives and Progressivisms 1890s–1920s* (New York: Oxford University Press, 2007), 218–220.

73. P. M. Cullon testimony, May 11, 1914, in Carson Court-Martial, p. 168, and in Taylor et al. Court-Martial, 379–380; C. A. Conner testimony, May 11, 1914, in Maurice Bigelow Court-Martial, case no. 6, folder 8, CNG Courts-Martial, pp. 111–112; John R. Lawson testimony, May 28, 1914, in Karl E. Linderfelt Court-Martial, case no. 11, copy in box 2, FF, p. 40; Pearl Jolly testimony, 7:6350.

74. Uncited quotation attributed to John Lawson, in L. S. Bigelow, untitled typescript report [1915?], box 25, CF&I-RAC, 66–73; Boughton testimony, CIR, 7:6367.

75. Boughton testimony, CIR, 7:6367–6370.

76. *Rocky Mountain News*, Apr. 23, 1914; *Denver Times*, Apr. 25, 1914.

77. LaMont Montgomery Bowers to John D. Rockefeller, Jr., Apr. 21, 1914, folder 211, box 23, CF&I-RAC; Jesse Floyd Welborn to McClement, May 27, 1914, ibid. "All the evidence," Welborn claimed, showed that with the exception of Linderfelt's attack on Tikas, "no acts that could be criticized were committed by any of the militia." The tents of the colony had caught on fire, he claimed, owing to "the act of someone within the colony"; the Snyder boy had been shot by a striker; and the victims in the so-called Black Hole of Ludlow had died of suffocation before the fire began. See also *Rocky Mountain News*, Apr. 25, 1914; *Denver Times*, Apr. 25, 1914; Jim Jam Junior, "The Truth about Colorado's Civil War," *Jim Jam Jems* (July 1914): 24 (excerpted versions of this article appeared in the *Oakland Tribune*, June 25, 1914, and other papers). Rev. Henry Pingree of Denver's Asbury Church declared, "What should have been done long ago, and what should be

done now is to organize a vigilante committee to call on these striking miners and say to them: 'Are you United States citizens? Do you intend to become United States citizens?' All who answer 'No' should be boxed up and deported to where they came from. Box up every man of them and deport them and you will end this reign of anarchy. There will be a wonderful roar set up if such a thing is done, but it is the only patriotic thing to do, the only religious thing to do." "Our Minister Speaks," enclosed in R. L. Hearon to William Ellis, June 5, 1914, folder 142, box 7, CF&I-CHS.

78. Edward Boughton testimony in CIR, 7:6367–6368; Robert Uhlich testimony, Dec. 27, 1913, in "Transcript of Statements of Witnesses Appearing before the Investigating Committee Appointed by John McLennan, President State Federation of Labor, Investigating Conduct of State Militia in the Southern Colorado Coal Fields," folder 3, box 1, John R. Lawson Papers, DPL; undated, unsigned report [1915], in folder 4, box 2, FF. See also Boughton, Memorandum, June 10, 1914, folder 200, box 22, CF&I-RAC; Jerome Greene to Boughton, May 24, 1914, folder 146, box 20, Organization: Industrial Relations—Colorado Fuel and Iron Co., 1914–1915, Administration, Program and Policy Series 900, Rockefeller Foundation Archives, RG 3, RAC; Green to A. Lawrence Lowell, June 3, 1914, ibid.; Charles Loughridge to Greene, July 11, 1914, ibid.

79. Telegram from UMWA to Wilson, quoted in *Denver Times,* Apr. 21, 1914; Horace Hawkins quoted in *Denver Times,* Apr. 22, 1914; telegram from Owen Roberts, M. C. Davis, and N. Fowler to John R. Lawson, ibid. The rumors of incineration were eventually dismissed by the reporter Harvey V. Deuell, who visited the Ludlow colony with two doctors and two ministers and inspected all recently disturbed ground for evidence of human remains. *Denver Times,* Apr. 27, 1914. Even after this account, though, the incineration scenario remained plausible, though the UMWA's inability to supply the names of the supposed victims renders it highly unlikely that the militia had, in fact, burned additional bodies.

80. Circular quoted in *Denver Times,* Apr. 22, 1914; Doyle to McElroy quoted in "JLM" to Jesse Floyd Welborn, Apr. 21 1914, folder 144, box 7, JFW Papers. Some claimed that the militia was not only murderous but bent on raping and pillaging. State Senator Helen Ring Robinson told the *Denver Times,* for instance, "'One minister alone told me he had performed fifteen forced marriages resulting from the invasion of the southern field by gunmen since this strike began.'" *Denver Times,* Apr. 22, 1914.

81. *Florence Citizen,* Apr. 22, 1914; *Denver Times,* Apr. 23, 1914. Lying in state, the body of Louis Tikas provoked similar paeans to masculinity: "As the many bent on their errands pass him," Clara Mozzor reported, "they bow their heads and mutter softly: 'He was a true man.'" Ibid.

82. Anonymous telegram, Apr. 23, 1914, folder 144, box 7, JFW Papers; *Denver Times,* Apr. 22, 23, and 25, 1914; *Florence Citizen,* Apr. 29, 1914; Dan DeSantis interview, p. 3. It is not possible to determine with absolute certainty the sex of all of the fighting strikers. Oral histories, official testimony, and contemporary accounts universally described them

as "men," however, and there are no reports of any women getting killed or injured while bearing arms for the union. Taking great care not to inflict violence on the wives and children of scabs, mine managers, and miners who remained loyal to the companies, the strikers consciously tried to set themselves apart from enemies who had betrayed the manly code of honor and slaughtered women and children. "It was reported," wrote the *Denver Times*, "that John Lawson had issued instructions to the strikers to protect all women and children." *Denver Times*, Apr. 24 and 25, 1914; Mike Livoda interview, Aug. 1975, transcript in box 10, EM, p. 16; and anon. letter to editor, *Walsenburg World*, June 4, 1914. For contradictory rumors, see *Denver Times*, Apr. 23 and 24, 1914; *Rocky Mountain News*, Apr. 25, 1914. On tactics, see *Denver Times*, Apr. 26, 1914; and photo "An American Who Is Leading and Advising the Striking Miners in the Industrial Warfare in Southern Colorado," in *Denver Times*, Apr. 27, 1914. On the size of battalions, the sources are too numerous to cite.

83. *Rocky Mountain News*, Apr. 23, 1914; *Florence Citizen*, Apr. 22, 1914; Hamrock to Chase, Apr. 23, 1914, folder 144, box 7, JFW Papers; anonymous telegram, Apr. 21, 1914, ibid.; *Denver Times*, Apr. 21, 23, 24, and 27, 1914.

84. "Detection Rept.," enclosed in LaMont Montgomery Bowers to John D. Rockefeller, Jr., May 9, 1914, folder 203, box 22, CF&I-RAC.

85. Quotations from *Denver Times*, Apr. 25, 1914. On mistrust, see Aldace Walker to U.S. Adjutant General, May 11, 1914 (two letters), box 1, AG File. Union officials blocked a brass band from playing at the funeral of Louis Tikas. "They feared martial music would create unnecessary excitement," they explained to reporters. "A guard of Italians will also be on hand, it was announced, to see that quiet was maintained." *Rocky Mountain News*, Apr. 27, 1914.

86. *Denver Times*, Apr. 24, 1914; telegrams in folder 144, box 7, CF&I-CHS; communications in folder 1, box 26751, Ammons Papers; Martelle, *Blood Passion*, 222–223. Guards and militiamen often reported having killed many strikers in these engagements; although it is possible that some strikers were buried unsung, the comparative death toll in this phase of the fighting suggests the miners' adeptness at offensive tactics.

87. *Rocky Mountain News*, Apr. 25 and 26, 1914. News accounts identified the social class of the women. "Many of Denver's best known women" participated, but Mrs. H. T. Herlinger, "wife of a laboring man," was on the committee delegated to meet with Ammons in his chambers, and a few women from the strikers' colonies, such as Mrs. Fred Renshaw, Sylvia Smith, and Mrs. Lena Bullington, were also present. *Denver Times*, Apr. 25, 1914.

88. A remarkable photograph shows a sea of women's faces, with a handful of men's scattered among them. *Denver Times*, Apr. 25, 1914. Lafferty, who later testified before the Commission on Industrial Relations, was excoriated for her involvement, in LaMont Montgomery Bowers to John D. Rockefeller, Jr., May 21, 1914, folder 184, box 20, CF&I-RAC. For a critique of the Denver clubwomen allegedly written by a strikebreaker's wife,

see *Walsenburg World,* June 4, 1914. Denver businessman Lucius Hallett told John D. Rockefeller, Jr., "You are being abused and attacked by a gang of conscienceless rascals and emotional women." Hallett to John D. Rockefeller, Jr., May 1, 1914, folder 170, box 19, CF&I-RAC. Supposedly basing its accusations on an investigation of the strike and massacre, a reactionary journal scoffed: "Some of Colorado's tearful Miss Nancys have sobbed out tales of sensational fiction that would do credit to the most prolific writer of modern melodrama." Jim Jam Junior, "The Truth about Colorado's Civil War," 23, 46–47.

89. *Rocky Mountain News,* Apr. 26, 1914; *Denver Times,* Apr. 25, 1914.

90. The Women's Peace Association was quite conscious of the precedent it was setting: "Women," Dora Phelps Buell proclaimed to the assembly, "we are making history." An incident during the course of the meeting perfectly captured the feminist politics of the women. When "a man in the gallery attempted to interrupt the governor," Lafferty shut him up. "'This is a woman's meeting,'" she declared. *Rocky Mountain News,* Apr. 26, 1914.

91. *Denver Times,* Apr. 25 and 27, 1913.

92. Letter from Rockvale (between unnamed correspondents), Apr. 29, 1914, folder 143, box 7, CF&I-CHS; J. V. McClenathan to C. M. Schenk, Apr. 30, 1914, folder 2, JFW Papers; Juan Urbano Vigil to Edward Keating, May 1, 1914, box 1, AG File. For papers relating to the president's decision to call out troops, see Arthur S. Link, ed., *The Papers of Woodrow Wilson* (Princeton, N.J.: Princeton University Press, 1979), 29:525–533, 541–542. Rumors of continuing militancy among the strikers were particularly strong in the Crested Butte area. W. A. Holbrook to Charles J. Symmonds, July 8, 1914, box 1, AG File. Strikers also carried out a small attack on federal troops at Segundo. James Lockett to Lindley Garrison, May 27, 1914, ibid. In October, "strike-sympathizers" attacked and stabbed two suspected strikebreakers at Florence, prompting the arrest of forty-eight; eight of those "identified as committing assault [were] turned over to civil authorities." Major Elliott to Garrison, Oct. 2, 6, and 10, 1914, ibid.; *Florence Citizen,* Oct. 9, 1914. For reports of strikers "drilling" in November, see William Carman to Hildreth Frost, Nov. 10, 1914, env. 1, Frost Papers. More generally, see Holbrook to Garrison, July 17, 1914, box 1, AG File; *Trinidad Advertiser,* Oct. 22, 1914.

93. Bowers, disgusted, complained that the strike had returned CF&I to the "edge of bankruptcy," thus undoing the six years of work he had devoted to reviving the company after the depression of 1907–1908. LaMont Montgomery Bowers to John D. Rockefeller, Jr., Dec. 3, 1914, folder 190, box 21, CF&I-RAC. As of early 1915, a company operative within the UMWA claimed that the union had spent $870,000 on the Colorado strike. J. K. T. to Ivy Lee, Mar. 23, 1915, folder 15, JFW Papers.

94. Lockett to Garrison, May 13 and 15, box 1, AG File; Garrison to Lockett, July 9, 1914, ibid.; W. W. Wotherspoon to U.S. adjutant general, Nov. 3, 1914, ibid.; Garrison to McClure, Aug. 26, 1914, ibid. On the complications that arose as field commanders tried

to determine who qualified as a "Colorado resident" for the purposes of the order, see Charles O'Neil to DeR. C. Cabell, Sept. 15, 1914, ibid.; Garrison to Lockett, Oct. 9, 1914, ibid.; Morgan to Garrison, Oct. 15, 1914, ibid.

95. McClure to Garrison, July 28, 1914, box 1, ibid.; Jesse Floyd Welborn to Mc-Clement, Aug. 18, 1914, folder 211, box 23, CF&I-RAC; John D. Rockefeller, Jr., to LaMont Montgomery Bowers and Jesse Floyd Welborn, folder 203, Sept. 1, 1914, box 22, ibid.

96. *Denver News,* Dec. 9, 1914. Wilson detailed his course of action in "A Statement on the Colorado Coal Strike" [Nov. 29, 1914], in *Papers of Woodrow Wilson,* 31:367–369. See also Priscilla Long, *Where the Sun Never Shines: A History of America's Bloody Coal Industry* (New York: Paragon House, 1989), 301–304. Strikers killed at least thirty-nine strikebreakers, mine guards, National Guardsmen, and bystanders. Martelle, *Blood Passion,* 222–223.

97. *Denver News,* Dec. 9, 1914.

98. Ibid.; "Synopsis: Special Convention Proceedings, District 15, U. M. W. of A.," env. 10, Doyle Papers.

99. *Los Angeles Times,* Dec. 13, 1914; J. K. T. to Ivy Lee, Mar. 23, 1915, folder 15, JFW Papers; Jesse Floyd Welborn to John D. Rockefeller, Jr., Apr. 2, 1915, folder 16, ibid.

100. John D. Rockefeller, Jr., *The Colorado Industrial Plan* (New York: n.p., 1916); Howard M. Gitelman, *The Legacy of the Ludlow Massacre: A Chapter in American Industrial Relations* (Philadelphia: University of Pennsylvania Press, 1988); Ben M. Selekman and Mary Van Kleeck, *Employees' Representation in Coal Mines: A Study of the Industrial Representation Plan of the Colorado Fuel and Iron Company* (New York: Russell Sage Foundation, 1924); John Thomas Hogle, "The Rockefeller Plan: Workers, Managers, and the Struggle over Unionism in Colorado Fuel and Iron, 1915–1942" (Ph.D. diss., University of Colorado, Boulder, 1992); Denise Pan, "Peace and Conflict in an Industrial Family: Company Identity and Class Consciousness in a Multi-Ethnic Community, Colorado Fuel and Iron's Cameron and Walsen Coal Camps, 1913–1928" (M.A. thesis, University of Colorado, Boulder, 1994); Jonathan Rees, "What If a Company Union Wasn't a 'Sham'? The Rockefeller Plan in Action," *Labor History* 48 (2007): 457–475; and Jonathan Rees, "Rockefeller's Cross," unpublished manuscript.

Epilogue

1. John Greenway, *Songs of the Ludlow Massacre: Reprint from the United Mine Workers Journal* (n.p.: United Mine Workers of America, 1955); United Mine Workers of America, "The Ludlow Massacre," at http://www.umwa.org (accessed May 2, 2008).

2. H. Lee Scamehorn, *Mill and Mine: The CF&I in the Twentieth Century* (Lincoln: University of Nebraska Press, 1992).

3. Keith Dix, *What's a Coal Miner to Do? The Mechanization of Coal Mining* (Pitts-

burgh: University of Pittsburgh Press, 1988); Rick J. Clyne, *Coal People: Life in Southern Colorado's Company Towns, 1890–1930* (Denver: Colorado Historical Society, 2000).

4. Hal Clifford, "'They Want the Workers to Be Invisible,'" *High Country News* Dec. 23, 2002; Hal Clifford, "Ski Town Workers Find Homes in the Hills," *High Country News,* Sept. 11, 2000; David Frey, "Resort Counties Push for Legal Workers," *High Country News,* Nov. 19, 2001; and Rebecca Clarren, "'There Are No Support Networks Here,'" *High Country News,* Apr. 24, 2000.

5. Frederick Jackson Turner, "The Significance of History," in *The Early Writings of Frederick Jackson Turner,* comp. Everette E. Edwards (Madison: University of Wisconsin Press, 1938), 57. For an articulation of the impossibility of writing a truly integral history, see George Lipsitz, *Time Passages: Collective Memory and American Popular Culture* (Minneapolis: University of Minnesota Press, 1990), 21.

Acknowledgments

I worked on this project for nearly a decade, in the process logging thousands of hours of archival research, then devoting thousands more to the laborious process of formulating ideas, trying to capture them in prose, failing, starting again, not getting it right, and agonizing over every paragraph, every sentence, every word. This experience has led me to warn the aspiring scholars among the students I teach that history is not rocket science—it's harder. Whether this is true or not, this book has certainly cost me more than I care to disclose. Yet it has also brought rewards beyond those I could have imagined. And though the long slog has often felt very much like a solitary trek, I could not have completed the journey without the help of many, many people.

Writing this book required more time and patience, support and guidance and love, than I ever imagined. It also took an embarrassment of funding. A three-year Science to Achieve Results (STAR) fellowship from the United States Environmental Protection Agency (U-91560901-2) enabled me to hunker down in Denver-area archives for protracted research, travel widely to a wealth of other relevant collections, and devote myself to this project full-time. A Mellon Foundation grant from the history department at the University of Wisconsin, Madison, and a University Fellowship also helped immensely, as did two research grants from the Rockefeller Archive Center. A W. M. Keck Young Scholars Fellowship from the Huntington Library, the National Endowment for the Humanities Summer Institute program on "the redemptive West" at the Huntington, the inaugural Los Angeles Posse of Westerners Fellowship from the Autry National Center, and the John Topham and Susan Redd Butler Faculty Fellowship from the Charles Redd Center for Western Studies at Brigham Young University helped me to shore up my evidence and reformulate my argument and narrative, as did extensive support from Dean Stella Theodoulou of the College of Social and Behavioral Sciences at California State University, Northridge (CSUN), and CSUN's Whitsett Foundation. Finally, the History Department and the College of Arts and Liberal Sciences at the University of Colorado Denver were kind enough to give me the light teaching schedule I needed to finish the book, while the Walter Rosenberry Fund generously picked up the tab for the maps and illustrations that grace this volume.

I am even more indebted to the librarians and archivists who made my research so enjoyable and productive. David Hays at the University of Colorado, Boulder; Peter Blodgett at the Huntington; Marva Felchlin and her colleagues at the Autry and Braun Research Libraries at the Autry National Center; Jay Trask at the Bessemer Historical Society in Pueblo, Colorado; George Miles at the Beinecke Rare Book & Manuscript Library, Yale University; Thomas Rosenbaum and his colleagues at the Rockefeller Archive Center; and the staffs of the Cañon City Public Library, the Carnegie Public Library in Trinidad, the Colorado Springs Pioneer Museum, the Kansas State Historical Society in Topeka, the Museum of New Mexico in Santa Fe, the Center for Southwest Research at the University of New Mexico Library, the Marriott Library at the University of Utah, the National Archives and Records Administration facilities in Denver, College Park (Maryland), and Washington, D.C., the Pikes Peak Library District in Colorado Springs, the Pueblo Public Library, and the Tutt Library at Colorado College. Special thanks go to Barbara Dey, Rebecca Lintz, and everyone else at the Colorado Historical Society; Terry Kettelsen and his staff at the Colorado State Archives; and the large and wonderful crew at the Western History and Genealogy Department of the Denver Public Library—all of whom tolerated my numerous and often strange requests with good humor, generosity, and professionalism.

David Fouser, a young historian of whom I expect great things, proved an invaluable research assistant. Philip Schwartzberg of Meridian Mapping translated my ambitious notions into elegant cartographic representations that exceeded my expectations in every way. Kathleen McDermott, my editor at Harvard University Press, shepherded me through the publication process with equanimity, professionalism, and vim. I am also indebted to Susan Abel for reining in my tendency toward rhetorical excess, setting me straight regarding innumerable grammatical improprieties, and maintaining her equanimity and good cheer throughout the copyediting process. Several friends and colleagues read portions of the manuscript: Steve Aron, Robert Chester, John Enyeart, Susan Fitzpatrick-Behrens, David Igler, Pamela Laird, John H. M. Laslett, Craig Loftin, Jenny Price, Steve Ross, Allison Varzally, Leila Zenderland, and the members of the environmental history group at the Huntington, the Los Angeles Social History Work Group, and the Western History Workshop at the Autry waded through inchoate arguments and unpolished prose; I am grateful for their generous and constructive criticism. Any residual mistakes and misunderstandings, of course, remain my fault alone. Katherine Morse and an anonymous reviewer for Harvard read through the entire manuscript, as did Jonathan Rees, pushing me to clarify my thinking and refine my argument even as they saved me from all sorts of embarrassing errors and oversights. Audiences at panel presentations and public talks at several conferences of the American Society for Environmental History, the Colorado State Historical Society, Colorado State University, and the University of British Columbia showed through their enthusiasm and engagement that I was onto something. Eric Margolis generously allowed me to quote from the oral histories that he and his colleagues had conducted in the Colorado coalfields in the 1970s and '80s, thus enabling me to let some of the people about whom I write tell their own stories.

Katherine Benton-Cohen, Flannery Burke, and Jenka Sokol have read many versions of what follows, including several that were shockingly bad. Their encouragement and friendship got me through some difficult years;

for that and our enduring collaborations I am ever in their debt. Flannery and I had the incredible good fortune to land jobs together at CSUN, and though we no longer get to work together every day, the example she sets of amazing teaching, thoughtful scholarship, and finely crafted prose continues to inspire me every day.

Thank you, too, to the many teachers and professors who inspired me over the years—Pat Baker, Harlan Bartram, Nancy Bosch, Jeanne Boydston, Skip Clopton, Charles Cohen, John Milton Cooper, Roger Craig, Colleen Dunlavy, Jerry Harrold, Karl Jacoby, Diane Lindstrom, David MacDonald, Florencia Mallon, Arthur McEvoy, Charlie Papazian, William Reese, Jean-Laurent Rosenthal, Francisco Scarano, Gaddis Smith, Mark Steinberg, Steve Stern, Louis Warren, and too many others to name—who I hope will find some hint of what I learned from them in this book, and to all my friends in the environmental history and Western history communities. I am also grateful to have had the pleasure of teaching so many fine students (including a host of wonderful teachers) as I worked on *Killing for Coal;* it is a better book because of all I learned from them. History is inherently a lonely pursuit, but I feel fortunate indeed to have worked with Myra Rich, Tom Maddux, Chris Agee, Jeffrey Auerbach, Shiva Bajpai, Joyce Broussard, Bill Conevery, Ron Davis, Tom Devine, Michael Ducey, Susan Fitzpatrick-Behrens, Susan Gustin, Richard Horowitz, Rachel Howes, Rebecca Hunt, Patricia Juarez-Dappe, Pamela Laird, Marjorie Levine-Clark, Charles Macune, Chris Magra, Tom Noel, Clementine Oliver, Merry Ovnick, Carl Pletsch, James Sefton, Alison Shah, Josh Sides, Michael Ward, James Whiteside, Greg Whitesides, Nan Yamane, and other illustrious colleagues both at CSUN and at the University of Colorado Denver. In Los Angeles, I was also blessed to get to know John Bowes, Lawrence Culver, Bill Deverell, Kathleen Donegan, Laura Mitchell, Jenny Price, Allison Varzally, Lissa Wadewitz, and a number of other fine scholars and great people. At key junctures, Elliot Gorn, Elliott West, Richard White, Donald Worster, and other eminent historians took the time to listen to me talk about this project; I thank them for lending their encouragement, as well as for demonstrating the benefits of making sophisticated analyses accessible to broader audiences. Finally, I must express my immense appreciation to the genial workers who served up tea, pastries, and conversation at the dozens of coffee shops in which I worked on this book, particularly Common Grounds, St. Marks, and Fluid in Denver, the 18th Street Café in Santa Monica, and Peets in Westwood.

Much as I enjoyed L.A. and learned from my time there, Colorado has always been my home. I am forever indebted to the three people who, more than anyone else, helped me get back to my native ground. Patty Limerick took me under her wing while this book was still in the conceptual stages; her friendship, generosity, and unfettered brilliance continue to strike me speechless. Ari Kelman became my unofficial mentor several years ago; since that time, he has given me unfailingly good advice, opened more doors for me than I could have imagined, while injecting wit into every corner of every conversation—all while asking nothing in return. Last but hardly least, Bill Cronon has guided me for years. His immense intelligence and strong moral sensibility, his passion for drawing connections and belief in reaching non-academic audiences, have helped me become a better historian, just as his sometimes fierce critiques of this project and his unfaltering belief in me made this a stronger book.

On a more personal note, Shawn Patrick became my brother, gave me much-needed breaks from my work, and shared his own writerly dilemmas on the concert circuit. Steve Wagner and Katka Vujich generously shared their home with me during Washington research trips. Through their hospitality Dena Gaussoin and Gary and Sandra Haug made a research trip to New Mexico more enjoyable than I had any right to expect. Jennifer Gay, Dru Jacobs, Brad O'Donnell, and a number of other friends stuck with me throughout it all. The friends I have met through my wife, Amy—Karen and Ted Buelow, Rosemarie Burke, Phyllis Currao, Kendra and Mark Fadil, Chrisy and Will Gottlick, Kristen and Luis Peña, Mark Tetrault, and many others—have welcomed me with open arms and helped Amy deal with a grumpy husband who too keenly felt the responsibility for this book hanging over his head. My wonderful extended family in Colorado, New York, England, and beyond supplied me with endless encouragement throughout. My sister, Melissa, and her family—Matt, Jamison, Landon, and Finley—often gave me better things to think about, not to mention lots of love. Finally, I thank my parents, John and Martha Andrews, for their love, generosity, and patience. They made the past real to me before I even knew there was such a thing as history, endured and actually enjoyed my incessant curiosity, and sacrificed so that I could have the best education possible. This book is for them, because it could not have happened without them.

Last and most of all, I thank Amy for helping me put the pieces back together again, for restoring my faith in the universe, for bringing Santiago into the world—and most of all, for loving me fearlessly and absolutely. Long may we walk the path together!

Index

conditions; Safety issues

Hearne, Frank, 229–231, 233, 245

Heartz, Evangeline, 280

Herrington, Cass, 216

Herrington, Frank, 153

Hezron camp, 210

Hill, Nathaniel B., 63

Hill, Zeph, 242–243

Hills, R. C., 146

Hinsdale County, Colo., 79

Hispanos, 12, 17, 39–40, 42, 64, 79, 88–89,
    91, 93–94, 98, 103–110, 112, 116, 138, 158,
    166, 172, 184, 188, 192, 205–207, 210–211,
    213, 218–219

Hixon, A. J., 96

Holbrook, W. A., 13–14

Homestead strike, 4

Hopi nation, 222

Horses, 38–39, 56, 131

Hospitals, 150, 187, 199, 214

Howells, William, 195

Hrusovsky family, 64

Huerfano County, Colo., 40, 53–54, 95, 98,
    101, 103–104, 132, 141–142, 158, 160, 181,
    184–186, 189, 192, 205, 210, 216, 235, 247–
    248, 254, 258

Hungarian immigrants, 100, 103–104, 106, 115,
    118–119

Hungaro, Tony, 167, 172

Hunt, A. C., 41

Idaho Springs, Colo., 240

Ihlseng, M. K., 55

Illinois, 28, 102–103, 156

Immigrants/migrants, 17, 44, 48, 55, 64, 86–121,
    197, 199, 234, 248, 252; emigration agents/com-
    panies, 114–115. *See also specific ethnic groups*

Industrialization, 4, 18, 22, 32, 48–50, 58, 60–61,
    64, 71, 73, 78, 93, 111, 159–160, 200, 233–234,
    286. *See also* Fossil-fuel dependence; Mineral-
    intensive industrialization

Industrial Workers of the World, 287

Inside-outside technique, 235

Inspectors, mine, 151–153, 167

International School of Mines, 98

Iowa, 102, 179

Irish immigrants, 89, 102, 104, 109, 112–113,
    154–155

Iron, 25, 32, 61–62, 104, 205

Irrigation, 40, 79–80

Italian immigrants, 12, 64, 88–90, 96, 99–100,
    103–104, 106–110, 112–121, 135, 138, 159, 161,

166, 171–172, 184–185, 189, 192, 206, 218–219,
    234, 243, 252

Ito (miner), 118

Jackson, J. B., 188

Jackson, William Henry, 58–60, 71, 73

Japanese immigrants, 18, 100–101, 103, 105, 107,
    109, 112, 115–116, 118–119, 166, 215

Jefferson County, Colo., 53

Jews, 64, 219

Jim Crow laws, 106, 171, 197, 213

Johns, Henry, 97–98, 100–102, 108

Johns, Margaret Thomas, 97–98, 104

Jokerville mine, 122–126, 138, 145, 153–156, 163,
    168–169, 185

Jones (state mine inspector), 152

Jones, David, 93, 95

Jones, Mary ("Mother"), 4, 238–239, 242, 268,
    283

Jones, William, 97

Judiscak, Mickey, 107–108

Kansas, 28, 38, 40–41, 43, 79–81, 100, 160, 242

Kansas City, Mo., 244

Kansas Pacific Railroad, 27–29, 32, 35, 37–40,
    42–44, 46–48, 53

Katcina camp, 222

Keating, Edward, 268

Kebler, J. A., 181, 183

Kenehan, Roady, 257, 270

Kessler, Ed, 12

King, William Lyon Mackenzie, 286

Knights of Labor, 97, 118, 158–159, 173, 178–179

Korean immigrants, 103, 109

Ku Klux Klan, 14

Lafferty, Alma, 280–281

Lake City, Colo., 229

Lambert, John J., 85

Lamont, Tony, 237

Landscape. *See* Political landscape; Vernacular
    landscape; Workscapes, mine

Lane, W. E., 12, 18

Larese, Primo, 272

Las Animas County, Colo., 11, 40, 53–54, 90,
    103, 116, 132, 140, 142, 145, 153, 157–158, 160,
    174–176, 181, 183–184, 186, 189, 191–193, 205,
    216–217, 235, 242, 247, 254, 258, 278

Laslett, John, 103

Lavatore Italiano, 243

La Veta, Colo., 192, 289

Lawrence, D. H., 174